SYNGRESS FORCE
EXPERT ADVISORS

D0870396

SYNGRESS FORCE announces its latest n.

ABOUT SYNGRESS FORCE

Syngress Force, comprised of Syngress authors who are among the world's most accomplished IT security professionals, now delivers "right-sized" professional security training and content expertise to your enterprise. Syngress Force designs a two day, on site deployment that matches the content of our best selling security titles to the unique needs of your enterprise. Our objective is simple: To quickly create and deploy solutions to your specific problems while providing key employees with the necessary tools and knowledge to manage thereafter. As your enterprise evolves, choose additional modules and schedule another deployment.

ABOUT INSIDER THREAT

The best Firewalls, Intrusion Detection Systems and Pen Testing systems may be useless in protecting your enterprise from the employee two offices down. That's why Syngress Force formed its newest unit on Insider Threat Protection. Team leader Dr. Eric Cole is author of *CyberSpying* and *Insider Threat.* Eric spent seven years with the CIA and is currently chief technology officer (CTO) and chief scientist at The Sytex Group, Inc. (TSGI). He has appeared on 60 Minutes and CNN News.

Deploy the Syngress Force team on site now to help design and implement secure IT systems as well as security and human resource policies. Key objectives include:

- Identifying the types of insiders who are most likely to pose a threat.
- Understanding the likely weapons used for attacks, including encryption, steganography, and social engineering.
- Design effective security systems to prevent insider attacks and how to investigate insider security breeches that do occur.

Register for Free Membership to

solutions@syngress.com

Over the last few years, Syngress has published many best-selling and critically acclaimed books, including Tom Shinder's *Configuring ISA Server 2004*, Brian Caswell and Jay Beale's *Snort 2.1 Intrusion Detection*, and Angela Orebaugh and Gilbert Ramirez's *Ethereal Packet Sniffing*. One of the reasons for the success of these books has been our unique **solutions@syngress.com** program. Through this site, we've been able to provide readers a real time extension to the printed book.

As a registered owner of this book, you will qualify for free access to our members-only solutions@syngress.com program. Once you have registered, you will enjoy several benefits, including:

- Four downloadable e-booklets on topics related to the book. Each booklet is approximately 20-30 pages in Adobe PDF format. They have been selected by our editors from other best-selling Syngress books as providing topic coverage that is directly related to the coverage in this book.

- A comprehensive FAQ page that consolidates all of the key points of this book into an easy-to-search web page, providing you with the concise, easy-to-access data you need to perform your job.

- A "From the Author" Forum that allows the authors of this book to post timely updates and links to related sites, or additional topic coverage that may have been requested by readers.

Just visit us at **www.syngress.com/solutions** and follow the simple registration process. You will need to have this book with you when you register.

Thank you for giving us the opportunity to serve your needs. And be sure to let us know if there is anything else we can do to make your job easier.

SYNGRESS®

SYNGRESS®

Insider Threat

Protecting the Enterprise from
Sabotage, Spying, and Theft

Dr. Eric Cole
Sandra Ring

KEY	SERIAL NUMBER
001	HJIRTCV764
002	PO9873D5FG
003	829KM8NJH2
004	GHVV56329M
005	CVPLQ6WQ23
006	VBP965T5T5
007	HJJJ863WD3E
008	2987GVTWMK
009	629MP5SDJT
010	IMWQ295T6T

PUBLISHED BY
Syngress Publishing, Inc.
800 Hingham Street
Rockland, MA 02370

Insider Threat: Protecting the Enterprise from Sabotage, Spying, and Theft

Printed in Canada
1 2 3 4 5 6 7 8 9 0
ISBN: 1-59749-048-2

Publisher: Andrew Williams   Page Layout and Art: Patricia Lupien
Acquisitions Editor: Gary Byrne   Copy Editor: Michelle Melani
Cover Designer: Michael Kavis   Indexer: Julie Kawabata

Distributed by O'Reilly Media, Inc. in the United States and Canada.
For information on rights, translations, and bulk purchases, contact Matt Pedersen, Director of Sales and Rights, at Syngress Publishing; email matt@syngress.com or fax to 781-681-3585.

Acknowledgments

Syngress would like to acknowledge the following people for their kindness and support in making this book possible.

Syngress books are now distributed in the United States and Canada by O'Reilly Media, Inc. The enthusiasm and work ethic at O'Reilly are incredible, and we would like to thank everyone there for their time and efforts to bring Syngress books to market: Tim O'Reilly, Laura Baldwin, Mark Brokering, Mike Leonard, Donna Selenko, Bonnie Sheehan, Cindy Davis, Grant Kikkert, Opol Matsutaro, Steve Hazelwood, Mark Wilson, Rick Brown, Tim Hinton, Kyle Hart, Sara Winge, Peter Pardo, Leslie Crandell, Regina Aggio Wilkinson, Pascal Honscher, Preston Paull, Susan Thompson, Bruce Stewart, Laura Schmier, Sue Willing, Mark Jacobsen, Betsy Waliszewski, Kathryn Barrett, John Chodacki, Rob Bullington, Kerry Beck, Karen Montgomery, and Patrick Dirden.

The incredibly hardworking team at Elsevier Science, including Jonathan Bunkell, Ian Seager, Duncan Enright, David Burton, Rosanna Ramacciotti, Robert Fairbrother, Miguel Sanchez, Klaus Beran, Emma Wyatt, Krista Leppiko, Marcel Koppes, Judy Chappell, Radek Janousek, Rosie Moss, David Lockley, Nicola Haden, Bill Kennedy, Martina Morris, Kai Wuerfl-Davidek, Christiane Leipersberger, Yvonne Grueneklee, Nadia Balavoine, and Chris Reinders for making certain that our vision remains worldwide in scope.

David Buckland, Marie Chieng, Lucy Chong, Leslie Lim, Audrey Gan, Pang Ai Hua, Joseph Chan, June Lim, and Siti Zuraidah Ahmad of Pansing Distributors for the enthusiasm with which they receive our books.

David Scott, Tricia Wilden, Marilla Burgess, Annette Scott, Andrew Swaffer, Stephen O'Donoghue, Bec Lowe, Mark Langley, and Anyo Geddes of Woodslane for distributing our books throughout Australia, New Zealand, Papua New Guinea, Fiji, Tonga, Solomon Islands, and the Cook Islands.

Author

Dr. Eric Cole is currently chief scientist for Lockheed Martin Information Technology (LMIT), specializing in advanced technology research. Eric is a highly sought-after network security consultant and speaker. Eric has consulted for international banks and Fortune 500 companies. He also has advised Venture Capitalist Firms on what start-ups should be funded. He has in-depth knowledge of network security and has come up with creative ways to secure his clients' assets. He is the author of several books, including *Hackers Beware: Defending Your Network from the Wiley Hacker, Hiding in Plain Sight,* and the *Network Security Bible.* Eric holds several patents and has written numerous magazine and journal articles. Eric worked for the CIA for more than seven years and has created several successful network security practices. Eric is an invited keynote speaker at government and international conferences and has appeared in interviews on CBS News, "60 Minutes," and CNN.

Coauthor

Sandra Ring is the founder of Pikewerks Corporation (www.pikewerks.com), an information security company that specializes in Insider Threat. Previously, Sandra was the deputy director of research for The Sytex Group, Inc. While working at Sytex, Sandra participated in original research of rootkit detection, volatile memory forensics, self-healing, and zero configuration networks. Sandra has worked for the Central Intelligence Agency, operated closely with the National Security Agency, and conducted research at the National Aeronautics and Space Administration's Langley Research Center. She is an author of *Cyber Spying: Tracking Your Family's (Sometimes) Secret Online Lives* (Syngress Publishing, ISBN: 1-931836-41-8) and a contributing author to the *Network Security Bible.*

Contents

Part I
Insider Threat Basics

Chapter 1

What Is There to Worry About?

Topics in this chapter:

- The Devil Inside
- The Importance of Insider Threat
- Why the Insider Threat Has Been Ignored
- Why the Insider Threat Is Worse Than the External Threat
- The Effect of Insider Threats on a Company
- How Bad Is It—Statistics on What Is Happening
- Targets of Attack
- The Threat Is Real
- New World Order
- Future Trends

Introduction

I was sitting at my desk when my phone rang. I answered the phone and it was a large pharmaceutical company who was interested in consulting services. They started off the conversation stating that they had some problems and thought that my company might be able to help. They had noticed a trend with one of their foreign competitors. Every time they went to release a new product (in this case a new drug), one of their competitors would release a similar drug with a similar name several weeks before them and would beat them to market. If you understand the drug industry, you'll know that this is a serious problem. The first company to get a product to market usually is able to obtain a higher market share and higher demand than its competitors. Therefore, this represented a huge monetary loss to the company and the executives were concerned.

This initially sounded like a potential problem but I needed more details. My follow-up question was how often had this occurred and over what time period. The executive I was talking with said it had happened eight times over the prior 12 months. I was sitting there thinking: You *think* there is a problem? My next question was, "Why did you wait so long to call someone?" Their answer was, "We figured it was just a coincidence, because the only way this could have happened was if an insider was giving the information to a competitor and we trust all of the employees so this could not be the case." Over the next several months they were going to realize how wrong that previous statement was.

I led an internal assessment team and over the course of several months found three different groups of people (each consisting of 2-4 people), working for two different competitors. Actually, one group was working for a foreign competitor and the other two groups were working for a foreign government.

The fact that this story is true is scary, but what makes it even more troubling is that this happened more than 18 months ago and I have worked on and am aware of at least 15 other similar cases. The average monetary loss of the case I worked on was estimated at $350 million annually.

The Devil Inside

"I trust everyone, it is the devil inside that I do not trust," is a great line from the movie *The Italian Job*. Everyone has the potential do to harm, including your employees. If you look at the minimal background checks that most companies perform on their employees, you have to wonder what that trust is based on. Why is it that once a total stranger is hired at your company, you now completely trust that person? Just because they are now called an employee does not mean they have loyalty to your organization and would do nothing to hurt the company. We do not want you to be so paranoid that your company cannot function, but a healthy dose of paranoia is good.

Aldrich Ames, Robert Hanssen, and other spies had one thing in common: they passed the polygraph (lie detector test) with almost a perfect score. How could a machine that tests whether people are lying not catch the biggest liars that cost so many people their lives? The reason is a polygraph does not detect lies, it detects guilt. In these cases, either the people felt justified by their actions and did not feel guilty about them or they were trained to be able to bypass and deceive people. Only by closely watching people over time will you start to understand that there are certain people who cannot be trusted.

Insider threat and corporate espionage rely on the fact that it is sometimes better to live in denial and be happy than to know the truth and have to deal with it. One of my associates recently found out his wife was cheating on him and was very annoyed with the person who told him. The person who told him said, "Why are you mad at me? Didn't you want to know?" And the person's response was, "No." It was easier to live with a lie than deal with the truth. While most executives might not be bold enough to admit this, it is very true in corporations and governments around the world. It is easier to trust your employees and keep life simple, than to suspect everyone and deal with the complexities it creates. However, if it will put your company out of business, cause hundreds of millions of dollars' worth of loss, or cause people to die, you might think differently about the answer.

Nobody wants to believe the truth, but corporate espionage via the insider threat is causing huge problems. Many companies either do not have the proper monitoring to realize or do not want to admit that it is happening to them. For some reason, with many crimes, including insider threat, victims feel embarrassed and ashamed. They are the victims, they did nothing wrong, but for some reason these criminals turn the tables on who is at fault. I have heard rape victims say that it was their own fault they were raped. I have also heard numerous times that it is a company's fault if they are stupid enough to be a victim to insider threat. With that mentality, who is going to admit that this happened to their company? The only person at fault is the attacker—not the victim.

The Importance of Insider Threat

Organizations tend to think that once they hire an employee or a contractor that that person is now part of a trusted group of people. Although an organization might give an employee additional access that an ordinary person would not have, why should they trust that person? Many organizations perform no background checks and no reference checks and as long as the hiring manager likes them, they will hire them. Many people might not be who you think they are and not properly validating them can be an expensive, if not a fatal, mistake. Because many organizations, in essence, hire complete strangers who are really unknown entities and give them access to sensitive data, the insider threat is something that all organizations must worry about.

If a competitor or similar entity wants to cause damage to your organization, steal critical secrets, or put you out of business, they just have to find a job opening, prep someone to ace the interview, have that person get hired, and they are in. The fact that it is that easy should scare you. Many companies have jobs open for several weeks and it could take a couple of weeks to set up an interview. That gives a competitor focused on your company a four-week period to prep someone to ace an interview. This is what foreign governments do when they plant a spy against the U.S. They know that a key criterion for that person is passing the polygraph, so they will put that person through intensive training so that he or she can pass the polygraph with no problem. This points out a key disadvantage that organizations have. The attacker knows what process you are going to follow to hire someone and all they have to do is prep someone so they ace that part of the process.

In terms of the importance, I often hear people say that it is only hype and that it cannot happen to us. This is synonymous to thinking that bad things only happen to others, they never happen to you; until they happen to you and then you have a different view of the world. I remember several years ago when my father got diagnosed with having a cancerous brain tumor. It shocked me, devastated me, and changed my views forever. Prior to that I knew that people had brain cancer but it was something that I could not relate to or understand because I never thought it could really happen to me or someone I love. Bad things happened to others, not to me. This is the denial that many of us live in, but the unfortunate truth is bad things do happen and they could be occurring right now and you just do not know about it.

Insider threat is occurring all the time, but since it is happening within a company, it is a private attack. Public attacks like defacing a Web site are hard for a company to deny. Private attacks are much easier to conceal.

Because these attacks are being perpetrated by trusted insiders, you need to understand the damage they can cause; how to build proper measures to prevent the attack; how to minimize the damage; and, at a minimum, how to detect the attacks in a timely manner. Many of the measures companies deploy today are ineffective against the insider. When companies talk about security and securing their enterprise, they are concerned with the external attack, forgetting about the damage that an insider can cause. Many people debate about what percent of attacks come from insiders and what percent of attacks come from outsiders. The short answer is who cares? The real answer is this:

- Can attacks come from external sources?
- Can an external attack cause damage to your company?
- Can an external attack put you out of business?
- Can attacks come from internal sources?
- Can an internal attack cause damage to your company?
- Can an internal attack put you out of business?

Since the answer to all of these questions is YES, who cares what the percent is? Both have to be addressed and both have to be dealt with. I would argue that since the insider has access already, the amount of damage they can cause is much greater than an external attacker and the chances of getting caught are much lower. If an attacker comes in from the outside, he has access only to systems that are publicly accessible and he has to break through security devices. If an attacker comes from the inside, she has full access and minimal if any security devices to deal with. As our digital economy continues to grow and the stakes increase, anyone who wants serious access to an organization is not even going to waste his time with an external attack, he is going to go right for the trusted insider.

Finally, to highlight the importance of insider threat, everyone is getting on the bandwagon. The Unites States Secret Service is conducting a series of studies on the insider; conferences are popping up on the subject. Why? Because billions of dollars are being lost and something has to be done to stop the bleeding. You will never be able to completely remove the insider threat because companies need to be able to function. If you fire all your employees, you might have prevented the insider attack, but you will also go out of business. The key is to strike a balance between what access people need and what access people have.

Insider Threat Defined

Since everyone uses different terminology, it is important to define what we mean by insider threat. The easiest way to get a base definition is to break the two words apart. According to *www.dictionary.com*, insider is defined as "one who has special knowledge or access to confidential information" and threat is defined as "an expression of an intention to inflict pain, injury, evil, or punishment; an indication of impending danger or harm; or one that is regarded as a possible danger." Putting this together, an insider threat is anyone who has special access or knowledge with the intent to cause harm or danger.

There is a reason that the insider threat is so powerful and most companies are not aware of it; it is because all the standard security devices that organizations deploy do little if anything to prevent the insider threat.

However, as much as we do not want to admit it, this is no longer true (if it ever was). The problem with insider threat is that it takes only one person who is disgruntled and looking for a quick payoff or revenge and your company is compromised. Unfortunately, it is really that easy and one of the many reasons that the problem has gotten so out of hand.

The world is also a different place than it once was. Most people today, by the time they are at the age of 30, have had more jobs than both their parents combined across their entire careers. In the past, people worked for one company for 30 years and retired. Having worked for one company for an entire career builds loyalty. However, today people switch companies fairly often and while most people are not intentionally out to perform corporate espionage, there is a high chance they can inadvertently perform it. When you switch companies, you most likely are going to stay within the same industry, unless you are making a complete career change, which is unlikely. Therefore, the chance that you are going to work for a competitor is very high. This means some of your knowledge from your previous employer, despite your best efforts, will leak over into this new company.

People do not like to hear it and employers do not like to admit it, but the biggest threat to a company is their internal employees. Your employees or anyone with special access (like a contractor) have more access than an outsider and therefore can cause a lot more damage. However, most organizations and media still focus on the external threat and pay little attention to the insider threat. Why? The short answer is the external threat is easier to see and easier to defend against. If an external attacker defaces your Web site, it is easy to detect and defend against. It is also difficult to deny because everyone can tell that it happened. However, if an employee makes copies of all of the customer credit cards and walks out with it on a USB drive that fits in his or her wallet, it is very difficult to detect and defend against.

Authorized versus Unauthorized Insider

An insider is anyone with special or additional access and an insider attack is someone using that access against the company in some way. The key question to ask is why does that person have the access they have and how did they get that access? One of the best ways to defend against the insider threat is to institute a principle of least privilege. Principle of least privilege states that you give an entity the least amount of access they need to do their job. There are two key pieces to this. First, you are giving your employees additional access. For employees to be able to perform their job at a company, it is obvious that they will need to be given special access that a normal person does not have. This means that every employee, contractor, or anyone else performing work at your organization has the potential to cause harm. The second key piece is needed to do their job. This focuses in on how critical access is to an organization. You know that every employee is going to be given special access; you just want to limit and control that access to the minimum possible subset.

The problem with most organizations is that employees are given a lot more access than what they actually need to do their jobs. Although the risk of insider threat is present with every employee, giving them additional access just increases the damage and increases the number of people that could cause harm. If only five people out of 3000 have access to a sensitive database within your organization, one of those five people would have to be motivated for an insider threat problem to arise. However, if 300 out of 3000 people have access to that information, the odds of finding or motivating someone is much higher. Therefore, the more people that have access to a piece of information, the greater the chance it could cause harm to your organization.

In addition, the more access that a single person has, the greater the damage that person can cause. If 10 different managers each have access to only 10 different pieces of sensitive data, for all 10 pieces of data to be compromised, 10 people would have to be involved. However, if one person had access to all 10 pieces of data, then it would take only one person to cause a grave amount of damage to the organization.

Based on this analysis, two criteria are critical for analyzing the potential for insider threat: number of people with access to a piece of information and number of pieces of data a single individual has. Carefully tracking and controlling critical data and people with critical access can minimize the potential for insider threat.

We have clearly shown that access is the avenue in which insider threat is manifested. The question is how did they get that access? If they were given the access then they are authorized to access the information. If they were not given the access, but stole, borrowed, or acquired it without permission, then it is unauthorized access. The reason the distinction is important is that it helps determine the countermeasures that could be put in place. Security devices like firewalls, passwords, and encryption protect against unauthorized access. If an unprotected wireless access point is set up, people who are unauthorized to connect to the corporate network can still connect and access sensitive data. Someone who is unauthorized to access the file server can walk up to an unlocked computer and access sensitive data. However, if proper security is put in place with firewalls, encryption, and passwords, an unauthorized person should no longer be able to connect to an unprotected wireless access point or to sit down in front of an unlocked system. So the security measures that are present today can prevent unauthorized insider threat.

However, all the current security measures today will not prevent the authorized insider. You can set up all the security you want on a network, but that will not stop someone with proper authorization. An authorized insider is someone with a valid reason for accessing the data but who uses that access in a way that was not intended by the company. The NOC manager is given access to customer passwords, because he needs that access to do his job. However, it is very hard to stop him from giving that information to an attacker or a competitor. When talking about authorized insider threat, intent plays a key role. People need access to do their jobs, but what are their intentions once they get access? Luckily, as the case studies in the later chapters will demonstrate, negative intentions rarely go without warning.

Categories of Insider Threat

Depending on the levels of access someone has, there are different categories of insider:

- Pure insider
- Insider associate
- Insider affiliate
- Outside affiliate

Each type has different levels of access and different motives.

Pure Insider

A pure insider is an employee with all the rights and access associated with being employed by the company. Typically, they have keys or a badge to get access to the facility, a logon to get access to the network, and can walk around the building unescorted. They can cause the most damage because they already have most of the access they need.

Elevated pure insider is an insider who has additional privileged access. This usually includes system administrators who have root or administrator access on the network. These people were given the additional access to do their jobs; however, in many cases, they are given more access than what they need. Very often when companies try to mitigate the risk of an insider threat, the best area to focus on is limiting the access of the elevated pure insider. This is also called the "principle of least privilege," or giving someone the least amount of access they need to do their job. Notice the key factors in this definition: you are not stopping people from doing their job, you are just taking away the extra access that they do not need.

With the pure insider, the key areas to focus in on to detect or prevent damage are access, behavior, and money. Throughout this book you will see that an underlying factor of insider threat is access. If someone does not have proper access, it makes their job much harder. Limiting and controlling access is key.

The second factor that comes into play is behavior. In many cases, when someone commits an insider attack, there have usually been personal behavior patterns that were predictive of such behavior. Usually they openly talked bad about the company or management. They tended to be unhappy and angry at work and might even have stated that one of these days they were going to get back at the company.

A third driving factor with the pure insider is money. Many of the people who perform these attacks have financial issues. A normal employee would not commit insider threat. However, if you add in stress and financial issues and someone comes along and offers a large sum of money to make all of their problems go away, there is a chance that person might be tempted. Therefore, tying this in with the second point, good managers should understand and watch for unusual behavior patterns. If a certain employee is complaining about financial issues and child support and three months later is driving a new Lexus, you might want to be concerned.

Insider Associate

Insider associates are people who have limited authorized access. Contractors, guards, and cleaning and plant services all fit under this category. They are not employees of the company and do not need full access, but they need limited access. Limited access usually takes the form of having physical access to the facility but not access to the network. This is best illustrated by a scene in the movie *Wall Street*. Charlie Sheen needed access to stock trading information. The easiest way he found to obtain it was to get a job at the company that provided the janitorial services for the company who he needed information on. He was given access to all of the offices after hours and as he was cleaning the offices he looked at and made copies of sensitive information that was left on people's desks. We tend to forget that in an office building, locking a door really does little to protect the security of the information in your office. With one company I worked for, everyone left sensitive data on their desks and locked their doors. The problem was that a master key was kept in a central location that anyone could use to gain access to an office. We have to remember that there are other people who can gain access to our offices and therefore sensitive data must always be properly secured.

To minimize the damage an insider associate can cause requires user awareness and controlling access. Raising awareness is meant to change someone's behavior as compared to training that is meant to teach someone a new skill. Many employees feel that their building, floor, and office are properly secure and leave systems logged in and information out that they shouldn't. User-awareness sessions can help change behaviors patterns, as people understand that locks do little to protect information. They must understand that a lot of people have potential access and that they should always properly secure sensitive data and lock systems before they walk away from them. In addition, you should carefully examine any activity that requires access to a facility. For example, why does the cleaning staff need access to everyone's office every night? I recommend that the cleaning staff not have a master key to each office. Instead, when people leave at the end of the day, they can put their trash can in the hallway. If they want their office vacuumed, they can leave their door open; if they do not want someone to have access, they can lock it. If employees leave their doors open, they know others can gain access and therefore will make sure that all sensitive date is properly secured.

Insider Affiliate

Pure insiders and insider associates have a legitimate reason to access the building. The next two categories of insider do not. An insider affiliate is a spouse, friend, or even client of an employee who uses the employee's credentials to gain access. This can be as simple as a friend coming to visit you, so you get them a badge for the building. When you take a phone call they go to use the rest room and on the way back they wander around looking at what is on people's computers and on their desks. While this can cause some problems it can usually be controlled.

The more damaging insider affiliate is someone who directly acts as an employee using the employee's credentials. The most common is remote access. Your spouse wants to sit on the couch and surf the Web and wants to borrow your laptop. You give him your user ID and password so he can log on and access the Internet. But what else is he accessing either deliberately or on purpose? I have also seen cases where a spouse is running out for the day and hands over his access card for the building and PIN number and says, "Can you swing by the office and pick up a few papers for me?" Once again, people think this is harmless, but if you stop and think about it, you'll realize the results can be very damaging.

To prevent insider affiliates, the best measure is to implement policies and procedures. You should never take for granted that employees will do the right thing. I have seen people say, "Well, of course everyone should know that they should not let someone borrow their user ID and password." But then I see others saying, "Why can't I, I am not doing any harm and I did not know that I wasn't suppose to."

The short answer is to never make assumptions. You should have clearly written policies and procedures, explain them to all employees, and require that they sign off that they understand them. Then, any deviation from the policy can be taken as a deliberate action on the part of an employee.

Outside Affiliate

Outside affiliates are non-trusted outsiders who use open access to gain access to an organization's resources. Today, one of the best examples is wireless access. If a company sets up an unprotected wireless access point, what stops an outsider from connecting? Nothing. Therefore, if an outsider is sitting at a Starbucks across from your office building and connects to your wireless network, are they breaking into your network? No. You are leaving the door wide open and they are wandering in. This is the same as leaving the front door unlocked with no access controls or guards, allowing anyone to walk in off the street.

Although the outside affiliate seems obvious, it is often overlooked by many companies. Protecting against the outside affiliate requires proper access controls in place for all types of access, including virtual and physical access.

Key Aspects of Insider Threat

The key thing to remember when dealing with insiders is that they have access and in most cases will exploit the weakest link that gives them the greatest chance of access, while minimizing the chances that they get caught. Why try to break through a firewall and gain access to a system with a private address, when you can find someone behind the firewall with full access to the system? I know it has been emphasized many times, but taking advantage of access is a driving force in the insider attack.

Most people, when they think of attackers, think of someone with a huge amount of technical sophistication that can walk through virtual cyber walls and gain access to anything that they want. However, insiders take advantage of the fact that they already have access, so many of the attack methods tend to be very low in technical sophistication. In some cases, if a pure insider or insider associate has partial access, they will sometimes use additional techniques to increase their access. However, since they are typically not dealing with any security devices, most of the methods tend to be fairly straightforward.

It is also important to remember that to launch an effective attack, attackers need knowledge of the organization they are trying to attack. External attackers could spend weeks, if not longer, trying to acquire the information they need to launch a successful attack. In some cases, if they cannot gain enough knowledge, they might decide to go against a different target. However, in the case of the insider, they have full knowledge of your operations. They know what is checked and what is not checked and can even test the system. For example, when they are trying to access their private shares, they could click on someone else's and see if anyone says anything. If they do this multiple times and nothing ever happens, they have now gained valuable knowledge that either access information is not being logged or not being watched. Because they have access to the operations, they either have detailed knowledge of how things operate or they can gain it quickly by testing the system.

NOTE

A private share is a folder on a file server that is only accessible by that individual and meant to hold personal or sensitive information. For example at most companies each person has his or her own private share to store files.

Acceptable Level of Loss

Everyone has heard the phrase no pain no gain or no risk no reward. Every company in business has to take some level of risk; otherwise, the company will not be able to survive. If you say that your company will have no risk of insider threat, then do not hire any employees. However, the second you hire one employee your chances of having an insider attack increase; as you hire more employees the risk keeps increasing. From a naïve standpoint, you might ask, if your risk keeps increasing why would you keep hiring people? The short answer is so that the company can grow and revenues and profits can increase and most companies are willing to take that risk.

This is also true of external attacks. As soon as you provide e-mail and Web services to the Internet, your chances of being attacked from the outside increase. However, your level of service and revenues also increase so it is a risk worth taking.

The bottom line is, you have to figure out what your acceptable level of loss is and then build in proper measures to protect against it. Many companies do not do this, throw caution to the wind, lose large amounts of money, and potentially go out of business due to insider attacks. It is much better to realize that there will be some level of loss but build in measures to minimize it to an acceptable level.

For example, hiring and giving everyone administrator access would be a huge potential for loss and not one that I would be willing to accept. On the other hand, if you require that anyone needing administrator access has to justify why they need it, get sign off by two executives, and go through a series of additional background checks before he or she is given the access, this will help reduce the risk. You might also put measures in place to rotate out key positions so it would be harder for a person to cause damage over a long period of time. In the chapters that follow, you will see how rotation in particular could have drastically shortened damage in many insider threat cases, such as when Mel Spillman stole nearly five million dollars over 15 years. In addition, you might set up separation of duties in which two people are required to perform a certain function, which prevents a single person from causing damage. This could have been monumental in reducing some of the visa fraud cases we will discuss, such as when Hsin Hui Hsu sent fraudulent letters inviting potentially hundreds of unauthorized Chinese nationals into the United States for "discussions" that were never meant to take place.

None of these measures mentioned would stop a determined attacker, but they enable you to properly manage risk to an acceptable level.

Insider attacks are likely to occur against your organization; the questions is whether you will be able to prevent most of them and in cases where you cannot prevent them, can you detect them in a timely manner?

Prevention versus Detection

One saying that I use a lot is, "Prevention is ideal but detection is a must." You always try to prevent attacks as much as possible and in cases where you cannot prevent an attack, you try to detect it in a timely manner and minimize the damage. The problem with insider threat is that prevention does not scale very well. If someone wants to compromise a piece of data he is going to do it. Therefore, while prevention measures should be put in place, they must always be teamed with detective measures. You have to assume that someone with inside knowledge and access will be able to work around the prevention measures; the key is, can you detect them and then take follow-up action to control the damage?

When I work with many companies on insider threat, they tell me that they want to put measures in place to detect attackers, not prevent them. Their logic is: if we prevent someone from doing something, they will just get more sophisticated and those more-sophisticated measures we might not know about. On the other hand, if we detect that someone is doing something, we have the proof and can take follow-up action to stop them by prosecuting or taking other measures against them.

In reality, what we are striving for is covert detection with reactive prevention. The reason this is the case is that there is so much going on in a network it is very difficult to find the malicious behavior. Many people say it is like finding a needle in a haystack. I think it is a lot worse than that and is like finding a single grain of sand among all the beaches in the world.

The problem with insider threat is finding enough information or having a high-enough level of confidence to know that someone is committing an insider attack. Most of us would agree that if we are 99 percent sure that someone is committing an insider attack, we would take action against them; if we were one percent sure, we would not take action. It is always easy to define the extremes, but what about the area in the middle that is gray? What is the burden of proof for your organization in which you have enough information to take action?

I want you to re-read the preceding paragraph. At first you might wonder what it has to do with prevention versus detection, but as you read it closely, you'll see it is talking about behavior: having enough indication that someone is up to no good. To gain the proper level of confidence, you must gather information, which is a category of detection. With detective measures you are monitoring and gathering information; when you have enough data points, you take action.

I am not saying that prevention should never be used against insider threats; I am just saying that you need a fine balance between prevention and detection. Preventive measures will stop a basic insider, which is what you want. A low-grade attacker you just want to stop and make go away, they are not worth additional effort. However, when it comes to high-end attackers who will put in whatever measure is necessary to accomplish a task, prevention will not stop them. It will just cause them to dig deeper and make it harder for you to find them the next time they come back. In these cases, detective measures will be key for finding and stopping them.

The bottom line is, to stop the insider threat problem, an organization has to put together a comprehensive and integrated solution of preventive and detective measures that encompass both host- and network-based solutions.

Insider versus External Threat

Arguing over whether insider versus external threat causes the most damage is what I categorize across the industry as a holy war. A holy war is a situation where you have smart people on both sides who disagree and the disagreement has gone on for so long that a stalemate has occurred. Regardless what the other side says, the group in disagreement will not listen. This is a no-win situation. The short answer that I stated previously in this chapter is: they both can cause damage and they both have to be addressed.

The problem to date is that most security efforts and focus have been on the external threat. At most organizations more energy and effort have been put against the external threat than the internal threat. The reason is simple: it is easier to stop, easier to control, and more visible. If you have system x you can state that it should not be accessible from the Internet and put measures in place to prevent it. Then if someone accesses it externally, it sets off a flag. The problem with the insider threat is, people are suppose to access server x but only for legitimate purposes. Now you have to measure intent when someone accesses data, which is almost impossible to do.

In addition, the outsider threat is more understood. We understand the means and methods and exploit scripts that are utilized to attack systems because we have a lot of case study. With insider threat we know it is occurring and it is damaging, but we have less factual data to base conclusions on.

Companies that are going to survive and thrive in the coming century are going to have to turn their focus to the insider and take action against these types of threats. Otherwise, by the time they do, there will not be much of their company left to save.

Why the Insider Threat Has Been Ignored

At this point you might be saying that if the insider threat is so damaging, why has it been ignored and why haven't people been focusing on it early? There are many reasons for this. First, it is not an easy problem. It is very hard to understand and almost impossible to get your arms around. Both the CIA and FBI knew of the damages of insider threat and took many measures to prevent it. However, over the past ten years they have still been severely impacted by it.

There are three key reasons that the insider threat has been ignored:

- Organizations do not know it is happening.
- It is easy to be in denial.
- Organizations fear bad publicity.

Each of these three areas will be examined in the following sections.

Organizations Do Not Know It Is Happening

Many companies do not even realize it is happening to them. Companies have good quarters and they have bad quarters; they have times where revenue is high and they have times when revenue is low. When the bad times occur, there are usually reasonable explanations for them. If a company had poor earnings in a given quarter because a new product they released did not do as well as they thought because a competitor came out with a similar product two months earlier, it is easy to write this off to poor market analysis. Because insider threat is a relatively new area for companies, their first thought is not going to be that it was because of an insider attack.

As insiders keep increasing in sophistication, it is going to be harder and harder for companies to know it is happening to them and are going to find other explanations for why the damage occurred.

We are not trying to turn companies into Chicken Little, where they run around saying the sky is falling, but we are trying to raise companies' awareness of what is happening and potentially give them an alternative explanation to what is happening when none of the conventional explanations seem to make sense. It is a hard problem and difficult to investigate, but the key thing to remember is: it will not go away. If you ignore it, it will only get worse. Therefore, if you think there is the potential that your organization is the victim of an insider attack, the sooner you start working the problem, the easier it will be and the less energy you will have to put in down the road. Insider threat is like a fire. The sooner you can detect a fire, the easier it is to deal with it. Ignoring a fire will not cause it to go out; it will keep getting worse and worse over time.

I would argue that if your company has been in existence for a while and has employees, the internal attack is occurring at some level. It might be a frustrated employee deleting some files, or someone bringing supplies home for the children, or people leaving sensitive documents at another location. While these might not seem damaging, think of the fire example. Do you want to put the fire out now while it is small or wait until it becomes a big problem?

It Is Easy to Be in Denial

After you admit you have a problem, you have to deal with it. One of my friends had a drinking problem and he would never admit to it. Everyone around him kept saying that they do not understand how he cannot recognize he has this problem. It turned out that it was twofold. First, he always justified it in his mind and downplayed it so he thought it was not as bad as it really was. Second, he knew that once he admitted he had a problem, he would have to do something about it, which he did not want to do.

These things are true with any problem that a company or person faces. It is sometimes easier to live in denial than to accept the truth and have to deal with it. Also, some companies write it off saying that they are willing to accept a certain level of loss to insider threat. That would be okay if they could answer these two questions: How much are you losing to insider threat? And what is your level of tolerance? If companies knew the answers to these questions and could live with them, that would be acceptable. The problem is that most companies have no idea how much money they are losing.

When it comes to insider threat, you are going to have to pay now or pay later and the sooner you pay, the less you will have to pay. While it is easier to live in denial for a short period of time, it is easier to identify and deal with the problem now than allow it to grow worse over time.

Fear of Bad Publicity

In some cases, companies are acknowledging they have a problem and dealing with it but not telling anyone because of the fear of bad publicity.

If a financial institution had three large clients compromised because of an insider attack and they publicly announced it, how many other clients would change banks because they fear that it could happen to them? The funny thing is a bank admitting they had a problem and fixed it is more secure than a bank who claims they never had any problems. However, when it comes to bad publicity, logic does not always hold up. Therefore, many places would rather keep their dirty secrets inside than expose them to the public. The real question that most executives ask is: what benefit or good will come of publicly announcing we had a problem? Except for raising awareness across the industry, little direct benefit will come to the company.

Why the Insider Threat Is Worse Than the External Threat

We have talked about the difference between the insider and external threat and why the insider threat has been ignored. In this section we are going to look at why the insider threat is potentially worse and what action must be taken to prevent and detect these types of attacks.

Although any type of attack can cause damage, the insider threat is usually worse for the following reasons:

- It's easier to implement.
- Current solutions do not scale.
- There's a high chance of success.
- There's less chance of being caught.

Easier

In many cases the insider attack is fairly easy because the person committing the act either has all or most of the access she needs. In addition, she has the knowledge to pull off the attack with less chance of being caught. A person committing an external attack has no idea what is going on at the other end. Fifteen people could be watching and ready to take legal action against him or they could be ignoring him. He could be very close to success or very far from it. He receives little knowledge and information and because the details of the site he is attacking are unknown, he is executing a blind attack, which is very difficult.

While some inside attacks are sophisticated, many of them are very straightforward because the attacker has the knowledge and access needed to commit the attack in a seamless manner.

Current Solutions Do Not Scale

Most security devices that are deployed at organizations are meant to stop the external attack. Firewalls, intrusion detection systems (IDS), and intrusion prevention systems (IPS) are based off some attack vector that they are trying to prevent. Firewalls block access to certain ports, which stops an attacker but does not stop an insider. If an insider needs access to certain information to do his job, a firewall will allow it. If that person uploads data to an external site or e-mails it to an unauthorized party, it is almost impossible for a firewall to prevent. IDS and IPS work off known signatures of attack. Most external attacks have known signatures, most internal attacks do not. In addition, most security devices are deployed at the perimeter. Once you get past the perimeter there are minimal internal protection measures.

As we have talked about, limiting access and implementing policies and procedures are key to preventing the insider threat. It should not be surprising that most organizations do a terrible job at controlling access and an even worse job at having clear, consistent policies. While companies claim they are doing this, they are not doing a good job. The analogy I like to use with security policies is that of sex when I went to high school. When I was in high school, everyone talked about sex and said they were having sex, but in reality, very few people were having sex and those that were having it were doing it incorrectly. Sorry for the bluntness, but that perfectly describes the state of security policies today.

Security measures that are in place are mainly for the perimeter and do not scale to the insider. Measures that will protect against the insider are hard to implement at a large organization and do not scale very well.

High Chance of Success

If someone gives you all the details and gives you the access you need, success is almost guaranteed. Now, I want to be careful not to over hype how easy the insider threat is, but I would at least argue that it is going to be easier than the external threat. One of the reasons there are more case studies on external threat in this book is because more people get caught. Particularly in the chapter on commercial threats you will notice that more than half the insiders were caught when the competing company they offered their proprietary information to contacted the authorities. What about the companies that are not so honest and ethical? How many other cases are out there that we are not aware of? The more people that get caught, the better you can understand a given problem.

Even if companies have proper access control in place and solid policies, the insider threat will be easier than the external threat for the foreseeable future.

Less Chance of Being Caught

If you know the environment and have access, you are technically not breaking in. If you are not breaking in, the chances of being caught are much lower. If an attacker has to maliciously compromise a firewall and use a zero-day exploit to break into a system and is doing things that are not suppose to be done, he has a higher chance of being detected. However, if he is accessing data that he is allowed to access but using it a manner that he is not supposed to, it is much harder for that action to be detected.

The Effect of Insider Threats on a Company

We have spent a lot of time laying the foundation for the insider threat and why an organization needs to be concerned with it. This section is where the rubber hits the road and we start to show how it can really impact your company and potentially put you out of business. It is one thing to know that the insider threat exists; it is completely different to see how it can affect your company's bottom line.

The obvious types of insider activity focus on disgruntled employees and usually revolve around destroying data or modifying data to cause harm to an organization (sabotage). Although these attacks cause monetary loss, they usually are easy to detect after the fact because the insider wants to take credit for his actions. Based on that, these are usually one-time attacks, where once the attacker performs his actions, he either disappears or is caught.

Other types of attacks are more damaging because they are done for different reasons, mainly financial gain, and therefore are much harder to stop or detect. The first area is fraud. According to *www.dictionary.com*, fraud is defined as:

"Deception carried out for the purpose of achieving personal gain while causing injury to another party. For example, selling a new security issue while intentionally concealing important facts related to the issue is fraud."

Releasing false information to outsiders or intentionally misrepresenting a product internally, all fall under the category of fraud. The more knowledge that you have, the easier it is to present false information to obtain the desired results that you are after.

One of the most damaging forms of insider threat is theft of intellectual property (IP). Although some companies do not recognize or admit to it, every organization that is in business has IP that must be protected. If this IP is compromised or given to the wrong person it could undermine the financial stability of the company. If a company understands, recognizes, and protects its IP, it can still be compromised, but it will be much harder. What is devastating is situations were a large percent of internal employees have access to sensitive IP. It only takes one person to cross the line and cause damage to the organization. In many cases, IP cases revolve around theft or breach of confidentiality of IP.

A twist on this is sabotage or modification of critical IP. One way to damage a company is to take sensitive IP and give it to a competitor. Another method is to modify the IP so it does not work or causes harm, which would cause the company to discontinue the use of that IP, which in some cases can be even more damaging. Would you rather have a viable product that has strong competition or no viable product regardless of the competition?

Fraud, theft of IP, and sabotage can all lead to the following:

- Monetary loss to the organization

- Financial instability

- Decrease in competitive advantage

- Loss of customers

- Loss of consumer confidence

There are many indicators that insider threat is happening at your company but companies have to be looking in the right area to see them. If your eyes are closed or you are looking the wrong direction, you might never realize that there is a problem.

What you have to remember is that insider attackers rarely think about the consequences of their actions or when they do, they obscure the facts to justify them in their minds.

How Bad Is It—
Statistics on What Is Happening

I can talk all day about the damage insider threat is causing companies and the cases that I have seen, but I thought it would be helpful to list some statistics across the industry and from recent reports. This section will show statistic, charts, and information from external sources, to validate the damage insider threat is causing across the world.

Insider Threat Study

The first set of findings is from a recent report titled "Insider Threat Study: Illicit Cyber Activity in the Banking and Finance Sector" that was written by the National Threat Assessment Center of the United States Secret Service and the CERT Coordination Center. The full report can be found at: www.sei.cmu.edu/ publications/documents/04.reports/04tr021/04tr021.html

The following are some critical points from the study. Each conclusive point from the study will be listed followed by brief analysis:

Conclusion

In 87 percent of the cases studied, the insiders employed simple, legitimate user commands to carry out the incidents. Only a small number of cases required technical knowledge of network security. For example, very few cases were carried out via a script or program (nine percent), and only slightly more involved spoofing or flooding (13 percent). There was no evidence that any insider scanned computer systems to discover vulnerabilities prior to the incident.

Analysis

This report highlights that this is not a technical problem but predominately an access problem. For external threat it is mainly a technical problem that can be solved with security devices like firewalls, IPS, and IDS. The insider already has access and is just using the access they have in an unauthorized manner.

Conclusion

In 70 percent of cases studied, the insiders exploited or attempted to exploit systemic vulnerabilities in applications, processes, or procedures (for example, business rule checks, authorized overrides) to carry out the incidents. In 61 percent of the cases, the insiders exploited vulnerabilities inherent in the design of the hardware, software, or network.

Analysis

One of the big problems with insiders is that they have knowledge. External attackers cannot exploit something they do not know about. An insider knows your organization's deepest, darkest secrets and will utilize them to her advantage. A trusted insider might know about a security hole and purposely not fix it so she can use it to gain access later. She might also create security holes that no one else will find, so she can get back in later. In most organizations, if a security engineer or system administrator wanted to create a back door that no one else knew about and that was virtually undetectable, he could. The reason is that most organizations do not have enough people to implement full checks and balances and they trust that their employees and contractors will always do the right thing.

Conclusion

In 78 percent of the incidents, the insiders were authorized users with active computer accounts at the time of the incident. In 43 percent of the cases, the insider used his or her own username and password to carry out the incident.

Analysis

In most cases, insiders are not really breaking into a system. They are just taking advantage of access they already have. What is also interesting is that they are using their actual accounts, so they are not trying to hide anything. Either they know the organization's security is so bad that they are not even looking at the logs; they do not care if they get caught; or they are so unsophisticated about technology that they do not even realize that someone could be watching them. With regards to the first item, in most cases insiders will test the waters. They will try something minor and see if anyone notices. If no one notices they will be a little more aggressive. If after several times no one notices, they figure they are in the clear. This is typically how an insider is caught because over time they let their guard down and push the limits (they get greedy) and someone notices.

Conclusion

There were some cases in which the insider used other means beyond his or her user account to perpetrate the harm. Twenty-six percent of the cases involved the use of someone else's computer account, physical use of an unattended terminal with an open user account, or social engineering (that is, gaining access through manipulation of a person or persons who can permit or facilitate access to a system or data).

Analysis

When performing an insider attack, even if the company is fairly secure, the weakest link in any organization is the human link. One person leaving his terminal unlocked for one hour on one day when he goes to a meeting provides the opportunity for an insider attack. In cases where an insider cannot find an unlocked terminal, she can usually obtain some level of access through social engineering attempts (just asking).

Conclusion

Only 23 percent of the insiders were employed in technical positions, with 17 percent of the insiders possessing system administrator or root access.

Analysis

This is no longer a revenge of the nerds situation. When insider threat is mentioned, most people think it is perpetrated by the technical staff. On the contrary, it can be anyone with a computer across your entire organization. Anyone who has access to the physical building that houses your organization has the potential to commit insider threat. This is why the problem is so difficult to detect and prevent: any one of your employees or contractors has the potential, means, and methods to cause harm.

Conclusion

Thirty-nine percent of the insiders were unaware of the organizations' technical security measures.

Analysis

This is one of my favorite statistics. A little less than half of the people committing insider threat did not know and did not care about any technical security measures that were in place. Reading deeper into this, the technical measures did nothing to detect or stop the attack. Reading even deeper, the reason technical measures were ineffective is because almost 40 percent of the attacks were non-technical.

Conclusion

In 81 percent of the incidents, the insiders planned their actions in advance.

Analysis

Initially, insider attacks were mostly reactive attacks by disgruntled employees. Now it is turning into a pre-meditated crime. People are carefully thinking about what they want to do, learning the environment, and carefully planning the crime so they do not get caught. Pre-meditation also implies that there is more to gain, for example monetary rewards. If an attacker just wants to cause loss to the company, he doesn't have to plan too much and it is usually a one-time event. If he wants to increase compensation to himself, it takes longer to plan it so he does not get caught, because he wants the crime to be a recurring event.

Conclusion

In 85 percent of the incidents, someone other than the insider had full or partial knowledge of the insider's intentions, plans, or activities. These included:

- Individuals involved in the incident and/or potential beneficiaries of the insider activity (74 percent)
- Coworkers (22 percent)
- Friends (13 percent)
- Family members (9 percent)

Analysis

No matter how good you think you are, there are always going to be others who know about what you are doing. You see this all the time in the media after someone is caught committing a crime and they interview their friends. There is always a friend or co-worker who says, "We always knew Johnny was suspicious and was up to no good; this does not surprise me at all." The question is: why didn't they say anything? If you want to catch an insider, you must raise awareness among co-workers to report suspicious activity.

Conclusion

In 31 percent of the incidents, there was some indication that the insider's planning behavior was noticeable. Planning behaviors included stealing administrative-level passwords, copying information from a home computer onto the organization's system, and approaching a former coworker for help in changing financial data.

Analysis

A crime is never composed of a single incident. There are many sub-components that have to occur before the actual crime is committed. In this case, the sub-components of insider threat are usually obvious actions that can be detected, prevented, and acted upon before the actual crime is committed.

Conclusion

Sixty-five percent of the insiders did not consider the possible negative consequences associated with carrying out the incident.

Analysis

There are many things that make an insider tick, but most of them are selfish reasons related to the individual. Financial gain, frustration, anger, and payback are all examples. In many cases the insider fails to look at the negative actions that could occur to them or the organization. This also ties in with the previous conclusion that other people, including family members, knew something was going on. Clearly letting people know the consequences of their actions and what could happen is often a solid deterrent against insider threat.

Conclusion

The motive and goal for most insiders studied were the prospects of financial gain (both 81 percent). Twenty-seven percent of the insiders studied were experiencing financial difficulty at the time of the incident.

Analysis

Money is a drug that entices almost everyone to become its prisoner. Money is a strong motivator and most people think if they had more money, that all their problems would go away. Therefore, it should be no surprise that one of the strongest motivators of committing an insider crime is money. There is a reason that government agencies that handle classified information require their employees and contractors to fill out financial disclosure forms. Money problems can be a big indicator of someone who might commit espionage attacks against an organization. It means they are highly susceptible to bribes when approached with an opportunity to earn fast money. When foreign governments are trying to recruit spies, money is usually the number one incentive and is usually a factor they look at to determine who they should recruit.

Conclusion

In 27 percent of the incidents, insiders had multiple motives for engaging in the incident.

Analysis

Although money is a primary motivator, there are usually secondary motivators. This is the straw-that-broke-the-camel's-back syndrome. In many cases there is usually a seemingly minor event that tips the scales to someone committing corporate espionage. During analysis, many people ask how Johnny not receiving a three-percent raise would cause him to try to destroy the company. What these analysts fail to realize is that that was just the last straw. If you go back two years, what caused Johnny to do this was his divorce, financial trouble, sick parent, not getting promoted three times, and working longer hours than anyone else. Not getting the three-percent raise just pushed him over the edge.

Conclusion

Insiders ranged from 18 to 59 years of age. Forty-two percent of the insiders were female. Insiders came from a variety of racial and ethnic backgrounds and were in a range of family situations, with 54 percent single and 31 percent married.

Analysis

For every crime, people like to put together demographics of the people who are most likely to commit the crime. For different types of robberies, law enforcement can tell you the demographic profile of someone likely to commit the crime. This helps law enforcement in preventing and investigating the crime because they can focus in on a smaller group. However, with the insider, there is no demographic profile. The people committing these crimes are all across the board. Therefore, anyone at your organization could be committing corporate espionage. From the summer intern to the 30-year-tenured executive, they all have the potential of committing internal espionage.

Conclusion

Insiders were employed in a variety of positions within their organizations, including:

- Service (31 percent)
- Administrative/clerical (23 percent)
- Professional (19 percent)
- Technical (23 percent)

Analysis

This conclusion drives home our previous point that there is no profile that can be generated of someone who will commit insider threat. Almost every position in your organization has sensitive information and access is all that is needed to commit this crime. In cases where a given position does not have access, it is usually fairly easy to obtain that access.

Conclusion

As reported earlier, only 17 percent of the insiders had system administrator/root access prior to the incident.

Analysis

The reason the insider threat is so devastating to an organization is that almost every position has more access than they need to do their job. So when someone decides to turn to the dark side, they already have access to the information they need. If organizations did a better job of controlling access to sensitive data, it would make the insider threat more difficult, easier to detect and easier to control.

Conclusion

Twenty-seven percent of insiders had come to the attention of either a supervisor or coworker for some concerning behavior prior to the incident. Examples of these behaviors include increasing complaints to supervisors regarding salary dissatisfaction, increased cell phone use at the office, refusal to work with new supervisors, increased outbursts directed at coworkers, and isolation from coworkers.

Analysis

Many organizations say that they wish there were indicators of people who will commit insider-threat activities. The answer is: there are. Insiders that cause harm to the organization have visible showed behavioral and professional problems at the office. In many cases, organizations never tie these people back to causing damage, but this conclusion shows that those people need to be isolated and removed from the organization.

Conclusion

Twenty-seven percent of the insiders had prior arrests.

Analysis

What makes this conclusion even scarier is that most of the employers probably had no idea that their employees had prior arrests. Most employers don't perform background or financial checks during the hiring process. If someone aces an interview, she is hired. However, validating the background and knowing the individual you are dealing with are critical.

Conclusion

In 61 percent of the cases, the insiders were detected by persons who were not responsible for security, including

- Customers (35 percent)
- Supervisors (13 percent)
- Other non-security personnel (13 percent)

Analysis

Firefighters are responsible for putting out the fires not for detecting the fires. The population is responsible for detecting the fires and calling them in so the experts can do their jobs. While this makes perfect sense, many companies don't follow it. Many companies say it is the security department's responsible for finding security breaches. That is one of the reasons the problem is so bad today. It is the security department who is responsible for dealing with the problems, but it is the entire company that is responsible for calling in the problems. Everyone must be trained to notify the appropriate people if they see suspicious behavior.

Conclusion

In at least 61 percent of the cases, insiders were caught through manual (that is, non-automated) procedures, including an inability to log in, customer complaints, manual account audits, and notification by outsiders.

Analysis

Because many of these attacks are low-tech crimes, in many cases they are detected with low-tech methods. Automated devices will help, but nothing can replace the analytical capability of a human. Humans must be involved and must perform the analysis to determine if there is a problem.

Conclusion

Eighty-three percent of the insider threat cases involved attacks that took place physically from within the insider's organization. In 70 percent of the cases, the incidents took place during normal working hours.

Analysis

Your organization is going to be the crime scene of the attack. Many people think that these attacks are done covertly in the middle of the night and therefore they look for anomalies in access time. However, many attacks are committed during normal works hours as part of a person's job.

These conclusions should help to lay the groundwork that many of the ways that people look at insider crime and who is committing these crimes are different from what was originally thought. While this section focused on a specific report, CERT also tracks computer crimes across the Internet.

The attacks are increasing exponentially and will continue to get worse. What is interesting is that because there are so many attacks occurring and it is getting so out of hand, CERT no longer tracks this information.

Beware of Insider Threats to Your Security

The next set of information on insider threat is from an article titled, "Beware of insider threats to your security." The full article can be found at www.viack.com/_download/200408_cdm.pdf.

The following are some of the key findings from the article:

Conclusion

The Gartner Group estimates that 70 percent of security incidents that cause monetary loss to enterprises involve insiders.

Analysis

When executives ask why they should be concerned about internal threat, this statistic is the driving theme. The reason is, it could cost your organization a significant amount of money and potentially put you out of business.

Conclusion

Credit reporting agency TransUnion recently stated the top cause of identity theft, which the FTC reported as generating business losses of nearly $48 billion in 2003, is now theft of records from employers that maintain records on many individuals.

Analysis

This is starting to show that the inroads of insider threat are deep and wide. Identify theft is being traced back to the trusted insider that is using and compromising information that they should not have access to. For any organization that maintains sensitive information about their clients, this is a huge concern. If client information is compromised because your organization did not properly protect it, your organization could have liability issues. Also, many states and the federal government are looking at making it a requirement that if you think that personal information might have been compromised, you must report it to the individual and potentially to the government.

Conclusion

Recent FBI statistics show that 59 percent of computer hackings are done internally (based only on what is reported).

Analysis

A long-debated issue is what percent of attacks occur from within the organization. Although the number can be debated, the recent CSI/FBI Computer Crime Report states that more than half of all attacks and monetary damage to an organization is done by a trusted insider. Regardless of whether you believe the statistic or not, insider threat is a huge problem and will only continue to get worse.

Conclusion

A source inside the United States intelligence community stated that more then 85 percent of all incidents involving the attempted theft or corruption of classified data involved an individual who had already been thoroughly vetted and been given legal access to that data.

Analysis

Controlling access is critical, but producing granularity of controls is even more important. For classified information to be publicly revealed, it almost has to be an inside job, because only insiders have access to the information. Therefore, the only way this information can be compromised is if someone trusted either deliberately or accidentally reveals it to someone who should not have access. Now if the US government, which takes extensive measures to protect classified information, still has internal compromises, is there any hope for small, non-governmental organizations?

Espionage: A Real Threat

Many companies do not even realize they are being attacked and victims of corporate espionage; and in cases where they do realize it, they are not reporting it. This is the basis for the next article we are going to cover, "Espionage: A Real Threat," which can be found at: www.optimizemag.com/article/showArticle. jhtml?articleId=17700988&pgno=3

This article shows that economic espionage is on the rise.

Preliminary System Dynamics Maps of the Insider Cyber-Threat Problem

The next report is an exercise that was undertaken as part of CERT. The report displays the results of what is to be deemed a work in progress. It is important to note that it is not a complete report or a finished product. In addition, many of the findings are based on expert opinion and not factual data. Nonetheless, I though that several of the key diagrams from the study were worth inclusion in this section with some additional explanation. The full report can be found at: www.cert.org/archive/pdf/InsiderThreatSystemDynamics.pdf

What is important to note is that all of the attacks included both high and low-tech attack methods. In addition, the motivation of the attacks covered the broad range. Nonetheless, you can see that the coverage of insider threat and the potential damage is very broad.

Do You Really Know What Your Programmers Are Doing?

Anyone with any access to critical data could represent a threat to your organization. A key group of people who have a large amount of control in an organization are the programmers. Programmers implement applications that are either used internally or sold externally to a large number of customers. Backdoors and other problems in code could represent a large threat to intellectual property of an organization

The article "Do You Really Know What Your Programmers Are Doing?" which can be found at www.mintaka.com/whitepaper/White%20Paper%20-%20Security.pdf, talks about the impact of insider threat.

What is of interest is the breakdown of human threats. Although human threats can be non-malicious and can come from outsiders, many of the threats come from insiders.

How Much is Too Much Data Loss?

Finishing up this section, we are going to look at the article "How Much Is Too Much Data Loss?" which can be found at http://internetnews.com/security/print.php/3503331.

This article highlights some of the similar points that we have seen, but it is also a good summary of the problem insider threat represents to an organization.

The following are some of the key points:

Conclusion

According to the Gartner Group, 70 percent of security incidents that occur are inside jobs, making the insider threat arguably the most critical one facing enterprises.

Analysis

Although the insider threat is one of the most critical risks facing an organization, very few organizations either recognize it or know that it exists. Many organizations that I have worked with on insider threat recognize it as a major problem only after there is a problem or huge monetary risk to the organization.

Conclusion

One out of every 500 e-mail messages contains confidential information, customer data, employee data, financial information, intellectual property, or competitive information," said Kelly. She offered another way to look at it: a company with 50,000 employees, each sending 10 e-mail messages outside the company per day, would incur nearly 1,000 potential data security violations per day.

Analysis

This emphasizes that the problem is occurring on a regular basis and is a part of normal business. One of the reasons so many companies suffer from insider threat is because it is so difficult to solve. If it were an isolated problem or one that infrequently occurred, it would be easy to solve. However, since it is ingrained in how people normally operate, it would require an entire paradigm shift to solve.

Conclusion

The Ponemon Institute, a private research company, recently released its 2004 Data Security Tracking Study with alarming results. Of the 163 companies participating, 75 percent, or 122 companies, reported a data-security breach within the past 12 months. The majority of the companies were Fortune 1000.

Analysis

What is scary about this is that only a small percent of companies actually know about and detect security breaches. If 75 percent admitted having a breach, the actually number of breaches and monetary loss is much higher.

Conclusion

A recent survey by the FBI and Computer Security Institute found that between 2000 and 2003, about 40 percent of all companies confronted an attempted information snatch each year.

Analysis

The good news is that organizations are starting to crack down on internal threat. The problem is that in many cases, it is too little to late.

Targets of Attack

If you do not know what someone is trying to do or target it is hard to stop them. Therefore in order to build appropriate protection measures and to understand the real threat, you need to understand what is being targeted. After you understand what the attacker's end objective is, you can not only build appropriate defense measures, but you can also test those measures to make sure they are effective.

If someone is committing insider threat, he is targeting your company; more specifically, he is targeting your IP. At the center of the bulls-eye is your organization's IP. That is what ultimately differentiates your organization from the competition; it is what makes your organization unique and is the financial engine behind its success.

There are different levels and types of IP that can be a target of attack. The obvious types of IP that would represent the greatest loss to your organization fall along the lines of formulas, source code, customer lists, and marketing plans. This obvious, or primary, IP is what forms the core of your business line. If someone asks you what your organization does, the primary IP is most likely highlighted in that description. For example, if you ask someone what Pepsi does, they would say they produce soda. Even in that brief description, their primary IP is identified: the recipe and methods for producing their brand of soda. Microsoft produces software. Once again, even in a two-word description the organization's IP is quickly identified. Therefore, the first step in the protection of your organization is to create a list of the primary IP in your organization, minimize and control who has access to it, and focus your attention on protecting that information.

Although primary IP is often the main focus, you cannot lose sight of the non-obvious, or secondary, IP for your organization. While it might not be as critical as the primary IP, it can still cause damage and has to be identified and tracked. Secondary IP is the street address of your building, system configurations, routers, access to critical areas, etc. These do not represent the core business line, like primary IP does, but they support the primary IP and could still be targeted by an insider.

To illustrate the difference between primary and secondary IP, let's look at two examples. If a pharmaceutical employee takes the recipe for a new drug and gives it to a competitor, she is clearly attacking the company's primary IP. However, if a disgruntled employee of an Internet sales company disconnects the primary Internet connection so customers cannot get to the company's e-commerce site, he is targeting the secondary IP.

In both cases, it is critical to know what your primary and secondary IP are because they will be the targets of attack. The more you can do to protect them, the better off you will be. Although this seems easy, correctly identifying IP is often the hardest and most-overlooked area of most companies. I guarantee you if you go up to any key stakeholders in the company and ask them what the primary and secondary IP are for your organization, they will either miss items or be incorrect on what those items are. Sometimes things that seem obvious and straightforward are very difficult to identify. Therefore, do not take the task of identifying IP lightly. Spend the time and energy to do it correctly because the better job you do in identifying the prospect of attack, the easier your job will be in protecting and preventing those attacks.

Just to show you how bad the problem is, let's assume that you have correctly identified the IP for your organization. Now ask yourself who has access to that information. If you are not scared enough, ask yourself the follow-up question of even if you knew who had access, would you know who is accessing the data, when they are accessing it, and what they are doing with it. What seemed like an easy question is growing rapidly in complexity as you start to develop a plan of attack. In reality, the problem of dealing with insider threat is not easy. I often compare it to accounting for each grain of sand on a beach and making sure they do not move. However, it is worthwhile to make the investment because if you do not, since the threat is growing rapidly, there might not be any part of your company left once the attacker is done. You have to always remember that the ultimate goal of an attack is to cause harm to your company.

Now that we have looked at the main target, let's briefly examine what an attacker could do to your primary or secondary IP. In dealing with what they can do, we can map it back to the core areas of security: confidentiality, integrity, and availability. After you identify the IP, you have to ask yourself what the primary attack vector is going to be. Would they try to reveal the information to someone who should not have access (confidentiality), modify it to reduce the value (integrity), or destroy it (availability)? Typically, the high-end insider primarily focuses on confidentiality with integrity as a secondary goal. The lower-end attacker, for example, a disgruntled employee, will usually focus on availability with integrity as a secondary goal.

The Threat Is Real

Insider threat is no longer a fictitious concept that people write about and that you see in movies. It is real and it is happening all the time and those who do not take it seriously may be hurt by its results.

Think of the damage that viruses and worms cause to organizations. These are attacks that start on the Internet and manage to get through organizations' firewalls, perimeters, and security devices and cause severe loss. If an external worm can penetrate an organization with ease, what can someone who is behind the firewall and security perimeter do? The short answer is: almost anything they want. Although people can argue over the validity and strength of firewalls, IDS, and perimeter security, at least there are some measures in place. When it comes to insiders, there is little stopping them because they are a trusted entity. What is even worse than not preventing them is not trying to detect their actions. This means that not only is nothing stopping an insider but nothing is watching or recording their actions to even tell something is happening.

As we talked about earlier, many organizations would rather live in denial than fix the problem. Unfortunately with a real threat, denial will only cause more harm. The insider threat is like a tumor; if you realize there is a problem and address it, you will have short-term suffering but a good chance of recovery. If you ignore it, it will keep getting worse and while you might have short-term enjoyment, it will most likely kill you.

You might be saying that you acknowledge that the threat is real, but that your company is not vulnerable. The reality is that almost every organization is vulnerable because almost every organization has minimal if any controls in place and they do not carefully control access to data. Some organizations might have some basic access controls in place, but that is not good enough. If even one person has more access than what they need to do their job, that is too much access. Giving everyone the least access they need to do their job is critical, plus putting auditing measures in place to track behavior, even if you know that access is strictly controlled. What stops someone who has legitimate access from e-mailing it to someone who should not have access? Not only do you have to strictly control access, you must also monitor it. Since too-much access it what leads to ultimate compromise and too-little monitoring is what leads to someone not being caught or controlled, both play a critical role in your insider threat arsenal.

More and more organizations are starting to recognize that insider threat is important; the problem is it is after the fact. I know of a ton of companies that have been victims to insider threat; I do not know of any that have successful stopped an insider threat initially. All of our case studies, histories, and knowledge of insider threat are after the problem occurs and a company gets compromised. The real problem is, we are finding out about the problem because of the damage not because the insiders are being caught. At least if we caught the insider after the fact we could stop that person from doing it again. Unfortunately, we know it is happening but we do not know who did it. This creates a double-edged sword. Most executives do not believe what they cannot see, so they initially do not take insider threat seriously. Then, after it happens and there is critical damage, they ask why no one warned them or told them it was a problem so they could have fixed it.

So far in 2005 it is estimated that more than 10 million identities have been stolen, with a loss of more than $50 million resulting from it. What more proof do we want that this is a real threat? You might ask what stolen identities have to do with insider threat. The answer is: there is a direct correlation. How is personal information taken to steal someone's identity? Through an insider who has access to that information for the company they work for. Credit card fraud and identity theft are both caused by insiders stealing information they should not have access to.

The Bali bomber wrote a manifesto from jail urging terrorists to take terrorism to cyberspace. Why? Because he knows that is a weak link that can easily be exploited. Organizations and countries have critical infrastructures all stored in computers. If that information is compromised, it could have the same impact as an actual bomb.

The book *Unrestricted Warfare*, by Qiao Liang and Wang Xiangsui (Beijing: PLA Literature and Arts Publishing House, February 1999), which can be downloaded at www.terrorism.com/documents/TRC-Analysis/unrestricted.pdf, talks about how cyber weapons will become the weapons of the future. The key fact is that this levels the playing field across all countries. Who can compete with the nuclear arsenal of the U.S.? However, with cyber weapons, all the barriers to entry and monitoring are gone. Just think if you put together two or three of the cyber weapons together in a coordinated fashion, you would have the cyber version of the perfect storm.

Insider threat needs to be moved up in importance and discussed in boardrooms prior to attacks, not after significant monetary loss. Proactive measures need to be to taken to stop insider attacks from occurring, not reactive measures to clean up the mess.

What is scary is there is really minimal skill needed to launch these attacks. You really do not need to know anything if you have access. You just drag and drop information you should not be sending outside the company and you e-mail it to a competitor or a Hotmail account. Years of company IP can be extracted in minutes. Even if you do not have access, there are tools you can download and run to get access. If you can install MS Office, you can install and run these tools. Unfortunately, they are really that easy to use. The days of knowing how to write, compile, build, and exploit are gone. These tools are publicly available, free for the taking.

The sale of stolen IP makes the stolen car industry look small time. It is happening constantly and is such a norm, that people do not even realize it. An unprotected computer is an insider threat even if the user of the system is the most ethical employee on the planet. The computer and account has trusted access, not the person, and if someone can compromise the system because the person went to lunch and left his system unlocked, that is a huge source of insider threat and loss for a company.

We can predict with high reliability snowstorms and severe weather before they occur. This early-warning system enables people to prepare and take action to help minimize the damage. The reason we can predict weather is because we look for indicators using radar and other advanced techniques. We need to develop cyber indicators. Some initial indicators that could show a company is vulnerable are: no or weak policies, weak passwords, and no list of critical assets. If we can better identify and track these cyber indicators, we will have a better chance of reacting to the problem.

Profiling the Insider

One problem with the insider threat is there is no single profile that can be used to help identify who might be committing these crimes. With other crimes there are clear profiles you can look for. There is a set profile for the person who would rob a gas station or commit rape. However, with insider threat there is no demographic profile. People who have been caught vary in age, sex, social background, and education and cover the entire range of categories of people.

There was one report that had a profile for the person most likely to commit insider threat. The profile was someone in their mid 30s, works long hours, logs into the company at night, sometimes works weekends, drinks, smokes, and is divorced. I laugh because that covers almost everyone I know. Therefore rash attempts like this never really generate anything meaningful in terms of a demographic profile.

One of the biggest indicators of an attacker is someone who is highly frustrated with his company and/or boss and who openly admits to his frustration and dissatisfaction with his job. You unfortunately see this all the time, when someone goes into work and shoots someone and they interview their co-workers and they say, "Johnny always talked about doing this, we knew it would happen someday and was only a matter of time." You think, why didn't anybody say anything or the boss do anything about it. The problem is in the past people never took this very seriously. Management and co-workers have to realize that these verbal outbreaks could be a pre-cursor to additional actions and if acted upon early, the crime could be prevented.

Most of the attacks were never very technical in nature. Based on the wide range of access most people have, it is fairly easy for people to commit these crimes. Many people committing the crimes have been at the company for 3-5 years, so they are viewed as trusted entities. Finally, many of the people committing the crimes justify the crimes in their minds and do not fully understand the repercussions of their actions. In one case a spouse said, "I knew my husband was doing this but I never thought he would get arrested and be put in jail. I wish I had said something sooner." In another case, the person blamed the company because he had to get an expensive operation and since the company would not give him a bonus he felt it was his right to commit the crime.

The motives for committing the crimes cover a broad spectrum, but the main areas are financial gain, revenge, and retaliation for a negative work environment. In addition, most of the insiders that were caught got caught because they were greedy, they bragged, or they got sloppy. Unfortunately, this means that the good criminals rarely get caught.

Preventing Insider Threat

There is no single thing that you can do to prevent an insider threat. The concept of defense in depth applies here as it does to all areas of security. No single solution is going to make you secure. Only by putting many defense measures together will you be secure and those measures must encompass both preventive and detective measures.

Some of the key things that can be done to prevent or minimize the damage of the insider threat are the following:

- **Security awareness** Employees, contractors, and any other insiders need to be educated on how to protect corporate assets. They need to understand the dangers and methods of social engineering and be careful what information they give out. They also have to be cognizant that insiders could exist at their company and not only do their part to protect corporate assets (for example, locking their workstations), but they also have to look for indications of insider threat and report them to the correct parties.

- **Separation of duties** Any critical job function or access to critical information should involve two or more people. This prevents a single person from committing an inside attack.

- **Rotation of duties** All critical jobs should have multiple people who perform the roles and those people should be rotated through periodically. If a person knows that someone else is going to be performing a given role in two months, it will be much harder for them to commit fraud or other insider attacks, because there is a good chance someone might catch it later.

- **Least privilege** Any additional access that someone has can be used against the company. Although access is needed for people to perform their jobs, this access should be carefully controlled. People should be given only the access they need to do their jobs and nothing else.

- **Controlled access** Access is what someone is going to use to compromise an organization. The more a company knows what access people have, the better they can control it.

- **Logging and auditing** Organizations must know what is happening on their network and this information must be reviewed on a regular basis. If someone's actions are not logged, a company will have no idea who did what and will not be able to detect the insider. Even if this information is logged, if it is not reviewed on a regular basis, an organization will not be able to catch an attacker in a timely manner.

- **Policies** A policy states what a company's stance is on security and what is expected of anyone with inside access. A policy is a mandatory document that is clear and concise and that everyone must follow. If a policy does not exist, how do insiders know what is expected of them? I once knew an employee that bragged about making copies of software when he left a company. When I questioned his concern of legality and theft, he replied simply by saying, "I never signed anything." This information must be presented to them in a way that they understand and it must be made clear that they have to follow it.

- **Defense in depth** When it comes to network security, there is no silver bullet. No single solution is going to make you sure. Organizations must deploy a layered security model, with checks and balances across each layer.

- **Look beyond technology** Many inside attacks are not technology driven. Organizations must realize that non-technology-based solutions need to be implemented across the company.

- **Archive critical data** Any critical information must be properly archived and protected. This way all the IP is not in one place if a system gets destroyed or compromised.

- **Complete solution** Any solution that is implemented must include all aspects of the company: people, data, technology, procedures, and policies.

New World Order

The world is a different place than it used to be. Insider threat is occurring and it is increasing at a rapid pace. Organizations that do not understand it or are not willing to get on the bandwagon are going to suffer damage and loss. Organizations that are going to survive have to realize the threat is real and take action immediately, because most likely the damage has already begun beneath the surface.

Organizations must understand that security is an ongoing task that must constantly be done and readjusted. Security goes way beyond technology and is never complete. There is no such thing as 100 percent security. Which means you will never get it right but you have to keep trying to get it close enough. In order to properly implement security you must understand the organization's structure, mission, and politics so security can be seamlessly integrated. Security is a means to an end but it is not an end state.

There are some insiders who will do anything they have to in order to compromise your organization. However, there are a lot of insiders who just take advantage of opportunity. They are working on a system, they find a problem, no one is watching and they take advantage of it. The determined insider will always be a problem, but the opportunistic insider can be stopped by organizations with comprehensive, integrated security solutions.

Many people, who have been at companies for several years and have been caught committing insider threat, were found to have less-than-perfect backgrounds when they were investigated. They had criminal records that the company never new about. Think of the damage that could have been saved if the company did the proper checks prior to the incident as opposed to after.

If you want to find where the hole is in a tire, you put it under water and see where the bubbles come out. Now, we are not suggesting that you hold your employees' heads under water until they confess, but we are saying that if you tighten down security you will quickly see the problem areas emerging.

Future Trends

We have covered a lot of ground in this chapter and felt that an appropriate summary would be necessary to cover the future trends that we see occurring in the industry.

Policies and Procedures

Many companies, from a cyber perspective, lack clear control and direction in terms of protecting and controlling access to their critical assets. While companies are focusing on long-term strategic plans for their organizations, they need to address the critical IP and put together clear guidelines for what is expected of their insiders. As we move forward, the lack of solid policies is going to manifest itself more and more in companies. Companies that are serious about the insider threat are going to realize that the old style of inefficient policies is no longer going to work. Therefore, instead of trying to re-work existing policies, companies are going to realize that they are going to have to re-write their policies from scratch.

It is critical with any organization that everyone is on the same page with regards to protection of information. Just because you have a policy does not mean people will follow it; however, without the policy as the starting point, there is no way you can perform consistent enforcement across an organization. While it is difficult, and executives never want to put things in writing, it is critical that a clear, concise policy with appropriate repercussions be put in place.

Access Controls

Access is the gateway in which the insider threat is manifested. Typically, in most organizations, access control is poorly implemented and poorly understood. Moving forward, companies are going to have to change this. Those that have been burnt in the past by insider threat or those that want to make sure they do not get burnt moving forward, will have to take the time to properly control access to critical data. This is a multi-staged process, involving identifying critical IP, determining who should have access to it, and controlling and tracking that access.

Miniaturization

Data and critical IP is at the heart of any organization and extracting and compromising that information is at the heart of insider threat. As technology continues to advance, storage devices are going to become smaller and smaller and embedded in other devices. Storage devices that fit in watches or pens and that are the size of pennies will make it much harder to be able to track and control this information. Attackers are always going to take the easiest path or exploit the weakest link when they are compromising an organization, and with storage technology getting smaller and smaller, the physical attack will become that much easier.

Even with guards and other physical security measures, it is too easy for someone to walk out with large amounts of information. Therefore companies are going to have to do a better job of locking down computers. In reality, do most individuals at a company need access to USB, serial, and parallel ports on their computers? The short answer is no. They have backup and storage across the network, there is not a legitimate reason we should be handing out laptops and desktop computers that make it trivial for this information to be extracted. Through software and hardware, these devices can be disabled and locked down to stop someone from using them in an inappropriate manner. As storage devices become so tiny that they can pass through any guard, companies will have to react by implementing a principle of least privilege at the hardware level.

Moles

As perimeters continue to be tightened down and new security devices get added to the perimeter arsenal, external attacks are going to become more and more difficult. As external attacks become more difficult it is not going to be worth the attackers' efforts. They are going to rely more on the use of moles to extract the data and cause damage to organizations. Planting an insider as a mole is as trivial as putting together a résumé, acing an interview and getting hired. Taking an insider and converting them to a mole is as easy as finding a weakness and exploiting it. Two common weaknesses are money and blackmail. It is usually easy to find someone who has some financial trouble. Offering them money to help them out is a temptation some people cannot resist. In addition, most people have deep, dark secrets. Finding out those secrets and threatening to reveal them is another way to convince people to cooperate.

Since moles are so easy and extremely effective, attackers are going to rely more and more on this method to accomplish their goals. This is why performing thorough background checks and validating employees and monitoring them is going to be even more critical.

Outsourcing

Outsourcing is becoming a norm for companies of all sizes. The cost-benefit analysis not only points to the fact that it is here to stay but that it is going to increase in popularity moving forward. This section is not implying in any way that outsourcing is bad, it is just pointing out that with outsourcing comes new challenges and concerns that a company has to be aware of.

With outsourcing, you are taking the zone of insiders and increasing it to the outsourcing company. In most situations, any source code that would be outsourced is considered IP for the company. Therefore, there is now a whole new group of people that will not only have access to the source code but could also make inadvertent changes to the code or create backdoors. Confidentiality can be controlled thought NDA, contractual agreements, background checks, and internal isolation by the outsourcing company. Integrity checks require that any code, whether it is outsourced or not, be validated by a separate party. Whether code is developed inside your company or outside there is the potential that an insider can create back doors to cause problems at a later point in time. Therefore third-party testing and code review must be performed to minimize the potential damage.

Porous Networks and Systems

As new functionality and enhancements are added to networks, they are and will continue to become more porous. A more porous network means the number and chances of having outside affiliates increases. As more holes are punched through the firewalls and wireless and extranet connections are set up, the exposure of the critical infrastructure increases and the number of potential people who can access critical IP also increases.

Therefore, organizations need to understand that these phenomena are happening and build in appropriate controls at the host and server level.

Ease of Use of Tools

Attack tools are not only increasing in ease of use but also increasing in capability and functionality. In the past, manual methods were required to use tools to gain access. In the future, the tools will become completely automated. Now, an insider who does not have proper access can gain access through the use of one of these tools. Because the landscape is going to continue to increase in complexity from a defense standpoint, the sooner that companies can start to defend against the insider threat the easier it will be.

Relays on the Rise

Attackers do not want to spend money on expensive resources or attack from their own systems because it is traceable. Instead, attackers use relays. A relay is a site that has weak security; the attacker breaks into the site and sets up a safe haven. From this site she can load all her tools and launch attacks. Now she is using someone else's resources and if a victim traces back the address it will go to the relay site and not the real attacker. This concept is not new, but moving forward it is going to be taken to a new level.

Attackers are going to start to compromise and infiltrate entire companies and use them as massive control centers for insider attacks. In essence, corporations will inadvertently be sub-funding illicit activity because they have poor security. If I am going to launch a massive insider attack, I need resources, I need Internet connectivity, and what better place to find it than a large company that has redundant T1 or T3s and extra servers? In essence, attackers are finding that organizations provide them "free" collocation services.

You might ask, while a company would prefer this does not happen, what is the big concern? The biggest concern with this happening to an organization is downstream liability. This means that if your company has such weak security that they allow themselves to be a launching-off platform, they could potentially be held liability for being grossly negligent in securing their enterprise. Not only could this cause serious monetary issues for a company, but if legal action is taken, the case is public and that could result in bad reputation, loss of customer confidence, and loss of customers.

Social Engineering

The weakest link in any organization is the people. Since most insiders had full access it has always been easy to just compromise an insider. However, as companies start to tighten controls, full access is going to be limited and taken away. Therefore, attackers need other ways to get the information or access they need; the solution: social engineering.

Social engineering is human manipulation where you pretend to be someone you're not with the sole goal of gaining access or information you otherwise would not have.

Social engineering is a very powerful, yet easy tool at the attacker's disposal. As social engineering attacks increase, organizations need to do a better job at education, making people aware, and defending against these types of attacks.

Plants

When many people think of insider threat they think that as soon as someone has access, they will commit the act immediately. While this would seem logical, it is easy to trace and the person is usually limited in access and capability. A good insider knows that patience is the key.

More and more governments are putting plants in competing companies in foreign countries. They view this as a long-term investment, so they will give you a fully qualified candidate to work at your company. This person will work their butt off for many years, learning the process, gaining trust, getting promoted, and then eventually will slowly start to extract sensitive information from the company.

This model is highly effective and very hard to detect and trace. No one thinks that someone would get hired at a company and work very hard so that in five years he could compromise data. To many of us it does not make sense, but to the skilled attacker or government organization it is a worthwhile investment.

Tolerance Increasing

As attacks increase, people's tolerance for pain increases. There are worm outbreaks and other attacks that three years ago would have made the front page of every paper, but today they do not even get a mention because people's tolerance for this type of behavior is increasing. Instead of doing something about it, we are accepting it as a norm.

This model is very dangerous because as soon as you get in the acceptance mode, the problem will keep getting worse and worse and no one will notice.

Something has to change; otherwise, the impact of the insider will cause such financial loss that it will impact the entire economic infrastructure.

Framing

As attackers get more sophisticated, they are looking for ways not to get caught. Especially in the case of the plant, if you worked three years in an organization you would want to get a lot of mileage out of it and not commit one act of insider threat and get caught. The easiest way to not get caught is to frame someone else. Instead of using your own identity, more and more attackers are compromising and using someone else's identity so that person gets blamed for the attack. If a skilled attacker does this properly, he can build up so much evidence against the person he is framing that there is no questioning or doubt in anyone's mind who committed the insider attack.

This trend is very scary because now you have innocent people becoming victims, in addition to the company. Therefore it is very critical that companies carefully examine the facts to make sure they are not punishing the wrong person.

Lack of Cyber Respect

It is amazing, but we are raising a generation today that has minimal respect for the cyber world. The total lack of appreciation and understanding of cyber ethics is downright scary. Many people would never think of stealing someone's wallet, but they have no problem reading people's e-mail or compromising their user ID and password.

As organizations put together new policies and procedures, they have to realize that they have a long road ahead of them in changing how people perceive and act towards information that exists in a digital format. By covering the future trends, you will help your organization properly build defensive measures against the insider threat that will not only work today but scale tomorrow.

Summary

This chapter was meant to serve as an introduction to how bad the problem is and why you should be concerned about it. Some problems if you ignore them they will go away, this problem will only continue to get worse. It is important that organizations understand the risks that insider threat can have, realize it is occurring today and take action to minimize or prevent the damage that it can cause.

Chapter 2

Behind the Crime

Solutions in this chapter:

- Overview of Technologies
- Information Extraction
- Hidden Files
- Network Leakage
- Cryptography
- Steganography
- Malicious Acts
- The Human

Introduction

In the previous chapter we laid the foundation for insider threat. We raised awareness and showed that it is a serious problem that requires serious attention. Insider threat has always been around, but with the widespread use of the Internet and computers, it has created a new arena that will allow insider threat to flourish like we have never seen it before. In an office full of paper there was always the potential for someone to copy a piece of paper that they were not supposed to copy, carry a paper copy of a document out of a facility, or tell someone what they read about. This problem of having a trusted insider use his or her access and knowledge to hurt the company always existed, but it was bound.

The methods that could be used before computers and the Internet to commit insider threat were limited:

- Extraction of a document in its original form
- Copy with potential miniaturization
- Faxing
- Verbal word of mouth
- Modification of information
- Destruction of information

To commit insider threat an attacker has to focus on compromising the confidentiality, integrity, or availability of critical IP across the organization. Even though there were methods to do this prior to the widespread use of computers and the Internet, they were controlled and bounded.

The easiest and most straightforward method, which still works today, is extraction of a document in its original form out of the organization. This could also entail physical relays, where someone gives the document to another department or group, who eventually transferred it out of the organization. One of the best and easiest ways I have seen attackers do this is via mail. Many organizations had guards that checked your bag when you left so it would be hard to walk out with a classified document in your briefcase. However, if I took that document from within the building and put it within an envelope with a stamp, no one would check it. There was a case where an organization would actually check mail and briefcases, but not FedEx packages. The reason is that there was a separate process and approval for being able to use FedEx, and when they set it up they were not thinking about insider threat. Yet an insider quickly found this as the best path for extracting information from the company. Although we might not always think about it, attackers will always find the weakest link and exploit it.

This is one of the reasons why it is critical to have a document classification scheme in place. In this book we are talking about classification scheme in a general sense. It does not matter if you are a government intelligence organization or a Fortune 500 company; you need some way to be able to mark and protect information. The government might use the term "top secret," and a commercial company might use the term "company proprietary" or "trade secret"; however, the level of protection remains the same. The documents must be marked and done so in a clear and consistent fashion. If documents are not properly classified and marked, how would a guard or anybody be able to determine that you should not be leaving with a sensitive document? Some easy criteria have to be used so that spot checks can be performed.

Traditionally organizations would mark documents just at the bottom of the document. The problem with this method is if someone was quickly looking at the document, they might miss the marking at the bottom. Based on the limitations, organizations would then mark at the top and bottom of the document. Although this was easy to spot, it still had some limitations. The main limitation was that if someone made a copy of the document they could cover up or cut off the labels at the top and bottom and conceal the actual level of the document. This is why today companies use a watermark on the page that goes behind the text. This can be seen in the Figure 2.1.

Figure 2.1 A Watermark

This makes it much harder for someone to try to remove and cover it up. I have seen cases where someone has tried to use white out to cover it up, but that does not work very well. Another method used is to mark each paragraph with a sensitivity label. Although this method works, it is harder for the person creating the document, plus a spot check could easily miss it because you would have to look much closer at the document.

A slight twist on this is to make a copy of the document and take the copy out with you. One advantage of making a copy is if the document has document control, where it has to be checked in or out if you left with the original, someone would know the document was missing. However, if I made a copy, I would be able to return the original to document control and take the copy home with me. The other advantage of copying is many copy machines have advanced features. These features could be used to make the document smaller in size and easier to conceal. If you have a single-sided document that is 100 pages, making a copy double-sided can cut the document in half.

Copy machines also having settings where you can reduce the contrast and make the copy either lighter or darker. I have seen cases where the watermark is so light that you could reduce the contrast by making a copy and removing the watermark. If you make a second copy with a darker contrast, the text will darken back up but the watermark will have been removed.

Many copiers also have size reduction capability. This is advantageous for many reasons. First it allows you to make a document much smaller in size. If I have a 100-page document and I reduce each page to 50%, now I can fit two pages per one printed page. If I use full duplex, I can reduce the document down to 25 pages. If I am a trying to remove a large number of documents, this can be the difference in slipping some documents in my briefcase and having to carry out a big box, which raises the suspicion level.

In addition to using copy machines to do this there are miniaturized cameras that have been developed just for this purpose. The cameras are very small and can easily fit within a pocket or embedded within a watch or a pair of glasses to make it very hard to detect. Now the attacker can take pictures of the document, leave with them on the tiny device, and then develop the pictures once they are at a safe facility. This technique and method has been around for a long time and is best illustrated in the movie, "Wall Street." It is actually not a bad movie to watch, but in the movie, the main character wants to commit insider trading. He works at the company but does not have access to his boss's office. He uses his internal knowledge of the organization to figure out where the sensitive documents are kept and when his boss leaves. Now he knows what he has to do and when he has to do it; he just needs to get access. To get access he interviews with the cleaning service that cleans the offices and gets a job working in the evening. To perform his job with the cleaning service he needs keys to all the offices. Since the cleaning company times you for each floor, he actually cleans some of the offices very quickly so he can spend more time in his boss's office and not have it look suspicious. When he is in his boss's office, he pulls out a miniature camera that he bought at the local electronic store and starts taking pictures of all the sensitive documents. Although this method works, I have also seen cases where you could look through the garbage to extract data. An ideal case that would also fit well is if I have access and can make copies but I cannot leave with a large amount of documents. I could also get a job with the cleaning service and us the large trash can on wheels as a means for getting the document out of the building. I then come back later that night and extract the documents from the dumpster. There are lots of opportunities and unconventional methods people will use to accomplish their task of insider threat.

Although simple and straightforward faxing is a method that, despite all the technological advances today, still has its spot in the office. Prior to computers and even today, if you needed to send a document to someone very quickly, faxing was a method for doing this using traditional phone lines. Most organizations have or had fax machines on almost every floor, so it would be relatively easy for someone to be able to take a document and extract it out of the company using the fax. Once again, even companies that have guards checking bags when you leave usually do not have checks at the fax machines. One company I know of actually had checks at the fax machine. The fax machines were locked in a person's office and they had to perform all faxing. This allowed them to be able to review the fax prior to sending it out. Even in this case, the system could be bypassed if this person was on vacation or not in the office. However, there was even an easier way that an insider found. Fax machines could be purchased relatively cheaply. This person bought a fax machine, plugged it in at the office, shut the door, and began faxing, allowing him to bypass all corporate controls. In this case, the funny part about it is the insider expensed the fax machine back to the company and the boss approved it.

Although fax machines and miniature cameras present their own challenges, at least there is still physical IP leaving the organization so proper perimeters and checking can still potentially flag it. The harder problem is when there is nothing to catch or stop, and the information is stored in an intangible format—someone's brain. Unless technology advances there is no way to scan someone's brain and make sure that he or she is not leaving with anything critical, and even if we could, it would be much harder to determine that the person intends to do harm with that information. Verbal word of mouth is probably the easiest and still one of the most common methods for extracting data out of the organization. I read a sensitive document, remember key facts, and walk out of the organization with nothing tangible.

No matter what checks are in place, there is no way they can stop you. Then you would meet up with someone at a remote location and give them a data dump of the critical data.

There is no way someone will remember a 50-page document word by word, but most people can remember the key or critical facts that could still result in a compromise. You can perform this experiment with a book. After someone reads a book, ask them to recite the entire book, word by word—they will not be able to do it. However, if you ask them for the general plot, the critical facts, and even the key characters, I am sure they will be able to do it. This is a big problem and comes down to controlling access. If someone is not able to read a document, they will never be able to repeat it to someone else. This problem is where the saying during World War II came from: "Loose Lips, Sink Ships." People have to learn that what happens at work stays at work.

All the methods we talked about apply mainly to disclosure of information: someone who has special access revealing sensitive information to someone who should not have access. This is the main thrust and focus of insider threat, and it requires removal of information from the organization in some format, which could be hard and risky in some organizations. In cases where you cannot extract data from an organization, having access within the walls of the organization, an insider can still cause harm in two other areas: modification of information (integrity) and destruction of information (availability).

Ideally as an insider spy, my ultimate goal is to be able to get a copy of the data; however, I do not want to blow my cover and get caught. Therefore if I cannot get the information out of the company, if I can modify the data I still provide a better service for the ultimate company I am working for by causing harm to its competitor. If I modify sales projection, I can cause reputational damage. If I can modify a proposal with the wrong numbers, I can cause financial harm to the organization. If I modify critical formulas or controls for critical systems, I could cause lawsuits that would result in both financial and reputational harm. Though integrity is not always the first choice, it can still provide benefit.

Destruction of information is typically the main form of a disgruntled employee who is not looking for a direct benefit but trying just to cause harm to the organization or punish the organization for the way he or she has been treated. Destruction, depending on the level and technique that is applied, can be very easy and simple to do. It can also be used as a last resort if extracting the data out of the organization does not work. Ideally a competitor wants to be able to get a copy of the latest proposal a company is submitting so they can underbid them. However, if you cannot find out that data, but you can destroy all copies of the proposal two days before it is due, in essence you have accomplished the same net effect. By destroying the proposal you will not be able to bid, and now since your company is not submitting a proposal I no longer have to worry about outbidding you. In some cases this could offer a big advantage because if you know you will be the only bid then price really is less important than before.

It is important to note that although these methods were used before there were computers, these methods will still work today. This is why organizations have to be so careful and make sure they look at the big picture. I have seen companies that are so focused on computers, they forget about the obvious and let people walk out the front door with documents in their brief cases. Their cyber security is so secure that you would not be able to do this electronically, but their physical security measures are so overlooked that an attacker could exploit that area with ease.

Although these traditional methods we just discussed could still cause harm to the company, it was something you could get your arms around and defend and detect. It was a known problem that was bounded in its methods and complexity. Therefore there were methods that could be used to counter this activity and the methods were known and understood, and if performed correctly, worked.

The following were some of the methods that were used to protect against this type of attack:

- Marked, color-coded covers
- Locks
- Guards
- Locked rooms with checks
- Spot checks
- Separation of duties

There is no such thing as 100% preventive measures, but the trick is to try to defend as much as possible and hope with proper awareness and training that most people will do the right thing.

One way to prevent information from leaving the organization is to carefully mark documents, both top and bottom, and with a watermark, as we discussed earlier. Something else that is helpful is putting a cover sheet on every document. A red cover sheet means the document should never leave the company, a yellow cover sheet means it can leave only if it is properly secure, and a white cover sheet means the document contains no sensitive information. Now you can argue that someone can just remove the cover sheet. However, a document without a cover sheet is an immediate flag because every document must have a cover sheet. If removing a cover sheet is easy I can just as easily remove a red cover sheet and put a white cover sheet on top. Although that is correct, that is still a little harder.

There is no perfect solution—the trick is to keep modifying the solution to the point where is comes prohibitively harder for someone to bypass it. At one Fortune 500 company, they used the color-coded sheets, but each cover sheet had to have the document's name printed on it and a manager's signature verifying that the cover sheet and document named matched. Once again, people can always be tricked but this made it a lot harder for someone to bypass. Now you would have to involve other people to bypass the system, and even if you think your boss may not actually check, it is still a risky thing to do.

Fear of being caught is a big driving factor, an advantage of using this method. Most people will not chance having the boss sign a form in which the cover sheet does not match the title. With proper training, bosses should be made aware that checking documents on a regular basis is vital, plus periodically telling employees they are going to review documents to make sure they match the covers keeps people on their toes. If you are a boss that is known for carefully reviewing documents, once you catch one or two people and the word spreads, the chances of someone else trying to do this would be very slim.

Locks, though fairly basic, can be very effective at controlling and preventing access. If someone cannot get into a room or cabinet it becomes harder for them to cause harm. If you cannot get access to something you cannot disclose it, you cannot modify it, and you cannot destroy it. The effectiveness of this control depends on the type of lock you are using and how the key to the lock is controlled. The lock is not what protects the data, it is the confidentiality and control of the key that keeps the data secure. Key accountability and key control are the driving success factors behind the effective use of locks. Therefore the more carefully you can control the key and track accountability, the higher the effectiveness of the lock.

Standard locks such as key-based locks controls access, but there is not a high grade of accountability of the key. People can give the key to someone else, they can make copies of the keys, and they can loose the keys. If 20 people all have a key to a given room and something is missing from the room, it will be very difficult to tell which of the 20 people did it. The other problem with standard locks that is often misused is the master key. A master key can get into any office. Even if I am the only one with a key to my office, but three people have a master key, we still have not achieved accountability.

The next general category of locks is something that can be tied to an individual, such as an access card. Each person has a different access card and is given permission to the areas needed to access in order to work. Even though 20 people have access to a room, since they each have a different access card, we can still have accountability and know at any instance which specific individual gained access. The problem with access cards is people can still lend them to others and lose them.

Biometric-based locks are the final general category of locks. Here, the key of the lock is tied to a personal attribute such as a hand scan, a retina scan, or voice recognition, just to name a few. The advantage of this method is that it is tied to the person and cannot be borrowed or lost. It is always with you and depending on the method is usually good for 15 or more years. The disadvantage is that these devices can be fairly expensive and some people are still distrustful of giving away their personal attributes so the company can always track them.

Guards also serve as an effective measure for preventing insider threat. Guards can provide effective choke points and have detailed analytical capability if they are trained correctly. Guards can be trained to be located at all critical perimeters and perform spot checks, looking for suspicious activity and stopping individuals. They can also ask people what they are leaving with and why. Some people do not see the value in questioning because they say that it will catch only honest people because attackers will lie, but combined with other techniques, it can show intent. If I ask you as you get off the elevator if you have any laptops or data storage devices that you are leaving with and you say no, then at the exit another guard checks your bag and finds a laptop, now we know that you have intentionally lied and tried to bypass the system. Without the first step of asking you a question, during the spot check you could have claimed that you did not know you were not supposed to have a laptop. However, now because we used a two-step process, you were caught red-handed.

In addition to being placed at perimeters, guards also have value walking around the facility looking for suspicious activity and performing random spot checks. If I know that no one else is around, I can make copies and fax sensitive data without anyone knowing. However, if I now know that a guard could walk by at any moment looking for unusual activity, and the activity I am currently performing is highly suspicious, I might be less tempted to continue my activities. In addition to looking for suspicious activity the guards can also do what is termed a traditional spot check just to make sure people are following procedures and doing what they are supposed to be doing. If all sensitive documents are supposed to be locked up if they are not in your possession and a guard finds a sensitive document on a desk with no one around, this represents a security violation. Just because a person left a document on a desk does not mean they are out to cause harm. However, the fact that anyone else could walk by and see the document represents an avenue where an untrusted entity could take the document or read it and gain access to information they should not have access to.

If a document is very sensitive, it should be locked in a room and not allowed to be removed. Now people can come in read the document and leave but the document can never leave with them. If the room containing the document does not contain any phone lines, copy machines, or other electronic equipment the chances of someone being able to extract the document is very slim. In addition, if the room requires two different people to open and you have to sign in and out and you are being monitored as you are examining the document, this also adds additional measures of protection.

We alluded to it when we talked about locked rooms, but separation of duties is another effective measure to defend against traditional insider threat. If only a single person is responsible for performing a task it is easy for that person to abuse privileges and cover up any malicious activity he or she is doing. However, if two people are involved with any task it would be much harder for any one individual to cause harm on his or her own.

Although these security methods seem basic and straightforward, they work and they solved the problem. Before computers, insider threat was still a problem, but companies knew how to control it and if they were concerned enough about it they could take action. It was not a problem that was out of control, where the attacker clearly had the upper hand.

Now that you have added computers, the Internet, and the mobile work force, just to name a few, we have a whole different ball game. Now, the potential for loss is huge and the methods they can utilize are numerous.

However, do not discount these measures. Even though they are not the main focus of this chapter, they still have value and use today, and sometimes the simple solutions work better than the more complex solutions.

Overview of Technologies

Technologies typically are going to serve as the basis for insider threat attacks. Even though simple, nontechnical attacks still work and are effective, they are not the focus of this chapter. They were covered in the introduction to lay the foundation. The main focus is to give an overview of key technologies and how they can be used to cause harm and damage across your organization.

It is important to remember that this is not a comprehensive list, and technologies are always changing. However, there are certain technologies that must be understood so you can try to stay one step ahead of the malicious insider.

The key technology areas that will be addressed are:

- Information extraction
- Network leakage

- Encryption

- Steganography

- Malicious attacks

- Beyond computers

- Humans

As you read through each section and start to understand each technology, how it works, and how it would be used, remember to think about the entire scenario in which this could be used to cause harm by a trusted insider. Understanding the core technologies is critical, but thinking about the big picture and how it would be used in an attack scenario will get you the best value in understanding how the malicious insider operates and how to defend against them.

Information Extraction

As we covered in the introduction, insider threat was occurring long before computers and long before the Internet was created. As long as organizations had sensitive data that they did not want anyone to obtain, insider threat existed. Even Julius Caesar had to worry about insiders and how they could hurt his organization. Probably the most famous example of insider threat is that of Jesus and Judas. Jesus' trusted disciples knew sensitive and critical data that no one else knew, and though Judas was a trusted insider, he was paid off to cause harm to Jesus.

In most cases computers do not invent new areas of crime, they just bring it to a whole new level. Computers and the Internet and companies having LANs did not create insider threat, it always existed. This new technological infrastructure just made the area of insider threat a more fertile ground for attackers because now their options and means and methods for causing harm are almost endless.

Before computers the main method of committing insider threat was information extraction; taking a sensitive document, taking it outside of the company, and giving it to someone else. Since technology did not create the problem of insider threat as we apply technology to the problem, the problem does not change. The main issue with insider threat in the current digital age is extraction of information, now using networks as opposed to putting a hard copy in a briefcase and walking out.

Therefore we will start looking at technologies in the area of information extraction, and then at additional technologies. The core technologies in the insider threat tool chest that we will examine are the following:

- Hidden files

- Removable media

- Wireless exfiltration

- Laptops

- PDAs/Blackberrys

> **NOTE**
>
> For most of the examples we will be using Windows. Everything that can be done with Windows can be done with UNIX. We are doing this for many reasons: First, many attackers are not that technical and therefore most likely will be using Windows as their primary OS. Second, most insiders are going to be using their desktop to commit insider threat and once again, Windows is the primary OS for desktops.

Hidden Files

Data exists in a digital form on your computer, on a server and in packets that are flying across your network. A simple but effective way to extract data out of your organization is to hide those files on your computer so if someone does a basic directory search they will not be able to see or find the documents on your system. In this section we are not talking about data hiding or steganography; that is such a broad topic in and of itself that it deserves its own section later. We are talking about basic file hiding on your system.

Similar Directory

The first method of hiding files on a system is to find a directory that contains a lot of files with similar names and create a new file or directory with a similar sounding name. The chances that someone knows or will check every single directory is slim. From a directory standpoint, c:\windows is a great spot for creating new directories that will never be spotted. Figure 2.2 is a screen shot from a portion of the c:\windows directory.

Figure 2.2 A Portion of the C:\Windows Directory

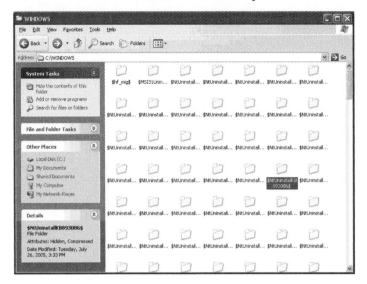

Can you tell me which directory is supposed to belong and which one is not supposed to? If I go in and create a new directory that starts with $NTUninstall, it will blend in and be virtually invisible. Adding to the fact that most people are very leery of deleting directories in the Windows main folder, and that there is minimal information on the correct folders that should be there, means most people when examining their system will ignore it. Add that with the fact that the folders are constantly changing based on the running of the system, no one is going to take the chance of trying to delete files that could cause their system to stop operating.

Similar File

From a file hiding perspective a great area to hide files is in c:\windows\system32, especially if you pick a file name beginning with ms (see Figure 2.3).

Figure 2.3 The C:\Windows\System32 Directory

In this directory you have many files beginning with ms and of a variety of file types, once again making the attacker's job very easy to perform.

File Extension

Another variant to hidden files that works very well is to change the file extension. If I have an .exe and I change it to a file type of .dll or .doc, it will make it harder for someone to find. If attackers think I have a malicious .exe on my system, they are going to go into my system and look for it; if they do not find it, some people would stop looking. Now when you want to run the program you would have to rename the file type back to an .exe and run the program. Anyone who has worked at a company and has had to use e-mail is probably very familiar with this tactic. This is probably one of the most common tactics to get past e-mail filters. If your e-mail filter blocks Word documents or .exe files from coming into the mail server because they can contain viruses, you would just change the file extension on the file, attach it to your e-mail, and have the person on the other side just rename it back. To do this you would either right-click on the file and rename it or use the rename command from a DOS prompt to change the file type.

Hidden Attribute

Getting slightly more advanced than what we have been doing, you can use the hidden file attribute to hide the files. Files have attributes that can be set; one is the ability to hide the file. By right-clicking on a file and clicking **Properties**, you can see the two main properties for a Windows file: Read-only and Hidden (see Figure 2.4).

Figure 2.4 Properties for a Windows File

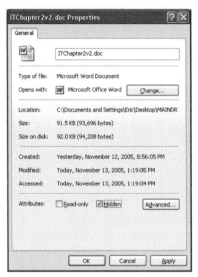

With the hidden attribute selected, you will not be able to see the file. You can also use the **attrib** command from a cmd prompt to change the attribute of files (see Figure 2.5).

Figure 2.5 Changing the Attribute of Files

In this example we started off by showing a directory with two files in it. We used the **attrib** command to add the hidden attribute (+h) to the file. Then we did another directory listing and you can see that the file is no longer displayed. However, if you use the **attrib** command with no arguments you can quickly see that the file is still listed, with the H or hidden flag. Finally if you use the **attrib** command with the –h, you can remove the hidden attribute and the file will once again appear.

It is very easy for someone to hide files on a system, and if you are not aware of it, it is easy for you to miss them. I recommend always configuring Windows Explorer to always display all files, including hidden files. This way there are no surprises and you see everything that is on the system. If you are ever performing any analysis across a system it is recommended to always configure Windows Explorer to show all files.

From Windows Explorer, select the **Tools** menu and click **Folder Options**, then select the **View** tab. The penultimate item under hidden files and folders is set by default to Do not show hidden files and folder. My recommendation is to always change the setting to Show hidden files and folders as it is set in Figure 2.6.

Figure 2.6 Windows Folder Options

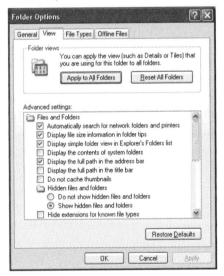

Even though attackers can still find ways around this technique, it still provides a basic level of protection.

Alternative Data Streams

The next technique we are going to look at, which is fairly advanced and very powerful, is alternative data streams. This is a feature that is available with NTFS file partitions on Windows. Since it is recommended that you always use NTFS as the file system, this technique will work on most systems. By right-clicking on a disk and selecting **Properties** you can quickly see what the file partition is (see Figure 2.7).

Figure 2.7 Local Disk Properties

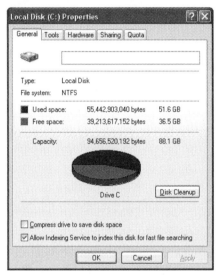

In Figure 2.7, you can look under file system and tell that it is NTFS, the default on most systems.

With NTFS there is a feature called Alternative Data Streams that turns every file into a file cabinet, and each file cabinet can contain many files. When I open the draw of my file cabinet at home I have my files, one for each of my clients, one for my bills, and so on. Here you can do the same thing. The file cabinet is the name of the file, and then I can attach additional files to the main file and each of the additional files are hidden and cannot be seen. When a secondary file is hidden within a main file using alternative data streams, the secondary file cannot be executed, but whenever the main file is copied or moved, the secondary file automatically moves along with it. Then if you want to use the secondary file, you have to unattach it from the main file and use it.

This is a technique used by inside attackers to hide sensitive data on a system and unless you know it is there it is almost impossible to find. Now I can take my sensitive files, hide them in an alternative data stream, and either leave it on my system or copy the file somewhere else. Anyone looking at the file would have no idea that there are other secondary files, filed away in the main file.

There are two ways to create alternative data streams:

- **Attaching to a file**. Use the cp program from the NT resource kit. The format for issuing the command is:

```
cp hiddenstuff.exe boringfile.exe:stream1.exe
```

- **Attaching to a directory**. Use Notepad to open a file stream connected to a directory using the following command:

```
c:\ notepad <directory_name>:<stream_name>
```

Attaching to a File

To create an alternative data stream you have to use the cp command from the resource kit. Figure 2.8 shows the sequence for creating an alternative data stream.

Figure 2.8 Creating an Alternative Data Stream

Typically this method is used if the file you want to hide already exists so you can attach it to a primary file as an alternative data stream. Notice there is nothing unusual about the file that has changed. It still looks the same in terms of size. Even if you check Properties from within Windows Explorer, there is nothing unusual that stands out (see Figure 2.9).

Figure 2.9 File2 Properties

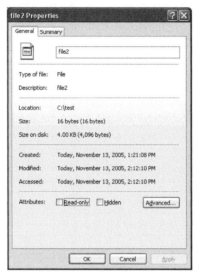

Alternative data streams are fairly nasty, since if you know the file is there you can extract it, but if you do not know it is there is could be very difficult to find.

Attaching to a Directory

Attaching a stream to a directory works best if you are creating a new file from scratch; however, it can also be used if the file already exists. If you start Notepad with a filename of a directory and a filename, it will create an alternative data stream attached to the directory. If it is a new stream, Windows will prompt you on whether you want to create a new filename (see Figure 2.10).

Figure 2.10 The Notepad Prompt

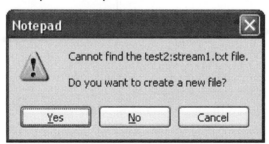

Select **Yes** and then type or paste the contents of the information you want in the stream. When you are done close the file and the stream will have been created. This can be seen in Figure 2.11.

Figure 2.11 Creating an Alternative Data Stream

We open up Notepad and create a stream attached to directory test2. After we are done you can see that there are no visible signs of the stream in either directory.

Removable Media

Although alternative data streams and hidden files are interesting concepts, we still have to be able to walk out the front door with our information. Hidden files will make it harder for someone to find, but we still have to put the information on something so we can leave the company with it.

One of the best ways to remove information from an organization in a covert manner is with removable media. Technology is an amazing thing, especially in this regard. The longer you can wait the more storage you can get in a smaller form factor. Memory sticks that used to contain 128 MB of memory now, for the same size, can contain over 4 GB of information. In many cases you can find something half the size that contains twice as much data storage capability. The real question is how much do you want to spend; today you are not talking that much money.

As I write this chapter, I am sitting on a train with a USB drive the size of the key to my car that contains 4 GB of data. While this is very powerful, because as I travel I can back up my data on the fly, it also raises interesting questions with regards to security. What if I lose the USB drive and someone else gets hold of it? During the train ride I can back up all my critical data in a few minutes on a device that easily can be concealed. What if someone else can get three minutes with my laptop when I am at a meeting or presenting and I step out to take a break? One of my themes that really drive home this point is that anything that can be used for good, can be used for evil. Organizations and IT people love these new portable devices, but we have to step back and think about the implications this technology poses.

Based on the ease with which someone can extract data out of the organization, the real question is whether allowing USB drives on work computers is worth the risk. People can back up their work, but they can also use it to cause significant harm to the company. Since most organizations have file servers, does it make sense to force all users to back up and store sensitive files on the file server and not run the risk of having USB ports accessible? You might bring up the point that for traveling users they would need this capability, but laptops present their own problems (covered in the following section).

So far with removable media we covered only small USB drives. There are many other storage types, however, that plug into serial and parallel connections and even use local wireless. Once again the decision has to be made on which is the lesser of the evils, allowing the access or not allowing the access. Since there are alternative ways for users to accomplish the same task in a more secure manner, my recommendation is to lock them down.

Removable media also comes in different form factors. There are watches and jewelry that contain USB plugs, and some of it is quite good. You could detect the earlier versions because they were unusual—geek-wear that most normal, self-respecting people would not wear. However, the new USB watches that contain over 8 GB of storage are no bigger than and look similar to the Tiger Woods self-charging Tag watch. There are also rings, earrings, and necklaces with storage capability very well concealed. Now if you see any people at your organization wearing an extra amount of bling, you might want to keep a closer eye on them.

Probably the biggest culprit of them all I saved for last, because it always creates quite a stir when I bring it up at conferences: iPods. Yes, I am actually saying that organizations should have policies about bringing iPods to work, and should restrict and control the usage. I have no problem with people listening to music at work, but I do have a problem with people bringing a 4+GB hard drive to work in which they can copy and store anything they want conveniently disguised as a music device. I am not against iPods (I actually own several); it is an awesome invention, but you just have to realize the risk it presents.

Put aside all your personal preferences and biases on the matter, and ask yourself if your organization should take the risk of allowing people to bring in personal devices that can store large amounts of data, remembering that it is their personal device and you have no control over it. In essence if you allow them to come into work with it and you have no policy stating they cannot, then since it is their personal property you have to allow them to leave with it.

Laptops

Laptops are probably one of the greatest, most powerful weapons for insider threat available to the attacker today. At this point I know some people must think I have lost my mind. First I insult iPods and now I am going after laptops. You are probably thinking that in the next section I am going to say Blackberrys are evil too (well, just wait until you read the next section). The point is control of IP is what companies should be focusing their energy and attention on, and any device that can provide a convenient avenue for circumventing those controls should be examined very carefully. I agree that laptops play a critical role in the IT arsenal of any organization, but we have to be aware of the threats that they pose and put measures in place to carefully control them.

Just to prove my point on how dangerous a laptop can be if it is not carefully controlled, I want you to do this simple exercise. Randomly walk around and borrow someone's laptop at your organization. Before you look at it ask yourself how much the laptop is worth. You are probably thinking $1K to $2K, focusing on the price it would cost to replace the physical equipment. Then I want you to do a quick analysis of the laptop looking at what files, data, e-mail, and such is on the laptop, and what damage it would cause if that information was exposed to the media or a competitor. Do not spend a lot of time analyzing it; 45 minutes max will be able to give you a good idea of what is on the system. *Now* ask yourself how much the laptop is worth (really thinking how much monetary loss and damage the company would suffer if this laptop was put into the wrong hands).

Many executives or managers before they travel dump all the critical data from the file server onto their laptop so they have all the information they need while they are on the road. In many cases the laptop is no longer used just for traveling, it is also their desktop system. The term portable desktop has emerged, showing that laptops are no longer computers that people use just when they travel; they are now systems that are used all the time, and for smaller companies that do not have file servers, the laptop is the file server and contains *all* the critical IP belonging to a company.

Laptops are a necessary evil, and we have to make sure that we understand the inherent risks and put measures in place like encryption, and minimize wireless to make sure the information stays protected as possible. Purging is also a good practice, where any unnecessary information or data that is not needed is removed from the system. Now if for some reason the system is compromised, the amount of data loss is minimal.

We have to make sure we avoid being digital pack rats. We would jokingly tease my grandparents that everything they ever bought they still had, because they would never throw anything out. Their garage and closets are filled with things that they can't even identify, and could not find even if they wanted to. We say we do not understand why people do that, but then I look at my office and realize that anything I ever created digitally I still have. Half the stuff I probably could not find if I wanted to, but I have it somewhere. Especially because laptops are so easy for someone to take, we have to make sure we do not become digital pack rats. Store the minimal amount of information needed and minimize your overall risk with what you are carrying around with you.

PDAs/Blackberrys

I definitely could not live without my Blackberry, and I am not sure if it is a quality-of-life addiction, but nonetheless, a Blackberry and PDA enhance our lives by bringing information to our fingertips anywhere we might be. You can be in a meeting and not be able to take a cell phone call but can quickly look down at a PDA or Blackberry and pick up emergency messages or even send quick replies to messages that might be very urgent. Why make the person wait six hours to get an answer to a question because you are tied up in a meeting, when you can just shoot them a quick reply back on your mobile device in less than 30 seconds?

With PDAs, however, take all the problems and issues associated with a laptop and multiply them. Essentially, PDAs have the same information that a laptop might contain, except with even less protection and in a much smaller form factor. At least laptops have a password that is required to log in before you can access the data, and even though it can be bypassed it still provides some level of protection. With most PDAs, though, there is no security, or if there is, most people turn it off. If I lose my Blackberry, someone can get access to e-mails, files, contacts, and credit card numbers, social security numbers, and other very sensitive information that many people store (not that I would) on their PDAs.

I had a client that started having some strange problems where their servers were being accessed and data was being copied, but there was no sign of attack, no visible break-in, no back doors or Trojans that you normally would see with a typical account. To make a long story short, one of the admins lost his Blackberry, purchased a new one, and never made a big deal about it. However, within all his e-mails and files were all the IP addresses, passwords, configuration information, and so on, and evidently someone got hold of it and started using that information to log in remotely. Therefore we quickly had to go in and change all the passwords on critical systems and control external access into the network. Even though the attacker came from the outside, I would clearly list this as an insider threat because a trusted insider with special access, in essence, took all the passwords and gave them to an untrusted entity so they could come in and do whatever they wanted to do. It wasn't on purpose, but unfortunately in this game that does not matter. Whether it was done intentionally or accidentally, the fact remains that an insider created an open door for an outsider to gain access.

The really scary part about this case was when I questioned why they did not have procedures and formal notification when critical equipment with sensitive data is lost, so immediate action can be taken. The response was that it happens all the time, and it would be too much work to change passwords every time it happened. If that is the case, you have a few options:

- Limit the information that is on the PDAs.

- Limit who actually has PDAs.

- Put together better awareness methods to minimize the chance of equipment getting lost.

- Do not use PDAs, because if you are not willing to accept the responsibility that goes along with them, then the organization should not have to accept the risk.

The other scary thing about PDAs is that people leave them lying around. During authorized insider threat penetration tests that I performed, people left PDAs on their desk when they went to meetings or lunch. Since it was authorized and I had permission, it was easy hypothetically to take the PDA, download the data to my computer (which takes about five minutes), and then put the PDA back. In most cases the person does not even know it is gone. In one case, when I went to return it, the person was sitting there, so I had to think quickly. I said I found the PDA in the break room, and the person admitted to often forgetting where he put it, and said he must have left it behind. As I stated earlier, the information that is found on PDAs is scary and organizations must do a much better job in protecting and controlling the information.

Wireless Exfiltration

The last technology that we are going to cover under information extraction that requires no introduction at all is wireless. Wireless is probably one of the easiest ways for an outsider to become an insider. There are many maps showing all the wireless access points in a given city; Figure 2.12 shows a map of commercial wireless antennas in the United States (from http://www.cybergeography.org/atlas/wireless.html).

Figure 2.12 Commercial Wireless Antennas in the United States

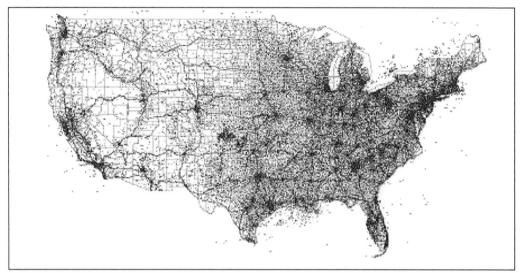

If you do not think wireless is a problem you might want to look closely at the map in Figure 2.12 and at other war driving maps that have been produced for almost every city (available on the Internet). War driving is the technique of driving around an area with a wireless antenna and GPS locator and a preloaded map, and plotting out the location for all wireless access points, both protected and unprotected. If you think you can put up wireless and not be found you are wrong. Not only will other people be able to find you relatively quickly, but with tools like Network Stumbler anyone can quickly find wireless access points in a given area (see Figure 2.13).

Figure 2.13 Using Network Stumbler

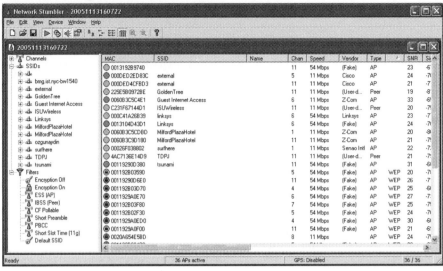

As I was writing this section I just opened up Network Stumbler to see what I would find and a whole list of APs popped up including at least a dozen that are not protected. Even the ones that are protected are not necessarily protected with strong security. Encryption on just means some from of encryption is being used, but many of them have weaknesses and ways to be broken if they are not configured correctly.

There are three general categories of wireless that we are concerned with:

- Authorized wireless
- Rogue wireless
- Ad-hoc wireless

Authorized Wireless

Even authorized wireless connections can create problems for an organization. They can be misconfigured and cause harm just like authorized users can make mistakes and cause harm. The first problem with authorized wireless is not properly restricting who can gain access to the device. There is still a large percent of authorized wireless access points that anyone could connect to.

I still remember talking with a friend, who is a financial advisor, about wireless. He said that his very large company does not allow wireless use, so some people are setting up rogue access points. He said that he usually just connects to Company X, which is a large government contractor, and uses their wireless because it is not properly secured and seems to work fine for him. I quickly told him never to send me an e-mail again, because I do not want all my sensitive data to go through that other company's network. He sheepishly said that he had a feeling that was a bad idea.

The second problem with authorized wireless is that they are connected directly to the private network. Even if proper security is put in place, wireless should be used as a means of access and still terminate at a perimeter, preferably the firewall. Then if the firewall determines the access is OK, then and only then should it be allowed onto the network. A wireless access point is not a firewall and it is not an IDS, therefore do not let it bypass your firewall and IDS. Any connection needs to be validated by your security devices, no exceptions.

Even if proper authentication is used, your data still might be going across the air, unencrypted. Even though you have slightly reduced the problem it is not much better. Now someone sitting in the parking lot or building across the street cannot directly connect to your network and access your data, but they can sniff all the traffic and if any sensitive data is being sent over the wireless network, they can still intercept it and analyze it. There is a lot of confusion on what companies actually are getting and what a given protocol will provide, but the best way to know for sure is to test it. When was the last time you set up a sniffer and examined your traffic to make sure it is really encrypted? People tell me all the time, we are fine because the product provides encryption. Great, but are you using the encryption and did you set it up correctly? The only way you will know for sure is if you test it.

One of the big reasons why authorized wireless is still causing problems is because many companies are being forced into wireless sooner than they would prefer and therefore are not taking the time to set it up correctly. With many organizations, rogue wireless has gotten so out of hand, that many companies feel the only way to stop people from setting up rogue points is if they provide wireless to their employees. However, this solves the rogue problem only if it is set up correctly; otherwise you are spending a lot of money to have the same problems you did before you set up your own sanctioned company wireless network.

Rogue Wireless

Wireless is truly a plug-and-play commodity. From your favorite electronic store you can buy a wireless access point for around $50; an insider goes into work, unplugs the cat5 cable from his or her computer, and plugs it into the wireless access point. Then they take a second cat5 cable, plug one end into the wireless access point, one end into the computer, and you now have a rogue access point at your facility. Five minutes and $50 is all it takes. Many users know the dangers of rogue wireless and set it up anyway because the convenience is more important. Others do not understand the dangers and think that if you buy something it must be secure, because stores would not be selling and setting up a rogue AP unintentionally.

Either way a rogue AP presents an easy way for an attacker to gain access to a network. The problem is, your organization needs to be prepared to detect and defend against rogue APs. Since they have become such a problem, there are actually commercially available wireless solutions that will access, track, identify, and disable rogue APs. These solutions work very well—the only thing you have to be careful about is that you do not take what you believe to be a rogue AP offline, when in reality, it is not on your network and does not belong to you, it belongs to another company that has office space in your building. As with any solution, measure twice before you cut.

Ad Hoc Wireless

By default with most configurations of Windows Operating Systems, when you turn on your wireless card, ad-hoc wireless also is turned on by default. With wireless ad-hoc or host-to-host wireless your computer is advertising itself as an open connection that someone can connect to. This vulnerability is shown in Figure 2.14 with the two bottom wireless connections.

Figure 2.14 Vulnerabilities in a Wireless Network

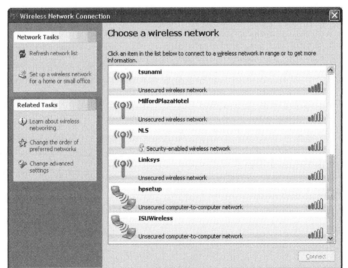

Now if someone connects to these connections they most likely will not have Internet access but they potentially could access any files or programs that are on that computer. Based on our earlier discussion of laptops, you can now see how bad the problem can get. Now you have an executive who has all the critical IP of the company on his laptop. He leaves his laptop and wireless on and goes to dinner, and as he is sipping a martini, someone is accessing and copying all the sensitive IP off his system. When he comes back from dinner, he has no idea what just happened and how bad it really is.

Regardless of which method of wireless is used, this provides an easy gateway for someone to get access to critical resources, and unfortunately in most cases, bypassing the perimeter. The typical rule of strong perimeter design is all connections must go through the firewall. However, for some reason, with wireless, many organizations decide to put it behind the firewall so if it is not configured correctly (which in most cases it is not), it allows an untrusted outsider to become an insider, putting your entire network at risk.

Wireless is so easy to perform today that people tend to forget what a huge risk it could present. Therefore it is critical that measures be put in place to control and secure wireless, otherwise the base of trusted users on your network could be a lot larger. In one case a security administrator said I was given an unfair advantage based on how the wireless was configured. I have 8,000 users, which I thought was what I was up against in combating the insider threat problem, but to do misconfigured wireless, the number of trusted users I had to deal with was more than 20 million. Although wireless has value, make sure the reward is worth the risk you are taking.

Network Leakage

Acquiring access to information does not accomplish anything if you cannot extract it from the organization. In prior sections we talked about walking out the front door with the IP either in paper form or digital form. However, that can still be cumbersome and risky. Ideally from an insider's desk they would like to be able to extract data from the organization via the network. The network provides an avenue and connection to the rest of the world. From your desktop computer you have full access to the entire world via the network connection that is connected to the Internet: full access to the Internet, anytime that you need it. Therefore it should come as no surprise that network leakage is a major problem for organizations. If people have the access not only are they going to use it, they are also going to abuse it.

We have talked a great deal about controlling access and limiting access, and one of the key principles that we have talked about is principle of least privilege—giving someone the least amount of access they need to do their jobs. Although we understand and adhere to this principle in some parts of our company, why is it that the one area that has the most power and the most potential for abuse is the one area in which we ignore the principle of least privilege: the network, or more specifically, network access?

Being able to access any systems or resources on the Internet from within a trusted private network is clearly a problem. The potential for people to take sensitive documents and tunnel them through the opening in the network to any resource on the Internet is an insider threat's dream come true. Changing this will require a major paradigm shift. My first question in most organizations is to ask why people need access to the Internet to do their job. Give me a reason why every employee needs to access the Web, e-mail, instant messaging, and so on, with little or no protection. Some organizations are slowly understanding that the risk is too great, and are implementing solutions like proxy servers. With a proxy server the employees have to authenticate to a server that will then analyze and service all requests. The employee never directly talks with resources on the Internet; the proxy will perform the actions on his or her behalf. Although this is a good start, it is still not as properly or finely grained controlled as it needs to be.

Most perimeters at organizations are set up to block or limit inbound connections, and perform little filtering outbound. Even organizations that are starting to filter outbound traffic still allow certain traffic out. Two types of traffic that are always allowed out of an organization are Web and e-mail traffic. Those two protocols/applications are the life-blood of any organization, and are needed to flow so employees can do their jobs. Therefore in this section we are going to look at both Web and e-mail in additional detail.

Web Access

The Web is no longer just a source of information; it has turned into a front end for almost any application or protocol that you would want to run. Initially there were separate protocols for performing e-mail and file transfers and sending messages back and forth. Although they still exist, the Web has transformed itself into a multipurpose protocol in which almost anything can be done by utilizing the simple power of a Web browser.

E-mail has always represented a potential risk (it is covered in the next section), but at least there was a central server that could limit and control e-mail leaving the company. Now with the power of the Web, users via a Web browser can send and receive e-mail, bypassing most of the filters that are in place. Even proxies that are starting to filter out Web-based e-mail has had difficulty via the use of encryption. Now Web-based e-mail is setting up SSL connections that look similar to e-commerce sites, which are allowed, but now all the content is encrypted. Not only is it almost impossible to block, but now you cannot even monitor or see what is going on. Figure 2.15 shows one of the more popular Web-based e-mail programs, Hotmail.

Figure 2.15 The Hotmail Login Screen

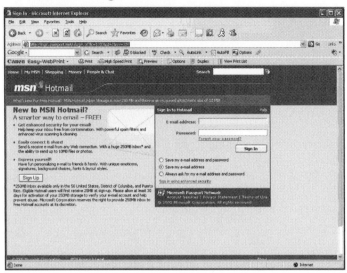

No messy clients, no special protocols—all through the power of the Web you can send and receive e-mail and even attach sensitive documents out of an organization.

Although this is a specialized application, most corporate e-mail servers also have Web front-ends set up so people can check e-mail anywhere, anytime. The problem with these front-end applications is that many people use them so if they do no have their computers with them, they can access e-mail from a Web kiosk at a hotel or airport, to log in, check e-mail, and disconnect. The problem with many of these Web-based applications is that information could be cached or locally stored and if not done correctly, other people could quickly retrieve the information and log into your mail server. Once again, what type of information usually is stored in your mail box? Almost everything, including critical IP for your organization.

If surfing the Web was not bad enough, now there is a whole suite of products called *anonymizers*, with the goal of making your Web surfing experience anonymous to anyone watching. Now if your company is trying to watch or carefully control Web surfing, via an anonymizer they now no longer know where you are going or what you are actually doing. One of the more popular sites for doing this is http://www.anonymizer.com (see Figure 2.16).

Figure 2.16 The Anonymizer Home Page

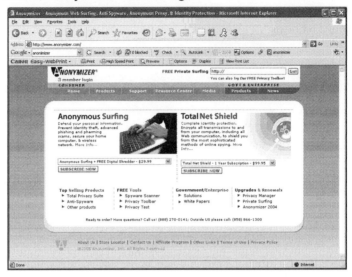

This site currently charges, but there are many sites that are still available for free. More and more corporate sites are blocking or not allowing access to these sites from within the corporation. Although this strategy is effective, so all user surfing can be watched and controlled, the well-versed employee usually will find a way around the controls.

E-mail

E-mail is another application that has huge potential based on the power of being able to send information, including attachments, to anyone in the world with the click of a button. If you are looking for an easy and simple way to perform an insider threat and extract data from the organization, e-mail is your answer. As you will see later, even if it is being monitored, the use of encryption or steganography can make it harder to track and block. Even in the ideal case you could just use a Web-based client that we talked about earlier to bypass the corporate mail server.

Just to show you how simple, yet powerful e-mail can be, let's look at e-mail basics. In order to send e-mail out to another system, your e-mail client has to connect to a mail server. The mail server then connects to the destination's domain mail server and transfers the message. There is a little more that goes on behind the scenes, but the key point to remember is in order to send out e-mail you have to connect to an e-mail server. Most organizations tighten down and properly secure their e-mail server, but there is an obvious solution for the insider that most people miss. Why not run an e-mail server on your local desktop? Now you are controlling everything. You can configure your local e-mail server to do whatever you want and it will make outbound connections. There are several of these programs available for download. A quick search of Tucows gives a long listing (see Figure 2.17).

Figure 2.17 Searching for E-mail Server Programs on Tucows.com

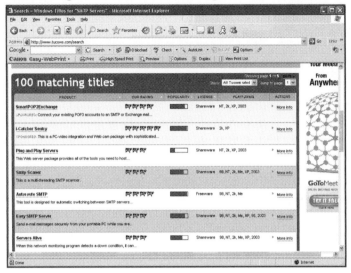

One of the programs that I have found very useful is SL Mail (see Figure 2.18).

Figure 2.18 SL Mail

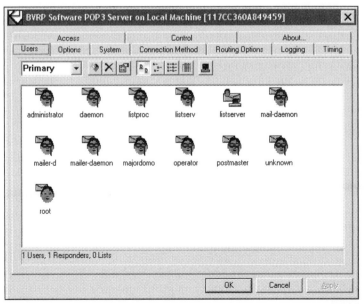

It is highly configurable, very powerful, and runs on a local desktop. Now if you want to send mail out or perform any tricks with e-mail aliases or spoofing addresses, you no longer have to worry about e-mail servers filtering out the message or not allowing them to run. You are running your own e-mail server and can configure it any way that you like (see Figure 2.19).

Figure 2.19 Configuring Your E-mail Server

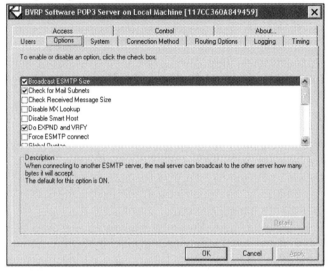

Figure 2.19 shows some of the many options that you can use to configure or set up the system to send e-mail from your local system. These programs have legitimate uses, an attacker can always use them to bypass the controls that are in place.

Spoofing e-mail is also just as easy. You just have to go into your e-mail settings and create a new account (see Figure 2.20).

Figure 2.20 Spoofing E-mail

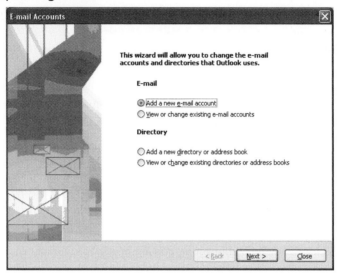

Once you are within the e-mail accounts, just select **Add a new account** and enter whatever information you would like (see Figure 2.21).

Figure 2.21 Adding Information to a New E-mail Account

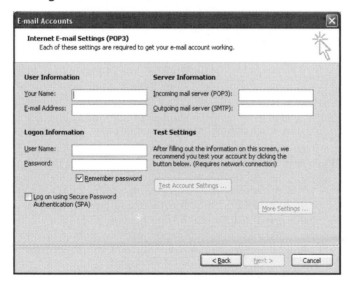

You can create a spoofed e-mail address for a competitor or just play games with your friends. The only trick is getting your e-mail server to send it out, but since you control your e-mail server, that is trivial. It is important to remember that if you are spoofing a legitimate e-mail address, when the person receives the message and replies back it will go back to the real person's e-mail address. Therefore if they realize they are getting responses to e-mails they never sent out, they might figure out there is a problem. However, if you are an insider attacking the system and trying to trick someone into getting access, it might work. For example at many companies you need to get an e-mail from your boss approving access to a certain resource. In this case it is usually a one-way communication, so if I can send a spoofed approval, it could work to get the additional access.

Cryptography

One of the main measures of protection organizations are using to protect sensitive information from leaving the organization is by monitoring traffic. They either are looking for keywords, actual filenames, or the content of critical IP to track and prevent information from leaving the company. To keep from being caught, one of the technologies that insider attackers are using is encryption. Cryptography garbles a message in such a way that its meaning is concealed.

With cryptography you start off with a plaintext message, which is a message in its original form. You then use an encryption algorithm to garble a message, which creates ciphertext. You would then use a decryption algorithm to take the ciphertext and convert it back to a plaintext message. During the encryption and decryption process, what protects the ciphertext and stops someone from inadvertently decrypting it back to the plaintext message is the key. Therefore the secrecy of the ciphertext is based on the secrecy of the key, not the secrecy of the algorithm.

Therefore to use an encryption program you have to generate a key. The key usually is tied to a username and e-mail address (see Figure 2.22).

Figure 2.22 Using an Encryption Key

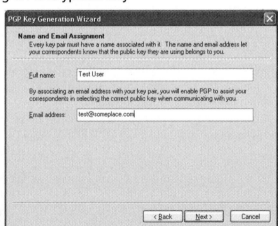

However, no validation is performed so you can put in bogus information that could be used later to launch a man-in-the-middle attack where you can trick someone into using a false key. If you know the public key for a user you can encrypt a message; but only if you know a private key can you decrypt a message. Therefore the public key can be distributed via a trusted channel, but your private key should never be given out. If someone can get access to your private key, then they can decrypt and read all your messages.

Detection

The benefit of encryption is that someone cannot read the content of the original message; however, encryption is detectable.

From a nonmathematical standpoint, if you are expecting to see ASCII characters and English text in a message and you see the following, clearly you can tell there is a problem.

dUTiR9wm+A0b3RFqJnpghU0QkyFpXliyt+c/lQkk1M5Q60azvBCi+XRJW/k7p15Y
d8fK/k5pSDiH+YwxDE62j8hs27sT7srttcEj+X4WcBimnUxIh2m22UARtGgXJOmp
zITSRgP9E6gab/iXiygH3IutNG2ovzgILaIeR7YTnYoGLVRgUjtuuRjSgX7aKLtz
7NcNLLtrNmdNZwCX0QlXdVi2NUOJPA96CSFgRfHw26GZ+3Jx4T4F7xRMDx2zIAsRBl
T7zqujZozh1hAqXpiVxk4bkkdeBBUuv8DXayLd96+ADnXlLBwU4DK+4i4J2T
rp8QB/9zVTo0sfigXAR8vI78EQrq/U225kXHLqPwPVgwuBOkZhlaTfEhTRZDmK84
rJZWwGUZAcEwTGPNzm/SYiJf2rS1ziP/hdyblfm3jgUkxi3pAoWAtyukLdwT1O+4
+9I3bnTnxjgE4olo/WRGJx/CV0ou2PQYjMOJsKWBZrR3pL8fhgO3kBT3Sx2OimCG
8HzZV5C0KZVnVyiFQKi1uBETtbUDXHjvdzmqFzfksght5+P+H+98SDu0MyvqrHaJ
hOHMTXwKdohLwTlrpBbe9ZT26oV+8nLlQlVca72mFACWyEfc4AH52BouOyIEQ/g8Yuthl
uxTvHjvY7JdtGJKLhEhYV5B/0ZjCtHa1fSBhY011ZrBZthVr9YjruWvDBo
/UukEcHOGyrw0UXEte3YmQceZOSVQCe1V3k675gvUi/HnAWG8dfneT5v/f1u2Vjp
WWdKMNcloeI4gQE8V91aA9AXPycG6wR/4KsInOB57WD5nsAC/FHE9sShLHsJ/2Cl
QyarhpGikhUNLGKFBNc5RYameGrp37pZn44ev4OgGLsAKzt99lST2cT8cXrglHgE
igbnp6xbHkLF2mkXm0nsA7B1cDm4dZ959IOp8mCFFbcsUzY3zPDMD69kPVPBa6q4
+pK89ioZ8fIqlf5Arip1IqSJhy2DGiZChzjij9ldWL5blppD0q5/0sGFAQNphq2h
hfWZyWRiY6Gz9LmwpyOmdI7YnCS5XQ2lbFpkKtLVy6flhVdyjxAscBkoqMcmUgc0
HKgcQlRXC/syLvpk3tEgiivVYBDq7VWGHYoh4swwqA4VOZDHKjoaO/FaIPayWo0f
RrWosMmKPtySgnD8WDZKyCXEshyx7jApapsxIeoTI5Z7soAHta5Yvl1Li8H8+KKB

Although this is not a mathematically sound way of doing the analysis, it works at a high level. However, mathematically, there is also a way to detect encryption. One of the qualities of strong ciphertext is that the output of encryption is random. This is important because given the ciphertext of a message, there should be no way to determine the plaintext message. If the ciphertext is not random, that means there are patterns that can be used to predict the plaintext message, which is not a good thing. However, this quality of strong encryption can also be used as a detective message.

With a normal message, all characters do not appear with the same frequency; some appear more than others. This should be evident if you have ever watched the Wheel of Fortune—people will always try some letters before others. Samuel Morse, who invented the Morse code, wanted to make it as efficient as possible, so he would give the simplest codes to the letter that appear with the highest frequency and the longer codes to the letters that appear with less frequency. He determined frequency by counting the number of letters in sets of printers' type. The following are the values he came up with:

12,000	E	2,500	F
9,000	T	2,000	W, Y
8,000	A, I, N, O, S	1,700	G, P
6,400	H	1,600	B
6,200	R	1,200	V
4,400	D	800	K
4,000	L	500	Q
3,400	U	400	J, X
3,000	C, M	200	Z

Therefore E, followed by T, are the letters that usually appear with the highest frequency. Based on this analysis if you plot a histogram of the letters in a typical document, you would get a very uneven histogram that would look like the one shown in Figure 2.23.

Figure 2.23 A Histogram Plotting Letters in Normal Text

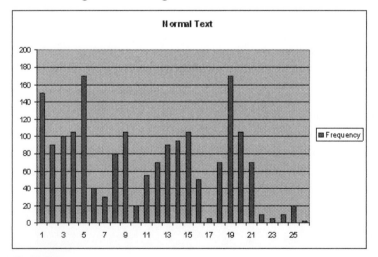

However, if you plot out the histogram for encrypted information, since ciphertext by nature is random, you will get a very flat histogram (see Figure 2.24).

Figure 2.24 A Flat Histogram Plotting Letters in Encrypted Text

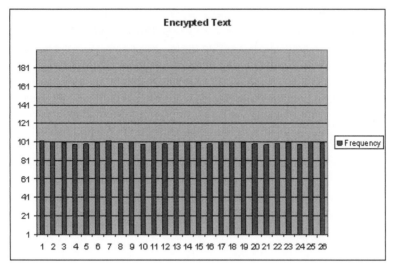

By looking at character frequency of the data you are examining you could detect whether the information is encrypted or not.

The good news is an organization can tell if information is encrypted; the bad news is if robust encryption is used you might never be able to decrypt the information and figure out the meaning of the message. However, in many cases, the mere fact that someone is encrypting information is enough to suspect them and watch them closely. If the organization does not have a sanctioned encryption program, in essence no one should be using encryption. The fact that someone is using encryption means they are using their own noncompany-sponsored program. This immediately raises a question. Second, the insider probably is only using encryption for certain communication, not all communication. Now the question becomes, who is the insider talking to and what are they saying that is so sensitive that he or she feels the need to encrypt the data during this transmission? Even though you might never know the actual content of the original message, you should be able to perform enough analysis to be able to warrant a more detailed investigation, and watch the person very closely.

Steganography

Steganography is data hiding, and is meant to conceal the true meaning of a message. With cryptography, you know someone is sending a sensitive message, you just do not know what it is. With steganography, you have no idea that someone is even sending a sensitive message because they are sending an overt message that completely conceals and hides the original covert message. Therefore cryptography often is referred to as secret communication and steganography is referred to as covert communication.

The analogy I like to use to differentiate between the two is the following. If I inherited a lot of gold I would want to keep it safe and protected. One option would be for me to purchase a big safe and keep it in my living room with all the gold locked inside. If you came to my house for a drink you would see the big safe in my living room. It would be locked so you could not open it. Even though the information inside was protected and you had no idea what was inside, you would know I must have something very valuable to lock it in such a big safe. That is cryptography. You do not know what I have but you know I am protecting something.

Another option would be for me to cut out the sheet rock on one of the walls, make a shelf, and stack all the gold on the shelf. Then I would put a picture on top of it on the wall. Now if you came to my house there was nothing unusual. I have some pictures on my walls, but it is quite normal for people to hang pictures on the walls. In this case nothing looks strange and you have no idea that I have anything of value. That is steganography. The sensitive gold is hidden and you have no idea it is there. The problem with straight steganography is if you noticed that the picture was crooked and went over to the wall to straighten it out, you would notice the wall is cut out behind the picture, and when you lifted up the picture you would see all my gold.

To maximize the efficiency of both technologies they often are used together. First I would install a wall safe and put the gold in the wall safe (cryptography). Then I would put a picture on top of the wall safe to conceal the safe (steganography). Together they provide a robust solution for inside attackers to protect their data and hide their information so no one at the company has any idea of what is going on.

To illustrate the power of steganography, we will use a program called S-tools. S-tools uses a simple drag-and-drop interface to perform steganography (see Figure 2.25).

Figure 2.25 The S-tools Interface

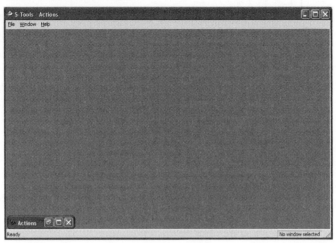

When S-tools hides information within a file it not only uses a pass-phrase to protect the information, it also uses encryption to keep the information secure (see Figure 2.26).

Figure 2.26 Using S-tools to Hide Information within a File

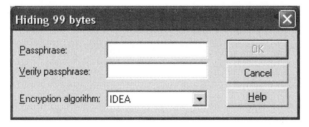

After you type the required information, S-tools automatically will hide the covert message within the overt message (see Figure 2.27).

Figure 2.27 Hiding a Covert Message within an Overt Message

The image on the left is the original image and the image on the right is the one with data hidden in it. Based on the how the algorithm works there is no visual difference between the two files. The binary composition of the two files are different, but visually, they are identical.

Steganography is a very popular technology for attackers because it allows them to completely conceal the true meaning of the communication and hide it in an overt image of any type.

There are two general ways to protect against steganography on your network: removal and detection. In some cases an organization does not care if someone is using steganography, they just want to make sure sensitive information does not leave the organization. Typically the easiest way to remove steganography is to convert the image to a different file type. For example the most common type of files on the Internet today are .jpeg files. The reason .jpeg files are so popular is because they are compressed files and are smaller than normal files. Therefore if you take a .jpeg file, convert it to a .bmp file, and then convert it back to a .jpeg file, although the image will look the same, the binary content will be different. During uncompression and decompression, the least significant bits are modified and this is where data is hidden with steganography. This conversion will remove any data that has been hidden within the file.

The second method is detection. For each steganography technique there are different ways to detect whether data has been hidden, but with S-tools it is fairly straightforward. S-tools works by making duplicate colors in the color table.

Therefore by writing a simple program to check for duplicate colors, you can tell whether data has been embedded within an image.

Normal File:

D:\DH\Data\BMP>bmpmap test.bmp

Filename: test.bmp

Actual size: 66146

Reported: 66146

Near duplicate colors: 2

Embedded File:

D:\DH\Data\BMP\STools>bmpmap test_h.bmp

Filename: test_h.bmp

Actual size: 66614

Reported: 66614

Near duplicate colors: 1046

You can see that in a file without data embedded within it the number of duplicate colors is less than 20. In a file that has data embedded within it, the number of duplicate colors is much higher than 20. Therefore a simple check of the duplicate colors would allow an organization to be able to detect steganography.

Malicious Acts

Malicious attacks typically are used by external attackers to gain access to a system. Since someone on the outside does not have access to critical systems or files they often need to use exploitation methods to attack a system and get access. Typically with an insider attack, the insider has access and the challenge becomes how to hide and extract the data from the organization. In addition, since most insiders are non-technical, exploitation methods are used only as a path of last resort.

Although the use of malicious acts as the primary measure for insider attack often does not happen, to gain additional access or elevated privileges malicious acts do come into play. In a situation where I have some access but not all the access I need to access the data, I might use a malicious attack to elevate my privileges or gain access to a system. These attacks usually involve running exploit code against a system. Some insiders may write their own exploits or even find their own zero day exploits, but many will use tools that already have been written. The advantage of utilizing zero day code is because most IDS would not be able to detect it or find it because there is no known pattern or signature.

Malicious attacks can also take other forms including the following:

- Deceit and deception
- Perception management
- Information corruption
- Theft
- Destruction
- Unlocked system

Although not the main focus or technology normally used for insider threat, in some cases an insider can reach deep into his or her arsenal and use these techniques to gain access to the information needed or to cause harm to the organization.

The Human

The weakest link in any security problem is the human factor, and insider threat is no different. No matter how well thought out your security plan is, no matter how much technology you utilize, no matter how many resources you have, humans still will be one of the key areas of focus for the insider to do harm.

Even though the insider typically has some access needed to do the job, often additional access is needed in order to acquire the access he or she needs to fully compromise critical IP. There are many ways that can be done, and we looked at several already, from malicious attacks to using out-of-band systems like voice mail. One of the easiest methods is to compromise the human element and have a human tell you the information you need, or at least give you enough data points to be able to make your job as the attacker easier.

This concept of essentially tricking someone into giving you information they normally should not give you is called *social engineering*, and it has been around forever. When my wife accuses me of lying to her, I respond jokingly that I am not lying, I am social engineering her (which, by the way, I do not recommend if you are married!). In short, social engineering is lying, it just sounds better than saying you are a liar.

The formal definition of social engineering is pretending to be something that you are not, with the goal of tricking someone into giving you information they normally should not give you and that you should not have access to. Essentially, if the person knew your true intent, he or she would not tell you the information, but since you are "in disguise" you are able to trick him or her. Some simple but effective examples of social engineering are:

- Calling the help desk requesting a new account to be set up

- Calling IT and acting like a vendor to find out how a piece of software is configured or where it is installed

- Impersonating a manager to get an employee to send you a proposal

- Impersonating a manager to get approval to access a sensitive directory

The interesting fact about social engineering is that many people overlook it because it seems so simple. But remember, just because something is simple does not mean that it is not extremely powerful.

Most people have a default level of trust—if you do not do anything to convince them otherwise, they generally trust you. Some of the other reasons why social engineering is effective include the following:

- **Exploits human behavior**. As we stated, if you are nice and friendly most people will trust you. Most people's personalities assume it is better to have a default mode of trust unless you do something to change their minds, than to go through life paranoid and not trusting or talking to anyone.

- **Trust is good**. Some level of trust is not a bad thing. When I meet someone for the first time it is much better to start talking and assume some level of trust than to sit in the corner thinking everyone is evil. But always remember the saying from the movie, *Italian Job*, "I trust everyone, it is the devil inside I do not trust."

- **If you are nice you must be honest**. Despite all the effort that we spend teaching our children not to trust strangers, most people grow up still thinking that it is OK to talk and socialize with nice people. Although interacting with people you do not know can be intriguing and give you a new outlook on life, you always have to be careful that there is a distinct difference between friendliness and trust.

- **People love to talk**. This is probably one of the biggest reasons social engineering is so effective. If you just give someone an opportunity and ask questions that are nonthreatening, you can get someone to tell you almost anything.

- **If you listen, you must be trustworthy**. Many people are lonely, and one of the signs of loneliness is that they have no one to talk to. Actually, the real sign is that they have no one who listens to them. Many people just want to hear themselves speak and when they talk with someone it is a competition of who can get more words in and dominate the session. Many people are not good listeners. Therefore if you are a good listener people are more prone to talking. It is critical to remember there is a difference between listening and not talking. I had one person tell me that when he talked with someone, he let the other person talk 90 percent of the time, therefore he was a good listener. You cannot make that correlation. Just because someone is not talking does not mean he is listening; he could be daydreaming or thinking about other things. Listening is a process of engaging with another person, understanding what he is saying, and being sincere. If you talk with someone who hardly talks, it could be because he could tell you were not interested and not really listening.

- **People love to tell secrets**. By having a secret that no one else knows people feel empowered. However, that empowerment is diminished if you do not tell anyone about the secret. Therefore the fact that someone knows something no one else knows, they have this eagerness to tell someone. In addition many people love to gossip and find out what other people are doing. Taking this and carefully planning a conversation can be a perfect avenue into social engineering.

The other item that makes social engineering so popular is that you need minimal, if any, information to perform social engineering. Although no information is required to perform social engineering, the more information you have, the higher the chance of success. If you are going to pretend to be a manager or from a different department, the more supporting data you can use or names you can throw out to put the person you are talking to at ease, the greater the chance of the attack being successful. Typically with an external social engineering attack, some general recon is appropriate so you are not going into it blind. However, if you are talking about internal social engineering, although you can perform additional recon, most insiders just by nature of their job have enough information to make the attack highly successful.

Social engineering can come in many flavors and types. I have found that just by being nice and helpful, usually you can get whatever information you need. However, in cases where that does not work, the following are some additional types of social engineering that can be used:

- **Just asking**. The most general type of social engineering and the one that often is overlooked because it is so obvious is just asking for the information. In many cases if you are confident about how you present yourself and you ask for something with authority, many times people will give it to you. Many buildings have guards in the front of a building but if you walk in the building you do not need an escort. If you walk in and look around and act like a visitor you will be stopped and have to sign in. However, if you walk with confidence as if you belong and know where you are going, in many cases, you will not be stopped.

- **Impersonation**. Pretending to be someone else is probably the most popular method of social engineering. If I pretend to be from the help desk I can probably get an executive assistant to open a CEO's office so I could supposedly fix a problem he was having. Even if the assistant says I do not know about any problem, you can say he was complaining to my boss about a problem, but if you prefer I just leave it and wait until he gets back that is fine. Most people do not want to be the one to be blamed for not having a problem fixed, so in most cases you would be given access.

- **Misleading and redirection**. With both of these you are giving someone false information with the purpose of misleading them, confusing them, or causing them to make a decision they normally would not make. For example, I heard a rumor that we had a fire code violation, and sometime this weekend they are going to come in and inspect the office. If they cannot get into an office, they might fine the company, so make sure you leave your office open this weekend. Clearly you are presenting someone with false information so you can gain access after hours.

- **Anger**. Although I would recommend using this method as a last resort, it will work in some cases. Instead of being nice, kind, and trying to sweet-talk someone into doing something, you get very angry and raise you voice. Some people do not like conflict so if you start getting upset and angry they would rather just give you what you want than risk making a scene. The risk of anger social engineering is that you could annoy the other person and he or she could get angry; then nothing would get accomplished.

To defend against social engineering, the best defense measure is to raise user awareness on the dangers that social engineering can pose to a company. In addition, strict policies with clear guidelines that are tightly enforced will also limit the chances that people could be tricked into given access. Employees have to realize that a company is taking social engineering seriously, and if it is enforced and proper measures are taken, the amount of social engineering attacks will decrease. This is not a problem that will be solved instantly, but with time it will get better.

Summary

This chapter covered a wide range of technologies and methods that can be used by an insider to cause harm to a company. Just like with viruses and other attacks, attackers often are taking a base method and modifying or creating variants of it to make it more powerful and difficult to attack. The same thing will occur with the insider threat. This chapter covered the base technologies and some variants, but expect to see additional variants and new methods evolve. As companies become more and more savvy on prevention and detection techniques for the insider threat, attackers are going to be forced to enhance their means and methods of using these technologies, and even in some cases, developing new technologies.

This often is referred to as the leap-frog approach. Either the "good guys" (security professionals) or the "bad guys" (attackers) can start the game, but usually it is the attackers. Most security measures are put in place because of a need; if there is a not a need, why spend money on something? Remember from our analysis that threat drives the train. If there is not a threat, than whether there is a vulnerability or not is irrelevant. Threat is tied back to possible danger and created by attackers. Every time an attacker develops a new method or technique for exploiting a system, he or she is creating a new threat, and in most cases, there is a high chance the company has a resulting vulnerability. The reason is simple: attackers develop methods to break in and cause harm, which is manifested through a vulnerability. If there is not a vulnerability then the attacker will spend all this effort on a technique that will never amount to anything of value. Attackers are very smart and clever and usually develop threats out of a need because they saw an opportunity they want to take advantage of.

Based on these reasons, we assume that the attacker will start the game. The attacker will leap-frog over the security professionals. This usually is done by the attacker finding a way into a system or a way to compromise data from an insider perspective, that a company has not thought about and has an inherent vulnerability to the attack. Once this starts being exploited by the attacker, security professionals start figuring out a way to fix the problem and stop the attack. Once they are able to do this they leap over the attacker. At this point the attackers' chance of success is either stopped or greatly diminished, and they have to figure out a new way to accomplish their goals, which usually entails the compromise of sensitive IP. In most cases they will modify an existing attack, or in some cases, create a whole new attack that once again is successful. Now they have leap-frogged over the security professional. This game usually continues, and is what guarantees that security professionals will be employed for a long period of time.

The problem with any new area, and insider threat is no exception, is the time it takes for security professionals to leap over the attackers. This usually takes a long period of time; however, the time it takes for attackers to leap-frog over the security professionals is usually fairly quick. Therefore it is critical that we are properly prepared going into this battle. The more we can understand the technology that is behind the attack, and start thinking about both prevention and detection measures, the better chances we will have at protecting our organizations from attack.

We covered a lot of different technologies that are used by attackers. Some of the technologies you might have known about and we presented a different perspective; some were very cool, and ones James Bond might use, and others seemed very basic. You might have questioned why something this basic was in this chapter. Remember that this chapter is not titled, "Cool and Crazy Technologies," it was meant to give you some insight to what is used to commit the crimes. Attackers do not care if the method is cool or not, they care about getting the job done. If the technology will help them accomplish the goal, they will use it. In most cases, if you have two ways to accomplish something—one that is very complicated and high tech and one that is simple and straightforward—and they both have the same chance of working with the same success rate, an attacker would always pick the more straightforward one. The simpler something is, the less chance for mistake. Also, if a simple method will work as good as a more advanced technique, why waste the advanced technique? An attacker only wants to use just enough energy to get the job done. Anything else could raise there profile, have a higher risk of getting caught, and give away an advanced technique.

Therefore, you have to look at how effective any technology that we review is going to be. Even though it might seem basic, the question you have to ask yourself is whether it work in your organization. If it will get past your security defenses and cause an attack to be successful, then you have to worry about it. The good news you should say to yourself is, if it is a basic attack, it should be easier to defend against than a more complicated attack.

In this chapter we dissected each technology by looking at each one separately; however, in practice, many are used together. Traditionally some form of social engineering usually comes into play before someone actually extracts IP out of the company. Essentially the social engineering piece is a good way to test the waters to try and find out as much information as possible to minimize the chance of getting caught and maximize the chance of being successful.

Another example is that if I am going to use steganography, I am always going to use it with encryption. This way if someone actually determines that steganography is being used, they will not be able to read the content of the message. In addition, if my ultimate goal is to get sensitive IP to a competitor, even if steganography is going to be used, I am not going to send it directly to someone at the competitor's e-mail address. Even though it might be pictures of my vacation, it could raise the suspicion level and create a link that I would prefer didn't exist. Therefore I would encrypt the IP, then hide it with steganography and send it to an e-mail alias outside of the company. Then from my personal home connection with no link to the company, I would download the message, extract the content, and even use relays before I send it to the competitor. Even though my company would have a hard time of finding out, I do not want anyone to put a link between me and the company; therefore relays provide an extra level of protection.

As you think back about the chapter, think about how an attacker would mix and match these different technologies to cause harm to your organization. The more you can think like an attacker and understand how they operate, the better you will be at defending the insider threat.

Technology is the foundation for how an attacker would compromise a company, but it is the raw materials of the attack that have to be fashioned and refined to come up with an actual attack. The refinement from taking a core technology and putting together an attack is the means and methods of how attackers operate. That is the level we need to think about. Understanding the technology is important, but what would be the means and methods an attacker would use to launch the attack is the end state. Being able to prevent and defend against a given technology is critical, but being able to protect against an entire attack is the ultimate goal. By knowing the means and ways an attack is going to use a technology against you will help you build the best defense possible. By understanding the full method, there might be easier ways to be able to defend against the attack ,and ultimately the more you know, the more in-depth defense you can apply to securing your organization.

The way this usually is done in practice is to create scenarios. Taking the information you learned in this chapter about the technologies and by understanding the real threats, you should build a series of scenarios of how an insider would compromise your organization. Try to put as many details into the scenarios as possible. Once you have the scenarios, figure out how you would defend against it and what changes you need to implement so the attack will not be successful. In order to do this it is critical that you put the scenarios in priority order, focusing heavily on likelihood of the attack. If the scenario has a high chance of occurring and could have a huge loss, you would spend more time defending against it than if it had a low likelihood of success.

Just to give you a sample, the following is a high-level scenario that can be used as a starting point:

- **Executive targeting**. After careful analysis, one of the employees working at your organization has identified that whenever the CEO travels, he has all the critical corporate IP on his laptop. By accessing help desk tickets they know that this executive has complained numerous times while on travel that he does not have the information he needs to do his job. To fix the problem they load all the data onto his system prior to his trip. The insider also knows that the executive has been locked out of his system many times and therefore his password is always set to the same password. Through social engineering they can acquire the password from the executive assistant. The insider checks corporate bulletins and knows the CEO is giving a presentation in California next Tuesday, so he will be traveling on Monday. By watching the pattern of the executive, the help desk loads his system with all the data prior to him leaving and then he comes in the morning of his trip, picks up his laptop, and goes on the trip. By talking with the help desk they are going to configure the laptop on Friday and leave it on his desk Friday evening so the CEO can pick up the laptop on Monday. This represents a window of opportunity over the weekend to go into the office, log in to the computer, copy the data to a USB drive, and leave.

  Likelihood: Very high.

  Impact: Very high.

  Problems: Once you put together a scenario and determine that it has a high likelihood of occurring and the impact could be high, you then want to figure out what the problems are, and possible solutions. The problems are people not being properly training on social engineering: the CEO not being made aware of security and presented with alternatives to accomplish what he wants with the same ease but more secure. Finally, sensitive corporate records and the laptops they are stored on are not properly protected.

For purposes of this book we listed a high-level scenario to serve as a starting point, but it should be developed in a lot more detail to make sure your company is ready and prepared to deal with the insider no matter what method of attack is used.

Scenarios are critical because the more planning you perform the better off you will be in the long run. Although you can never predict the future with 100 percent accuracy, the more you can do to figure out what is going to happen and plan for it, the better off you are. In the military they are constantly running scenarios and training against them because they know it is not 100 percent accurate, but it will be pretty close, and the more your organization can be prepared the better off you will be. The more time you take to create the scenarios, the more valuable they will be in a preparedness and training tool. The less time and thought you put into them, the less value they will have.

Although this chapter talked about some cool technologies, the chapter was about awareness and allowing you to use that knowledge to build defenses before attackers strike.

Part II
Government

In the previous section, we opened your eyes to the very real concern of insider threat and detailed the specifics that characterize this problem. We talked about why detection is so difficult and why it is often covered up to prevent bad publicity and additional disclosure of sensitive intellectual property. We identified the general motives of insiders and described common methods that are used.

After you grasped exactly what there is to worry about in Chapter 1, we moved on to the technology used and misused by many insiders. We talked about information hiding, encryption, steganography, and malicious acts such as information theft and corruption. In addition, we stepped beyond computer networks and addressed concerns of other technological systems, such as voicemail and biometrics, that can be manipulated by rogue insiders. We then turned our attention to one of the most common victims/tools of corruption... the human.

Now we will apply your understanding of both the threats and the tools to real cases that have been tried within the legal systems of the United States and other countries. Although they are not as glamorous as Hollywood fiction, our cases studies are entirely factual. We believe that this will give you a better understanding of what has truly happened in the past.

Cases are organized by venue. In this section we discuss crimes that are committed within the government. This starts within the confines of state and local institutions and ends with unique threats within the United States federal government. According to the May 2005 U.S. Secret Service and CERT Coordination Center/SEI Insider Threat Study titled "Insider Threat Study: Computer System Sabotage in Critical Infrastructure Sectors," 16% of insider activity occurs within government organizations. (To read this study, go to www.secretservice.gov/ntac/its_report_050516.pdf.)

Although the lessons learned can be equally applied to each type of organization, specifics on the type of access employees have, such as the manufacturing of identification cards verses national secrets, changes what type of malicious activity they conduct. Case studies include: misuse of official network access, incidents involving fraud and tampering with property (including confidential or controlled information), and sabotage.

In section three we will turn our attention away from public safety and stability to financial interests of the commercial sector. For each, we describe threats, provide real-world case examples, and analyze prevention, detection, and remediation strategies.

Chapter 3

State and Local Government Insiders

Topics in this chapter:

- Threats You May Face
- Incidents
- Prosecution Statistics

"I was their contact inside of the DMV."

— Former Nevada Department of Motor Vehicles employee, Dalva Flagg, Speaking to U.S. District Judge Robert Jones while being tried in 2003

"He was very good. He knew the system. He knew from practical experience; he knew the people involved, and he knew the legal side of it. He was on the inside."

— Assistant District Attorney, Cliff Herberg

Speaking about a case involving former county clerk Mel Spillman in 2002

"A city government employee who was passed over for promotion to finance director retaliated by deleting files from his and a coworker's computers the day before the new finance director took office. An investigation identified the disgruntled employee as the perpetrator of the incident... No criminal charges were filed, and, under an agreement with city officials, the employee was allowed to resign."

— 2005 U.S. Secret Service and CERT Coordination Center/SEI Insider Threat Study

Introduction

In this chapter we discuss unique insider threats to state and local government institutions. This includes organizations such as mass transit, utilities, and licensing agencies (for example, Department of Motor Vehicles/Bureau of Motor Vehicles [DMV/BMV]). Although threats of sabotage are very real, and we discuss the possibilities in depth, thankfully, at the time of writing this book, most of the cases revolve around *fraud*. Unlike some of the motivations that you will see in the next chapter, most of this fraud is strictly tied to greed and the desire for additional income.

One such instance that we will discuss is when a DMV employee sold sensitive information about individuals to a private investigator. Other examples we will cover in this chapter are the numerous cases in which DMV/BMV employees used their access to produce fraudulent identification cards for those that could not legally acquire them. As another example of a prevalent insider threat, we will talk about cases in which insiders used their access to fraudulently "give" money to friends and family.

While we detail what happens in each case, in your mind identify how they apply to you. Although your company or organization may not have Electronic Benefit Transaction (EBT) cards like the victims in this chapter, you probably provide access to corporate charge cards that could be misused in the same manner. Just as the DMV has databases of sensitive information about local citizens, you may have a database of sensitive client and employee information, both of which could be disclosed by a malicious insider.

For each case, put yourself in the position of the employee's supervisor or an auditor. How could this have been prevented? Why were they able to get away with this for so long? What can you do to ensure that the same does not happen to you or your organization?

Threats You May Face

In our research we discovered that although rarely publicized, state and local governments are frequent victims of insiders. According to the United States Department of Justice in 2003 alone, 94 state officials were charged with corruption, 87 were convicted, and 38 more awaited trial. In addition, 259 local government officials were charged with corruption, 119 were convicted, and 106 awaited trial.[1] When statistics for the past decade are combined, on average 249 state and local officials are charged with corruption each year, 206 are prosecuted, and 92 await trial.

In a society where everything has a price, corruption does happen, and on a consistent basis. Unfortunately, this is often caused by the proportionally larger number of employees when compared to most companies, and the low salaries of many entry-level workers. In general, the equation of low pay and high access to sensitive data rarely turns out positively. These employees are frequently susceptible to being bribed to leverage their access in a malicious manner. Steps to prevent and mitigate this type of insider threat must be continually implemented and reassessed.

The first stage to preventing any type of crime is to be aware of potential threats. Recognizing vulnerabilities allows for preventative measures to be implemented before they can be exploited. This type of analysis comes in two forms: 1) identifying anticipated problems and 2) examining what whet wrong in previous cases. That is precisely what we intend to do in the following chapters. We start by identifying areas that have a high potential for exploitation, followed by specific examples of insider activity that have happened in the past.

In this chapter we focus on where the government ties closest to its citizens: at the state and local level. These entities are primarily responsible for ensuring the welfare and safety of residents and economic health of local companies. Threats at this level can be generalized as a loss of safety or a loss of property (see Figure 3.1).

Figure 3.1 Threats and Subsequent Effects from Insiders at the State and Local Level

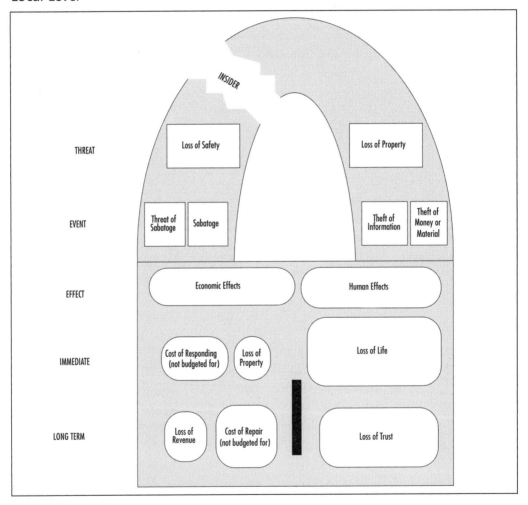

Threats that involve loss of safety are the least common, but the most dangerous. In general, the specific event that triggers this category of threat is sabotage, or in

some cases even the "threat" of sabotage. For example, a true emergency that causes a substantial response from emergency personnel leaves citizens vulnerable to other threats. This is because response time will be significantly slower due to the fact that personnel and equipment are already in route to, or on location at the first emergency. Similarly, the "threat" of a widespread emergency can also cause the same deployment and leave citizens vulnerable to a true crisis if it were to happen at the same time.

Beyond the potential for loss of life, sabotage can have other immediate and long-term effects. As it happens, the event may cause loss of property which takes away access to a resource needed by others. This may impact jobs, irreplaceable records, or expensive equipment. In addition, the cost of responding must be accounted for. After the July 2005 bombings in the London mass transit system, popular mass transit systems across the United States (and other countries) dramatically increased their number of security personnel. Even though the event did not happen in these locations, the "threat" of the event occurring became realized and therefore those cities were impacted with the burden of non-budgeted economic effects.

The impact of this non-budgeted cost is not insignificant and causes considerable ripple effects in unrelated areas. For example, consider that if positioning five additional patrols at a single subway system may cost $200,000 ($40,000 x 5). Next imagine what this means to a city that has 20 subway stations. This cost is now $4 million. Then apply this to a state that has two mass transit systems, $8 million, and a country that has thirty, $120 million. This means that there will be $120 million dollars less for programs that were originally earmarked to receive this funding. This shortcoming is often compensated for by temporarily shuffling priorities of other important programs. For example, this might mean that this year the DMV of each state cannot hire the additional auditing personnel that are needed to protect against their threats, or it may mean that local schools may not have the same number of patrols and crossing guards.

After the event itself has taken place, costs of repair must be accounted for. Beyond costs of new construction, there is the cost of demolition and removal. Redirection of this money may mean that the local fire department does not have the funds to purchase the two new fire trucks that are necessary to accommodate a growing population, or it may reduce funds for "ice and snow" removal in the winter, which in turn can mean more dangerous roads for motorists. Costs must be accounted for, and they have unavoidable side effects to the needs of others.

The second category of threat at the state and local level is loss of property. This loss can come in the form of information theft, or the theft of money or materials. When information is stolen, there are costs associated. Some of these costs are in the form of money such as when irreparable harm has been caused to an innocent citizen, or it may have a human effect such as loss of trust by citizens that rely on the organization.

In the next section we will analyze each of these threats caused by events, and their immediate and long-term effects. We start at the home or office, and then expand outward.

At the Home or Office

Call it paranoia, but threats from rogue state and local government employees can even reach into the sanctity of your home or office. This is because of our sense of "community." We gather together to share services such as first responders when emergencies occur, fresh water, sanitary sewage removal, electricity, natural gas, telephone service, and Internet service. Although in the United States most of these services are not provided directly by the government, many are "privatized" and for the sake of organization in this book we will treat them as if they are. Without their proper operation, the health of both citizens of the community and local businesses are at risk.

First Responders

Safety and public well-being requires confidence that first responders such as fire and rescue will provide the help needed. Imagine calling 9-1-1 and not having anyone answer. Even the most equipped fire and rescue department in the nation will be useless if they are not dispatched when they are needed. Similarly, a fire department that attempts to dispatch a crew to a fire, but determines that their engine is malfunctioning does no good. Just look at the impact one person with malicious intent had when he used an e-mail attachment to launch a distributed attack against a 9-1-1 service. [2] Luckily he only sent the e-mail to 20 users, only 10 of which triggered responses from emergency personnel. Just imagine the impact if he had sent it to hundreds or thousands instead.

Although there are many safety measures in place for these organizations, they are still vulnerable to insider attack. Employees within these ranks must be stringently screened (even in the case of volunteer organizations). Otherwise, one rogue insider with malicious intent can disrupt the services of others.

Access granted to technologies such as computers used to process and dispatch during emergencies must be strictly limited and should be frequently audited for security. Automated integrity checks could be implemented daily, if not hourly, to ensure that records have not been corrupted or deleted. Back-ups should be made on a frequent basis and be easy to reinstate. Employees should be trained on how to handle this type of threat just as they are trained to handle external emergencies.

Water

Water is a necessity of our well-being and we take its cleanliness for granted as we fill our glasses and pitchers for drinking. Much of the coverage on this threat is highly sensationalized and highly credible reports do illustrate the difficulty of tampering with our water supply on a large scale. However, it should be said that like first responders, employees within these organizations should be screened. Even steps such as verifying past employment records on a résumé or application, or verifying past claims of residency, can go a long way in preventing someone with a shady history from causing damage.

Electricity

An easier target than water, and as effective (if not more), is electricity. Electricity goes far beyond watching television and surfing on the Internet. Most buildings over three floors high need electricity to pump water. This means apartment complexes, hospitals, and office buildings need electricity for water alone. Even with generators, electricity can hinder emergency personnel from responding in a comprehensive fashion.

An insider can be a service person that purposefully disables access by cutting power lines or an operator that stops access through computerized controlling equipment like SCADA devices. Both can cause significant damage.

Over the past two years, Washington, DC, has been plagued with "exploding manhole covers." These explosions that send the covers flying through the air are caused by problematic underground electrical wiring igniting accumulated sewage gas. At periods these explosions occur daily and are almost comical when viewed independently of their side effect to the community. Besides the costs of response and repair, these tend to occur in areas of heavy population. Each instance usually causes ten or twenty stores to lose power, and thousands of commuters are impacted with heavy traffic. Businesses without power lose revenue for the day, and in the case of groceries and restaurants, also lose their stock of fresh and frozen items. These are examples of a series of accidental problems, but a targeted insider could do significantly more damage.

Natural Gas

Similar to the example of the manhole covers, several aging neighborhoods in Maryland have had houses literally explode because of gas leaks in the sewer lines. Instead of the leak being in appliances within the home as one might expect, the gas lines outside the house are faulty and require repair. The leaking gas is held underground by soil and is guided into homes through other conduits such as the "extra" space around water and sewer pipes. Once inside the house they accumulate and explode. Incidents such as this have the capability of leveling buildings and injuring or killing everyone inside. Like electrical sabotage, this example shows the extreme danger caused by an accidental problem. If an event such as this were caused through sabotage, the results could be catastrophic.

Telephone

With the exception of access to first responders discussed previously, not having access to the telephone may impact the welfare of its citizens but will have little impact on their actual health. However, not having access to telephone service can have a major impact on the health of a business. Reliable communication is the lifeblood of all companies. Customers expect businesses to be available for questions, consultation, and sale. Businesses need continual access to their employees (especially those traveling or working remote) and partners. Without this access, economic impact is inevitable.

Other than sabotage, an insider with access to telephone service records could still cause damage to a company. For instance, if the competitor of a consulting company had access to their telephone records, they could easily identify who their customers are. From this list they could contact those customers and offer them reduced prices. Protection of databases such as these is essential to the economic health of local companies that rely on this service.

Internet

Businesses also rely on communication across the Internet to complete day-to-day tasks. E-mail and Web site availability can often be more important than telephone access for some e-commerce businesses. Also, with the increased popularity of VoIP (Voice over Internet Protocol) in both government and private communications, network and Internet security must be taken much more seriously to prevent information loss.

A bribed insider within an Internet service provider has the potential to intercept large amounts of unencrypted network traffic, as well as to spoof traffic with malicious intent. One example of a similar case happened a few years back when the owner of an Internet service provider monitored the traffic of his clients. When they searched for or purchased books he would redirect their traffic and send them advertisements for his own store. You could argue that this was unfair access for any competing bookstores.

Miles from the Home or Business

Moving the radius out from the home or business we come to other vulnerable areas. Some of these include traffic control, mass transit, voting safety, and licensing organizations.

Traffic Control

In our current technological state, many seemingly simple devices have become automated with extremely complex systems. The traffic control mechanisms are one of the many devices that have become autonomous. Although most of the systems are extremely robust and rarely experience problems or long-term downtime, many are still vulnerable to compromise via malicious insiders.

Many of us take advantage of these seemingly mundane controls, expecting they will always be operational. Imagine a large city environment during the peak of rush-hour traffic. Then imagine what would happen if all the traffic control mechanisms (traffic lights, warning signals, etc.) stopped operating as one would expect them to. What if all the traffic lights turned green? Would anyone notice in time to prevent an accident? Or would they just presume that because their light was green that they should be able to safely venture into an intersection. Now imagine this as a widespread phenomenon. This type of disturbance could cost lives, cause panic, and drastically disrupt the U.S. economy. This may seem like a scare tactic, but it is not far from the truth. A single insider with enough information has the potential to craft such an attack.

Mass Transit

Airlines, trains, and public transportation all rely on technology to accomplish their end goal: getting their passengers where they need to go in a safe and reliable manner. As we have seen in suicide attacks across the world, mass transit is highly vulnerable to attack. In some cases attackers leveraged identification cards and papers that were supplied by malicious insiders.

As inspection prior to boarding grows, attackers may attempt to make even more use of insider access. Many theorize that the crash of EgyptAir 990 60 miles south of Nantucket, Massachusetts on October 31, 1999, is an example of this. In March 2002, the National Transportation Safety Board (NTSB) released the following statement: "The National Transportation Safety Board today determined that the probable cause of the crash of EgyptAir flight 990 was the airplane's departure from normal cruise flight and subsequent impact with the Atlantic Ocean as a result of the relief first officer's flight control inputs. The reason for the relief first officer's actions was not determined." [3]

Voting Safety

Voting is an extremely important component of every democratic society. Unfortunately, like any competition where power or money is at stake, there will always be individuals who wish to tip the scale in their favor. Vote buying is nothing new, and now that many voting systems have become electronic, there is an even higher risk of compromise. One unique problem of this risk is that detection is extremely difficult. We will explore this topic further in the case studies.

Licensing Organizations

Any type of licensing organization is vulnerable to fraudulent license distribution and the exposure of sensitive information. In many cities public access is freely granted to blueprint drawings stored for homes and businesses that have acquired licenses. In other cases, these sensitive drawings are only available to city clerks and investigators. The drawings explicitly indicate rooms and their type of use. For a thief, knowing the window that goes to the "office" in a home can lead them directly to documents they can use to steal your identity.

DMVs and BMVs also have two common threats. The first is concern over sensitive personal information being misused. With identification information an ever growing commodity among thieves, these databases are a prime target. The second threat is the manufacture and sale of fraudulent licenses. This becomes obvious with the tremendous number of case examples on the subject in the following section.

NOTE

In the next chapter we will discuss some of the large and organized threats that the federal government faces from foreign intelligence organizations. Although in general, state and local governments are not direct targets of intelligence activities like the federal government is, increased sharing of databases and information may change that.

As organizations work closely together, the lines between some may blur and thus insiders may look to leverage their access for espionage. State and local governments are "new" to this type of threat and therefore may be easy targets for attackers.

Incidents

Looking at potential areas of weakness can help to protect against attacks before they take place, but analyzing attacks that have already taken place can be just as (if not more) important. Just as transportation safety officials gather statistics and review case studies of accidents that occur, we will review cases where insiders have misused their access. Most of the cases we will discuss involve fraud or the theft of information and/or property.

A Closer Look...

Is There Power behind Fear?

According to early 18th-century philosopher Jeremy Bentham (1748–1832), there is power behind fear. He writes in his work, *An Introduction to the Principles of Morals and Legislation,* that humans are controlled by desire for gratification and contemplation over negative effects of such action. [4] Fear, he defines, is "the prospect of pain." When describing his view of our decision process, Bentham writes:

"... the other of danger. The pain which it produces is a pain of apprehension: a pain grounded on the apprehension of suffering such mischiefs or inconveniences, whatever they may be, as it is the nature of the primary mischief to produce. It may be styled, in one word, the alarm. The danger is the chance, whatever it may be, which the multitude it concerns may in consequence of the primary mischief stand exposed to, of suffering such mischiefs or inconveniences. For danger is nothing but the chance of pain, or, what comes to the same thing, of loss of pleasure."

The two government-produced posters in Figure 3.2 show images of former federal employees Aldrich Ames (left) and Earl Pitts who were both convicted of espionage. These posters were designed to deter against espionage. The poster of Ames is available at www.wasc.noaa.gov/wrso/posters/Security_Awareness_Posters-i0327.htm; the poster of former FBI Special Agent Earl Pitts is available at www.wasc.noaa.gov/wrso/posters/Security_Awareness_Posters-i0015.htm.

Continued

Figure 3.2 U.S. Government-Produced Security Awareness Posters

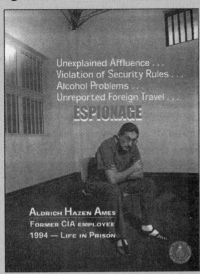 

The interesting point about each of these "security awareness" posters is that they make the statement that if you commit this crime, you *will* be caught. When you are caught, you will look just like these traitors sitting in a prison uniform with concrete walls and bars. Their purpose is to place fear of being caught in the mind of anyone contemplating this crime.

Corruption in the DMV

When threats related to state and local governments are considered, corruption within the DMV or BMV immediately come to mind. It is easier than you think for someone to acquire one or more fraudulent licenses using different names and ages. When placed side by side you may be able to identify that two pictures of the driver in Figure 3.3 are of the same individual. In both cases the same shirt is being worn, but they have different haircuts which can dramatically change appearances.

Figure 3.3 Photographs of Two Fraudulent Licenses of the Same Person

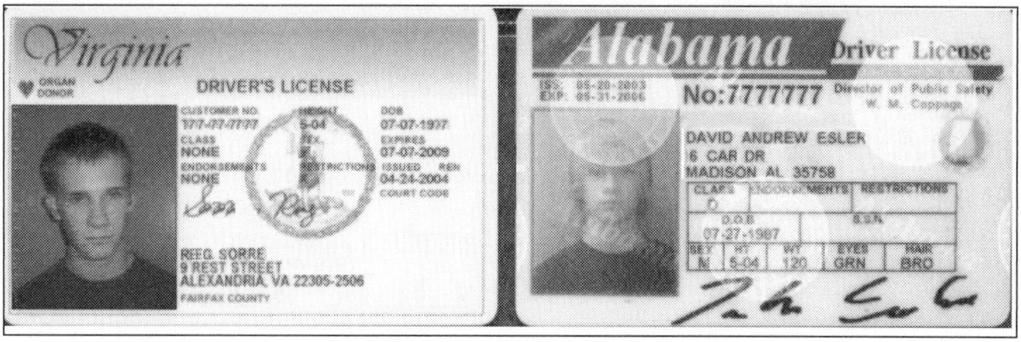

In an electronic database, however, these licenses are far from similar. On the left the driver is named "Sorre Reeg", but on the right he is "David Esler." In each case, addresses, birthdays, and signatures are totally different. Verifying the integrity of one or the other electronically by the data alone is difficult. We must place some level of trust and reliance on those that legitimately manufacture these licenses to validate their integrity. Unfortunately as we discuss next, this trust is sometimes taken for granted.

In this section we have a selected listing of cases involving corrupt insiders within these state-run organizations. This list is far from complete, but we have chosen a diverse collection to bring many different threats to light.

- **BMV Employee Allegedly Offered To Validate a Suspended License for $100 (March 4, 2001)**   In Ohio, a BMV employee, Reginald Spence, 34, allegedly offered to validate a suspended driver's license for $100. Following this, the women who received the offer called the authorities. She aided police to set up a meeting with Spence to catch him in the act. According to reports, an undercover police officer met with Spence and provided the $100, at which time he also solicited her to have sex with him.
  www.enquirer.com/editions/2001/03/04/loc_bmv_employee_accused.html

- **Three Insider DMV Employees Allegedly Approved Fake Licenses (February 26, 2002)**   In New York State, nine people were arrested following a two-year investigation of an illegal criminal ID scheme. Of those arrested and charged with accepting bribes were three DMV employees: Hettie Little, 43; Michelle Francis, 32; and Daniel Vega, 35. According to investigators, these clerks allegedly approved as many as 100 fake licenses and state ID cards. In a scheme such as this, a DMV clerk would earn between $300 and $500 for illegally approving each fake license. A broker would be paid about $1,600 for negotiating the arrangement. In this case, six brokers were arrested.

http://tianews.com/tianews/SFTHBR/09-25-04/20020226a.htm

■ **DMV Employee Allegedly Stole an Identity to Write Bad Checks (December 3, 2003)** In Washington, DC, a DMV employee allegedly used an old driver's license that was supposed to be shred to steal a person's identity. According to reports, this stolen identification was used to write over $2000 in bad checks.

www.cdt.org/privacy/030131motorvehicle.shtml

■ **DMV Insider Accepted More Than $300,000 in Exchange for Fake IDs (December 10, 2003)** In Nevada, former DMV employee Dalva Flagg, 49 pled guilty to felony charges of bribery, conspiracy, use of a false Social Security number, money laundering, and filing a false tax return. Flagg admitted taking more than $300,000 in bribes in exchange for providing illegal identification documents to immigrants. During her plea she told U.S. District Judge Robert Jones "I was their contact inside of the DMV. I knew it was wrong. I knew it was not the right thing to do, but I did it."

www.sfgate.com/cgi-bin/article.cgi?f=/news/archive/2003/12/10/state1315EST0071.DTL

■ **BMV Translator Sentenced for Forgery and False Use of Passports (July 23, 2004)** In Indiana, former BMV translator Ricardo Herrera, 42, was sentenced to 16 months imprisonment after he pled guilty to forgery and false use of passports. Herrera forged and falsified five passports by stamping them with a counterfeit I-551 stamp. This stamp is used to indicate that a non-citizen has been granted permanent residence in the United States. Herrera, who is Peruvian, will face mandatory deportation when he is released from prison.

www.justice.gov/usao/ins/pressrelease/imgroffense/20040721.hererra.io.pdf

■ **BMV Translation Fraud Ringleader Sentenced (April 5, 2005)** In Indiana, former BMV translator Elizabeth Lang, 41, was sentenced to 27 months imprisonment after she pled guilty to conspiracy to unlawfully produce identification documents, unlawful production of identification documents, fraud and false use of passports, and fraud and misuse of visas and other immigration documents. Lang (with assistance of others) illegally aided thousands of Chinese nationals to acquire Indiana driver's licenses and identification cards.

www.usdoj.gov/usao/ins/pressrelease/imgroffense/20040624.lang.io.pdf

www.usdoj.gov/usao/ins/pressrelease/Pressrelease05/20050404. Lang.io.pdf

Analysis of Fraudulent IDs Supplied at DMV/BMV

Although each instance is unique when it comes to the details, they all stem from an employee misusing their insider access in a fraudulent manner. One highly successful preventative measure would be to require that each transaction be verified by another party prior to completion. This would ensure that a "lone" insider could not utilize their access to fraudulently grant passports, licenses, etc. However, we realize this solution is virtually impossible to implement because of the shear number of transactions that take place every day, and the limited resources that these organizations have to operate. Instead, we suggest that random spot checking may be a good alternative to help deter and identify this type of fraudulent activity. Technological solutions such as automated monitoring and biometrics may also prove to be lucrative in detecting this type of threat:

■ **Consider video taping employees and the applicants.** Video recordings could be time stamped and made to correspond to transactions. Automated analysis could be made to flag new entries that are created prior or after standard work hours and snapshots of the video could be sent to an auditor. If the video shows that no applicant is present, then the transaction could be investigated further. Video recording will also act as a deterrent to the employee misusing their access.

■ **Make use of biometrics technologies.** In the case of the two driver's licenses in Figure 3.3, biometrics would have been able to successfully identify that the photos are of the same person. It seems feasible that systems could be put in place to scour DMV databases in an automated fashion searching for images that appear to be identical. In the case of the 9/11 hijackers for instance, many acquired multiple identification cards using aliases.[5] Computerized checks such as this could help to identify these anomalies.

Case Study: Using Insider Access to Sell Private Information

In this case an insider uses access not to sell false documents to someone, but to profit by selling sensitive information to an investigator. We as private citizens expect that the *personal* information we provide to BMV/DMV licensing agencies and taxing organizations like the Internal Revenue Service (IRS) will not be disclosed outside of those environments. As this case demonstrates, insiders can break this critical trust.

Topic

An insider sells personal information from a New York DMV database to a private investigator.

Source

New York State Attorney General Press Release
www.oag.state.ny.us/press/2001/dec/dec07d_01.html

Details

In New York State, former DMV employee Catherine Puckett, 41, owner of Protrac, Inc., a private investigations firm; Vincent Liptak, 57; and Liptak's secretary, Stacie Kalbacher, 44, were arraigned on a 20-count indictment in the theft of information from DMV computers. Liptak and Kalbacher allegedly bribed Puckett to repeatedly steal sensitive personal information from a DMV computer database over the course of two years.

This stolen information was sent using the DMV e-mail system to Liptak and Kalbacher. At the time, Puckett was an eight-year veteran of the DMV. According to the New York Attorney General's Criminal Prosecutions Bureau, Puckett pled guilty on January 2, 2002, to receiving a reward for official misconduct and was sentenced to pay restitution March 2002.

Analysis

This case is an example of how someone used their insider access to sell sensitive information for profit. The following are countermeasures that we recommend to prevent this form of insider threat in your office:

- **Only employees that need continued admission to sensitive information should be given access.** Access to databases and other electronic data containing sensitive personal information should be restricted to the furthest extent possible.

- **Access to records in sensitive databases should be frequently audited.** Each employee should have his or her own username and password. A monitoring system should be implemented to identify who accesses what records when. This monitoring can identify unusual after-hours activities as well as identify when as an employee accesses records beyond legitimate work requirements. This monitoring system should be advertised to help deter curious employees.

- **Records should not be cut-and-paste capable and printing should be monitored.** Records that can easily be copied can easily be distributed electronically. By preventing cutting and pasting of information, insiders are forced to type, write, or print the information.

- **Outgoing e-mail and messaging should be automatically monitored for sensitive information.** This case is an example of how monitoring of e-mail for outgoing sensitive information could have detected this activity. Items such as Social Security numbers can be scanned in outgoing e-mail and messaging using technologies available today. In addition, the occurrence of large amounts of encrypted traffic is identifiable and can indicate someone trying to hide sensitive information that is being transmitted.

A Closer Look...

Is Prevention the Same as Deterrence?

While the following definitions from Merriam-Webster (www.webster.com) are similar, and the end goal of stopping an event from taking place are the same, the means of researching that goal are significantly different:

Prevent (pronunciation: pri-'vent) Function: verb

Etymology: Middle English, to anticipate, from Latin praeventus, past participle of praevenire to come before, anticipate, forestall, from prae- + venire to come — more at **COME**

transitive senses

1: archaic a : to be in readiness for (as an occasion) b : to meet or satisfy in advance c : to act ahead of d : to go or arrive before

2: to deprive of power or hope of acting or succeeding

3: to keep from happening or existing

4: to hold or keep back : HINDER, STOP—often used with from

Deter (pronunciation: di-'t&r, dE-) Function: transitive verb

Inflected Form(s): de·terred; de·ter·ring

Etymology: Latin deterrEre, from de- + terrEre to frighten—more at **TERROR**

1: to turn aside, discourage, or prevent from acting

2: **INHIBIT**

When applied to our context, prevention refers to eliminating the vulnerability that can be leveraged by an insider to do damage. In contrast, when the vulnerability cannot be eliminated, deterrence attempts to convince the insider not to exploit the vulnerability.

Although simple, an analogy can be drawn from a child and a piece of candy. You can prevent the child from having the candy altogether by placing it out of reach. Alternatively, you can attempt to persuade the child that he is not allowed to have the candy sitting in front of him and that you will punish him if he does. Anyone with young children knows that the first circumstance has a significantly better chance of success.

Removing the vulnerability altogether is the most desirable choice when possible. When this is not an option, you should attempt to dissuade and deter employees from committing the crime through overt types of monitoring. These include video cameras, advertised database transaction monitoring, and advertised e-mail content monitoring.

Case Studies:
Theft of Electronic Benefits

Theft and corruption of benefits such as food stamps is nothing new. However, with transitions from paper accounting to electronic databases, monitoring of these systems should help to reduce occurrences. Some may argue, although, that without proper safeguards it instead enables thieves to operate in a more efficient manner. In the next section, we discuss two cases that demonstrate how easily this can be done with computers using EBT cards (see Figure 3.4 for an example of a Virginia EBT card).

Figure 3.4 A Virginia EBT Card from www.co.henrico.va.us/dss/ebt.htm

Topic

Two Indiana Family and Social Services Administration (FSSA) employees are arrested and accused of fraudulently adding and changing food stamp assistance eligibility in an online database.

Source

Marion County Press Release
www.indygov.org/eGov/County/Pros/PR/FSSA+Scam.htm

Details

On June 27, 2005, suspended FSSA employees Geraldine Harper and Mary Miracle were both arrested and charged with theft, conspiracy to commit theft, welfare fraud, official misconduct, and corrupt business influence, among other lesser charges. Miracle was a 19-year veteran of the agency and Harper was nearing retirement, having worked there for 26 years.

Marion County Prosecutor Carl Brizzi said "these two women used their expertise to satisfy their individual greed. You and I and all of the taxpayers of Indiana are victims in this case, because the money taken out of our paychecks – supposedly going to those who have nothing – went to those who wanted everything."

While working at FSSA, both women were responsible for distributing funds from the Temporary Assistance to Needy Families (TANF) program. Families in temporary need were mailed an EBT card. This acted similarly to an ATM card and could be used as cash or food stamps in stores. Each family was evaluated and an amount, usually $500 to $1500 a month, was provided to them for up to six months.

According to Brizzi, "Harper and Miracle would create fictitious accounts and mail EBT cards to themselves or to family or friends. They would then take the cards to ATMs and drain all of the cash and use it for themselves. They would also sell the value of the food stamps contained in the cards on the black market, so they were making money two ways. They would then "refill" the card each month. We estimate that they made $100,000 in TANF funds and a like amount in food stamps. This had been going on since at least 2003."

Analysis

Harper and Miracle were reportedly detected because they repeatedly began adding auxiliary funds to cards that had already been maxed out. Because of this unusual occurrence, an FSSA supervisor became suspicious and determined that the cards were fraudulent. The supervisor determined that they had been obtained with fake Social Security numbers and sent to incorrect addresses.

Because this is an electronic system, it seems plausible that the Social Security number of the recipient could be tied into a larger database to determine its validity and prevent fake numbers. In addition, a change such as this could prevent one person from obtaining funds from multiple locations. This is also an example of how frequent random auditing is necessary in environments in which employees have access to financial transactions.

A few states issue EBT cards that carry photographs on them. By doing this the number of cards "issued" to one person could be drastically limited. It would be an interesting case study to investigate if those states have significantly lower levels of EBT card fraud than the ones that do not have photographs.

In addition, just as with driver's licenses, the databases could be searched using biometrics to identify duplicate cards issued to one person's photograph.

Topic

A Florida public assistance eligibility specialist is arrested and accused of fraudulently adding and changing food stamp assistance eligibility in an online database.

Source

Florida State Department of Law Enforcement Press Release
www.fdle.state.fl.us/press_releases/20050204_Glenda_Taylor.html

Details

On February 2, 2005, Glenda Taylor, 48, of Riviera Beach, Florida, was arrested and charged with grand theft, public assistance fraud, and offenses against intellectual property. According to a Florida Department of Law Enforcement press release, Taylor is accused of issuing more than $7,300 in fraudulent food stamp benefits. After receiving information from the Florida Department of Children and Families Benefit Recovery Unit back in 2003 an investigation was launched.

Taylor, an employee for 18 years, is accused of creating fraudulent EBT cards using the Florida Online Recipient Integrated Data Access (FLORIDA) system. In addition, she reportedly reopened closed cases (such as her deceased mother's) and changed eligibility information and the mailing address of the EBT cards. This is an ongoing investigation and authorities do not yet know who was receiving and using the fraudulent cards.

Analysis

Like the previous case, this demonstrates the need of oversight for employees that access and disburse large amounts of funds. It also demonstrates that database transactions can be logged and analyzed to determine if fraudulent access is taking place. Reopening closed and deceased cases should be audited to prevent events such as this.

Lessons Learned from Both EBT Cases

In most states EBT cards have only been around since the early 1990s. They are still making constant improvements in the way they are processed and in techniques to prevent against fraud. Here are some suggestions we have for these (and other) benefits cards used in state governments and elsewhere:

- Automated verification of address, Social Security information, and eligibility for benefits could prevent most cases of fraud.

- Transaction auditing, especially when "closed" cases are reopened or addresses are changed, should be implemented. When transactions occur before or after normal business hours they should be flagged and audited as well.

- Rotating employees to different positions occasionally can also help to limit and detect malicious activity such as this.

- Photographs on the cards could limit the amount of fraud.

A Closer Look...

What Is "Need-to-Know"?

Need-to-know is a phrase that describes a security policy requiring not only the correct level of clearance for information, but a genuine need to know the information in order to conduct official business. It is used throughout the government, especially in classified environments. From a United States military Web site discussing proper handing of sensitive information, it is described as follows:

Need-to-know is one of the most fundamental security principles. *The practice of need-to-know limits the damage that can be done by a trusted insider who goes bad. Failures in implementing the need-to-know principle have contributed greatly to the damage caused by a number of recent espionage cases*

Even organizations that do not guard classified information should use the need-to-know principle. For example, if an employee is not responsible for adding or changing entries within an EBT card database, then they should not be instructed on how to do it by anyone else. An employee desiring to commit fraud from a database such as this may act curious to another who has knowledge of how to log in and create transactions. In general, this starts as small talk and eventually ends with the employee unknowingly aiding in the crime.

The classified world has witnessed the phenomena too many times, specifically in cases involving espionage. Smoking areas used to be a particularly vulnerable area because they were a place where people went and talked on a scheduled basis. For example, an insider wishing to gain access to the information of another may observe that the employee tends to smoke just before lunch and again in the early afternoon. The insider may purposefully time himself to be in the same place at the same time as the employee to smoke. The two are now

Continued

standing outside together and they begin to talk. As time goes on and the two employees develop a bond, the insider may push with probing questions that otherwise would be alerting if asked by a stranger. Because of this, drawings such as the one shown in Figure 3.5 are generally posted around smoking areas to raise awareness. This reminds employees that just because someone asks a question, they are not obligated to answer. Smoking areas are an example of locations where the "need-to-know" principle was not practiced in the past and sensitive classified information was divulged to an insider. More can be read about this in the next chapter.

Figure 3.5 A Drawing from a Military Web Site Reminding Employees to Be Cautious about Where They Disclose Sensitive Information*

* Source: www.dss.mil/search-dir/training/csg/security/S1class/Need.htm

Case Study: Lottery Fraud

Lottery tickets would not sell if the game was thought to be fixed. Unfortunately, however, in at least one circumstance, that is exactly what happened. As the next case study demonstrates, access to knowledge such as the location of a winning multimillion-dollar ticket can bring out the worst in people. Although you will see that mistakes were made, particularly in lack of practice of the "need-to-know" principle, we would like to point out that this case is an excellent example of how insider threat *can* be detected.

Topic

Former Indiana lottery employee is charged with passing on the location of a winning ticket in the "$2,000,000 Bonus Spectacular" game.

Source

Marion County Press Release
www.indygov.org/eGov/County/Pros/Prosecute/WhiteCollar/Corrupt/home.htm

Details

According to accusations, former Indiana lottery security guard William Foreman, 59, knew the location of a winning $2,000,000 Bonus Spectacular scratch-off game ticket and passed it to two of his friends, Chad R. Adkins, 28, and Daniel J. Foltz, 31.

Authorities indicate that months before the winning ticket was claimed they thought the game had been compromised because someone (identified by Store Clerk Ragina Warner as Foltz) purchased the entire stock of $20 tickets from the Cross Plains store. This immediate $640 purchase in May was unusual.

In September, Foltz went to claim his prize at the lottery office. Once he explained that the winning ticket was co-owned by another individual, lottery officials indicated that the co-winner had to appear in person as well. When Adkins did appear the next day, he was immediately recognized by security chief Peter Byrne as a friend of the lottery security guard William Foreman. Given this, their payment was initially delayed and Foreman was asked to take a polygraph test. He refused and resigned from his position despite the fact that he was nearly vested in the state pension.

According to authorities, the compromise occurred on May 13, 2004, when lottery investigator Mathew Hollcraft was given a "ticket reconstruction list" from the manufacturer in Georgia. With sensitive information known only to people within the lottery system, Hollcraft was able to determine the location of all five winning tickets. Both Peter Byrne and Foreman had access to this list. Byrne was also asked to take a polygraph test, which he passed.

Former Indiana lottery security guard William Foreman was then arrested and charged with disclosing confidential information related to a lottery and theft.

The *Indianapolis Star* reports that Adkins and Foltz have filed guilty pleas agreeing to testify against William Foreman. [6] "This type of insider trading could devastate the public's confidence in the lottery," Marion County Prosecutor Carl Brizzi said. "This is one occasion when the game was fixed. Those responsible need to be held accountable." If Foreman is convicted of disclosing the secret location of the winning lottery ticket, he could serve up to fifty years in prison.

Analysis

This case is an excellent example of successful detection and remediation against insider threat. Although Foreman never should have been able to obtain the location of the winning lottery ticket, his actions were indeed detected. Luckily, one of the persons that went to claim the winnings was recognized to be Foreman's friend, and thus raised suspicions about the plot. From this case we learned the following countermeasures:

- **Practice "Need-to-Know."** Foreman never should have had access to where the winning lottery ticket was sold.

- **Audit employees that have access to sensitive information.** Foreman was asked to take a polygraph test, but he refused and resigned from his position.

- **Audit recipients of benefits.** Both of the "winners" were found to have ties to Foreman. If the recipients of the EBT cards were verified in this manner, the two previous cases could have been detected and possibly prevented.

A Look at Technology…

Is a "Real ID" the Real Answer?

On January 26, 2005, the Real ID Act was introduced to the House of Representatives. The Real ID is a method of identification meant to prevent suspected terrorists and illegal aliens from unlawfully traveling around the country. It is essentially a form of national ID that one would have to present at airports, train stations, and maybe elsewhere.

The ID will contain at a minimum: full legal name, date of birth, gender, driver's license number, digital photo, home address, signature, and a common machine-readable technology. Also, before receiving the ID, you must be able to present a photo ID, date-of-birth documentation, Social Security number, and proof of residence. All of this data will then be added to a state-controlled database. However, the databases will be shared from state-to-state, creating a national database of United States citizens.

Although the act was well perceived by the House, many argue that it is not a terribly effective tool. DMV employees will still issue the ID, so the threat of

Continued

compromise via an insider is still a very real problem. Also, those same DMV employees will have access to the entire national database, making the effects of compromise much more widespread.

As noted in this chapter, many DMV and BMV employees have accepted payment to produce drivers' licenses with falsified information and to reveal confidential information of citizens. Also, since the card is meant to be universal, and will contain a common machine-readable technology, it will be much easier for thieves to extract data from the ID. This threat could very likely lead to an increase in identity theft and similar fraud.

After reviewing the cases in this chapter you may come to the conclusion that the money being put into this mechanism may be better spent in reforming the screening process of DMV and BMV employees and adding detection mechanisms to prevent insiders from utilizing their access unlawfully. At any rate, Real ID deserves careful consideration, and more research needs to be done to determine the effectiveness to prevent illegal activity. Read the act for yourself at http://thomas.loc.gov/ and you be the judge.

Case Study: Clerk Steals More Than $4.9M from Estates

You may be familiar with this next story from news reports a few years back. No matter how many times you hear about it, it will probably still amaze you that this brazen theft was able to continue for so long without detection. Despite his lavish lifestyle, and even after this insider "retired" and the position was eliminated, he continued his path of crime without being caught.

Topic

A U.S. probate clerk illegally uses his insider knowledge to transfer estate properties to himself.

Source

The State of Texas V. Melvyn M. Spillman

Case Numbers: 2002-CR-0003/2002-CR-2004 District Court 290th Judicial District of Bexar County, Texas

Details

In the late 1990s, Mel Spillman was a well-known member of the Ferrari racing community. A quick search on Google for "Mel Spillman Ferrari" still details some of his expeditions and road races all across the United States. Some of the cars in his Ferrari collection are pictured in Figure 3.6.

Figure 3.6 Mel Spillman's Ferrari Collection: A 1990 Ferrari F40 Serial Number 87454 (top left), 1972 Ferrari 365 GTB/4 Serial Number 14279 (top right), and 1980 Ferrari 308/288 Conversion Serial Number 34555 (bottom center)

The photos in Figure 3.6 are reprinted with permission from Ferrari Specialist and Broker, Michael Sheehan at http://ferraris-online.com/.

Spillman liked racing so much, in fact, that he even started his own racing team with his own Formula One racing car. Interestingly enough, Mel Spillman lived on the modest salary of a Texas county clerk ($33,000 a year). Yet, as Assistant District Attorney Cliff Herberg said in a CBS interview, "He spent tons of money. A fuel injection system would be $15,000, tires would be $4,000. Wheels would be $4,000 or $5,000. He spent $250,000 on his American Express bill in one quarter."[7]

How did Spillman do it? With his home computer, a forged signature, and stolen county seals. Melvyn Spillman began his career as a Bexar County employee serving as a Probate Clerk in 1969. After this he was a Probate Court Administrative Assistant (Court Coordinator) and later became a Supervisor in the Probate Court until 1982. Spillman then served as a Consultant to the Probate Court until 1988 when he transferred out to the District Court's Office as a Departmental Supervisor. In 1999 he retired.

According to police, Stillman began committing this fraud at the Bexar County courthouse in 1986 while he was a Probate Clerk. Despite his retirement, the fraud did not end until July 2001 when he was arrested at a local bank attempting to close out the account of a decedent. In these years it is estimated that Spillman fraudulently misappropriated more than $4.9 million.

Now, you may be asking yourself, "how could he do this and not get caught?" As part of his job, he was responsible for settling the estates of deceased individuals that had no heirs. This included working in the medical examiner's office and handling funeral arrangements for these individuals. He was supposed to liquidate the property and turn over all the proceeds to the state. Instead, Spillman stole the money and illegally turned the estates over to himself.

In cases where he sold the property, he kept the money. In other cases he used his home computer to create forged documents. An example of one of these documents that enabled him to take control of the properties is in Figure 3.7. He put these houses up for rent under his name and ownership and retained the earnings. During estate liquidations, he claimed many of the antiques and valuables for himself prior to offering them to the public for sale. Some of these antiques can be seen in photos of property seized following his arrest (see Figure 3.8).

Figure 3.7 Seized Letter of Temporary Administration Fraudulently Created by Melvyn Spillman

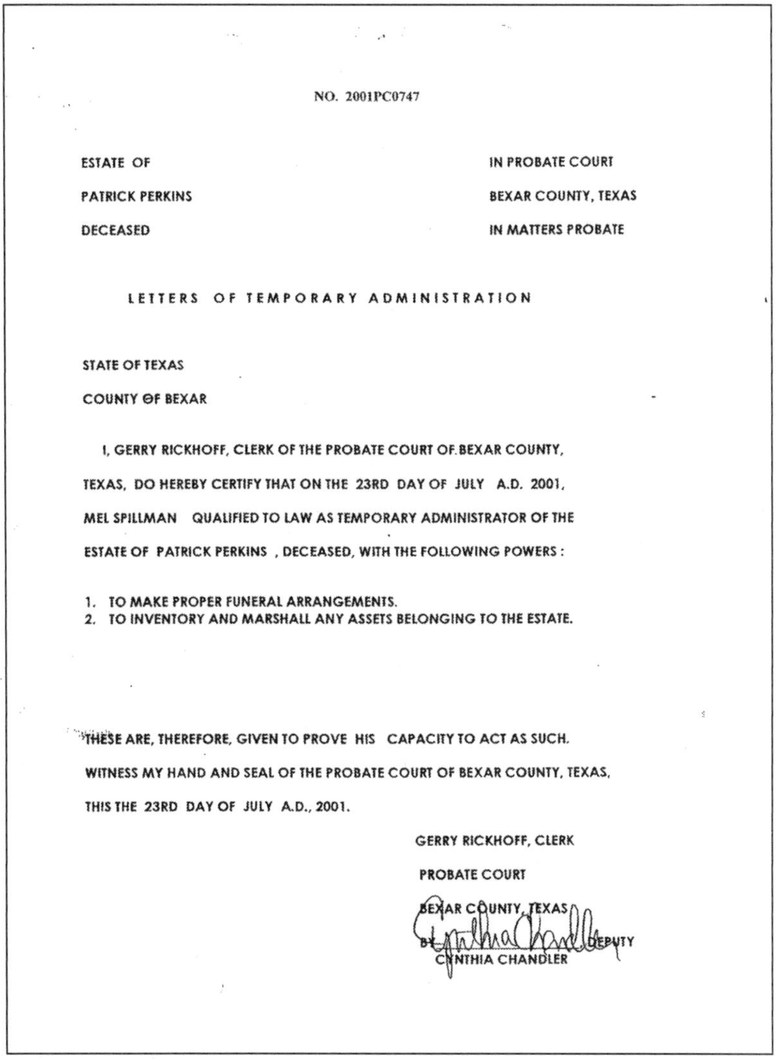

NO. 2001PC0747

ESTATE OF	IN PROBATE COURT
PATRICK PERKINS	BEXAR COUNTY, TEXAS
DECEASED	IN MATTERS PROBATE

LETTERS OF TEMPORARY ADMINISTRATION

STATE OF TEXAS

COUNTY OF BEXAR

I, GERRY RICKHOFF, CLERK OF THE PROBATE COURT OF BEXAR COUNTY, TEXAS, DO HEREBY CERTIFY THAT ON THE 23RD DAY OF JULY A.D. 2001, MEL SPILLMAN QUALIFIED TO LAW AS TEMPORARY ADMINISTRATOR OF THE ESTATE OF PATRICK PERKINS , DECEASED, WITH THE FOLLOWING POWERS :

1. TO MAKE PROPER FUNERAL ARRANGEMENTS.
2. TO INVENTORY AND MARSHALL ANY ASSETS BELONGING TO THE ESTATE.

THESE ARE, THEREFORE, GIVEN TO PROVE HIS CAPACITY TO ACT AS SUCH.

WITNESS MY HAND AND SEAL OF THE PROBATE COURT OF BEXAR COUNTY, TEXAS,

THIS THE 23RD DAY OF JULY A.D., 2001.

GERRY RICKHOFF, CLERK

PROBATE COURT

BEXAR COUNTY, TEXAS

BY _____ DEPUTY

CYNTHIA CHANDLER

Figure 3.8 Pictures of Seized Assets from Mel Spillman's Property for Auction outside San Antonio, Texas

The photos in Figure 3.8 are reprinted with permission from Ilan Jenkins at www.particleman.org.

His arrest was part of a sting operation conducted in Bexar County, Texas, (outside San Antonio). Charged with tampering with government records, impersonating a public servant using the fraudulent badge pictured in Figure 3.9, and forgery, Spillman pled guilty to forgery and impersonation.

Figure 3.9 Seized Badge Fraudulently Used by Melvyn Spillman after He Was No Longer a County Employee

Bexar County 290th Criminal District Court Judge Sharon MacRae sentenced Spillman to two maximum terms of 10 years each in prison for forgery and impersonation of a public servant. These sentences are being served concurrently and Spillman will be eligible for parole in 2007.

Analysis

According to police investigations, Spillman stole nearly five million dollars from the estates of 122 people. Even after his position was officially eliminated in 1988, Spillman continued to do the job. When he retired in 1999, he operated as a private consultant for the court and continued his fraudulent scheme. It wasn't until 2001 when a probate judge noticed Spillman's name incorrectly listed on papers as a "court administrator" that the situation came to light. The length of time that this fraud continued is unbelievable. The case illustrates the importance of the following countermeasures to prevent this from happening in your workplace:

- **Accountability of sensitive materials** Sensitive materials such as seals and badges must be closely accounted for.

- **Rotation of employees with sensitive access** Spillman was rotated, but unfortunately his previous position was never refilled. This left the door open for him to continue his fraud. If someone else had taken on his past responsibility, his actions would have likely stopped upon his rotation.

- **Auditing and Authentication**   It seems as if the distribution of estate funds to the appropriate recipients was never verified. Given the sensitivity of his access and the large amount of money at stake, these transactions should have been logged and audited. Similarly, if the fraudulent letters that he created on his home computer had been authenticated this could have, in theory, been detected much sooner.

Vote Tampering

Vote buying corrupts the very notion of democracy by maliciously providing one candidate a fraudulent advantage over the other. Hundreds of cases related to this topic have occurred in the past, and very likely hundreds of cases will occur in the future. In the next few sections, we discuss several cases that occurred within the Eastern District of Kentucky alone. These cases came to light following a federal investigation of the May 1998 primary election in Knott County, Kentucky. In 2003, these cases were tried in court. There were seven separate cases comprising a total of 10 defendants. Five pleaded guilty, two were convicted by a jury, and three others were acquitted.

United States of America v. Calhoun

On August 19, 2003, Jimmy Calhoun pleaded guilty to two counts of vote-buying. He paid two persons to vote by absentee ballot for candidates headed by Donnie Newsome who was the successful candidate for County Judge Executive in the election.

United States of America v. Conley

On March 28, 2003, Jimmy Lee Conley was indicted on five counts of vote-buying. He was accused of paying five people to vote by absentee ballot for candidates headed by Donnie Newsome. He was acquitted on June 19, 2003.

United States of America v. Madden

Patrick Madden was indicted on three counts of vote buying on March 28, 2003. He confessed to paying three people to vote by absentee ballot for candidates headed by Donnie Newsome. Madden pleaded guilty to one count of vote-buying on October 6, 2003.

United States of America v. Johnson

On June 2, 2003, Newton Johnson pled guilty to paying people to vote by absentee ballot for candidates headed by Donnie Newsome in the May 1998 Knott County, Kentucky, primary election. Johnson reached a plea agreement and participated with the government to uncover the larger conspiracy headed by Donnie Newsome.

Johnson testified that Newsome, the winning County Judge Executive, had offered to give him a road improvement and a county job in exchange for his actions. Given Johnson's circumstances of living in a remote mountain hollow in which he could not leave without the road improvement, and his illiteracy, which made it difficult for him to acquire a job, he agreed.

United States of America v. Pigman, Newsome, and Smith

On July 8, 2003, Keith Pigman pled guilty with a plea agreement to conspiracy to commit vote-buying as well as one count of vote-buying. Upon his agreement, he cooperated with investigators and testified against both Newsome and Smith. He verified the existence of a conspiracy to pay "numerous impoverished, handicapped, illiterate, or otherwise impaired persons" to vote for the candidates headed by Newsome. In addition, he explained that these people were purposefully chosen because they felt their credibility would be in question if an investigation did take place. In exchange for his part in the conspiracy, Newsome gave Pigman a county job.

County Judge Executive Donnie Newsome and his supporter Willard Smith were convicted on charges of conspiracy to commit vote-buying and several counts of vote-buying. Together the three approached and paid others to convince people to vote for the slate of Newsome candidates using absentee vote.

A Closer Look...

Is Electronic Voting Safe?

In short the answer to that question is no. If an attacker wants it bad enough and pairs with an insider who understands the ins and outs of the software, compromise is a very real threat. Just as fake IDs can be purchased, fraudulent identification information can be presented, or bypassed altogether, with the cooperation of an insider. Although widespread corruption of this type would be an extremely difficult task, it is possible. Especially in this technological age, the Internet is quickly becoming a convenient solution for voting both at home and abroad. Internet voting is still in its premature stages and is not the most reliable means of voting. Also, unlike other electronic voting mechanisms, there is no way to confirm, short of a re-vote, that the results were legitimate. Although most electronic voting systems are capable of detecting and mitigating anomalies, current Internet voting technology is extremely vulnerable to widespread undetectable compromise. However, electronic voting safety is a big concern of the U.S. government and they are currently looking for new ways to ensure the security and integrity of the process.

Examples of recently implemented security mechanisms can be found here: www.ss.ca.gov/elections/security%20measures%20for%20touch%20screen%20(dre).pdf

Prosecution Statistics

Figure 3.10 contains prosecution statistics taken from the Department of Justice Report to Congress on the Activities and Operations of the Public Integrity Section for 2003. You can see that the number of officials charged with corruption has remained fairly steady since 1984. The highest number of charges occurred in 1993 (309) and the lowest number in 1984 (203). Otherwise, on average 249 local officials are charged every year.

Figure 3.10 Chart of Local Government Officials Who Are Charged, Convicted, and Awaiting Trial

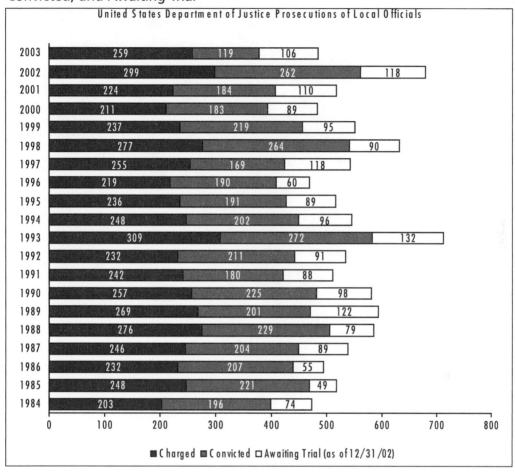

At the state level, on average 89 state officials are charged with corruption each year, 78 are prosecuted, and 32 await trial (see Figure 3.11).

Figure 3.11 Chart of State Government Officials Who Are Charged, Convicted, and Awaiting Trial

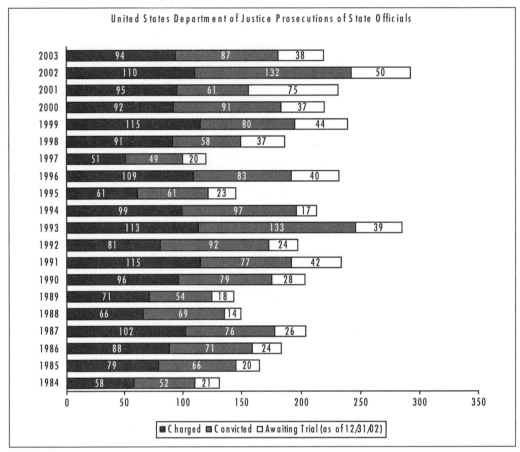

To help identify if your state is one of the problematic areas, we have correlated the statistics in the Department of Justice Report with Population data from the census bureau. Ratios for each state are calculated, and then states are ranked by the score of their ratio. From this chart you can see that in 2003 the top ten most corrupt states by population ratio are as follows:

- District of Columbia*
- North Dakota
- Mississippi
- Arkansas

- Kentucky

- Pennsylvania

- Louisiana

- New Jersey

- Illinois

- Virginia

* The District of Columbia may be unusually high because of the large number of senators and congressmen as well as other government staff centered in this area. States that had no public corruption charges for 2003 are:

- Alaska

- Kansas

- Rhode Island

- Vermont

The full chart of rankings can be found in Table 3.1.

Table 3.1 Alphabetic Chart of States Including Corruption Rankings by Population Ratio

State	Number of Incidents	Population	Ratio	Rank
Alabama	14	4,503,726	0.310853724	24
Alaska	0	648,280	0	49
Arizona	10	5,579,222	0.17923646	39
Arkansas	19	2,727,774	0.696538643	4
California	75	35,462,712	0.211489747	37
Colorado	7	4,547,633	0.153926229	41
Connecticut	12	3,486,960	0.344139308	16
Delaware	3	818,166	0.366673756	14
District of Columbia	20	557,620	3.586671927	1
Florida	55	16,999,181	0.323544999	20
Georgia	21	8,676,460	0.242034194	29
Hawaii	4	1,248,755	0.320319038	23

Continued

Table 3.1 continued Alphabetic Chart of States Including Corruption Rankings by Population Ratio

State	Number of Incidents	Population	Ratio	Rank
Idaho	4	1,367,034	0.292604281	26
Illinois	60	12,649,087	0.474342536	9
Indiana	20	6,199,571	0.322602967	22
Iowa	9	2,941,976	0.30591684	25
Kansas	0	2,724,786	0	49
Kentucky	26	4,118,189	0.631345477	5
Louisiana	25	4,493,665	0.556338757	7
Maine	5	1,309,205	0.38191116	13
Maryland	12	5,512,310	0.217694578	36
Massachusetts	22	6,420,357	0.342660073	17
Michigan	24	10,082,364	0.238039412	30
Minnesota	3	5,064,172	0.059239694	47
Mississippi	27	2,882,594	0.936656359	3
Missouri	10	5,719,204	0.174849507	40
Montana	2	918,157	0.21782767	35
Nebraska	2	1,737,475	0.11510957	42
Nevada	6	2,242,207	0.267593492	27
New Hampshire	3	1,288,705	0.232791834	32
New Jersey	41	8,642,412	0.474404599	8
New Mexico	2	1,878,562	0.106464413	44
New York	63	19,212,425	0.327912796	19
North Carolina	21	8,421,190	0.249370932	28
North Dakota	16	633,400	2.526049889	2
Ohio	37	11,437,680	0.323492177	21
Oklahoma	4	3,506,469	0.114074871	43
Oregon	3	3,564,330	0.084167291	46
Pennsylvania	74	12,370,761	0.598184703	6
Rhode Island	0	1,076,084	0	49
South Carolina	8	4,148,744	0.192829444	38

Continued

Table 3.1 continued Alphabetic Chart of States Including Corruption
Rankings by Population Ratio

State	Number of Incidents	Population	Ratio	Rank
South Dakota	3	764,905	0.392205568	12
Tennessee	21	5,845,208	0.359268652	15
Texas	49	22,103,374	0.221685612	33
Utah	8	2,352,119	0.340118846	18
Vermont	0	619,343	0	49
Virginia	30	7,365,284	0.407316269	10
Washington	6	6,131,298	0.097858561	45
West Virginia	4	1,811,440	0.220818796	34
Wisconsin	13	5,474,290	0.237473718	31
Wyoming	2	502,111	0.3983183	11

The source for number of convictions in each state Report to Congress on the Activities and Operations of the Public Integrity Section for 2003 (www.usdoj.gov/criminal/pin/AnnReport_03.pdf). Note that this report is incomplete and does not provide statistics for Tennessee through Wisconsin. Despite attempts to collect this information from the Public Integrity Section, we could not determine these values. For these states, we used their statistics from 2002 instead.

Closing Thoughts

State and local governments are frequent victims of insiders. In some cases, these employees use their access and knowledge to steal benefits such as those from EBT cards, and in one case those benefits actually came from estates of local citizens that had recently died.

State and local insiders within the DMV/BMV use their access to sell information from sensitive databases about private citizens, bribe applicants for illegal activities related to their accounts, or even produce fraudulent licenses for those that cannot legally obtain them.

In other cases, individuals used bribery to "buy" votes under the presumption that once they were elected they would use their insider access to provide favors such as road improvements, contracts, and government jobs. This threat will likely become even more widespread as more counties transition to mail-only and electronic voting to reduce crowds and increase voter turnout.

As we demonstrate, even the lottery is susceptible to insider threat.

These threats can be either prevented or deterred. Prevention helps to remove the possibility of its occurrence. For example, the lottery security guard should have been *prevented* from knowing where the winning ticket was located.

For those that must have access to the sensitive information, the threats can be deterred. As an example, DMV employees should be told that each of their transactions is monitored and audited and that they will face steep fines if they are caught making fraudulent entries. As the 18th-century philosopher Jeremy Bentham suggests, the perceived notion of being caught partnered with penalties that will outweigh the benefit of their actions is one way to prevent malicious activities.

Although the cases that we analyze in this chapter are examples of incidents within state and local government, the threats are not unique to these organizations. The federal government and even companies have similar situations that can (and probably do) result in insider attacks.

Summary

Corruption within state and local government does happen and on a consistent basis; on average 249 state and local officials are charged with corruption each year, 206 are prosecuted, and 92 await trial. Potential threats are categorized as a loss of safety and/or loss of property. Sometimes the threat of sabotage can be almost as damaging as the act itself. Examples include the additional unbudgeted costs that resulted from increased security worldwide after the July 2005 London mass transit bombing.

At the home or office possible threats include first responders, water, electricity, natural gas, telephone, and Internet service. Away from the home or office threats include traffic control systems, mass transit, voting safety, and licensing organizations. The difference between prevention and deterrence is that the first removes the vulnerability whereas the latter attempts to convince the individual from not exploiting it. Whenever possible, always prevent and use deterrence as a last resort, or as an additional layer of security.

Philosopher Jeremy Bentham suggests that our decisions are based on contemplation of the likelihood that we will be caught versus the benefit we will acquire from the act. Your organization should take the following measures to detect an inside threat:

- Practice "need-to-know."
- Frequently audit access and transaction records for sensitive databases.
- Disable "cut and paste" functionality from records and monitor printing.
- Automatically monitor outgoing e-mail and messaging for sensitive information.
- If possible, automatically check and confirm identification information such as biometric images, addresses, Social Security numbers, and eligibility for benefits for each transaction.
- Rotate employees to different positions occasionally to limit and detect malicious activity.
- Audit employees that have access to sensitive information.
- Audit recipients who are granted benefits such as EBT cards, lottery payouts, and corporate credit cards in the commercial environment.
- Have an accountability program for sensitive materials such as seals, badges, and official letterhead.

■   Require auditing and authentication of sensitive letters and requests such as corporate credit card accounts and letters that indicate temporary administration power beyond normal access.

Endnotes

1. "Annual Report to Congress on the Activities and Operations of the Public Integrity Section." United States Department of Justice, 2003, www.usdoj.gov/criminal/pin/AnnReport_03.pdf.

2 "Louisiana Man Pleads Guilty to Sending E-mail with Attachment That Caused Internet Service to Dial 9-1-1." United States Attorney of the Northern District of California, February 14, 2005, www.usdoj.gov/usao/can/press/html/2005_02_14_jeansonne.html.

3 "Aircraft Accident Brief." National Transportation Safety Board, March 13, 2002, www.ntsb.gov/Publictn/2002/aab0201.htm.

4. Jeremy Bentham. An Introduction to the Principles of Morals and Legislation, 1781, http://socserv.mcmaster.ca/econ/ugcm/3ll3/bentham/morals.pdf.

5. "9/11 and Terrorist Travel." National Commission of Terrorist Attacks upon the United States, http://www.9-11commission.gov/staff_statements/911_TerrTrav_Monograph.pdf.

6. "Three Interesting Stories." The Lotto Report, www.lottoreport.com/sadbut-true8.htm.

7. "Scammed: County Clerk Cashes In." CBS Interview Containing Quotes from Assistant District Attorney Cliff Herberg, November 8, 2002, www.cbsnews.com/stories/2002/11/07/48hours/main528514.shtml

Chapter 4

Federal Government

Topics in this chapter:

- Threats

- IRS Employee Appeals Conviction of Wire Fraud

- FBI Employee Discloses Sensitive Files to Family and Friends

- FBI Employee Accesses Computer System without Authorization

- Department of Energy Employee Provides Price List to Competition

- Time Fraud in the Patent and Trademark Office

- Time Fraud in the Department of Commerce

- Time Fraud in the Defense Intelligence Agency

- Time Fraud in Defense Security Services

- **Time Fraud Using False Jury Duty Claims**

- **Government Credit Card Fraud in the State Department**

- **Government Credit Card Fraud in the U.S. Attorney's Office**

- **Department of Agriculture Employee Commits Massive Visa Fraud**

- **State Department Employee Commits Massive Visa Fraud**

- **United States Border Patrol and Customs Agents Smuggle Drugs**

- **NLM Programmer Creates Backdoor in Medical Computer System**

- **CIA and FBI Traitors**

- **Disgruntled Coast Guard Employee Deletes Database Records**

"America will never be destroyed from the outside. If we falter and lose our freedoms, it will be because we destroyed ourselves."
— Abraham Lincoln

"Audit trails performed by internal IRS auditors establish that Czubinski frequently made unauthorized accesses on IDRS in 1992"

— Court records describing the Appeal of Richard Czubinski on the grounds that his browsing was "intangible" and therefore did not deprive the IRS of any property

"Because she was familiar with these systems and she knew the user name and password information for several supervisors, she was able to submit payroll information without obtaining approval, which allowed her to conceal her excess overtime."

— Description of Untied States v. Patsy Ann Rock in the 2003 Department of Justice Report on the Activities and Operations of the Pubic Integrity Section

Introduction

Insiders within the ranks of the federal government have been around since the notion of government first existed. Many of the "founding fathers" of the United States had a rich background in espionage and practiced it extensively during the Revolutionary War.

In those days, insiders were generally depicted as patriots that risked their lives to infiltrate enemy camps. Today it is the face of traitors such as Aldrich Ames and Robert Hanssen, often motivated by greed, that come to mind instead.

In this chapter, we hope to draw your attention to the fact that insiders within the federal government do not *just* commit espionage. They steal taxpayers' dollars through time and attendance fraud, illegally charge personal items to government charge cards, expose sensitive information about citizens and undercover investigations, sell controlled privileges such as visas, plant backdoors in computer systems, and even use government vehicles to smuggle illegal drugs into the country.

To help you work to counter these activities, we identify many problems that result in possible threats to the federal government and discuss case examples of past insider activity within the federal government.

If you are an employee of the federal government, then we hope that reading this chapter will help you to better prevent and/or detect when these events occur in your office. We hope that we raise your awareness of the possibility of each threat and hope that you are able to take some of the corrective countermeasures that we suggest and put them into practice.

For those that work in commercial environments, particularly those that are government contractors, then this chapter also applies to you. Fraudulent awarding of contracts by employees that accept bribes, instead of conducting a fair selection process, impact your chances of surviving as a company. Time and attendance fraud is still a rampant problem, and as long as there are corporate credit cards with little monitoring, employees will misuse them. When we talk about sensitive FBI investigative information that is stolen or national intelligence that is sold by spies, consider the price tag of your own computer databases. Who would want to buy them, and who is in a position of selling them? If you are in the engineering business, you need to be concerned with your designs and drawings; if you are a consultant, imagine how upset your clients would be if their sensitive information were exposed because of someone in your company.

Threats

Like in state and local governments, threats are generally categorized by a loss of safety and/or a loss of property. Property can be in the form of money (for example, time and attendance fraud), physical property (such as the theft of computers), information (such as in cases of espionage, or even public trust).

It is necessary to first understand the importance of public trust to realize the extent to which fraud can affect it. If citizens cannot trust that police will protect them, where can they turn? If FBI informants believe that their name is going to be leaked to the public, will they continue to cooperate? Will our intelligence officers be able to continue acquiring information overseas if the Central Intelligence Agency (CIA) is infested with rogue insiders that sell their names for money? Beyond doubt, the answer to each of these questions is no.

Governments rely on public trust and integrity to maintain a sense of stability. In a country where media coverage is virtually unregulated, and public speech is thankfully an exercised freedom, this can be difficult. Organizations must constantly search for, investigate, and audit its employees. As you can see from this statement on the FBI Web site, the FBI identifies investigation of espionage and public corruption as one of their top priorities, second only to terrorism:

Public corruption is one of the FBI's top investigative priorities—
behind only terrorism, espionage, and cyber crimes. Why? Because
our democracy and national security depend on a healthy, efficient,
and ethical government. [1]

When you consider that in the case of sabotage, insiders are often terrorists, then
you see that the topics in this chapter are the top three focus areas of the FBI.

Loss of Safety

The primary threat of concern to the federal government is loss of safety. Security of
the government at this level is imperative to stability as a nation. In the past, concerns over safety stemmed from foreign governments, but in this day and age it
comes from terrorism.

The effects of successful infiltration as an insider within the federal government
by foreign or domestic terrorists would be devastating. Threats of this kind are
unfortunately limited only by the maliciousness and access that an attacker has.

Just imagine the outcome if a terrorist infiltrated the White House or Capitol
building staff, or if one was placed as an air traffic controller at a busy airport like
Chicago O'Hare.

To help keep this nation safe, never underestimate the importance of pre-
employment background checks. Even if the position that you are hiring for does
not directly lead to sensitive positions such as these, an attacker could use your organization as a stepping stone to begin a "credible" slate of references and history.

Loss of Property

The federal government has to spend a great deal of effort in the prevention, deterrence, detection, and ultimately the remediation, of traitors that commit espionage.
Figure 4.1 contains an image of a poster distributed by the government that lists the
names and faces of several convicted federal employees that have committed treason
against the United States (the poster is available for download at www.ncix.gov/
publications/posters_calendars/posters/poster_oneevil.php). At the bottom it has a
quote from George Washington that reads: "There is one evil I dread, and that is, their
spies. I could wish, therefore, the most attentive watch be kept...."

We will talk about two of these cases, but we also want to make the point that
theft within the federal government takes on many faces beyond espionage. It is the
secretary that fraudulently adds 10 hours of overtime to her paycheck every week; it
is the contracting officer that accepts bribes in exchange for a fixed award, impacting
the other companies attempting to conduct business in a fair and ethical manner; it

is the FBI agent that blows an investigation by leaking information, possibly placing sources and agents in danger; it is the administrator that processes government credit card applications who employees trust with their sensitive information such as social security numbers, bank accounts, and mother's maiden names; and it is the computer programmer that creates backdoors or purposefully destroys irreplaceable databases.

At the risk of sounding paranoid, threats are everywhere within these organizations and we have not even talked about the long-term impact such as loss of national and global trust.

Figure 4.1 U. S. Office of the National Counterintelligence Executive "One Evil" Poster with Images of Several Convicted Spies

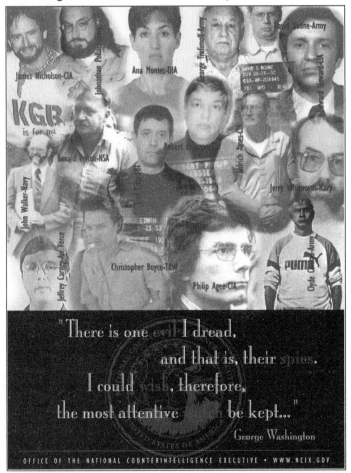

Time and Attendance Fraud

One rampant problem within the federal government is time and attendance fraud. In these situations, employees purposefully misrepresent the number of hours they work in an effort to increase the amount of money they are paid in a given period.

There is no doubt that fraud of this nature also occurs widely within private industry, but it is a particularly egregious act within the federal government, because taxpayers foot the bill.

As you will read in the following case studies, this fraud is often committed by the very people that are trusted to enter the time for others. We speculate that this is because they are generally in a position where they are responsible for forwarding timecards directly from a supervisor to the accounting office. This means that they have little or no oversight over their own timecard and what gets entered into it.

In addition, to make transactions fast and easy each week, many of these personnel had access to the user names and passwords of their supervisors. They easily approved their own overtime using this access without any fear of being detected. Most of the time the quantities of fraudulent time charged were small, and distributed across several months. This made detection significantly more difficult.

Government Credit Card Fraud

Far too often, greed gets the best of people when they have access to what they perceive to be the "easy money" of credit cards. Cases of this type of fraud can be especially dangerous in the bureaucracy of large government agencies in which accountability sometimes gets overlooked. The following are a small subset of the enormously large number of credit card fraud cases we found in our research.

Case Study: IRS Employee Appeals Conviction of Wire Fraud

In our first case study we write about a former Internal Revenue Service (IRS) employee that despite an initial guilty verdict was judged to be innocent of any crime upon appeal. This case makes the point that simply acquiring sensitive information in a *prohibited* manner does not automatically make it illegal.

Topic

A former IRS employee appeals his jury conviction of wire and computer fraud.

Source

UNITED STATES OF AMERICA
V.
Richard W. Czubinski
Case Number: 1:95-cr-10165-NMG

Details

Richard Czubinski was employed by the IRS as a local Contact Representative in the Boston office. His official duties included answering questions by taxpayers and performing searches in highly sensitive IRS databases such as the Integrated Data Retrieval System (IDRS).

With his access he could retrieve records from almost every account in the Martinsburg, West Virginia, "master record" site.

Despite this blanket access, IRS policies strictly enforced that records were only to be accessed on a "need-to-know" basis. Specifically, according to court documents, "Employees must make every effort to assure security and prevent unauthorized disclosure of protected information in the use of government-owned or leased computers. In addition, employees may not use any Service computer system for other than official purposes." Czubinski also received specific rules that addressed IDRS access, such as "Access only those accounts required to accomplish your official duties."

However, according to court records and evidence based on internal IRS auditors, he ignored these rules. In fact, audit trails ascertain that Czubinski carried out frequent unofficial searches of this database in 1992. As an example, he conducted searches related to:

- Two individuals with ties to the David Duke Presidential campaign

- An assistant district attorney (and his wife) that was prosecuting his father on a felony offense

- Boston City Counselor Jim Kelly's Campaign Committee (note that Kelly had previously defeated Czubinski when he ran for the Counselor seat of District 2)

- One of his brother's instructors

- A Boston Housing Authority police officer and his spouse (he was involved in an organization with one of Czubinski's brothers)

- A women he had dated; and

- Other social acquaintances.

In 1995 he was indicted under allegations of wire fraud because the database lines of communications crossed state boundaries. Although the government did not accuse Czubinski of disclosing the confidential information he had accessed during these searches, it contended that he had intended to use the information in disreputable ways. The indictment states that he:

> … defrauded the IRS of confidential property and defrauded the IRS and the public of his honest services by using his valid password to acquire confidential taxpayer information as part of a scheme to:

- build "dossiers" on associates in the KKK;

- seek information regarding an assistant district attorney who was then prosecuting Czubinski's father on an unrelated criminal charge; and

- perform opposition research by inspecting the records of a political opponent in the race for a Boston City Councilor seat.

In the meantime, Czubinski filed a motion to dismiss the indictment arguing that while unauthorized, the "browsing" did not deprive the IRS of any property, and hence, was not a crime. In addition, Czubinski claimed that the section 1346 (intangible right to honest service amendment to the mail and wire fraud statutes) was unconstitutionally vague in the context of his case.

To further complicate matters, according to one account, a newspaper had "just uncovered his righteous role" which was what they claim sparked the entire investigation.[2] Following this, Czubinski filed motions to prevent references to some of his white supremacist activities, including his membership in a KKK chapter, from trial. This was denied; however, special instructions regarding the relevance of these affiliations were discussed during jury instructions.

On December 15, 1995, the jury returned a guilty verdict on all counts except for wire fraud count 3. Following this verdict, Czubinski filed an appeal.

As the ruling on the appeal states, he was never found to actually take any action to use this information and the mere "searching" alone was not found to cause damage:

... The fatal flaw in the government's case is that it has not shown beyond a reasonable doubt that Czubinski intended to carry out a scheme to deprive the IRS of its property interest in confidential information...

... The government's only evidence demonstrating any intent to use the confidential information for nefarious ends was the trial testimony of William A. Murray, an acquaintance of Czubinski who briefly participated in Czubinski's local Invisible Knights of the Ku Klux Klan ("KKK") chapter and worked with him on the David Duke campaign. Murray testified that Czubinski had once stated at a social gathering in "early 1992" that "he intended to use some of that information to build dossiers on people" involved in "the white supremacist movement." Trial Transcript, Vol. 2 at 170, 188. There is, however, no evidence that Czubinski created dossiers, took steps toward making dossiers (such as by printing out or recording the information he browsed), or shared any of the information he accessed in the years following the single comment to Murray. No other witness testified to having any knowledge of Czubinski's alleged intent to create "dossiers" on KKK members.

This appeal was accepted and Czubinski was found to be innocent

Analysis

Although Czubinski was not found to be guilty of any crime in the end, this is an interesting case. The court found that his "browsing" of unauthorized information alone was itself not a crime. Because the defense could not demonstrate that what he had done deprived the IRS of property, he could not be charged. It marks the importance of recording transactions such as e-mail, transfers to removable media, and printing. We are in no way saying that Czubinski did these things, but if he had, and the transactions were recorded then the outcome of the case may have been different.

Czubinski's unauthorized queries were detected by auditors, but the lesson learned in this case is that beyond evidence of collection, intent and proof of the actual crime (i.e., depriving the IRS of its property) should be demonstrated.

Case Study: FBI Employee Discloses Sensitive Files to Family and Friends

Unlike the previous example, the subject in this case was found to be guilty. While you may observe striking similarities between the two studies, as you read further try to identify the key differences that changed the verdict.

Topic

FBI employee accesses FBI computer systems outside his "need-to-know" access rights and shares sensitive information with family and friends.

Source

UNITED STATES OF AMERICA
V.
Jeffrey D. Fudge
Case Number: 3:03-cr-380-R

Details

Jeffrey D. Fudge, 33, was an FBI investigative analyst who had worked for the bureau since 1988. He was responsible for serving subpoenas, analyzing phone records, assisting in criminal and administrative investigations, and conducting searches in highly restricted FBI databases. Given the sensitivity of the records in these databases, access to entries was limited to "need-to-know." Searches were allowed only within the bounds of official business. Because of the duties of his job, Jeffrey Fudge was granted access. In particular, through the course of his normal operations, he had access to the Automated Case Support system (ACS), the National Crime Information Center (NCIC), the Texas Crime Information Center (TCIC), the Texas Law Enforcement Telecommunications System (TLETS), and the FBI Network (FBINET) databases.

According to court records, around October 7, 1997, Fudge began misusing this position of trust and accessed FBI files and computer programs to search cases that were not part of his official business. This continued through the years and ended on or about April 25, 2003. During this time, Fudge conducted these unofficial searches to determine if the people he inquired about were being investigated. These people were often friends and prominent Dallas, Texas, citizens.

One case, however, was a little different: Fudge was passing the information he acquired on to his family. On May 18, 2004, Fudge pled guilty to illegally using the databases to search for information about his own brother who was currently being investigated by the FBI for HUD fraud.

In his plea, he confessed to conducting these searches on November 16, 1999, and on several occasions between October 1997 and April 2003. In one of these instances his brother called him (on April 14, 2003) and stated that he was being followed by vehicles. He asked Fudge to use his access to the FBI databases to determine if the cars were registered to law enforcement.

Fudge then conducted searches using the TLETS and ACS systems and, ironically, determined that the cars were not registered to law enforcement and told his brother that he was not under investigation. Note that the ACS, NCIC, and FBINET communications travel across interstate communication lines.

On November 5, 2003, a federal grand jury returned a ten-count indictment against Fudge and he was subsequently arrested and fired at the FBI headquarters. Following this, Steven P. Beauchamp, Special Agent in Charge of the Department of Justice – Office of the Inspector General, Dallas Field Office, stated:

> This indictment serves as a reminder that the Department will not tolerate the misuse and unauthorized disclosure of sensitive law enforcement information. In today's world, and with advancing technology, there is too much at stake. All of law enforcement must be vigilant and protect against those who would compromise our most important asset – our information.

During trial, Fudge entered a guilty plea agreement and was placed on probation for two years and ordered to pay restitution.

Analysis

This case is similar to the IRS case, except that Fudge disclosed the information he had unofficially obtained to others. This is an important distinction, because Fudge was found guilty whereas Czubinski was not. Like the previous case, this demonstrates the need to frequently audit searches and access to sensitive databases. The integrity and confidentiality of these must be protected at all costs. Keep in mind that the burden may be on you to prove that the insider either used, or intended to use, the information for something beyond mere curiosity.

Case Study: FBI Employee Accesses Computer System without Authorization

One could argue that in the last case Fudge was attempting to hinder an investigation when he conducted the searches for his brother. Luckily it appears that despite his attempt, Fudge was never able to compromise the case. In this next study, an insider did manage to obtain sensitive files, and she did disclose the acquired information to those being investigated.

Topic

An FBI employee searches for, acquires, and then distributes sensitive investigation information to subjects of drug investigations.

Source

UNITED STATES OF AMERICA
V.
Narissa Smalls
Case Number: 1:03-cr-00496-GK-1

Details

Narissa Smalls was a Legal Technician for the FBI. She worked in the Freedom of Information and Privacy Act Unit located at FBI headquarters in Washington, DC.

Her position was to search the FBI ACS computer system to collect information needed in administrative matters and in responses to Freedom of Information Act (FOIA) requests made by the public.

However, she also used her access to make unofficial searches into cases she had no need to know. In particular, she searched for information about people who were the subject of ongoing drug investigations. In at least one instance she printed the information and brought it to her home. She then shared this information with those people that were under investigation.

Smalls was sentenced to 12 months and one day in prison, followed by a two-year supervised release.

Analysis

Similar to the last case, this example describes someone that used their access to provide restricted information to others. It is interesting to point out that neither of these last two cases involved financial motivation. Instead actions of the insider were done for personal reasons or for friend/family motivations. In all cases the best advice to prevent this activity is to conduct thorough background checks, watch for the warning signs, and continually monitor and audit access.

Case Study: Department of Energy Employee Provides Price List to Competition

This next case may be discouraging to those in companies that compete for government contracts. It demonstrates that unfortunately the best company does not always "win" competitions due to the greed of others.

Topic

Employee at the United States Department of Energy accepts bribes and kickbacks in exchange for awarding contracts.

Source

UNITED STATES OF AMERICA
V.
James W. Brown

Details

James W. Brown was an employee of the United States Department of Energy (DOE). He worked as a General Supply Specialist. One of his responsibilities was to select and manage contracts related to carpet cleaning. He had the authority to make awards for bids that were under $25,000 without any supervision.

As a representative of the federal government, it was his responsibility to ensure that the lowest rate was always chosen. In addition, he was required to establish fair and honest selection criteria. Unfortunately for both the taxpayers of the United States and the vendors that participated in the bidding process, this was not the case.

He was found to have accepted bribes between $5,000 and $10,000 on multiple occasions; he had instead based his selection on enticements and kickbacks. In at least one instance, Brown even provided the fixed winner a copy of a competitor's price list. This enabled them to unfairly see their competitor's sensitive proprietary information and to place the lowest bid.

On January 13, 2003, Brown pled guilty to this charge, and on June 5, 2003, he was sentenced to one year of incarceration (six months in jail and six months home monitoring) and a fine.

Analysis

Bribery is an especially difficult threat to prevent and detect because it leaves such a small audit trail. In this case, Brown was authorized to make awards without any supervision whatsoever—an effort to reduce bureaucracy and lower the costs to taxpayers.

In addition, he did select the bids with the lowest price, so from the outside it appeared as if he were doing his job properly. One of the only telltale signs in this case is that he provided the price list to the competitor. Depending on how he did this it may not have even been detectable. In theory he could have had the list visible on his desk when the contractor came to visit, or he may have secretly taken a copy with him to visit with the contractor.

Our best recommendation for situations such as this is to implement an auditable computerized solicitation system. One example of such a system is utilized by the Department of Defense (DoD) small business program, and can be found at: www.dodsbir.net/submission/SignIn.asp.

In this system, all proposals and bids from qualified companies are solicited and must be received electronically by a specific closing date. Prior to that date, program managers making selections are not able to access the bids. After the date closes and all proposals/bids have been received, then they are evaluated. In the case of the DoD small business program they are evaluated by a committee, but in the case of smaller purchases such as carpet cleaning, the prices could be evaluated by an individual.

Because the individual cannot access any bid until all have been received at the solicitation's closing, an unscrupulous employee cannot accept bribes in exchange for disclosure of this information. In addition, even if the insider were to add favor to a particular company, the entire transaction would be auditable. The widespread advertising of this auditing could also help in deterring would-be insiders.

Case Study: Time Fraud in the Patent and Trademark Office

We will now shift gears to study a series of cases that involve time fraud. In each circumstance federal government employees misused their access to fraudulently profit from unearned income. We will start first with one example from the Patent and Trademark Office.

Topic

Patent and Trademark Office employee responsible for time and attendance fraudulently claims about $5,930 in hours that were not worked

Source

UNITED STATES OF AMERICA
V.
Kimberlee L. Clark
Case Number: 1:2002mj01070

Details

Kimberlee Clark was a personal assistant at the United States Patent and Trademark Office in Crystal City, Virginia. Part of her responsibility was to be the timekeeper for her group. In this position, she collected timesheet information from the employees and sent them on to the National Finance Center in New Orleans, Louisiana, for processing. She was also responsible for processing her own timesheet information.

In 14 different pay periods from 1999 to 2000, Clark claimed more hours than what was confirmed. In total, she fraudulently acquired approximately $5,930 in additional salary through these false claims. She pled guilty to this theft of government money and was sentenced to 20 days of incarceration during one year of supervised probation, four years of unsupervised probation, and restitution for the taxpayer money that she stole.

Analysis

We have had people ask us many times how time and attendance fraud can be prevented. In most cases it is our opinion that the supervisor should be responsible for verifying the hours and overtime worked by employees. That is part of their job to know who works, and when. However, in this case study and the following case examples on time and attendance fraud, there was a flaw in this reviewing system. The supervisor never had access to the claims made by the time and attendance clerks. While they may have approved one set of hours on paper, a completely different set was sent to the payroll department. Granted, continual checking and verification is what sometimes gives the government a bad name, and is why actions appear to take so long to process, but some additional verification can help detect and prevent this form of fraud. In the end, it is likely that the amount of unearned wages paid out illegally would be better spent on hiring additional auditing personnel.

Beyond distribution of statements for hours submitted back to supervisors, there are some technical means for verification that, while not foolproof, can be incorporated into an auditing system as well. There are several computerized accounting systems in which users must sign in at the start of work and sign out when they are finished. Time accounting systems like this are required for many government contractors. However, we should note that systems such as these can be offensive to employees and display a lack of trust in their dedication. When expectations are lowered for performance, more often than not, people lower their performance to meet the expectations.

More-silent accounting methods can also be implemented, such as automated verification based on login/logout or badge enter/exit logs. These will in no way be foolproof, but they can be helpful in identifying a habitual offender that often claims three hours of overtime on a Friday when the badge system placed them outside of the building for the weekend shortly after lunch. To help illustrate how rampant a problem this is, several similar examples of fraudulent claims follow. However, this is just a sampling of hundreds of cases that we identified on the subject.

Case Study: Time Fraud in the Department of Commerce

The amount of fraudulent salary paid in this case is three times that of the previous example. This is probably because it went undetected for about six years.

Topic

Department of Commerce employee responsible for time and attendance fraudulently claims about $18,564.91 in hours that were not worked.

Source

UNITED STATES OF AMERICA
V.
Brenda Dobbs
Case Number: 1:03-cr-00219-JDB-1

Details

Brenda Dobbs was a secretary and program support assistant for the National Oceanic and Atmospheric Administration's (NOAA) Office of General Counsel for Natural Resources, part of the Department of Commerce. Like Clark, Dobbs was the time and attendance clerk for her office.

In this position, Dobbs made false reports on her time and attendance reports. Her fraud continued from 1996 to 2001. The result was that she obtained $18,564.91 in additional salary. This salary was paid by taxpayers for work that she did not perform.

In addition, using an NOAA account number, Dobbs purchased Sprint and Verizon cellular phones services. She often used these phones for personal calls and accumulated $3,152 in unofficial charges. These charges were submitted to the government for payment.

After Dobbs was caught, she pleaded guilty to a charge of government property theft. On September 4, 2003, she was sentenced to three years of probation and restitution of the fraudulent charges she had accumulated.

Analysis

As described in the previous case, auditing, either manually by a supervisor or automatically using software, can prevent this activity from continuing. Similarly, when personal-type items such as cellular phones are provided to employees, they need to be monitored for potential misuse.

In the case of the government, regulations for monitoring are generally easily accepted because of the fact that taxpayers are the ones paying for the costs. It is fair, then, to assume that proper accountability should be made to assure taxpayers that their funds are not being misused. However, in the case of companies, the same concessions should be made for stockholders or investors. One could argue that they should be assured the same level of accountability for their investments.

Case Study: Time Fraud in the Defense Intelligence Agency

There are many more cases, but here are two interesting examples involving time fraud within the Defense Intelligence Agency (DIA). The subjects in both of these cases were also trusted time keepers.

Topic

DIA employees responsible for time and attendance fraudulently claim more than $10,000 each in hours that were not worked.

Source

UNITED STATES OF AMERICA
V.   and
Charelle Ferguson
Case Number: 1:03-mj-00247-AK-1

UNITED STATES OF AMERICA
V.
Angelique Speight
Case Number: 1:03-mj-00344-DAR

Details

Charelle Ferguson was a time and attendance keeper for the DIA. While in this position, she misused her access to the system and fraudulent submitted 337.3 hours of extra overtime. As a result, she was paid $10,169.31 in additional salary for work she did not perform.

Ferguson pled guilty to a one-count theft of government property charge and was sentenced to three years of probation, 10 hours of community service, and restitution for the money she had stolen.

Likewise, Angelique Speight was also a timekeeper for the DIA. While in her position she falsely claimed 336.27 hours of extra overtime, which resulted in $10,444.56 in fraudulent payment. She also pled guilty and was sentenced to two years of probation, 10 hours of community service, and restitution for the government funds she illegally obtained.

Analysis

Both of these cases in the DIA similarly demonstrate the need for auditing. Each individual was able to submit more than 300 hours of extra overtime prior to being detected.

Case Study: Time Fraud in Defense Security Services

At this point you may be amazed, like we were, at the prevalence of time fraud. Most of these cases were detected by internal reviews specifically focusing on time keepers. What about regular employees that slip overtime by an inattentive supervisor? What about supervisors themselves?

Also, we are not just picking on federal government employees. Examples of fraudulent claims in overtime do indeed happen regularly in commercial venues. The largest difference is that fraudulent employees identified in companies are often silently fired, but when it comes to the government they get charged in federal court systems for all to see.

To further complicate the problem, in this next case the trusted insider was given the user names and passwords of supervisors so that she could access the time submission and approval system. Here approval processes implemented to detect fraud were short-circuited and bypassed all-together.

Topic

Defense Security Services employee responsible for time and attendance fraudulently claims about $9,387 in hours that were not worked.

Source

UNITED STATES OF AMERICA
V.
Patsy Ann Rock
Case Number: 1:2002mj01214

Details

Patsy Ann Rock was an administrative secretary for Defense Security Services. Like the others in this chapter, she was responsible for entering time and attendance for employees within her organization. She was given full access to the computer system used to submit time and attendance information, including the user names and passwords of several supervisors. With this access, she could submit information without any approval.

Rock chose to use her access in a fraudulent manner as she claimed 346 hours of overtime that she did not work. This resulted in her being paid $9,387 in additional salary. She pled guilty to theft of government money and was sentenced on

February 11, 2003, to one year of probation and restitution of the funds she illegally acquired.

Analysis

Like the others, Rock managed to claim more than 300 hours of fraudulent overtime without being detected. In her case, she acquired passwords and user names that she never should have had access to. While it is not the fault of her supervisor that she misused her access and illegally stole funds from the United States government, it is the job of every supervisor and employee to protect these funds from insiders. Employees should be taught repeatedly not to give anyone their passwords and not to <u>ever</u> allow others to use their accounts.

Case Study: Time Fraud Using False Jury Duty Claims

Time fraud can take other and more creative shapes as well. In this case, an officer claimed court leave for eleven different days. This would normally not be a problem, but the officer was never actually present in court.

Topic

United States Government Printing Office (GPO) employee falsely claims jury duty responsibilities.

Source

UNITED STATES OF AMERICA
V.
Bobbie J. Sellers
Case Number: 1:03-mj-00002-DAR-1

Details

Bobbie Sellers worked as a freight rate specialist for the United States Government Printing Office (GPO). While working in this position, she was summoned to serve as a juror. She obliged and from July 16, 2001, through September 5, 2001, she served on a grand jury in the District of Columbia. During this time she was paid using court leave that had been granted.

However, on September 4, 2001, she presented a letter to her supervisor that was written on United States Attorney's Office stationary. The letter indicated that Sellers was required to serve two additional grand jury recall dates in September. Those dates came and Sellers took paid "court leave" for them. However, the letter she had given to her supervisor was fraudulent and she did not serve as a juror those days.

She continued to present these fraudulent "jury duty" letters and between October 21, 2001, and March 21, 2002, she had presented seven more. Based on these letters, she fraudulently took paid "court leave" for eleven additional days. Sellers claimed 127 hours for court leave that she never served and was paid $2,399.03 in fraudulent wages.

A plea agreement was reached and Sellers was sentenced to 16 months probation and $800 in restitution.

Analysis

Jury duty does not occur often, and when it does it is fairly easy to verify. Rather than using letters provided by the employee as your proof, request proof directly from the courthouse. Most are used to answering inquiries from curious employers verifying the participation of the employee.

Case Study: Government Credit Card Fraud in the State Department

This next subject is a topic that costs everyone money in the long-run through increased interest rates and insurance costs. We are going to talk about credit card fraud within the government.

Topic

Two Department of State (DOS) employees and a private citizen conspire to transfer money from government employee credit cards to Western Union offices where they can collect it for their own use.

Source

UNITED STATES OF AMERICA
V.
Crystal Green, Jameil Lloyd, and Jacemyein Morales
Case Number: 1:02-cr-00329-RMU-1 and CR 01-0529M-01

Details

Crystal Green was a contract employee with the DOS. Her job was to process paperwork for DOS employees who needed to acquire credit cards for official business such as travel and small office purchases.

Besides access to the sensitive credit card numbers on this paperwork, Green had access to private identification information for these DOS employees. She and her co-conspirators, Jameil Lloyd and Jacemyein Morales, used this access to commit fraud.

Crystal Green would obtain the credit card and identification information from the paperwork and provide it to Jameil Lloyd who was also a DOS employee. Lloyd would then call or access the Western Union Web site and make requests for money transfers from the cards. She would set payment to be for herself and others.

Jacemyein Morales was a private citizen associate of Green's and was generally responsible for picking up the money from the Western Union locations.

In one month alone, more than $4,600 was stolen from employee credit cards by these three individuals. They had attempted to steal more than $7,600.

Green pled guilty to wire fraud and was sentenced to six months imprisonment and six months home confinement. Lloyd pled guilty to conspiracy and agreed to cooperate in the investigation. She was sentenced to five years of probation, 100 hours of community service, and restitution of $4,654.16. Morales also agreed to cooperate with the investigation and was sentenced to three years of probation and $1,895 in restitution.

Analysis

Identify theft and credit card fraud is extremely difficult to prevent. Anyone who has had a legitimate charge denied because it looked suspicious can testify to how angry and embarrassed that made them.

I can remember one instance in which I was entertaining a candidate that I wanted to hire badly. Early that day I had used my corporate credit card to purchase some unusual computer equipment over the Internet. Because of this, when I tried to charge the dinner at the expensive out-of-town restaurant, my card was denied. As a start-up, I was attempting to convey a sense of trust that my company had stability and plenty of funds to cover the employee. Instead, having my credit card denied made the company look like it was hardly in business. I was terribly upset and let the banking company know that I would no longer do business with them if any of my charges were ever denied again. Unfortunately, there is always a tradeoff between usability and security, and credit cards are a prime example of this. In looking back, the card company was just trying to detect and prevent fraud just as they should. It is difficult to determine what is and is not an allowed charge. For in-person charges, one solution may be to request identification such as a driver's license, but this does not help when charges are made over the telephone or across the Internet. This is an area that requires much more research to mature technologies to detect misuse and identity theft.

Case Study: Government Credit Card Fraud in the U.S. Attorney's Office

This next study is an example of just how much financial damage one employee can cause with a credit card. Beyond just fraudulent charges, this employee went as far as *selling* the items that she bought with the government credit card and keeping the profit.

Topic

United States Attorney's Office for the Central District of California (located in Los Angeles) employee fraudulently uses a government credit card to pay for personal travel expenses and merchandise, which she eventually sold, even using the office's Federal Express account to ship it to customers.

Source

UNITED STATES OF AMERICA
V.
Dorothy Menyweather
Case Number: 00-CR-1253-ALL

Details

Dorothy Menyweather was an employee within the United States Attorney's Office for the Central District of California, located in Los Angeles. In this position, she had been granted access to office credit cards for official purchases. Instead, she used this access for more than $100,000 in personal travel and the purchase of non-official clothing, computers, and equipment. Her indictment claims:

> As alleged in the indictment, Menyweather used the credit cards to pay for travel expenses and personal bills for herself, and other friends and relatives. She also bought computers and related equipment, clothing, stereos, electronic games and gift certificates redeemable for cash and merchandise.

> As alleged in the indictment, Menyweather sold some of the com-
> puters and related equipment that she purchased with the govern-
> ment issued card for her benefit. She used the office's Federal
> Express account to ship the goods for delivery to her customers. [3]

In the end, Menyweather admitted to stealing more than $430,000 from the
United States Attorney General's Office and pled guilty to one count of honest services mail fraud. She was sentenced on September 22, 2003, to serve forty days of
incarceration (on weekends), restitution, 3000 hours of community service, and
reporting requirements.

Analysis

I find this case incredible. Menyweather never should have been able to charge such
large amounts of money without some supervision or auditing. I do not know what
the credit limit was for the card, but I can remember that the limit on my government card when I first joined the CIA was high. For someone just out of college
that has never been responsible for this amount of money, initial credit limits should
be reduced. Although regulations clearly state that purchases are for official business
only, we recommend that lower credit limits be issued and that they are raised only
as needed.

In addition, when Menyweather sold the items she had purchased fraudulently
with her government card, she used the Federal Express account number of the
office to ship them. Account numbers such as these are rarely audited, and they are
frequently misused. Although individual costs tied to these accounts may be small, by
tracking them, you may identify employees that are willing to cross over the line and
steal from an organization. If an employee is willing to misuse this account for personal purposes, they may be willing to misuse their access in other ways as well.
Further investigation of these charges can lead to larger discoveries of significant
theft and corruption.

Case Study: Department of Agriculture Employee Commits Massive Visa Fraud

As the next two case studies demonstrate, those with access to country admission
responsibility are also susceptible to fraud. Initially you may only think that
employees of embassies would be subject to this temptation, but as this next case
illustrates, it can happen in the most unlikely of places.

Topic

United States Department of Agriculture (USDA) employee and his wife assist hundreds of Chinese nationals to obtain fraudulently acquired visas to enter the United States.

Source

UNITED STATES OF AMERICA
V.
Hsin Hui Hsu
Case Number: 1:03–cr–00312–CKK–1

Details

Hsin Hui Hsu was an employee of the USDA. Part of his job was to identify and invite Chinese nationals that had experience in agriculture to come to the United States. The purpose of these trips was for Chinese nationals and USDA officials to meet, exchange information, and establish agreements.

However, in 1999, Hsu decided to leverage his insider position to commit fraud. He conspired with visa brokers to assist them in illegally granting access to Chinese nationals who otherwise could not obtain legitimate visas. The brokers were located in both California and China and were responsible for identifying people that were willing to pay $10,000 to enter the United States.

They would then provide names and fake biographical information to Hsu. With this information, Hsu would then illegally use USDA letterhead to write letters of support for these individuals. These official-looking letters would be taken to United States consulates in China so that the traveler could obtain a visa. Although these individuals had no background in agriculture, Hsu would write in the letters that they did, and that they were specialists that were invited to attend meetings in the United States. Hsu knew these meetings would never take place and that this was simply a ploy to grant them admittance into the country.

In addition, Hsu also created and signed letters representing his wife, Jing Ling Wu Hsu, and her company, Strathmore Enterprises, that "confirmed" the USDA invitations. The money that Hsu was paid by the brokers was paid into a Strathmore bank account.

Before being caught, Hsu and Wu had been paid approximately $82,000 by the brokers. It is estimated that hundreds of Chinese nationals were able to enter the United States illegally because of this.

Hsin Hui Hsu was sentenced on October 22, 2003 to two years of incarceration, supervised release for three years, and restitution of $77,400.

Analysis

Hsu misused his trusted access within the USDA. He utilized his knowledge of how official request letters could be used to invite foreign nationals into the country, and he fraudulently used official USDA letterhead. Employees with this level of access should be susceptible to continual security screening.

In addition, official letterhead should be tightly controlled, and a ledger could be used to log official requests such as the letters he issued. The problem with this case is that Hsu was doing the same tasks as his official position. Therefore prevention is difficult. Instead, the countermeasures are aimed at deterring him from committing malicious actions: The greater his perception of auditing and detection, the lower the chances that he will accept the bribes.

Case Study: State Department Employee Commits Massive Visa Fraud

This next study is a more typical example of some of the visa-bribe cases we found in our research. Here the insider was an employee at the United States embassy in Prague, Czech Republic.

Topic

A State Department employee misuses his access to illegally grant visa status to applicants in exchange for bribes.

Source

UNITED STATES OF AMERICA
V.
Alexander Meerovich
Case Number: 1:03–cr–00023–RMU–1

Details

Alexander Meerovich was a consular officer for the United States State Department. During part of his employment, he served as the Deputy Consul General at the United States Embassy in Prague, Czech Republic. He was responsible for reviewing cases for people requesting visas for travel to the United States. As part of this, he interviewed candidates and processed their applications. He did this job from August 1999 to July 2002.

In January 2000, he decided to use his insider access in a malicious manner. Visa brokers in Prague offered to pay Meerovich money if he would illegally grant access to their clients. He agreed and between April 2000 and May 2002 he illegally granted false visa status to at least 85 individuals. It is estimated that he made at least $50,000 for this illegal activity.

He was caught and on June 24, 2003, was sentenced to 24 months in prison and a fine of $5,000.

Analysis

Supervisors or co-workers should periodically review cases of others when decisions as important as visa travel are at stake. Having a single point of failure can be a breeding ground for this type of fraud. The difficulty is to strike a balance between being able to impose auditing without slowing down the approval process and adding layers of bureaucracy.

Case Study: United States Border Patrol and Customs Agents Smuggle Drugs

Unfortunately when it comes to the money, influence, and corruption associated with illegal drugs, the number of insider cases appears to be endless. We chose this case example because the actions taken by the insiders were so blatant that they were hard to believe. They used an official customs van to load and smuggle marijuana into the United States on several occasion, virtually undetected.

Topic

A Border Patrol agent and a Customs agent use their insider access to smuggle marijuana into the United States from Mexico.

Source

UNITED STATES OF AMERICA
V.
Juan Martinez

Details

Juan Martinez was a United States Border Patrol agent. He resided in Texas and was part of a special task force that was supervised by Customs Supervisory Special Agent Ramon Torrez. Torrez was a corrupt insider who, with assistance from Martinez and others, smuggled drugs from Mexico into the United States.

On several occasions Torrez asked Martinez to telephone the Border Patrol and indicate that they were returning from Mexico with an "official controlled delivery of narcotics." This request meant that the agents normally on duty at the inspection point would leave the area. This allowed Martinez and Torrez to pass through the gate without any inspection by just using the key he was assigned to open the gate.

Because they knew they would not be searched, Martinez and Torrez would load their large government vans entirely up with marijuana. This happened on at least eight occasions. In all it is estimated that they smuggled approximately 13,000 pounds of marijuana into the United States from Mexico using their insider access.

Martinez pleaded guilty to charges and agreed to cooperate with investigations. He was sentenced to five months in prison and five months of home confinement. Torrez was charged in a separate case.

Analysis

This is just one example of several dozen cases in which border and customs officers have illegally smuggled drugs themselves, or accepted bribes for allowing cars filled with drugs to pass inspection. A longtime border agent reflects on this overwhelming number of cases and says, "How do you stop corruption? You don't, as long as there is money and weakness in the system. You have to keep monitoring." [4] This case and this quote demonstrate that even the *watchers* need to be watched.

Case Study: NLM Programmer Creates Backdoor in Medical Computer System

After analyzing this case, we find it is hard to understand the intentions of this insider. The subject in this case created a backdoor in a government computer system that he had access to, but nothing indicates that he used it in a destructive manner.

Topic

Computer programmer implements a backdoor in a National Library of Medicine (NLM) computer and illegally accesses it after he no longer works there.

Source

UNITED STATES OF AMERICA
V.
Montgomery Johns Gray
Case Number: 1:99-cr-00326-TSE

Details

Montgomery Johns Gray III was a computer programmer for the United States NLM. NLM is an organization within the National Institutes of Health (NIH) and is the world's largest research library of health science information. While employed by NLM, Gray created a "backdoor" into the software he programmed.

In early 1999, NLM had identified that an intruder was illegally accessing a computer server that was relied on by thousands of doctors. Although Gray no longer had access to the computer system, it turned out that he was the intruder and was accessing it through the backdoor he had created. A search warrant was executed for Gray's computers. Analysis led to evidence of the intrusions as well as images of child pornography. Shortly afterward, Gray was arrested.

Gray pled guilty to receiving obscene images on the Internet and was sentenced to five months prison, five months halfway house, three years probation, and was ordered to pay $10,000 in restitution.

TERMINOLOGY: BACKDOOR

A backdoor, in software terms, is a program or service designed to clandestinely provide access to a user. Unlike standard "login" programs, backdoors are generally designed to bypass system authorization steps. Backdoors can either be standalone programs, or covert access capabilities built into existing applications. Both are generally associated with hacking and are often hidden and difficult to detect.

Websites such as *www.packstormsecurity.org* contain examples of this type of technology, and more can be found in the book *Hack Proofing Your Network* by Ryan Russell.

Analysis

Additional cases of misused access like this are described in the next chapter, on commercial insiders. Each case further illustrates the importance of proper auditing of administrators and application developers. In particular, great care must be given when they resign or are terminated, especially when they appear to leave in a disgruntled manner.

Case Study: CIA and FBI Traitors

Given our past employment in the Intelligence community, these next two cases are the most upsetting. Here the seriousness of insider threat is <u>magnitudes</u> larger when compared to all of the previous case examples we have written about. The two studies are of people that, while accepting salaries and taking advantage of the enormous opportunities within the federal government, were traitors to our country. People died because of what these men did.

Topic

CIA insider steals secrets and sells them to Russia.

Source

UNITED STATES OF AMERICA
V.
Aldrich Hazen Ames
Case Number: 1:94-cr-00166-CMH-1

Details

Aldrich Hazen Ames (pictured in Figure 4.2) began working for the CIA in 1963. His career at the agency was as a case officer who spoke Russian and specialized in the Russian intelligence services such as the KGB.[5] According to the FBI, his first overseas assignment was in Ankara, Turkey. While overseas Ames targeted Russian intelligence officers for recruitment. Following this assignment, Ames was stationed in New York City, Mexico City, and CIA headquarters in Langley, Virginia.

Figure 4.2 CIA Traitor Aldrich Hazen Ames

All photographs from the Ames case are reprinted from the FBI Web site: www.fbi.gov/libref/historic/famcases/ames/ames.htm.

While in Virginia, Ames was part of the CIA's Soviet/East European Division. According to the FBI, it was in this position on April 16, 1985, that he went to the USSR Embassy in Washington, DC, and volunteered himself as an insider spy. That summer Ames met with a Russian diplomat in Washington several times and passed classified information in exchange for money. He illegally disclosed sensitive information about CIA and FBI human sources (placing their lives in danger) and provided details about technical operations that were targeting the Soviet Union.

That winter Ames met with a KGB officer from Moscow while he was traveling in Bogotá, Colombia, and in July 1986 he was transferred to Rome, Italy. By the time his tour ended, Ames had received $1.88 million from the Russians in exchange for his insider activities. Before he left, his KGB handler instructed him on how to secretly communicate upon his return to Washington, DC. This communication was through a series of "dead drops" and clandestine letters. An example of one such letter can be seen in Figure 4.3.

Figure 4.3 A Letter Written by CIA Traitor Aldrich Ames to His Russian Handler

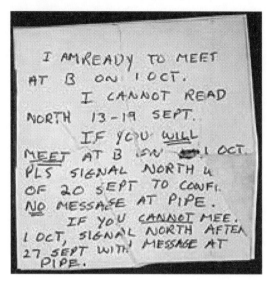

TERMINOLOGY: DEAD DROP

According to the FBI Web site, a dead drop is spy terminology for a "place that is used to hide packages, messages, or payments." These locations are sometimes used to allow people to exchange items without ever having to meet in person.

Although the damage committed in the case studies in the previous chapter on state and local government is serious, the actions taken by Ames reportedly caused people to be murdered. According to the FBI, they and the CIA began to discover that officials they had recruited were being arrested and executed. Given this, the FBI began to investigate and, given unusual circumstances surrounding Ames, such as his unexplained wealth, they began to focus on him as a suspect in May 1993. By October, an investigator had witnessed Ames make a chalk mark on a mailbox as a signal, and in November he was observed meeting with his Russian handler in Bogotá, Colombia. This gave authorities enough evidence to arrest him, and he was brought into custody.

Ames pled guilty and is now serving life in prison.

Analysis

Entire books have been written on the motivation and lessons learned of this case. We have included it to reiterate the seriousness of the damage that insiders can create. Because Ames was working with "handlers," he was instructed on communication tactics that would be difficult for United States counter-intelligence officials to detect. Cases such as this teach us to remain vigilant and to keep our eyes open for even the smallest hints that insider activity could be taking place. The combination of these anomalous events may be the only way to detect sophisticated spying such as this.

Topic

In a similar case, FBI traitor Robert Phillip Hanssen sells secrets to Russia.

Source

UNITED STATES OF AMERICA
V.
Robert Philip Hanssen
Case Number: 1:2001-cr-00188

Details

"Robert Philip Hanssen is a traitor. For all the words that have been written about him, for all the psychological analyses, the speculations about his motivation, and the assessments of his character, this is, at the end of the day, all that really warrants being said about Hanssen. He is a traitor and that singular truth is his legend."[6] This is how the sentencing memorandum issued on May 20, 2002, begins. Hanssen is pictured in Figure 4.4.

Figure 4.4 FBI Traitor Robert Hanssen

All photographs from the Hanssen case are reprinted from the FBI website: www.fbi.gov/pressrel/pressrel01/hanssenphotos.htm.

It all started on January 12, 1976, when Hanssen consented to an employment agreement to work for the FBI. According to court records, as part of this agreement he stated:

> I hereby declare that I intend to be governed by and I will comply with the following provisions:
>
> (1) That I am hereby advised and I understand that Federal law such as Title 18, United States Code, Sections 793, 794, and 798; Order of the President of the United States (Executive Order 11652); and regulations issued by the Attorney General of the United States (28 Code of Federal Regulations, Sections 16.21 through 16.26) prohibit loss, misuse, or unauthorized disclosure or production of national security information, other classified information and other nonclassified information in the files of the FBI;
>
> (2) I understand that unauthorized disclosure of information in the files of the FBI or information I may acquire as an employee of the FBI could result in impairment of national security, place human life in jeopardy, or result in the denial of due process to a person or persons who are subjects of an FBI investigation, or prevent the FBI from effectively discharging its responsibilities. I understand the

need for this secrecy agreement; therefore, as consideration for employment I agree that I will never divulge, publish, or reveal either by word or conduct, or by other means disclose to any unauthorized recipient without official written authorization by the Director of the FBI or his delegate, any information from the investigatory files of the FBI or any information relating to material contained in the files, or disclose any information or produce any material acquired as part of the performance of my official duties or because of my official status... .

(4) That I understand unauthorized disclosure may be a violation of Federal law and prosecuted as a criminal offense and in addition to this agreement may be enforced by means of an injunction or other civil remedy.[7]

However, while working for the FBI, he did not adhere to this agreement. He used his sensitive access to covertly provide information to the Russians in exchange for benefits such as money. One example is the $50,000 package collected by the FBI at the LEWIS dead drop site pictured in Figure 4.5.

Figure 4.5 Photograph of $50,000 That Was Recovered by the FBI at the LEWIS Dead Drop Site Used by Hanssen and His Russian Handlers

Hanssen provided sensitive information such as the following message, given to KGB officer Victor Cherkashin, October 1985:

I must warn of certain risks to my security of which you may not be aware. Your service has recently suffered some setbacks. I warn that Mr. Boris Luzhin… Mr. Sergey Motorin… and Mr. Valeriy Martynov… have been recruited by our 'special services'. [8]

Hanssen's insider activity cost people their lives. After their names were exposed by Hanssen, Motorin and Martynov were executed and Luzhin spent more than five years in prison. In addition, Hanssen compromised numerous technical operations, which resulted in "not only the value of its investments, but the priceless value of lost opportunities to gather intelligence of the most vital importance to the United States." [7]

At sentencing, a judge declared, "For his betrayal of our country, and for the unpardonable consequences of his misconduct, Hanssen deserves to forfeit his right ever to live again within our community and within our society."

Analysis

We are never ones to point fingers after the fact, because the truth remains that the acts Hanssen took were the crimes, not the lack of immediate detection. However, reviewing what happened in a meaningful way can help identify warning signs and be used to indicate problems in the future.

In this case, it does appear as if there were signs that, if followed up on, may have indicated a problem with Hanssen far earlier. For example, convicted spy Earl Pitts says that he identified Hanssen as being suspicious as early as 1997 (three years before the formal FBI investigation began). FBI spokesman John Collingwood said in a statement, "Pitts described as 'unusual' a computer hacking incident involving Hanssen. Pitts did not identify Hanssen as a spy." [9] According to a New York Times report:

> In the prison interview, Mr. Pitts recalled that a female supervisor from the F.B.I.'s counterintelligence operations had come to his security office - he did not recall when - and complained that Mr. Hanssen had broken into her classified computer. He recalled that the supervisor had said an F.B.I. computer expert had traced the hacking effort to Mr. Hanssen's computer. He added that she was "livid" at Mr. Hanssen.
>
> An F.B.I. official said that when Mr. Pitts raised the matter during his 1997 debriefing, the bureau concluded that he was referring to a 1992 incident in which Mr. Hanssen broke into the computer of Ray Mislock, a senior F.B.I. counterintelligence official. The F.B.I. official said that the incident involved the computer network in the bureau's

> counterintelligence office, and led several people in the office to believe that Mr. Hanssen had broken into their computers. [10]

Reports indicate that Hanssen was clearly involved in computer activity that should have been viewed as alerting: "…officials willingly accepted an excuse from Hanssen that hacking software used to steal passwords and bypass network limits found on his computer was used to connect a new color printer." [11] There are yet other altercations in which Hanssen misused his access to the computer network. Hanssen played these attacks off as demonstrations of lax security, but in reality he should have been investigated more for his actions. We always suggest following up on any potential security breach, no matter how small. Just as the Menyweather case illustrated that something as small as auditing of the Federal Express shipping ledger could have detected her massive fraud, further investigation into Hanssen's hacking activities could have potentially stopped his activity far sooner.

Case Study: Disgruntled Coast Guard Employee Deletes Database Records

Lastly we will discuss a case of sabotage. Although we did not find it to be nearly as prevalent as what you will read about in the next chapter, it does happen within the federal government. Here a disgruntled employee used her insider knowledge to purposefully disrupt a computer system. Because of faulty backups, the damage caused was far more than she ever anticipated.

Topic

Former U.S. Coast Guard Shakuntla Devi Singla pleads guilty to accessing a federal computer without authorization and intentionally causing damage.

Source

UNITED STATES OF AMERICA
V.
Shakuntla Devi Singla
Case Number: 1:98-cr-00109-LMB

Details

Shakuntla Devi Singla is a former Coast Guard employee who was responsible for helping to create an Oracle database containing personnel information. While working at the Coast Guard, Singla became increasingly upset by what she viewed as unresponsiveness to complaints of improper conduct of a contractor. In court documents, Singla said "I was frustrated and depressed because no one listened to my complaints of sexual harassment in the workplace."

On July 8, 1997, Singla dialed in to the Coast Guard network and used a "shared" password of another (unsuspecting) user. Seven other people were logged on to the system at the time. Using her access, she purposefully deleted entries within the database. After doing this, the server immediately crashed and became inoperable. "I wanted to get even with them," Singla said. "I did delete information, but I did not crash the system."

Because the back-up tapes were faulty, the entire data had to be manually re-entered. This cost approximately $35,000 and more than 1,800 hours to restore.

Singla was sentenced to five months in prison, five months of house arrest, and ordered to pay restitution for the cost of the damage.

Analysis

At the time, the Coast Guard was using the proprietary Convergent Technologies operating system. This release of the system had the weakness that enabled Singla to view the passwords of other users.[12] In addition, if the backup system had been operating properly, the deleted data could have been restored in a matter of minutes.

From this case we learn:

- To verify the correct operation of backup systems frequently.

- To educate employees not to share passwords.

- To not use systems that enable other employees (even administrators) to view the passwords of users.

- To council disgruntled employees

Summary

Threats from insiders are everywhere in the federal government. There is a difference between catching someone "browsing" sensitive information, even if it is outside of his or her official scope, and catching someone distributing the information to others who would otherwise not have access to it. Just as in state and local organizations, federal government agencies should restrict access to sensitive databases and log and frequently review transactions.

Agencies need to make improvements in contract procurement to prevent insider bribes and kickbacks. Monitor and audit time and attendance, especially of those that are responsible for submitting the cards after they have been approved by a supervisor. If requests such as repeated jury duty letters sound suspicious, take the time to confirm their validity.

Closely monitor and frequently rotate those employees that have responsibilities dealing with large amounts of money (such as government credit cards). Set credit limits as low as possible by default.

Audit even small charges, such as corporate or office Federal Express account numbers. Although the cost of misused account numbers may seem insignificant at first, you can use it to identify employees that are willing to misuse their access. If you investigation these small charges, you may uncover larger levels of fraud.

Any position involving visa processing is highly susceptible to bribes by brokers. Even in cases such as conferences and invited speeches, monitor those with the authority to write travel request letters to continuously ensure their truthfulness.

Verify that backup systems operate properly and ensure that several employees know the procedures for replacing data that has been corrupted. Make sure that employees know not to share their passwords, and do not use systems that enable anyone else (even administrators) to view the passwords of others.

When employees are terminated, verify that their badge and any other access devices are returned, that their e-mail and other accounts such as virtual private network (VPN) access has been disabled, and that all sensitive documents or letterhead have been returned. As we will further reiterate in the coming chapters, NEVER discount disgruntled employees. Their problems will not "go away", and their anger will only grow. Part IV of this book contains many suggestions we have to identify and mitigate their actions before they damage your organization.

Endnotes

1. Federal Bureau of Investigation. "Public Corruption," www.fbi.gov/hq/cid/pub-corrupt/pubcorrupt.htm (accessed 7 September 2005).

2. The Nationalist Movement. "United States v Czubinski," http://nationalist.org/docs/law/czubinski.html#2 (accessed 7 September 2005).

3. United States Department of Justice. "Los Angeles U.S. Attorneys' Office Employee Indicted on Fraud Charges," www.usdoj.gov/opa/pr/2000/December/691crm.htm (accessed 7 September 2005).

4. James Pinkerton. "Corruption Crosses the Border with Agent Bribes." The Houston Chronicle, (May 29, 2005). www.november.org/stayinfo/breaking3/AgentBribes.html (accessed 7 September 2005).

5. Federal Bureau of Investigation. "FBI History: Famous Cases: Aldrich Hazen Ames," www.fbi.gov/libref/historic/famcases/ames/ames.htm (accessed 7 September 2005).

6. Paul J. McNulty. "Sentencing Memorandum." United States District Court for the Eastern District of Virginia, Alexandria Division. http://news.findlaw.com/wp/docs/hanssen/ushanssen50602smem.pdf (accessed 7 September 2005).

7. "Affidavit in Support of Criminal Complaint, Arrest Warrant, and Search Warrants." United States District Court for the Eastern District of Virginia, Alexandria Division. www.fas.org/irp/ops/ci/hanssen_affidavit.html (accessed 7 September 2005).

8. Robert Philip Hanssen to KGB officer Victor Cherkashin, October 1985. www.cnn.com/interactive/law/0205/hanssen.quotes/1985.html (accessed 7 September 2005).

9. Jim Wolfe. "FBI Says Jailed Turncoat Warned of Spy Suspect." Los Angeles Times, (May 28, 2001). http://seclists.org/lists/isn/2001/May/0063.html (accessed 7 September 2005).

10. James Risen. "FBI Agent Jailed for Spying Fingered Hanssen 4 Years Ago." New York Times, (May 28, 2001). http://www.blythe.org/nytransfer-subs/2001cov/FBI_Agent_Jailed_for_Spying_Fingered_Hanssen_4_Years_Ago (accessed 7 September 2005).

11. Fox News and the Associated Press. "FBI Ignored Russia Tip on Hanssen." Fox News, (April 4, 2002). www.foxnews.com/story/0,2933,49520,00.html (accessed 7 September 2005).

12. Laura DiDio. "U.S. Coast Guard Beefs Up Security after Hack." Computerworld, (July 22, 1998). www.cnn.com/TECH/computing/9807/22/coastguard.idg/ (accessed 7 September 2005).

Part III
Corporations

Chapter 5

Commercial

Topics in this chapter:

- Companies and Insider Threats
- United States Code Relevant to Insider Threat
- Dismissed Computer Programmer Inflicts $10 Million in Damage
- Programmer with Access to System Passwords Deletes Payroll Data
- Former Forbes Employee Crashes Five (of Eight) Servers
- Programmer Launches Online Denial of Service Attack
- Telecommuting Employee Feels Cheated and Sabotages a Computer
- Company Goes Out of Business after Employee Allegedly Steals Proprietary Source Code

- **Former Employee Offers to Sell Proprietary Source Code to Competitors**

- **Customers with Access Become Insiders**

- **Loss of "Buy-in" Causes Employee to Turn Against His Company**

- **Eastman Kodak Is Victimized by a Retiree**

- **Former Employee Eavesdrops on Voice Mail for Competitive Advantage**

- **Newspaper Employees Attempt to Sell Customer Subscription Lists**

- **Former Employee Allegedly Sends Improper E-Mails to Clients**

- **AOL Employee Sells 92 Million Customer E-Mail Addresses to Spammers**

- **Cisco Employees Steal Almost $8 Million in Company Stock**

"Would it be of any profit to Owens-Corning to have the inside track on PPG?"

—A letter to Owens-Corning CEO that was allegedly written by Patrick and Daniel Worthing. Patrick Worthing admitted to stealing sensitive proprietary information from PPG.

"Boeing Co. recently acknowledged that two of its employees possessed competitor Lockheed Martin Corp.'s proprietary documents during a $2 billion rocket-launcher contract competition in 1998… Dean Farmer, a former Lockheed engineer – had the proprietary documents. Farmer reportedly brought the documents – 8,800 pages – with him to Boeing from Lockheed."

—Nikki Swartz, Information Management Journal, September 2003

"I had trusted Tim Lloyd completely. We relied on Tim Lloyd. He was responsible for the security of the system."

—Jim Ferguson, Omega Engineering Corporation plant manager speaking to the jury after Lloyd implanted a software bomb that cost the company $10 million dollars

"Smathers misused his position of employment within AOL, and misused the access to confidential and proprietary customer information to steal that data for his own personal use and profit, and the profit of others."

—David Kelley, United States Attorney and David Siegl, Assistant United States Attorney in a letter dated August 16, 2005 to Judge Alvin K. Hellerstein during USA v. Smathers

Introduction

Ever since a 1998 survey by the Computer Crime Institute in which they reported that approximately 70 percent of the organizations polled had been the victim of a computer network attack, and two-thirds of those attacks came from the inside, "insider threat" has been a recognized concern.[1] Sensitive information, such as trade secrets and other proprietary information, can be worth more than that which is normally stolen through time and attendance fraud, corporate credit card fraud, or theft of equipment, as discussed in previous chapters. Although the other threats are still a concern, protecting information from insiders is a primary focus of most corporations, and consequently of this chapter.

This chapter will discuss various threats to this information, such as sabotage and theft, the impact of these actions to the reputation and financial health of organizations, and will describe several real-life case studies involving well-known commercial companies. While some attackers were motivated by financial greed, most encountered through our research were simply disgruntled employees. Many of these angry employees had a grievance about the way the organization was operating, had recently had administrative action taken against them, faced future administrative actions, and/or had been dismissed from their position. This raises the sometimes difficult questions of: how to hire someone that you can trust, how to deal with a disgruntled employee, and how to fire an under-performing or problem employee.

As we describe the landmark case in which a former computer network administrator at Omega Corporation unleashed a software "bomb" that destroyed important design and protection programs, costing the company $10 million dollars, think about how your company or organization may be vulnerable to this type of attack. We also discuss other cases of sabotage, such as an administrator deleting necessary accounting databases, and in turn disrupting payroll, as well as an employee of Forbes deliberately crashing five (of only eight) primary servers.

Then we turn our attention toward theft of information, where companies were driven out of business by insiders that stole software source code and other proprietary information. We also analyze cases in which retirees and former employees had no hesitation in approaching competitors to sell stolen information.

We talk about how insiders can cause damage by impacting a company's reputation. In one case in particular, we tell you about an insider that allegedly e-mailed negative messages to every customer of an Internet hosting company, prompting the company to eventually go out of business when customers discontinued their contracts.

Toward the end of the chapter we address the direct financial losses that can be caused by malicious insiders. As we will show you, the material wealth of a company, such as its stock, is also vulnerable. Cisco found this out the hard way when two of its employees stole nearly eight million dollars' worth of company stock.

TERMINOLOGY: TRADE SECRET

According to US CODE, Title 18, 1839:

A "trade secret" includes all forms and types of financial, business, scientific, technical, economic, or engineering information, including patterns, plans, compilations, program devices, formulas, designs, prototypes, methods, techniques, processes, procedures, programs, or codes, whether tangible or intangible, and whether or how stored, compiled, or memorialized physically, electronically, graphically, photographically, or in writing if—

(A) the owner thereof has taken reasonable measures to keep such information secret; and

(B) the information derives independent economic value, actual or potential, from not being generally known to, and not being readily ascertainable through proper means by, the public.

Threats

Similar to the previous two chapters, we start by talking about threats that an organization *can* face. For commercial companies, this means the threats from sabotage, theft of intellectual property, theft of customer information, impacts to reputation, and direct financial losses. Unlike in the previous chapters, each one of these "possible" threats has actually been realized in at least one instance. We will talk about each of these circumstances in detail, but first let's identify the concerns.

Sabotage

Sabotage is commonly characterized by a disgruntled employee who was recently terminated and has decided to take some type of action in hopes of dooming the company to failure. Although most of the cases we found fit this mold, it is not always the case. Individuals can be targets too.

An employee unhappy with a specific supervisor or coworker can covertly (or even overtly) sabotage their performance, and in turn the overall productivity of the company. In one situation, a senior member of an engineering team swiftly changed the direction of the team over a series of lunches that the supervisor was not privy to. Because the senior employee interfaced with the team everyday, whereas the supervisor was only present weekly or bi-weekly, he was their *implied* leader. He had long since desired a change in the way the team operated, and he approached the supervisor with this request. The supervisor indicated that he was adamantly against it, and for good reasons refused. When this happened the employee spread his influence upon the other engineers. They respected him and before the supervisor realized it, the entire team was demanding this change. The senior member knew that the supervisor was against it, so he chose to sabotage his authority by convincing the team to support him. You could say that this is in some ways a type of mutiny.

Because sabotage is generally motivated by anger or dislike, versus greed, we believe that while it is capable of inflicting the most damage, it is also one of the easiest to prevent. There are warning signs.

A Closer Look...

Key Findings of the 2005 Insider Threat Study

Here is a selection of the key findings from the *2005 Insider Threat Survey: Computer System Sabotage in Critical Infrastructure Sectors* conducted by the United States Secret Service and the CERT Program at the Carnegie Mellon Software Engineering Institute. This annual report is a required reading for

Continued

anyone who wants to understand and prevent insider threat within their organization. Key findings this year include:

- Insider activities caused organizations financial losses, negative impacts to their business operations, and damage to their reputations.
- A negative work-related event triggered most insiders' actions.
- Most insiders held a work-related grievance prior to the incident.
- The most frequently reported motive was revenge.
- The majority of attacks were accomplished using company computer equipment.
- In addition to harming the organizations, the insiders caused harm to specific individuals.
- The majority of insider attacks were only detected once there was a noticeable irregularity in the information system or a system became unavailable.
- System logs were the most prevalent means by which the insider was identified.
- Insiders took steps to conceal their identities and their activities.
- Most of the incidents were detected by non-security personnel.
- When hired, the majority of insiders were granted system administer or privileged access, but less than half of all the insiders had authorized access at the time of the incident.
- Insiders exploited systemic vulnerabilities in applications, processes, and/or procedures, but relatively sophisticated attack tools were also employed.
- The majority of insiders compromised computer accounts, created unauthorized backdoor accounts, or used shared accounts in their attacks.
- Remote access was used to carry out the majority of the attacks.
- The majority of attacks took place outside normal working hours.

Source: www.secretservice.gov/ntac/its_report_050516_es.pdf

Theft of Intellectual Property

Competitors within the United States can steal intellectual property, or a foreign government attempting to provide economic advantage to companies in its own country can be the initiator. In either event, companies need to work relentlessly to prevent this theft. To help identify technologies that are frequent targets of this attack, we have included results from the 2004 Annual Report to Congress on Foreign Economic Collection and Industrial Espionage, prepared by the Office of the National Counterintelligence Executive.[2] This report highlights several key technologies that were targeted for theft throughout the 2004 fiscal year, including the following:

Information Systems

As in past years, information technology was the top target of foreign industries in 2004. To put it in perspective, 20 percent of all suspicious activity reported by Defense Security Services (DSS) and more than 15 percent of the Air Force Office of Special Investigations (AFOSI) was related to information systems threats. These statistics include both attempts to acquire technologies and attempts to instill technologies such as foreign-derived software within sensitive, classified environments.

Sensors

Slightly more than 10 percent of both DSS and AFOSI incidents involved sensor technology in 2004. Sensors are primarily used by the military and include technologies such as specialized high-speed cameras, night-vision equipment, and technology used to be the "eyes and ears" of unmanned aerial vehicles (UAVs).

Aeronautics

UAVs and other sophisticated aeronautics technologies take many years, and many millions of dollars in research and prototyping, to develop. That probably explains why 12 percent of DSS and 7 percent of AFOSI incidents were directly related to aeronautics technologies in 2004.

Electronics

It should be no surprise that electronics accounted for 11 percent of both DSS and AFOSI incidents. After designs have been perfected and finalized, they can easily be reproduced by virtually anyone with manufacturing capabilities.

Armaments & Energetic Materials

The United States military weapons systems rely on armament and energetic materials. These technologies are used in both attack and defense systems, and exposure of their capabilities and designs would be highly detrimental to US military forces. Therefore, they are an obvious target of foreign economic collection and accounted for approximately 10 percent of DSS and AFOSI incidents in 2004.

Theft of Customer Information

Customer lists are closely guarded within companies. With this sensitive information, competitors could approach the customers and offer them discounts for their service.

Examples of this can be seen everywhere and in marketing terms are ways that companies attempt to increase market share. Take grocery shopping for example—we humans are creatures of habit. When we buy something as mundane as orange juice we generally stick with a familiar brand. However, competitors of this brand desperately want customers to switch and purchase their product instead. That is why many cash registers include software that identifies you as a customer of specific products. They directly market to you through competing coupons for similar products printed on your receipt.

This is a simplified example, but one should be able to grasp the concept. Losing a single orange juice customer is not going to drive a company into bankruptcy; however, for a small business that relies on one or two sources of income, this could be a tremendous loss.

Impact to Reputation

A company cannot survive with a poor reputation. ValuJet is a prime example of this. When the company first started, business was booming—they had the reputation of low fares, casual dress, and a fun environment. After 110 people died on ValuJet flight 592, critics widely publicized problems with mismanagement and past safety issues involving the fire-related losses of several aircrafts.

In an attempt to free themselves from their former image and their path to bankruptcy, they made a change. On September 24, 1997, CEO Joseph Corr stated, "I'm pleased to announce that we are permanently retiring the name ValuJet and henceforth we will be know as AirTran Airlines."[3] ValuJet is not alone in this desperate effort to divorce from a bad reputation; many other companies have followed suit.

Financial Losses

Direct financial theft is the most obvious type of loss that can be caused by an insider. Unlike concerns involving theft of trade secrets or customer lists, direct financial losses are easier to identify and easier to put a dollar figure to than others. This includes most of the other concerns discussed in previous chapters such as time and attendance fraud; corporate credit card fraud; theft of other materials such as equipment; and bribes and kickbacks for contracts, subcontracts, and services. As we will demonstrate, stock and ownership is another area that is frequently targeted in commercial companies by insiders. Because nearly every stock transfer occurs electronically, theft can occur with lightening speed.

United States Code Relevant to Insider Threat

Throughout this chapter we make several references to US Code Title 18 complaints against former employees. In the next section of this chapter, we describe what each section covers, what is included in the charges in each, and their maximum penalties.

Section 1030 Fraud and Related Activity in Connection with Computers

Section 1030 violations are described as follows:

(a) Whoever—

(1) knowingly accesses a computer without authorization or exceeds authorized access, and by means of such conduct obtains information that has been determined by the United States Government pursuant to an Executive order or statute to require protection against unauthorized disclosure for reasons of national defense or foreign relations, or any restricted data, as defined in paragraph y. of section 11 of the Atomic Energy Act of 1954, with the intent or reason to believe that such information so obtained is to be used to the injury of the United States, or to the advantage of any foreign nation;

(2) intentionally accesses a computer without authorization or exceeds authorized access, and thereby obtains information contained in a financial record of a financial institution, or of a card issuer as defined in section 1602(n) of title 15, or contained in a file of a consumer reporting agency on a consumer, as such terms are defined in the Fair Credit Reporting Act (15 U.S.C. 1681 et seq.);

(3) intentionally, without authorization to access any computer of a department or agency of the United States, accesses such a computer of that department or agency that is exclusively for the use of the Government of the United States or, in the case of a computer not exclusively for such use, is used by or for the Government of the United States and such conduct adversely affects the use of the Government's operation of such computer;

(4) knowingly and with intent to defraud, accesses a Federal interest computer without authorization, or exceeds authorized access, and by means of such conduct furthers the intended fraud and obtains anything of value, unless the object of the fraud and the thing obtained consists only of the use of the computer;

(5)(A) through means of a computer used in interstate commerce or communications, knowingly causes the transmission of a program, information, code, or command to a computer or computer system if—

(i) the person causing the transmission intends that such transmission will—

(I) damage, or cause damage to, a computer, computer system, network, information, data, or program; or

(II) withhold or deny, or cause the withholding or denial, of the use of a computer, computer services, system or network, information, data, or program; and

(ii) the transmission of the harmful component of the program, information, code, or command—

(I) occurred without the authorization of the persons or entities who own or are responsible for the computer system receiving the program, information, code, or command; and

(II)(aa) causes loss or damage to one or more other persons of value aggregating $1,000 or more during any 1-year period; or

(bb) modifies or impairs, or potentially modifies or impairs, the medical examination, medical diagnosis, medical treatment, or medical care of one or more individuals; or

(B) through means of a computer used in interstate commerce or communication, knowingly causes the transmission of a program, information, code, or command to a computer or computer system—

(i) with reckless disregard of a substantial and unjustifiable risk that the transmission will—

(I) damage, or cause damage to, a computer, computer system, network, information, data or program; or

(II) withhold or deny or cause the withholding or denial of the use of a computer, computer services, system, network, information, data or program; and

(ii) if the transmission of the harmful component of the program, information, code, or command—

(I) occurred without the authorization of the persons or entities who own or are responsible for the computer system receiving the program, information, code, or command; and

(II)(aa) causes loss or damage to one or more other persons of a value aggregating $1,000 or more during any 1-year period; or

(bb) modifies or impairs, or potentially modifies or impairs, the medical examination, medical diagnosis, medical treatment, or medical care of one or more individuals;

(6) knowingly and with intent to defraud traffics (as defined in section 1029) in any password or similar information through which a computer may be accessed without authorization, if—

(A) such trafficking affects interstate or foreign commerce; or

(B) such computer is used by or for the Government of the United States;

shall be punished as provided in subsection (c) of this section.

(b) Whoever attempts to commit an offense under subsection (a) of this section shall be punished as provided in subsection (c) of this section.

(c) The punishment for an offense under subsection (a) or (b) of this section is—

(1)(A) a fine under this title or imprisonment for not more than ten years, or both, in the case of an offense under subsection (a)(1) of this section which does not occur after a conviction for another offense under such subsection, or an attempt to commit an offense punishable under this subparagraph; and

(B) a fine under this title or imprisonment for not more than twenty years, or both, in the case of an offense under subsection (a)(1) of this section which occurs after a conviction for another offense under such subsection, or an attempt to commit an offense punishable under this subparagraph; and

(2)(A) a fine under this title or imprisonment for not more than one year, or both, in the case of an offense under subsection (a)(2), (a)(3) or (a)(6) of this section which does not occur after a conviction for another offense under such subsection, or an attempt to commit an offense punishable under this subparagraph; and

(B) a fine under this title or imprisonment for not more than ten years, or both, in the case of an offense under subsection (a)(2), (a)(3) or (a)(6) of this section which occurs after a conviction for another offense under such subsection, or an attempt to commit an offense punishable under this subparagraph;

(3)(A) a fine under this title or imprisonment for not more than five years, or both, in the case of an offense under subsection (a)(4) or (a)(5)(A) of this section which does not occur after a conviction for another offense under such subsection, or an attempt to commit an offense punishable under this subparagraph; and

(B) a fine under this title or imprisonment for not more than ten years, or both, in the case of an offense under subsection (a)(4) or (a)(5) of this section which occurs after a conviction for another offense under such subsection, or an attempt to commit an offense punishable under this subparagraph; and

(4) a fine under this title or imprisonment for not more than 1 year, or both, in the case of an offense under subsection (a)(5)(B).

(d) The United States Secret Service shall, in addition to any other agency having such authority, have the authority to investigate offenses under this section. Such authority of the United States Secret Service shall be exercised in accordance with an agreement which shall be entered into by the Secretary of the Treasury and the Attorney General.

(e) As used in this section—

(1) the term "computer" means an electronic, magnetic, optical, electrochemical, or other high-speed data-processing device performing logical, arithmetic, or storage functions, and includes any data-storage facility or communications facility directly

related to or operating in conjunction with such device, but such term does not include an automated typewriter or typesetter, a portable handheld calculator, or other similar device;

(2) the term "Federal interest computer" means a computer—

(A) exclusively for the use of a financial institution or the United States Government, or, in the case of a computer not exclusively for such use, used by or for a financial institution or the United States Government and the conduct constituting the offense affects the use of the financial institution's operation or the Government's operation of such computer; or

(B) which is one of two or more computers used in committing the offense, not all of which are located in the same State;

(3) the term "State" includes the District of Columbia, the Commonwealth of Puerto Rico, and any other commonwealth, possession, or territory of the United States;

(4) the term "financial institution" means—

(A) an institution, with deposits insured by the Federal Deposit Insurance Corporation;

(B) the Federal Reserve or a member of the Federal Reserve including any Federal Reserve Bank;

(C) a credit union with accounts insured by the National Credit Union Administration;

(D) a member of the Federal home loan bank system and any home loan bank;

(E) any institution of the Farm Credit System under the Farm Credit Act of 1971;

(F) a broker-dealer registered with the Securities and Exchange Commission pursuant to section 15 of the Securities Exchange Act of 1934;

(G) the Securities Investor Protection Corporation;

(H) a branch or agency of a foreign bank (as such terms are defined in paragraphs (1) and (3) of section 1(b) of the International Banking Act of 1978); and

(I) an organization operating under section 25 or section 25(a) of the Federal Reserve Act.

(5) the term "financial record" means information derived from any record held by a financial institution pertaining to a customer's relationship with the financial institution;

(6) the term "exceeds authorized access" means to access a computer with authorization and to use such access to obtain or alter information in the computer that the accesser is not entitled so to obtain or alter; and

(7) the term "department of the United States" means the legislative or judicial branch of the Government or one of the executive departments enumerated in section 101 of title 5.

(f) This section does not prohibit any lawfully authorized investigative, protective, or intelligence activity of a law enforcement agency of the United States, a State, or a political subdivision of a State, or of an intelligence agency of the United States.

(g) Any person who suffers damage or loss by reason of a violation of the section, other than a violation of subsection (a)(5)(B), may maintain a civil action against the violator to obtain compensatory damages and injunctive relief or other equitable relief. Damages for violations of any subsection other than subsection (a)(5)(A)(ii)(II)(bb) or (a)(5)(B)(ii)(II)(bb) are limited to economic damages. No action may be brought under this subsection unless such action is begun within 2 years of the date of the act complained of or the date of the discovery of the damage.

(h) The Attorney General and the Secretary of the Treasury shall report to the Congress annually, during the first 3 years following the date of the enactment of this subsection, concerning investigations and prosecutions under section 1030(a)(5) of title 18, United States Code.

Section 1037 Fraud and Related Activity in Connection with Electronic Mail

Section 1037 activities are described as follows:

(a) In General— Whoever, in or affecting interstate or foreign commerce, knowingly—

(1) accesses a protected computer without authorization, and intentionally initiates the transmission of multiple commercial electronic mail messages from or through such computer,

(2) uses a protected computer to relay or retransmit multiple commercial electronic mail messages, with the intent to deceive or mislead recipients, or any Internet access service, as to the origin of such messages,

(3) materially falsifies header information in multiple commercial electronic mail messages and intentionally initiates the transmission of such messages,

(4) registers, using information that materially falsifies the identity of the actual registrant, for five or more electronic mail accounts or online user accounts or two or more domain names, and intentionally initiates the transmission of multiple commercial electronic mail messages from any combination of such accounts or domain names, or

(5) falsely represents oneself to be the registrant or the legitimate successor in interest to the registrant of 5 or more Internet Protocol addresses, and intentionally initiates the transmission of multiple commercial electronic mail messages from such addresses,

or conspires to do so, shall be punished as provided in subsection (b)

(b) Penalties— The punishment for an offense under subsection (a) is—

(1) a fine under this title, imprisonment for not more than 5 years, or both, if—

(A) the offense is committed in furtherance of any felony under the laws of the United States or of any State; or

(B) the defendant has previously been convicted under this section or section 1030, or under the law of any State for conduct involving the transmission of multiple commercial electronic mail messages or unauthorized access to a computer system;

(2) a fine under this title, imprisonment for not more than 3 years, or both, if—

(A) the offense is an offense under subsection (a)(1);

(B) the offense is an offense under subsection (a)(4) and involved 20 or more falsified electronic mail or online user account registrations, or 10 or more falsified domain name registrations;

(C) the volume of electronic mail messages transmitted in furtherance of the offense exceeded 2,500 during any 24-hour period, 25,000 during any 30-day period, or 250,000 during any 1-year period;

(D) the offense caused loss to one or more persons aggregating $5,000 or more in value during any 1-year period;

(E) as a result of the offense any individual committing the offense obtained anything of value aggregating $5,000 or more during any 1-year period; or

(F) the offense was undertaken by the defendant in concert with three or more other persons with respect to whom the defendant occupied a position of organizer or leader; and

(3) a fine under this title or imprisonment for not more than 1 year, or both, in any other case.

(c) Forfeiture—

(1) In general— The court, in imposing sentence on a person who is convicted of an offense under this section, shall order that the defendant forfeit to the United States—

(A) any property, real or personal, constituting or traceable to gross proceeds obtained from such offense; and

(B) any equipment, software, or other technology used or intended to be used to commit or to facilitate the commission of such offense.

(2) Procedures— The procedures set forth in section 413 of the Controlled Substances Act (21 U.S.C. 853), other than subsection (d) of that section, and in Rule 32.2 of the Federal Rules of Criminal Procedure, shall apply to all stages of a criminal forfeiture proceeding under this section.

(d) Definitions.— In this section:

(1) Loss— The term "loss" has the meaning given that term in section 1030 (e) of this title.

(2) Materially— For purposes of paragraphs (3) and (4) of subsection (a), header information or registration information is materially falsified if it is altered or concealed in a manner that would impair the ability of a recipient of the message, an Internet access service processing the message on behalf of a recipient, a person alleging a violation of this section, or a law enforcement agency to identify, locate, or respond to a person who initiated the electronic mail message or to investigate the alleged violation.

(3) Multiple— The term "multiple" means more than 100 electronic mail messages during a 24-hour period, more than 1,000 electronic mail messages during a 30-day period, or more than 10,000 electronic mail messages during a 1-year period.

(4) Other terms— Any other term has the meaning given that term by section 3 of the CAN-SPAM Act of 2003.

Section 1831 Economic Espionage (Foreign Government Involvement)

According to Title 18, Part I, Chapter 90, § 1831, Section 1831 violations are described as follows:

(a) IN GENERAL—Whoever, intending or knowing that the offense will benefit any foreign government, foreign instrumentality, or foreign agent, knowingly—

(1) steals, or without authorization appropriates, takes, carries away, or conceals, or by fraud, artifice, or deception obtains a trade secret;

(2) without authorization copies, duplicates, sketches, draws, photographs, downloads, uploads, alters, destroys, photocopies, replicates, transmits, delivers, sends, mails, communicates, or conveys a trade secret;

(3) receives, buys, or possesses a trade secret, knowing the same to have been stolen or appropriated, obtained, or converted without authorization;

(4) attempts to commit any offense described in any of paragraphs (1) through (3); or

(5) conspires with one or more other persons to commit any offense described in any of paragraphs (1) through (3), and one or more of such persons do any act to effect the object of the conspiracy,

shall, except as provided in subsection (b), be fined not more than $500,000 or imprisoned not more than 15 years, or both.

(b) ORGANIZATIONS — Any organization that commits any offense described in subsection (a) shall be fined not more than $10,000,000.

Section 1832 Theft of Trade Secrets (Individual Motivation)

(a) Whoever, with intent to convert a trade secret, that is related to or included in a product that is produced for or placed in interstate or foreign commerce, to the economic benefit of anyone other than the owner thereof, and intending or knowing that the offense will, injure any owner of that trade secret, knowingly—

(1) steals, or without authorization appropriates, takes, carries away, or conceals, or by fraud, artifice, or deception obtains such information;

(2) without authorization copies, duplicates, sketches, draws, photographs, downloads, uploads, alters, destroys, photocopies, replicates, transmits, delivers, sends, mails, communicates, or conveys such information;

(3) receives, buys, or possesses such information, knowing the same to have been stolen or appropriated, obtained, or converted without authorization;

(4) attempts to commit any offense described in paragraphs (1) through (3); or

(5) conspires with one or more other persons to commit any offense described in paragraphs (1) through (3), and one or more of such persons do any act to effect the object of the conspiracy,

shall, except as provided in subsection (b), be fined under this title or imprisoned not more than 10 years, or both.

(b) Any organization that commits any offense described in subsection (a) shall be fined not more than $5,000,000.

Section 2314 Transportation of Stolen Goods, Securities, Moneys, Fraudulent State Tax Stamps, or Articles Used in Counterfeiting

Whoever transports, transmits, or transfers in interstate or foreign commerce any goods, wares, merchandise, securities, or money, of the value of $5,000 or more, knowing the same to have been stolen, converted, or taken by fraud; or

Whoever, having devised or intending to devise any scheme or artifice to defraud, or for obtaining money or property by means of false or fraudulent pretenses, representations, or promises, transports or causes to be transported, or induces any person or persons to travel in, or to be transported in interstate or foreign commerce in the execution or concealment of a scheme or artifice to defraud that person or those persons of money or property having a value of $5,000 or more; or

Whoever, with unlawful or fraudulent intent, transports in interstate or foreign commerce any falsely made, forged, altered, or counterfeited securities or tax stamps, knowing the same to have been falsely made, forged, altered, or counterfeited; or

Whoever, with unlawful or fraudulent intent, transports in interstate or foreign commerce any traveler's check bearing a forged countersignature; or

Whoever, with unlawful or fraudulent intent, transports in interstate or foreign commerce, any tool, implement, or thing used or fitted to be used in falsely making, forging, altering, or counterfeiting any security or tax stamps, or any part thereof—

Shall be fined under this title or imprisoned not more than ten years, or both.

This section shall not apply to any falsely made, forged, altered, counterfeited, or spurious representation of an obligation or other security of the United States, or of an obligation, bond, certificate, security, treasury note, bill, promise to pay or bank note issued by any foreign government. This section also shall not apply to any falsely made, forged, altered, counterfeited, or spurious representation of any bank note or bill issued by a bank or corporation of any foreign country which is intended by the laws or usage of such country to circulate as money.

Internal Sabotage

Now that we have identified concerns that an insider could pose, we will tell you about several real-life cases in which they were realized. We will first start with one of the most damaging—sabotage.

The etymology of the word can be linked to two distinct origins: the first is from the Flemish, meaning to use a wooden shoe to jam machinery, [4] while the second originates in France and refers to how striking railway workers used to cut the metal sabot that held the tracks in place. [5] In either event, the intentions for both are to purposely disrupt. However, the question of why is not always clear. Most of the cases encountered during the process of writing this book are of employees or contractors who have been terminated. Some are angry with the company for terminating them, some have left of their own accord because the company was not giving them all they felt they deserved, and some have delusional concepts that through sabotage the company will appreciate them more. For example, according to reports, Michael Lauffenberger allegedly felt unappreciated and thought that by sabotaging critical General Dynamics Atlas Missile Program data he would be considered a savior to the company as a "highly paid and valued consultant" following his resignation. [6]

It is important that you realize that your organization is not invulnerable to this. While some of these arguments may not seem logical to you, to a disgruntled insider they may appear to make perfect sense. Study each case and ask yourself if it could happen to you, and what you can do to make sure that it does not.

Case Study: Dismissed Computer Programmer Inflicts $10 Million in Damage

The case of the dismissed computer programmer inflicting $10 million in damage is often considered a landmark event in the world of commercial insider threats. It marks the first widely publicized trial of a disgruntled employee that sought payback using insider knowledge and access. The study is of Timothy Lloyd and the Omega Engineering Corporation.

Topic

A former computer network administrator and programmer releases a software bomb that costs Omega Engineering Corporation $10 million 20 days after being dismissed.

Source

UNITED STATES OF AMERICA
V.
Timothy Lloyd
Case Number: 2:98-cr-00061-WHW-1

Details

Timothy Allen Lloyd, of Wilmington, Delaware, started as a machinist for Omega Engineering Corporation. He climbed up the corporate ladder and became a computer network programmer that was responsible for configuring and maintaining much of their Novell NetWare infrastructure at the company. In total, Lloyd spent 11 years working at Omega.

According to reports, these years were not always positive and productive. As the company grew larger, so did their network. Lloyd found many of his responsibilities being delegated to others and court records indicate that he perceived this as a demotion. After Omega decided to fire Lloyd, his supervisor asked him to train and grant access on the file server to himself and two other employees. Lloyd never did this. Following a series of performance and behavioral problems, Lloyd was fired on July 10, 1996.

Twenty-one days later, on the morning of July 31, 1996, it happened—a program that Lloyd had installed on the servers prior to his departure executed and deleted about 1200 critical programs. Despite their best efforts to restart the server, it would not function and the manufacturing machines that relied on tooling programs from the server could not operate properly.

Jim Ferguson was the plant manager at the time and his immediate decision was to rebuild the server from backup tapes as quickly as possible. However, the backup tapes were nowhere to be found. He then attempted to retrieve copies of the programs off individual workstations, but they had been deleted as well. "It was an awful feeling," Ferguson said. "We were starting to get an idea of all the impact and what it was going to mean and how it was going to affect us."

As a last resort, Ferguson ordered the manufacturing machines to continue operating with their last set of instructions—even though these orders had already been filled. He could not let production cease. According to Assistant U.S. Attorney Grady O'Malley, Ferguson next telephoned Lloyd and asked:

> "Tim, Tim, do you have the backup tapes? Tim, we need those tapes. Are you sure you don't have the tapes?" [7]

Lloyd told Ferguson that he did not have the tapes, and that they were left in his desk drawer. Knowing that his desk was completely empty, Ferguson went to Lloyd's home and pleaded in person. Still, Lloyd indicated that he did not have possession of the tapes.

Several different data recovery companies were hired to try to retrieve the deleted programs, but each told Ferguson that the task was impossible. Ferguson shut down machines, shuffled workers into other departments, and hired a team of programmers to rewrite the programs. "We were doing everything we could. The other step would have been to shut down and lay off everybody," Ferguson said.

One of the data-recovery companies, Ontrack Data International, made a copy of the damaged Omega hard drive and analyzed it. Greg Olson, their director of Worldwide Data Recovery Services, identified a number of anomalies with the disk. First, he identified the presence of a user account named "12345" with supervisor access, but no password. Second he found a program containing six strings that looked to be the cause of the damage.

Olsen determined that the event started with a specialized script that was triggered by the date July 31. He concluded that this script first called a program named "FIX.EXE" and second purged the drive. In his analysis of FIX.EXE he identified that it was actually a copy of DELTREE.EXE, a DOS program used to delete directories of files from Windows operating systems. The only difference between the two programs was that the standard output was changed to read "Fixing" versus "Deleting."

To prove that the incident occurred because of this program, Olsen recreated the scenario in his lab with an old copy of the Omega file server disk. Just as he had anticipated, when the system was configured for July 31, 1996, the script executed, and the server became completely disabled.

In the meantime, Omega executives reported the case to the U.S. Secret Service, and Special Agent William Hoffman came to Omega South to investigate. Because Lloyd was the only person that had the access necessary to cause this damage, and he was the last person known to possess the backup tapes on July 1, a search warrant was issued for his house. On August 12, 1996, his home was searched and about 700 pieces of evidence were seized. Some of the most notable included: computers, disks, CD-ROMs, 12 hard drives, and tapes. Two of the tapes, both reformatted, had in fact been labeled "Backup" for dates "5/14/96" and "7/1/96."

Olsen was given one of the confiscated "home" computers to analyze. He identified that it contained the exact same six lines of code that caused the damage on the Omega server.

Lloyd was indicted on January 28, 1998, by a Camden federal grand jury. They alleged he had "caused irreparable damage" to Omega's computer systems and transported computer equipment stolen from Omega interstate to his Delaware home.

The trial lasted four weeks, and the defense blamed Omega for not hiring a network administrator in place of Lloyd:

> These are the guys who didn't have a network administrator. These are the guys whose heads are on the chopping block. It's about going to your boss and explaining why you didn't have a network administrator. It's about explaining why you didn't have a backup protocol.

The prosecution argued that Lloyd was jealous and physically intimated his coworkers. As court records indicate, witnesses claimed that Lloyd "repeatedly elbowed, shoved, and bumped colleagues in the hallways, and that he became verbally abusive." They contended that Lloyd had been interviewing and had decided to leave Omega for another job. In their opinion: "This was [Lloyd's] parting shot to a company he was leaving, a going-away gift… And it was almost a perfect crime."

Following three days of jury deliberation, Lloyd was convicted of the computer sabotage charge and sentenced to three and a half years in prison and more than $2 million dollars in restitution.

Lloyd still maintains his innocence.

Analysis

Several problems come to mind in analyzing this case. First and foremost is that Lloyd appears to have been the only person with knowledge of the computer systems in this company. Court records indicate that Lloyd was the only person in the organization that was responsible for maintaining the backup information. It is important that you do not allow your organization to become solely dependent on one person for anything critical to success.

The second problem became evident when Ferguson realized that Lloyd needed to be replaced: he asked Lloyd to train others, but he refused. Unfortunately, at this point it was too late, and requests such as this further insulted Lloyd, causing him to become more disgruntled. As you will see throughout this chapter, an employee refusing to train others can be a *significant* warning sign for the potential of sabotage.

The third problem we identified was the out-processing of Lloyd. Many behavioral psychologists, such as Eric Shaw, maintain that firing is not always the best option. [8] This may have been true in this case; it is hard to say. In either event, the termination process was poorly handled. When Lloyd left, there was no verification that materials, such as the backup tapes, were properly returned. There was no analysis of the computer system to ensure that no backdoors or "ticking time bombs" were left behind. Even worse—they never even placed anyone in Lloyd's position to resume these responsibilities. Still, what happened is not the fault of Omega; they did not commit the crime. In addition, this occurred over ten years ago which was a time before insider threat was as widely publicized as it is now. Still, it is important that we critique cases such as this to ensure that these same lessons do not have to be relearned by others.

The lessons learned in this case are:

- **Do not allow yourself to have a single point of failure:** Place more than one person in charge of the critical aspects of your company (the two-person rule).

- **Deal with disgruntled employees immediately:** Don't let problems fester and escalate.

■ **Follow proper procedures during termination:** Verify that sensitive materials are returned and that the terminated employee no longer maintains access.

Case Study: Programmer with Access to System Passwords Deletes Payroll Data

The previous case introduced the notion that disgruntled employees can sabotage an organization. Like Lloyd, people complained that the subject of this next case was also allegedly difficult to work with. [9] Unlike Lloyd, who had left a time bomb behind to cause the damage, this employee went back to his former place of employment and did the damage himself. This was also a landmark case because it was one of the first trials in which a computer-generated display was allowed and considered as admissible evidence.

Topic

A former programmer and technical security officer for USPA logs on and deletes sensitive database information needed for monthly payroll two days after being fired.

Source

THE STATE OF TEXAS
V.
Donald Gene Burleson
Case Number: 2-88-301-CR

Details

Donald Burleson worked as a senior programmer and analyst for USPA, an insurance company based in Fort Worth, Texas. The company had about 450 agents employed, and most were distributed across the world.

The insurance agents entered their commission information into the USPA computer system each month, and a few days later they were paid their salaries. This payroll calculation system relied on the nearly 400,000 records stored on the server. Most months these commission-based salaries totaled over two million dollars.

Prior to being fired on September 19, 1985, Burleson had the role of administrator for the IBM System 38 computer used in the commission calculations. Because of his position, he was aware of passwords used by other employees to log on the server.

Two days after Burleson was fired, at 8:30 A.M., a USPA employee checked the payroll report for September. It failed to complete because many of the records could not be found.

Log files were analyzed, and they indicated that, oddly, several computers at USPA (including the one in Burleson's former office) had been turned on between 3:00 A.M. and 3:48 A.M. that same day. One of the computers that had been turned on belonged to USPA employee Al Wynn, who testified that he was not in the building at that time.

Initial thoughts turned to Burleson, but he had turned in his set of keys when he was fired. Through court testimony, however, it came to light that he had possession of at least one extra key to the building. From the court records:

> By backtracking various computer printouts, Duane Benson, USPA's programmer for the payroll commission system, testified that records were deleted from the payroll by a set of programs which were in turn triggered by instructions (jobs) entered into the system at 3:37 a.m. on September 21. The programs which actually deleted the records on September 21 were duplicates of a program (a source program) with a different name that had been created by September 4, 1985, when Burleson was still employed. By September 3, 1985, a program had been created that would duplicate programs, change their name, and move them around in the computer system...

> On September 23, 1985, the entire USPA computer system shut down... On September 28, 1985, Burleson went to Benson's home to pick up video tapes. Benson testified that Burleson admitted that he created the program responsible for shutting down the computer system as well as creating the programs responsible for deleting the records.

At the trial, Burleson denied being at USPA on September 3 and insisted that he and his son were visiting his father in Jasper, Texas. He even provided a Texaco credit card receipt for a flat tire repair outside town on September 3, 1985. Prosecution, however, demonstrated that the receipt he presented was fraudulent because it was printed in a form that was not used by Texaco until 1987. Furthermore, his son was placed at school that same day, and witnesses placed Burleson at a USPA staff meeting as well.

A jury convicted Burleson of "harmful access to a computer" and he was sentenced to seven years probation and $11,800 in restitution. Burleson appealed the case, arguing that:

1. The court did not specify the number of computer records deleted.

2. The court did not specify the programs he allegedly used to delete the records.

3. That evidence did not prove the data was deleted from the memory and storage.

4. That evidence did not prove the computer malfunctioned as claimed.

5. That the charge against him should not have been issued because there was not enough evidence to prove that he deleted the data.

For the first point, the court argued that the number of records deleted did not matter because even with vagueness of Texas Penal Code section 33.03, it was clear that the activity was criminal. The second point reaffirmed that the indictment was not based on how he did it, but the fact that he did do it. Third, the court decided that the evidence did prove beyond a reasonable doubt that the data had been deleted, and that it was correct to have assigned that same question to the jury. Forth, and the most historically important, the court announced that:

> The court did not err in overruling Burleson's trial objection to a computer-generated display showing the number of records missing from his employer's data file because such evidence was not hearsay, because it was shown to be accurate and reliable, because it did not violate the best evidence rule or the rules of optional completeness and related writings, because the sponsoring witness was qualified to testify, and because even if the court did err its err did not beyond a reasonable doubt contribute to Burleson's sentence or conviction in that there was other testimony showing that he deleted records from his employer's data file; and, furthermore, the court did not err in overruling Burleson's objection to any computer-generated printout because such printouts were admissible for the same reasons that the computer-generated display was admissible, and because any error which may have been committed did not beyond a reasonable doubt contribute to Burleson's conviction or sentence in that there was other testimony that he deleted records.

The appeal judgment was that the original trial was sufficient and that the sentence should stand. This case is important because it marks one of the first instances of computer-generated displays being accepted in courts.

Analysis

This case further emphasizes the importance of proper handling of sensitive company property such as keys. While Burleson did return his original set, court testimony indicated that other employees were aware that he had made backup copies for himself. Rarely do companies consider the consequences of the employee becoming a sabotaging insider when keys are handed out freely. When he was terminated, all of these keys should have been retrieved and accounted for.

NOTE

It is important to note that the 1996 Economic Espionage Act is *criminal*, not civil law. This means that investigations are handled by the FBI and United States Attorneys handle the prosecution. If a company cannot afford council, the government can provide help. In addition, because of the speedy trial provision in the Sixth Amendment, these cases will be resolved far sooner than most civil disputes. They generally don't last more than one year. However, conviction in federal cases is more difficult. Prosecution must prove "beyond a reasonable doubt" versus the much more lenient "preponderance of evidence" in civil trials.

Case Study: Former Forbes Employee Crashes Five (of Eight) Servers

In the case of the former Forbes employee crashing five servers, no one had complained publicly about problems with the subject. Nevertheless, he was disgruntled when his temporary status at Forbes was not extended and his employment was terminated. Here, the employee managed to obtain the user name and password of a current employee and remotely dialed into the system.

Topic

A former Forbes computer technician intentionally causes five of their eight servers to crash after he is dismissed.

Source

UNITED STATES OF AMERICA
V.
George Mario Parente
Case Number: 1:97-cr-01317-HB

Details

George Parente was a temporary computer technician at Forbes, Inc. When his employment was terminated, he leveraged the user name and password of a coworker and clandestinely dialed back into the network. With this unauthorized access he erased all the data and programs on five servers, subsequently causing them to crash.

Forbes' New York operations had to be shut down for two days, which cost the company more than $100,000.

Parente pleaded guilty on April 7, 1998, and was subsequently sentenced to five years of probation (four months to be served as in-home confinement), two hours a week of group therapy in an impulse—and anger-management program, 200 hours of community service, and restitution of $19,326 to Forbes, Inc.

Analysis

Without knowing more about the case, we find it is hard to say if Parente was motivated by his anger, his ego, or the delusional thought that this action would make Forbes want to rehire him. In any case, the point of failure here is that he was able to obtain the user name and password of a co-worker and could remotely access the computer network without authorization. If the user name and password were exposed to him because of technical means, that type of authentication system should not be utilized. Not even administrators should have access to the user names and passwords of other employees. Assuming that it was an unwitting employee that provided the information, this case further demonstrates the importance of insider threat training for everyone in your organization.

Explore More...

Are There Characteristics for Those That Will Sabotage?

According to many expert behavioral psychologists, such as Eric Shaw, Ph.D., who specializes in employee and organizational relations with security implications, there are warning signs for those that will do damage within a company.

Shaw calls this vulnerable type of personality a "proprietor." He writes that:

"Teamwork and cooperation are not the hallmarks of a proprietor. Typically, he will resist sharing information or training other employees in the intricacies of his specialized, exclusive knowledge of the company's systems. His self-imposed isolation is out of fear that allowing others on his turf will compromise his position... They don't respond well to criticism or change, and don't think twice about criticizing others. While they believe they have the best interests of the organization in mind, their attitudes will often poison employee moral... The reactions [when challenged] range from sulking to violent outburst, withdrawal to fighting back with the support of allies, ignoring and avoiding the problem to altering system components to eliminate the source of the criticism. The string that ties all proprietors together is that their reaction is always an attempt to preserve their position of control."

The signs Shaw defines to identify a proprietor are as follows. A proprietor:

- Feels he or she "owns" the system.
- Feels entitled to special privileges & exceptions to the rules.
- Won't delegate any vital responsibilities.
- Encourages customer dependence on him or her only.
- Denies others information and access and refuses to document vital codes and processes.
- Fights when his control is threatened, including making threats of violence.
- Encourages "us vs. them" culture with staff.
- Contributes to staff turnover by hindering others' upward mobility.

This personality trait is evident in many of the cases we have described thus far in this chapter and is seen throughout the remaining case studies. In Chapter 8, Profile, and Chapter 10, Survivability and Prevention, we will research more into this topic and address how you can detect and mitigate proprietors before

Continued

> any damage is done. You can also read more about this profiling in the book *Cyber Adversary Characterization: Auditing the Hacker Mind* by Tom Parker, Marcus Sachs, Eric Shaw, Ed Stroz, and Matt Devost (**www.syngress.com/catalog/?pid=2960**) and in Eric Shaw's article in *Information Security Magazine* titled "The Insider Problem: To Fire, Or Not to Fire?"
>
> http://infosecuritymag.techtarget.com/articles/january01/features4.shtml

Case Study: Programmer Launches Online Denial of Service Attack

A supervisor leaves and is replaced with consultants. Previous employees are upset and demand substantial payments. Those requests for payments are granted, but then the employees decide to request more. When those amended requests are not approved, the employees resign, and one seeks revenge using a denial of service attack.

Topic

A programmer is upset that his company will not meet his requests for a bonus and contract extensions so he resigns and sabotages the company with a series of denial of service attacks.

Source

UNITED STATES OF AMERICA
V.
Abdelkader Smires
Case Number: 1:00-cr-00392-RR-1

Details

Abdelkader Smires was a 31-year-old database programmer at Internet Trading Technologies Corp. (ITTI), located in New York. In the year 2000, ITTI was processing a considerably large number of transactions in the online stock trading business. Even still, the chief development officer, who was also Smires' supervisor, resigned from the company on March 6.

The company hired consultants to replace the employee, and asked Smires and the second programmer to train them. Like many of the other case studies we have observed, the two employees refused. In an attempt to maintain a stable environment, ITTI offered to pay the two employees large cash bonuses ($70,000), plus $50,000 in stock options and a one-year contract. Initially, on March 8, they accepted the offer, but then they changed their minds the very next day. For these two employees, this compensation was not enough and they made counteroffers to the company, threatening to quit if their larger demands were not met. The company refused their offers and within hours it found its trading network under attack from a computer in a Manhattan Kinko's copy center.

These attacks continued for three days. Eric Friedberg, computer and telecommunications crime coordinator at the U.S. Attorney's Office in Brooklyn, New York, said, "Although it was a potentially disastrous attack, it wasn't a highly sophisticated attack." Soon, investigators tracked down a launch point to a computer at the Queens College Campus in Flushing, New York. Identification of the attack location occurred in real time and within minutes they were onsite. Friedberg said, "Ten minutes after the defendant had left the building, we were able to find a witness to find out who had sat at this computer 10 minutes [earlier]."

On March 14 (two days after the attack concluded), a complaint was issued against Smires that he "did knowingly cause the transmission of a program, information, code, or command, and as a result of such conduct, intentionally caused damage without authorization to a protected computer in violation of USC 18 1030(5)(A)." He was immediately arrested and tried. On January 2, 2001, Smires pled guilty and was sentenced to 10 months (time served), house arrest for two months, two years' supervised release, and $20,001 in restitution.

Analysis

A $5,000 or $10,000 difference in bonus is probably not the root of the problem in this case. Even after Smires accepted a particular dollar amount, he went back and demanded more. In a sense, it is as if no amount would have been sufficient. I once had an employee demand that he receive a $5,000 increase in salary one year or he would quit. While on the surface that does not seem to be an outrageous demand, I felt that his demand had nothing to do with more money. The employee was not happy and was looking for a reason to leave. Hypothetically, it is possible that Smires may have felt that he was the next in line for his supervisor's position, and he may have been hurt when the consultants were hired from the outside. It is hard to say, but this demonstrates the importance of how careful you must be when you hire, fire, or transfer. There is a trickle-down effect from every decision; changes that you make can significantly alter group dynamics.

Case Study: Telecommuting Employee Feels Cheated and Sabotages a Computer

A telecommuting employee whose status changes to contract worker resents the situation and sabotages a computer. It is our opinion that this case demonstrates a breakdown in communication, further reiterating the importance of solving problems as soon as they become apparent. This is especially important when an employee telecommutes and is located away from everyone else.

Topic

An employee resents being forced to become a contractor when he moves to a different state.

Source

UNITED STATES OF AMERICA
V.
Patrick Angle
Case Number: 1:04-cr-10252-RCL-1

Details

Varian Semiconductor Equipment Associates, Inc., of Massachusetts, hired Patrick Angle to develop communications software to interface between the company and its vendors. He established a "work-from-home" arrangement with Varian so that half his time he could telecommute from his home in New Hampshire. One year after he started, his family wanted to move to Indiana. Angle asked permission to continue his employment in a full-time telecommuting status from Indiana. The company agreed to this change.

Varian did not have an Indiana business license or any other legal establishment with the state of Indiana. This meant that Angle had to become a contract worker instead of a standard employee. Contract workers are responsible for their own tax withholdings, health insurance, retirement, and other benefits. As court records describe, this upset him: "Angle resented this arrangement and later believed that his Varian supervisors had not fulfilled all of the company's obligations under the contract. Their relationship deteriorated." Given these problems, Angle was told around September 8, 2003, that his contract was going to be terminated in a month. This certainly did not help matters.

According to the charging document in this case, which was prepared by U.S. Attorney Michael J. Sullivan, Assistant U.S. Attorney Adam J. Bookbinder, and Trial Attorney from Computer Crime and Intellectual Property Section of United States Department of Justice Scott Garland, about one week later, Angle attacked Varian's computer systems:

> On September 17, 2003, from his Indiana home, Angle logged into Varian's Cypher computer server in Massachusetts, as he was authorized to do. This computer held the source code to the e-commerce software that Angle had been developing for Varian, as well as the source code to software projects that others at Varian were developing.
>
> To vent his frustration with Varian and in excess of his authorized access, Angle then intentionally and without authorization trans-mitted computer commands to the Cypher server that deleted the source code for the e-commerce software that he had been devel-oping, along with the source code for e-commerce software devel-oped by others at Varian.

After Angle sabotaged the system, he attempted to cover his tracks by editing the server's transaction log files. In addition, he changed the password for the system to something none of the other employees would know. When he was finished, he par-ticipated in a company teleconference and acted completely normal, not mentioning anything about what he had done to the computer system. When the teleconference was wrapping up, Angle announced to everyone that he was not going to complete the rest of the contract and that it was his last day at Varian.

Angle then preemptively notified Varian employees about the server problem by pretending as if he had just tried to log on, but could not. Varian kept backups of the server and after approximately $26,455 in recovery time, the deleted software had been replaced.

On August 22, 2004, Angle pled guilty to one count of intentionally damaging a protected computer, USC 18 1030(a)(5)(A)(i),(B)(i).

Analysis

After analyzing court documents in this case, it appears as if the company was being extremely flexible with Angle. It is hard to imagine how he was drawn to the point of committing sabotage. It was his own request to transfer to Indiana, and many companies at that point would have told him he had to quit. Perhaps it was the way in which it was handled (not being clear with him about his change of status until after he left), or perhaps the legal requirements associated with doing business in a particular state were never properly explained to him. It could also have been that he was disgruntled over something entirely different, and like in the previous case, he used this to fuel his anger. Luckily, Varian did keep backups of their software, because without them the damage he caused would have been significantly more severe. From this case we can observe:

- **The benefit of maintaining backups:** Although time was spent recovering the deleted data, significantly more time would have been required if the data was not backed up

- **The importance of clear and communicated expectations by all parties:** The entire event may have stemmed from a misunderstanding. Employees (especially those that are remote) need constant lines of communication. This cannot always be over the phone or through e-mail either; often problems can be solved much more efficiently in face-to-face meetings. For one thing, it demonstrates that the supervisor is *attempting* to work with the employee by making the extra effort of meeting with them. E-mails and phone calls also do not adequately convey the emotions or significance of problems to individuals.

Theft of Intellectual Property

Unlike sabotage, theft of intellectual property is not always done by disgruntled employees. People motivated by greed, those with prior loyalties, engineers and program managers with feelings of "ownership," and many, many others steal intellectual property. Theft of this type is terribly difficult to detect. It is not like when a company has all its computer equipment stolen by a thief. When information gets stolen it is silent—you may not ever know when it winds up in the hands of your competitors.

You will notice that, for the most part, it is the honest competitor of the victim company that raises the red flag. It is troubling to think about how many companies are not this ethical and how many fund and encourage the insider to provide further details.

Case Study: Company Goes Out of Business After Employee Allegedly Steals Proprietary Source Code

A former employee allegedly admits to selling proprietary software source code to another company, but because there was no legislation in place at the time, he is never proven guilty or sentenced. This case is from 1994 and is historically important to the protection of intellectually property. It occurred two years before the Economic Espionage Act of 1996 and is one of the prime reasons why it was created.

Topic

Ellery Systems, Inc. goes out of business when an employee resigns and allegedly sells proprietary software source code to a Chinese company.

Source

UNITED STATES OF AMERICA
V.
Liaosheng Wang a/k/a
Andrew Wang and
Jing Cui
Case Number: 1:1994-cr-00059

Details

Ellery Systems, Inc. was a small company located in Boulder, Colorado, that designed and built distributed computing devices. They were funded by both the United States Department of Defense and NASA to build a suite of innovative software applications. Their proprietary software cost $950,000 and was on the verge of full commercialization that is estimated to have been in the "tens of billions of dollars." [10]

One of Ellery's trusted employees was a Chinese citizen named Liaosheng Wang (a.k.a. Andrew Wang). While working at Ellery, Wang scheduled a trip back to China to "visit his sick mother." Only days after he returned, he suddenly resigned.

In a completely unauthorized activity, the next day proprietary source code that belonged to Ellery was allegedly downloaded across the Internet to a friend of Wang named Jing Cui who was also a Chinese citizen.

Wang confessed that he received $550,000 from a Chinese government-controlled corporation named Beijing Machinery Import & Export (Group) Corp to form a new and competing company.

At the time of this crime there was no federal statute against corporate/economic espionage and the charges were dropped. Ellery was left with nothing. The company promptly went out of business, and 25 employees were left without jobs.

Analysis

This case, and Congressional testimony by the former Chief Executive Officer of Ellery, Geoffrey Shaw, were driving forces in the creation of the Economic Espionage Act of 1996. The good news is that there is legislation in place to prosecute cases of this nature now, but it still remains that prevention is best when possible. In this situation, the actual downloading of the source code occurred one day after Wang resigned. Following his resignation, his access should have been limited and passwords should have changed to protect the intellectual property.

Explore More...

Will Trade Secrets Be Exposed If I Prosecute?

Section 1835 from the 1996 Economics Espionage Act includes oversight to ensure trade secrets of the victim are protected during prosecution:

"In any prosecution or other proceeding under this chapter, the court shall enter such orders and take such other action as may be necessary and appropriate to preserve the confidentiality of trade secrets, consistent with the requirements of the Federal Rules of Criminal and Civil Procedure, the Federal Rules of Evidence, and all other applicable laws. An interlocutory appeal by the United States shall lie from a decision or order of a district court authorizing or directing the disclosure of any trade secret."

Case Study: Former Employee Offers to Sell Proprietary Source Code to Competitors

The following case demonstrates the classic scenario of a disgruntled employee that loses his job, approaches competitors with offers of proprietary information, and those competitors approach law enforcement and/or the company. You should notice that several of the cases in this section follow this outline. This case happens several years after the Economic Espionage Act and therefore the subject is prosecuted successfully.

Topic

A former employee offers copies of proprietary software from the CVS repository to competitors.

Source

UNITED STATES OF AMERICA
V.
Timothy Kissane
Case Number: 1:02–cr–00626–RCC–1

Details

Timothy Kissane was a release engineer at the software company System Management Arts Incorporated (SMARTS). The company SMARTS had a product they called InCharge that was designed to monitor the status of large computer networks. SMARTS sold this product to telecommunications companies across the world and kept its source code a guarded secret. Like other SMARTS employees, Kissane signed a legally binding agreement to maintain this secrecy and not to disclose this proprietary information.

Kissane was terminated from SMARTS on November 28, 2001. Two weeks after this date, two competitors approached SMARTS and indicated that they received unsolicited offers for the sale of proprietary information. The offers had come from an e-mail alias for the Yahoo account of "Joe Friday." The e-mail offered proprietary source code, in particular, "cvs repository of SMARTS InCharge code, from 11/20/01 as well as custom code for specific bug fixes and customer-requested enhancements." Transmission of the e-mail was traced to a White Plains, New York, library. In addition, the Yahoo account was also accessed a number of times from the address of Kissane in Lavallette, New Jersey.

Timothy Kissane pled guilty to USC 18 1832(f), Theft of Trade Secrets, and was sentenced to two years' imprisonment with two years' of supervised release.

Analysis

Revision control systems such as CVS are a godsend for configuration management. However, because they enable developers to "check out" copies of sensitive source code quickly and without much oversight, they can be damaging to the protection of intellectual property. It is difficult to have employees operate in an efficient manner without freedom and trust. However, as in the previous chapter on the Federal Government, the "need-to-know" principle must be practiced.

However, even with need-to-know, Kissane still could have attempted to sell "his piece" of the work. When it comes to software development, there is a technology gap between convenience and protection. In the future it would be helpful if there were some sort of enforceable expiration of the software after some time. The feasibility (both technologically and its psychological impact on employees) remains to be seen.

A Closer Look...

Insiders May Not *Always* Have Bad Intentions

All throughout this book we provide descriptions of cases in which insiders purposefully sabotage, steal, spy on, and sell out the very organizations that provide them with salary and employment. While these cases take the limelight, it is fair to say that not *all* insiders have bad intentions. In fact, sometimes the very characteristics that make a good employee great, may in some ways be a vulnerability.

Take an academic conference for example. This is a chance for the top researchers in a field to get together to exchange cutting-edge ideas and "lessons learned." Especially in the case of workshops, the purpose is for participants to combine experiences and further enhance the sciences. Academic conferences are generally not tremendous business-development opportunities and for the most part discussions are held at the technical level. This means that attendees tend to be researchers and scientists who are not necessarily concerned over proprietary/trade secret boundaries.

As the Office of the National Counterintelligence Executive's Annual Report to Congress on Foreign Economic Collection and Industrial Espionage for 2004 describes, conferences such as these are a prime place where insiders may unknowingly leak sensitive information to foreign and domestic competitors:

"One of the oldest methods used to extract technologies is the targeting at conventions, expositions, and trade shows.... Standard collection procedures involve clandestinely filming equipment, stealing exhibitor's technical reference manuals, and engaging exhibitors in discussions that might yield classified material or fill collection gaps. Exhibitors, on occasion, have also had their equipment searched and photographed at ports of entry or have had their hotel rooms clandestinely entered and searched for sensitive information."

Similarly, the report also touches on the dangers that an ill-prepared insider can bring to a company while traveling:

"Foreign governments and businesses continue to acquire sensitive US proprietary information from all types of electronic storage devices, including laptop computers, personal digital assistants (PDAs), and cell phones carried by US businessman traveling abroad."

Unfortunately, environments such as these may not always be as safe as one might expect, and companies must instruct employees to watch for these types of threats. When traveling, all unnecessary information should be removed from

Continued

electronic devices and sensitive data should be protected. Conference attendees and presenters should be told to expect probing questions and should be taught to deal with them in an appropriate manner. When incidents arise they should be reported to your local FBI office.

http://www.nacic.gov/publications/reports_speeches/reports/fecie_all/ fecie_2004/FecieAnnual%20report_2004_NoCoverPages.pdf

Case Study: Customers with Access Become Insiders

This next case demonstrates that insiders are not just employees; they can also be customers with employee-like access. Here, two customers attend a training course for a product. However, the customers have more in mind then just training. One secretly copies and clandestinely stores copies of source code and other sensitive proprietary information that they should not have access to.

Topic

Customers use a "training" opportunity to illegally make copies of sensitive proprietary information.

Source

UNITED STATES OF AMERICA
V.
Yan Ming Shan
Case Number: 5:02-cr-20127

Details

3DGeo is a California-based company that has a software product capable of transforming seismic data into three-dimensional images. Oil companies use this software to determine where they should drill.

One of the clients of 3DGeo was a Chinese oil company named PetroChina. PetroChina purchased a copy of this software, and this purchase entitled them to a training opportunity for some of its employees. PetroChina sent Shan Yan Ming and Qiao Wei (both employees of DaQing Oil Field, a division of PetroChina) to the United States for training.

An affidavit by FBI Special Agent Richard Price describes that during their training on September 11, 2002:

3DGeo employee Ovidiv Fedorov and 3DGeo employee Iulian Musat discovered that Shan was in the process of organizing a large volume of copied files into one large master file. They were able to observe this from their own terminals when it occurred. As Fedorov and Musat watched, Shan changed the file from a visible file to a hidden file, thereby attempting to disguise what he was doing.

Fedorov began to search the file in more detail and discovered that Shan had made copies of 3DGeo proprietary software programs and source code, none of which is supposed to be accessible to Shan or Qiao. All of this information is password protected. Fedorov and Musat, acting on their own and without direction from any law enforcement agency, looked at Qiao's laptop computer. In it they found copies of the aforementioned programs and information, including the company's source code.

Additionally, Fedorov and Musat found a file containing 3DGeo's password file. In the same file, the two saw a program called "crack," which is used solely to penetrate encrypted software programs by decoding the protecting passwords.

On July 7, 2004, Shan pleaded guilty to USC 18 1030(a)(4), Unauthorized Access of a Protected Computer with Intent to Defraud and Obtaining Something of Value. He was sentenced to time served (24 months) and two years of supervised release.

Analysis

Enforcing security requirements on employees is both sensitive and difficult, but when you try to do the same for customers that have a check in their hand, it becomes even more complicated. Here a customer misused his access at a vendor's company to conduct economic espionage. The employees of 3DGeo should be commended for their vigilant work in the detection of this activity. Without it, the company may have found itself driven out of business like many of the other unfortunate victims in this chapter.

Economic espionage by customers is not as rare as you might imagine. Many of our clients have found out that their customers were actually "fronts" for competitors or foreign companies that are not allowed to acquire the technology. Beyond straightforward theft like what is described in this case, customers learn your rates, proposal style, key employee names and qualifications, and most of all… *capabilities*. Just as you would perform due diligence with a subcontractor you might hire, we suggest that you do your best to verify the background of customer organizations. This is especially necessary when dealing with export-controlled materials (refer to the US State Department Trade Controls Policy for more details). [11]

Case Study: Loss of "Buy-in" Causes Employee to Turn Against His Company

The subject in this case is the senior member of a company. When he finds out that the company is going to cease to exist in its current capacity he loses his loyalty and attempts to profit using economic espionage. He offers to sell intellectual property to a customer, who in turn contacts the authorities.

Topic

Disgruntled employee is upset with upcoming changes in an organization. He attempts to sell sensitive proprietary information to a competitor.

Source

UNITED STATES OF AMERICA
V.
Brent Alan Woodard
Case Number: 5:03-cr-20066

Details

Brent Woodard was the Director of Information Technology at Lightwave Microsystems, Inc. When the company announced plans to stop operations in late 2002, his loyalty ceased. This change triggered Woodard to secretly steal trade secrets and offer to sell them to one of Lightwave's biggest competitors.

Woodard accomplished this by copying information off proprietary Lightwave backup tapes. He then established an alias of "Joe Data" and sent an e-mail from the account "lightwavedata@yahoo.com" to competitor JDS-Uniphase. When the chief technology officer at JDS received the suspicious e-mail, he immediately contacted the FBI. The FBI then clandestinely took over the communications and began negotiating terms with Woodard. While these exchanges took place, investigators were able to trace the origination of the e-mails to Woodard's residence.

With evidence in hand, the FBI executed a search warrant of his home in December 2002, and an indictment for Woodard was issued shortly thereafter.

After many trial delays, on August 1, 2005, Woodard pled guilty to one count of theft of trade secrets under USC 18 1832. His sentencing is scheduled for December

5, 2005, at 9:00 A.M. The maximum penalty for this count is 10 years in prison with a fine of $250,000, after consideration of the U.S. sentencing guidelines and the federal sentencing statute USC 18 3553.

Lightwave Microsystems, Inc has since been bought by Neophotonics Corporation.

Analysis

Transition from one company ownership to another (most of us have done it at least once) is difficult. It is even more difficult when the company gets purchased by an organization that was previously considered a competitor. After you give time to a company, there is a natural tendency to lose loyalty after being told that it will cease to exist in one year. While that certainly does not make the crimes committed by Woodard right, it definitely makes the job of detection and prevention even more difficult than in regular situations. This is a very special circumstance that needs to be handled with great care and with tremendous oversight of the protection of proprietary information. It is a situation such as this that can cause someone unexpected, such as a director in an organization, to turn against the company.

Case Study: Eastman Kodak Corporation Is Victimized by a Retiree

Although there are not a lot of public domain details available on the following case, it does highlight the fact that insiders are not always disgruntled employees. They can be retirees who have dedicated their careers to an organization. Here an employee retired and then stole from a company after working there for 28 years.

Topic

When he retired from Eastman Kodak, Harold Worden approached competitors attempting to sell proprietary and trade secret information that he stole.

Source

UNITED STATES OF AMERICA
V.
Harold Worden
Case Number: 6:97–cr–06050–MAT–1

Details

Harold Worden is not your average insider. He dedicated the better half of his life (28 years) to Eastman Kodak. During this time, he was one of the key members of the team that designed something called "the 401 machine" inside Kodak. It was a machine to make the chemical acetate, an essential component of photographic film.

When he retired in 1992, he started his own consulting company. According to case records he actively recruited as many as 63 current and recently retired employees of Kodak to participate in his business. From this network he was able to obtain and sell confidential information that belonged to Kodak, including information about the 401 machine process. The activity was discovered when he attempted to sell information to Kodak officials that were actually posing as Chinese agents.

Worden was indicted on August 28, 1997, and immediately pled guilty to one count of transportation of stolen property, USC 18 2314. He was sentenced a month later to 12 months in prison, three years' supervised release including three months of home confinement and 100 hours of community service, and a $30,000 fine. When he was sentenced, Federal Judge Michael Telesca criticized Worden for attempting to sell his information to "not just any foreign national, but China."

Analysis

Educate, educate, and educate your employees about the harm of economic espionage against *everyone*. It is alleged that many of the individuals within this network were selling stolen information for $5,000 or $10,000. This amount of money means nothing when your entire organization can no longer afford to stay in business because *you* have just given your secrets to competitors. Enforce a strong zero-tolerance rule for misuse of information. Convey to the employees that your organization closely guards proprietary trade secrets and the importance of not disclosing them to anyone, not even friends or past coworkers and supervisors.

Theft of Customer Information

As the cases in this section illustrate, insider threat does not just target technical details such as engineering drawings or source codes. It includes sensitive proprietary information such as customer information and sales leads for competitive advantage. As this first demonstrates, you need to think beyond computer systems when dealing with insiders. Anything, including the telephone system, is vulnerable.

Case Study: Former Employee Eavesdrops on Voice Mail for Competitive Advantage

Lax telephone system security enables this former employee to use his insider knowledge of default passwords to listen to sales-related messages and gain competitive advantage.

Topic

John Hebel, a former employee of Standard Duplicating Machines Corporation, uses unauthorized access into their voice mail systems to gain competitive advantage for his new employer, Duplo Manufacturing Corporation of Japan.[12]

Source

UNITED STATES OF AMERICA
V.
John Hebel
Case Number: 1:96-cr-10288-JLT-1

Details

John Hebel was a field sales manager for the Standard Duplicating Machines Corporation and worked directly from his home. However, his position was terminated by Standard after two years and Hebel accepted a position with one of their competitors.

While working for this competitor, Hebel repeatedly broke into the voice mail system that belonged to Standard. The messages in this system contained sales leads and customer information and could be used for competitive advantage over Standard.

Hebel knew how to do this because he was an insider. He knew the phone number to call, and he knew that the default password for the mailboxes was the extension number and the pound sign. Unfortunately for Standard, Hebel also knew that most employees never changed their passwords from this default.

For one year he was able to access the system without detection. He did this several *hundred* times. According to one report, Standard learned about Hebel when a customer notified them that they had been solicited by Hebel after they left a voice message at Standard.[13] Shortly thereafter, Hebel was arrested, charged with wire fraud, and sentenced to two years of probation.

Analysis

Instruct and then periodically verify that employees change the initial passwords they are given. Default passwords should NEVER be used, not even for unimportant systems. They seem to migrate into places they should not. For example, one of my first jobs was as a developer in a large lab with many computers. Remembering all the passwords would be impossible so they were all set to one default. A few years later I left and began working somewhere else with some of my previous co-workers. Before I knew it, I began seeing a few servers at this new job set to this same password. It had migrated. Try not to encourage the use of one common or default password, or if you must have one, ensure that it is changed frequently (especially after people have been terminated).

Case Study: Newspaper Employees Attempt to Sell Customer Subscription Lists

The motivation in the following case is difficult to analyze. The employee appears to be attempting to assist in an investigation to reportedly uncover fraud, but at the same time he requests a large payment for the stolen proprietary information.

Topic

A circulation manager for the Gwinnett Daily Post in Georgia attempts to sell proprietary marketing plans and subscription lists to the Atlanta Journal-Constitution for $150,000.

Source

UNITED STATES OF AMERICA
V.
Carroll Lee Campbell, Jr.
Case Number: 98-CR-64

UNITED STATES OF AMERICA
V.
Paul Edward Soucy
Case Number: 98-CR-59

Details

The *Atlanta Journal-Constitution* and the *Gwinnett Daily Post* had an ongoing dispute about 34,000 newspaper subscriptions that involved a cable TV operator. The legality of how the *Gwinnett Daily Post* obtained these subscriptions was in question by the *Atlanta Journal-Constitution*.

At the time, Carroll Campbell, Jr., was a circulation manager for the *Gwinnett Daily Post* and Paul Soucy was a circulation manager for the sister newspaper,

Rockwell Citizen. While they were in these positions, Campbell used the alias "Athena" to communicate with prosecuting *Atlanta Journal-Constitution* attorneys for the case. In his letters, he offered to send copies of proprietary Post financial and business information, including a copy of the agreement with the cable entity that was being challenged. In exchange for this sensitive proprietary information, Campbell requested a payment of $150,000.

The *Atlanta Journal-Constitution* was instructed to place a personals ad in their newspaper if they were interested in purchasing this information. Rather than dealing with "Athena," they reported the offer to the FBI, which began investigating. At the instruction of the FBI, the *Atlanta Journal-Constitution* placed an ad to Athena in the personals.

After several correspondences, a meeting took place between "Athena" and an undercover FBI agent. Campbell (a.k.a. Athena) provided a sample of the proprietary information in exchange for $5,000. After he received it, he asked his wife (who was proven to be innocent in this case because she was not aware of the origin of the money) to give $1,500 of it to Paul Soucy. According to reports, Soucy was a "lookout" during Campbell's meetings with the FBI, who he thought was a representative from the *Atlanta Journal-Constitution*. [14] It is also alleged that Campbell offered another employee $300 in exchange for additional trade-secret information.

Campbell, Campbell's wife, and Soucy were subsequently arrested on February 6, 1998. Campbell pleaded guilty to conspiracy to sell trade secrets and was sentenced to three months' imprisonment, four months' "in-house" electronic monitoring arrest, and three years' supervised probation.

Analysis

This case is a bit different from the others because in theory Campbell seems to have been attempting to act as a whistle-blower to expose alleged corruption in his organization. However, when he accepted payment in exchange for this information, he jeopardized this defense. In conducting our research, we found a posting that was reportedly from C. Lee Campbell, Jr. [15] What is written in this e-mail (whether authentically written by Campbell or not) is important to reflect upon. It states: "A mistake does not define me as a human being. It was just a mistake." Motivations for people's actions are not always evident, and they are certainly not contained in court proceedings. It is our goal to help organizations prevent or identify incidents in which insiders have exposed, stolen, sold, or otherwise damaged the property of an organization. In no way do we intend to judge or criticize actions of any of these employees. Preventing this action by Campbell would have been difficult, because in his position he could easily acquire this information.

Impact to Reputation

Damage to a reputation can be as detrimental as theft or sabotage. Imagine the reputation of a computer security company being infiltrated by hackers, or even worse, insiders. What would customers of an accounting firm think if their information was found distributed to their competitors? While the actions themselves may or may not damage the company, the impact of these actions to their reputation can push them out of business.

Case Study: Former Employee Allegedly Sends Improper E-Mails to Clients

In the following case, someone breaks into a computer system and sends negative e-mail to every customer of the company. While there is an alleged confession from a former employee, this case has never been brought to court.

Topic

Former Elite Web Hosting employee allegedly breaks into the computer system and sends e-mails to customers claiming that the company was transitioning into the Web porn business.

Source

"When the Hacker Is on the Inside," December 13, 2000
http://www.businessweek.com/bwdaily/dnflash/dec2000/nf20001213_253.htm

Details

In September 2000, a disgruntled former Elite Web Hosting employee allegedly broke into company computer systems and sent vulgar e-mails to every customer "revealing" that Elite was transitioning into the Web porn business. The problem was that Elite was not shifting into this line of business and the e-mails were unauthorized. The angry e-mails even went as far as accusing majority owner Augustino Mireles of stealing from the company.

Thirty of Elite's customers stopped their service, which equated to an immediate loss of $150,000 a month in revenue. The company hired a computer-security company to try to rebuild their reputation and ensure the security of their servers, but it was not enough. Elite never made up the revenue and eventually went out of business. Charges were never filed against the employee from this incident because, as Mireles said, you "can't get blood out of a stone." The former employee was however

placed on probation following a second incident in which he pled guilty to physically assaulting Mireles.

Analysis

As has been discussed in previous cases, you should make it difficult for any one
person to obtain a complete listing of all customers. You should treat this information as confidential and should implement technology to prevent "spamming" of
your customers internally.

Case Study: AOL Employee Sells 92 Million Customer E-Mail Addresses to Spammers

Speaking of spam, in the following case an AOL employee uses his access to obtain
and then sell the ENTIRE client list to spammers.

Topic

An AOL employee sold 92 million screen names and e-mail addresses to spammers,
which resulted in approximately seven billion unsolicited e-mails.

Source

UNITED STATES OF AMERICA
V.
Jason Smathers
Case Number: 1:04-cr-01273-AKH-1

Details

Jason Smathers was a 25-year-old employee of America Online (AOL), a wholly
owned subsidiary of Time Warner, Inc when, according to court records:

> "From at least in or about April 2003, up to and including in or
> about April 2004, … unlawfully, willfully, and knowingly did com-
> bine, conspire, confederate [with others] and agree together and
> with each other to violate the laws of the United States, to wit,
> Title 18, United States Code, Sections 1037(a)(2), (b)(2)(C) and
> (b)(2)(E), and 2314."

Smathers illegally used the credentials of another employee to access the 2003
AOL customer subscription list (92 million e-mail addresses and screen names). This
list was retrieved from a computer located at AOL headquarters in Dulles, Virginia.

After he stole the list, Smathers sold it to Sean Dunaway, of Las Vegas. Dunaway had told Smathers that he intended to use it to advertise offshore gambling to AOL customers. However, Smathers admitted to knowing that the list may also be transmitted to others that intended to send unsolicited e-mails (SPAM). In addition, because Smathers worked with others in "deceptive practices to ensure that spam sent in connection with the stolen list reached its intended recipients, and would not be detected and filtered by anti-spam technology," he was in violation of the CAN-SPAM Act.

Smathers sold the list in its entirety for $28,000. However, the damage to AOL and its customers was enormous. It is estimated that approximately seven billion unsolicited e-mails were sent because of this crime, plus the list is still thought to be circulating and being used by spammers, which potentially puts the number even higher each day. For AOL, quantifying this damage is difficult. Original estimates are that the damage was $300,000, but others have speculated that it actually reaches in the millions when the cost to public reputation is considered. At one of the hearings in December, the judge himself admitted that he had cancelled his own AOL service because of the large amounts of spam he was receiving. In court, Smathers said, "I know I've done something very wrong." On August 17, 2005 Smathers was sentenced to one year and three months in prison. This was a lenient sentence owing to his cooperation during the case.

Analysis

It is extremely difficult to pinpoint how much of a financial impact this made to AOL. In theory, both this spam and the advertising of this case persuaded many people to discontinue their service with this provider. It is hard to quantify how many years these clients would have otherwise subscribed to AOL, or how many additional people discontinued their service, or chose not to select this provider because of what these former clients may have said.

As far as prevention, Smathers did not have legitimate access to the list he sold. At the time, AOL officials probably did not realize the extent to which spammers would go to obtain their e-mail addresses.

This case should be an eye-opener for large companies with many e-mail addresses. Few organizations protect this information. Your list could also be stolen and sold to spammers. Unsolicited e-mail wastes peoples' time, reduces performance on networks, and has been known to carry viruses. Consider treating your own distribution lists as sensitive information and educate your employees not to post their work e-mail addresses to mailing lists and Web pages, because these are also places where spammers look to collect information.

Financial Losses

Perhaps the most straightforward loss is a direct financial impact. The past two chapters covered this topic in detail with regard to time and attendance and credit card fraud. In this section, we address losses that are unique to companies: theft of stock.

Case Study: Cisco Employees Steal Almost $8 Million in Company Stock

In the following case, two Cisco insiders develop and implement a plan to steal nearly $8 million worth of company stock. Their fraud scheme is complex and well thought out, which makes it extremely difficult to detect.

Topic

A financial analyst and an account manager divert 97,750 shares of Cisco stock into their personal brokerage accounts.

Source

UNITED STATES OF AMERICA
V.
Geoffrey Osowski and Wilson Tang
Case Number: 01–cr–20055–ALL

Details

Geoffrey Osowski was a financial analyst and Wilson Tang was an accounting manager for Cisco Systems. As insiders they knew the ins and outs of the Sabrina computer system that was used to manage stock options for the company. The pair eventually used this knowledge in a malicious manner to break in and issue themselves 230,000 shares of the stock. They then sold this illegally obtained stock and purchased lavish items such as a new Mercedes 320 for $52,000, a diamond ring for $44,000, and a Rolex watch for $20,000.[16] According to the sentencing announcement:

"… the first time that they did this, in December 2000, they caused 97,750 shares of Cisco stock to be placed in two separate Merrill Lynch accounts, with 58,250 of the shares deposited into an account set up by Mr. Osowski and 39,500 shares deposited in an account set up by Mr. Tang. In February 2001, they caused two additional transfers of stock, in amounts of 67,500 shares and 65,300 shares, to be transferred to brokerage accounts in their name."

Their new-found wealth was suspicious to others and they were eventually investigated and their fraud was uncovered. On August 20, 2001, the pair pled guilty and was sentenced to 34 months in prison, three years of supervised release, and $7,868,637.50 in restitution.

Analysis

Fortunately, general auditing of financial components of an organization are conducted on a frequent basis, and in general is a more mature field compared to intellectual property protection. As this case demonstrates, however, it is still vulnerable to insiders. You will see many more cases involving theft of stock and insider trading in the next chapter.

NOTE

According to the 2005 Insider Threat Survey, the majority of insiders are actually *former* employees. The report states that:

- At the time of the incident, 59% of the insiders were former employees or contractors of the affected organizations and 41% were current employees or contractors.
- The former employees or contractors left their positions for a variety of reasons. These included the insiders being fired (48%), resigning (38%), and being laid off (7%).

http://www.secretservice.gov/ntac/its_report_050516_es.pdf

Summary

Protecting information from insiders is a primary focus of most corporations. Our research indicates that most of the subjects in current cases are disgruntled employees who were upset over ways companies operated (whistle-blowers), had the perception that the intellectual property legitimately belonged to them, became angry after recent administrative action was taken against them, were knowledgeable of future administrative action they faced, and/or had been recently terminated by the company.

However, we do not overlook the rare circumstance in which insiders appear to have allegiances to other companies, or even other countries, that can be a strong motivation. The *2004 Annual Report to Congress on Foreign Economic Collection and Industrial Espionage*, prepared by the Office of the National Counterintelligence Executive, identifies the following as key technology targets of economic espionage: information systems, sensors, aeronautics, electronics, and armaments and energetic materials.[17] Beyond pure technological intellectual property theft, companies need to be concerned over theft of customer information, theft of financial assets such as stock, and negative impacts that insiders can make to their reputation.

Endnotes

[1] 1998 Computer Crime Institute Survey. www.gocsi.com/contact_us.jhtml.

[2] Office of the National Counterintelligence Executive (ONCIX). "Annual Report to Congress on Foreign Economic Collection and Industrial Espionage—2004." www.nacic.gov/publications/reports_speeches/reports/fecie_all/fecie_2004/FecieAn nual%20report_2004_NoCoverPages.pdf (accessed September 22, 2005).

[3] Corr at a press conference, September 24, 1997. www.cnn.com/TRAVEL/NEWS/9709/24/valujet.presser/ (accessed September 22, 2005).

[4] I. Perrin Weston. "Guerrilla Warfare," LATimes.com, February 4, 2001. www.rtmark.com/legacy/more/articles/latimes20010204.html (accessed September 22, 2005).

[5] David Wilton. "Etymologies & Word Origins." www.wordorigins.org/wordors.htm (accessed September 22, 2005).

[6] Eric D. Shaw, Ph.D.; Keven G. Ruby, M.A.; and Jerrold M. Post, M.D. "The Insider Threat to Information Systems." www.dss.mil/search-dir/training/csg/security/Treason/Infosys.htm (accessed September 22, 2005).

[7] Sharon Gaudin. "The Omega Files: A True Story." June 27, 2000. http://archives.cnn.com/2000/TECH/computing/06/27/omega.files.idg/ (accessed September 22, 2005).

8. Eric D. Shaw. "The Insider Problem: To Fire, or Not to Fire," *Information Security Magazine*, January 2001. http://infosecuritymag.techtarget.com/articles/january01/features4.shtml (accessed September 22, 2005).

9. "Malicious Code 101: Definitions and Background." Spectria InfoSec Services. www.securitywebsites.com/Spectria-MalaciousCode101.htm (accessed September 22, 2005).

10. "Espionage Killed the Company." www.hanford.gov/oci/maindocs/ci_i_docs/ellerysys.pdf (accessed September 22, 2005).

11. Directorate of Defense Trade Controls: U.S. Department of State. "U.S. State Department Trade Controls Policy." www.pmdtc.org/ (accessed September 22, 2005).

12. "Annual Report to Congress on Foreign Economic Collection and Industrial Espionage—1998." www.hanford.gov/oci/maindocs/ci_r_docs/arc1998.pdf (accessed September 22, 2005).

13. Defense Personnel Security Research Center (PERSEREC). "Voice Mail." http://rf-web.tamu.edu/security/secguide/V2comint/Voice.htm (accessed September 22, 2005).

14. R. Mark Halligan, Esq. "Reported Criminal Arrests and Convictions" Trade Secrets Home Page. www.rmarkhalligan2.com/trade/articles.asp?id=prev&currentId=15 (accessed September 22, 2005).

15. See note 14.

16. U.S. Department of Justice Press Release, "Former Cisco Systems, Inc. Accountants Sentenced for Unauthorized Access to Computer Systems to Illegally Issue Almost $8 Million in Cisco Stock to Themselves," November 26, 2001. www.usdoj.gov/criminal/cybercrime/Osowski_TangSent.htm (accessed September 22, 2005).

17. See note 2.

Chapter 6

Banking and Financial Sector

Topics in this chapter:

- Financial Sector and Insider Threats

- Disgruntled USB PaineWebber Employee is Charged with Sabotage

- Allfirst Bank in Baltimore Loses $691 Million to Rogue Trader

- Barings Bank is Bankrupted by $1 Billion in Unauthorized Trades

- Daiwa Bank Loses $1.1 Billion to Rogue Trading

- Insider Helped in Armed Bank Robbery

- Insider Sold Consumer Credit Information

- Financial Insiders Conspire to Fraudulently Use Customer Account Information

- Finnish Wireless Hacker Is Suspected to Be a GE Money Insider

"Bankers who hire money-hungry geniuses should not always express surprise and amazement when some of them turn around with brilliant, creative, and illegal means of making money."

— Linda Davies, Financial thriller writer

"A lot of banks do not want to admit the fact that there are organized groups that are laundering money and getting away with it."

— Howard Palmer, a computer security expert who works for the Banking Academy

Speaking about the attempted heist of £220 million ($420 million) in March 2005 when keylogging software was discovered on several computers at the London branch of the Japanese Sumitomo Bank, and an attempt was made to illegally transfer money.

"The defendants took advantage of an insider's access to sensitive information in much the same way that a gang of thieves might get the combination to the bank vault from an insider. But the potential windfall was probably far greater than the contents of a bank vault, and using 21st century technology, they didn't even need a getaway car."

— Kevin Donovan, the Assistant Director in Charge of the New York Field Office of the FBI, November 25, 2002, referring to the defendants in a case that authorities believe to be the largest identify theft case in U.S. history.

Introduction

Examples of insiders participating in bank heists have been around nearly as long as banks themselves. Because of technology, today the threat is much more complex. Besides traditional armed robberies, which we will demonstrate still occur with help from insiders, banking and financial institutions need to be prepared to prevent and mitigate the larger threat of damage from electronic transactions. Like the other cases discussed in this book, these transactions can include sabotage and theft. Several real cases demonstrating this will be studied within this chapter.

Explore More...

Insider Threat Study: Illicit Cyber Activity in the Banking and Finance Sector

Here are the key findings of the 2004 United States Secret Service National Threat Assessment Center (NTAC) and Carnegie Mellon University Software Engineering Institute's CERT® Coordination Center (CERT/CC) Insider Threat study, which focused on banking and finance sector incidents. The findings come from analysis of 23 cases that involved 26 insiders.

1. Most incidents required little technical sophistication.
2. Perpetrators planned their actions.
3. Financial gain motivated most perpetrators.
4. Perpetrators did not share a common profile.
5. Incidents were detected by various methods and people.
6. Victim organizations suffered financial loss.
7. Perpetrators committed acts while on the job.

Some of the interesting statistics from the study include the following:

In 70% of cases studied, the insiders exploited or attempted to exploit systematic vulnerabilities in applications and/or processes or procedures (for example, business rule checks and authorized overrides) to carry out the incidents. In 61% of the cases, insiders exploited vulnerabilities inherent in the design of the hardware, software, or network.

In 85% of the incidents, someone other than the insider had full or partial knowledge about the insider's intentions, plans, and/or activities (22% of those were co-workers).

In 31% of the incidents, there was some indication that the insider's planning behavior was noticeable. Planning behaviors included stealing administrative-level passwords, copying information from a home computer onto the organization's system, and approaching a former co-worker to get help in changing financial data.

Twenty-seven percent of the insiders had prior arrests.

Eighty-tree percent of the insider threat cases involved attacks that took place physically from within the insider's organization. In 70% of the cases, the incidents took place during normal working hours. Thirty percent of the incidents were carried out from the insiders' homes through remote access. Of those attacks, 57% involved actions both at the workplace and from home.

Continued

> We encourage you to download (www.cert.org/archive/pdf/bankfin
> 040820.pdf) and read this study in its entirety. Although only a fraction of the
> cases discussed in this chapter overlap with the cases in the studies, there is a
> remarkable parallel between the main findings.

Threats

The banking and financial sector has most recently suffered through the seemingly constant stream of databases containing identity information being "lost" and stolen. In most of these cases, an outside hacker did not access the databases. Insiders sold them, or inside information was used to acquire them. Although these threats have grabbed recent headlines, they are not the most significant concern of these institutions. Unlike all the other sectors we have discussed, the foundation for banks is currency. This means that instead of stealing trade secrets and selling them to competitors, insiders can skip right to embezzling money.

However, motivation is not always this simple. When it comes to this sector, we will study another situation: rogue trading. Traders are paid to use their experience and fine-tuned judgment to make investment decisions that will eventually turn over a profit. When these traders make mistakes, they lose money. However, ego and/or management style sometimes push these traders to hide their mistakes. By hiding the problems they use insider know-how to bypass necessary checks and balances within organizations. As we will demonstrate, this can be a costly event for a company because the losses can grow unfettered.

Sabotage

Like with the insiders we've seen in previous chapters, banking and financial sector insiders usually show signs of being disgruntled. Unlike those in previous chapters though, financial sector insiders demonstrate that they understand concepts of investment. We will describe a case involving an employee of USB PaineWebber that purchased a large number of "put" options for his company prior to allegedly causing damage to their computer network. It is alleged that in addition to disrupting the operations of the company, he anticipated that the price of the stock would plummet from his actions, and that he would benefit financially through his put options.

Theft

Theft involving banking and finance is complex. Insiders can steal, embezzle, make poor decisions with money, and compromise intellectual property as in previous cases.

Financial Theft

Financial theft is fairly straightforward. An insider that knows the system and knows how to exploit it is likely to do so. The insider either helps to arrange a robbery at a large institution, or transfers money to secret accounts. Some cases are even more intriguing. One we will discuss occurred recently when the Helsinki branch of GE Money realized that someone "broke" into their network and stole money. Records pointed to a neighborhood apartment complex. This apartment had unsecured wireless access, and, as it turns out, a bank insider is suspected of illegally transferring the money from this access point.

Rogue Trading

From the late Rear Admiral Eugene Carroll, U.S. Navy (retired), we learn that "there is an old military doctrine called the First Rule of Holes: If you find yourself stuck in one, stop digging." This is a rule that the perpetrators in the cases that follow would have benefited greatly from. As Nick Leeson, one of the rogue traders said, "It had started off so small, but had rapidly seized hold and was now all across me like a cancer."[1]

Rogue trading is a problem that we will explore in depth. Besides its obvious implication to the banking and finance sector, it has consequences for all organizations. Rogue traders are highly motivated employees that make mistakes. These mistakes are compounded with their belief that the mistake was a one-time occurrence that they can make up for without reporting the problem. The issue comes when their belief is incorrect and instead of one mistake that can be easily corrected for, the problem is compounded. Their losses grow and practically double in size with each attempt to make up for the problem. We will discuss cases such as John Rusnak who lost $691 million at AllFirst Bank and Nick Leeson who bankrupted Barrings Bank with $1 billion in losses, among others.

Intellectual Property

Like any institution, banks and financial sector companies have intellectual property. Unlike engineering firms that guard trade secrets, these organizations generally have large collections of confidential customer information. In the wrong hands, this information can lead to identity theft and fraudulent purchases.

Case Study: Disgruntled USB PaineWebber Employee Charged with Sabotage

We study this case first to illustrate that financial institutions are not immune to sabotage, and second to show that insiders in these organizations are savvy of the financial consequences. The employee in this case allegedly caused significant damage to the computer network of the organization, but before he did this he purchased a large number of "put" options. He anticipated benefiting financially from these options.

Topic

A disgruntled employee allegedly sabotages USB PaineWebber and attempts to benefit from the damage.

Source

UNITED STATES OF AMERICA
V.
Roger Duronio
Case Number: 2:02-CR-00933-JAG-1

Details

Roger Duronio allegedly launched a software logic bomb that caused more than $3 million in damage to his company. Unlike previous cases of sabotage, reports indicate that Duronio had a plan to financially benefit from this event. Although this event took place in 2002, this is a complex case and the trial is ongoing.

It all started in Weehawken, New Jersey, where PaineWebber hired Roger Duronio on June 28, 1999. He was a system administrator who had access to and responsibility for the entire USB PaineWebber computer network. His base salary was $115,000 and his contract allowed for $60,000 a year in bonuses. However, he continually expressed his dissatisfaction with his earnings. Then, on Friday February 22, 2002, he quit. One week later, approximately 1,500 networked computers for the company failed.

At the same time, Duronio purchased put option contracts for $21,762 that expired on March 15, 2002; he had anticipated that the stock price would soon go down.

A put option enables someone to sell his or her stock at the pre-designated strike price rather than the current market price. If the actual price is less than the stock price, the owner of the put options makes a profit when it is exercised: strike price – current price = profit.

In Roger Duronio's case, he purchased options at an average strike price of $42.91 for 31,800 shares of USB stock.[2] If the price of stock had fallen to $35.00 he would have made $7.91 off each share:

($42.91 - $35.00) x 31,800 = $251,538

However, the attack that occurred was not made public at the time, and the price of stock in March never fell lower than $45.00.

http://biz.yahoo.com/opt/basics4.html

Early in the morning on Monday, March 4, 2002, more than 1,000 of USB PaineWebber's UNIX systems (AIX and Solaris) had their entire hard drives deleted. As described in the Evidentiary Summary from court documents:

The logic bomb had three basic parts: (1) a trigger, (2) an initiator, and (3) a payload. A trigger—a compiled binary named "rpc.logd" and "syschg"—caused the infected computers to execute the payload at 9:30 a.m. on Mondays in March, April, or May. The initiator —an OS-specific shell script named "rc.nfs" for AIX and "S71rpclog" for Solaris—ensured that the trigger executed even after reboots. The payload—a copy of the UNIX "rm" command— deleted the entire hard drive of the infected computers.

One of the central servers was used to distribute this attack throughout the network. This server first scanned to ensure that the computers were capable of running the "rc.nfs" shell script. If they were, the program "rsh_scan2.ksh" did the following (verbatim from the Evidentiary Summary):

- *Connected to each target computer;*

- *Copied and ran a shell script on each target computer, which stopped the trigger ("rpc.logd") from executing;*

- *Updated the trigger by placing copies of the trigger into two files: /usr/sbin/rpc.logd and /usr/bin/syschg;*

- *Instructed each computer to create "mrm" by saving the "rm" command as "mrm";*

- *Restarted to "rpc.logd" trigger (not the "syschg" version) by using the nohup command — which ensured that the trigger will keep running even though the executor is no longer logged in;*

- *Deleted the shell script mentioned above that killed the trigger; and*

- *Deleted a file called "ll_list," which is a file very similar to the list of target computers.*

There was a third scan, basically identical to the previous one, that was scheduled to execute March 1, 2002.

When Duriono's house was searched, they found several copies of the source code named "wait_tst.c", which corresponded to the trigger program. One copy found during the search was a printout left on his bedroom dresser. Backups recovered from his home contained copies and recorded history of the root user accessing and compiling this file. When analysis of histories took place it is interesting to point out that:

> By searching the 111 user's command history files from the November 2001 and December 2001 backups, it was determined that "root" and "rduronio" were the only users to access this directory and that when accessed as "root" or as "rduronio," the same "walk and talk" was used.

As an example, in December, "root" typed:

```
cd /y2k*/y2k*
tail -f nohup.out
ps -ef | grep scan
```

In January, "rduronio" typed:

```
ps -ef | grep scan
cd /y2k*/y2k*
ls
ls -al nohup*
tail -f nohup.out
su -
```

Both behaviors (commands and the syntax used) are very similar.

It is calculated that this attack cost USB PaineWebber $3,228,692 (including forensics analysis). This is an ongoing case. Duronio is charged with one count of securities fraud and one count of computer fraud, each of which can bring him up to10 years in prison, and combined the fines can be as high as $1.25 million.

Analysis

If Duronio is found guilty, this case will illustrate a clever attempt at profiting from an intentional act of sabotage. It also further enforces the argument that there are visible warning signs of employees that are at the point of sabotage. Court records indicate that Duronio was not happy in his position and frequently complained about his compensation.

Because records point to "root" as the user responsible for most of the damage, this case also highlights the problem that can occur when several employees are allowed to share the same administrator account. When one acts in a malicious manner, it is difficult to determine (and prove in court) exactly who is responsible. Consider using better authentication by not allowing root to log in directly. Force administrators to log in using their name, and "su" to root level access. To maintain proper records, configure syslog for remote logging. Additionally, privileged non-root accounts can be made to help segregate activities from one administrator to the next.

NOTE

From http://en.wikipedia.org/wiki/Hedging:
   Hedging is a strategy, usually through some form of transaction, designed to minimize exposure to an *unwanted* business risk.

Case Study: Allfirst Bank Loses $691 Million to Rogue Trader

This next case example is typical of rogue trading. An Allfirst Bank employee is pushed to achieve high profits so he takes risks that lead him to large losses.

Topic

John Rusnak becomes a rogue trader at Allfirst Bank.

Source

UNITED STATES OF AMERICA
V.
John M. Rusnak
Case Number: 1:02-cr-00280-WMN-1

Details

John Rusnak was a foreign currency trader. He gambled on what forthcoming conversion rates would be in other countries, particularly between the yen, euro, and U.S. dollar. Rusnak's career began in 1986 at Fidelity Bank in Philadelphia and then moved to Chemical Bank in New York two years later. In the early nineties he was looking for a change, and interviewed for a position at AllFirst Bank in Maryland. When he told AllFirst Treasurer David Cronin that he would "consistently make more money by running a large option book hedged in the cash markets, buying options when they were cheap and selling them when they were expensive,"[3] he was offered a job.

When Rusnak was hired by AllFirst in 1993, the yen had been rising against the dollar for three years solid. Rusnak believed that this trend was going to continue, and purchased large amounts of yen for future delivery. This was essentially a bet that the price of the yen was going to continue growing stronger against the dollar. However, as Figure 6.1 illustrates, this was not what happened. Unfortunately for Rusnak, the Toyko market fell after an earthquake struck Kobe on January 17, 1995.

Figure 6.1 Currency Exchange Rates over Time between the Yen and the U.S. Dollar*

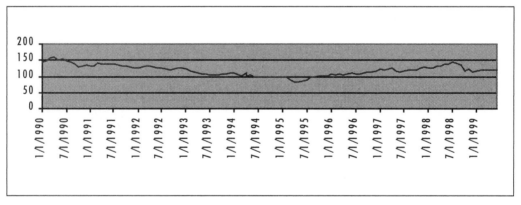

*Quantity shown is the number of yen needed to purchase one dollar.
Source: Wikipedia at http://en.wikipedia.org/wiki/Yen

For Rusnak, this meant trouble. Forward contracts are binding, and he had no choice but to take the losses. By the end of 1997 he had lost $29.1 million. Rather than immediately accounting for the large losses caused by the Asian market crisis, he hid them. Like the other cases we will discuss in this section, Rusnak believed that the mistakes he made were not repeatable, and that if he continued he would be able to recover. He continuously created fake options, backed up by falsified documents to cover up these problems.

By early 1999, his supervisor, a trading manager, left the company. Because of budget concerns, this position was never refilled. Instead, Rusnak reported directly to the treasurer. At this time his debt had nearly doubled, up to $41.5 Million. To attempt to overcome his losses, he made larger trades using prime brokerage accounts. He leveraged the fact that these types of contracts, historical rate rollovers (HRRO), could be used to hide losses. Despite a previous warning by the Federal Reserve Bank of New York:

> The Foreign Exchange Committee believes that rolling contracts at historical rates is a dangerous practice which should be avoided absent compelling justification and procedural safeguards. Because of the special risks, the Committee urges dealers that continue to accommodate customer requests for historical-rate rollovers to take the following three steps: (i) inquire about the customer's motivation in requesting an off-market rate trade to gauge the commercial justification; (ii) make sure that senior customer management is aware of the transaction and the special risks involved; and (iii) obtain the informed consent of one's own senior management to take on the additional risk and any effective credit extension.[4]

However, Rusnak was never questioned. Furthermore, despite having a Value at Risk (VaR) of $1.5 million by the end of 1999, his losses had doubled again to $90 million. He cleverly hid his problem by manipulating this calculation. By entering fake options, his true (losing) open forward positions looked like he was hedging them. In addition, because he was the one that reported his VaR, he distorted the values in the spreadsheet. Because there was no auditing or confirmation of this data, he was never challenged.

Rusnak had to worry about the stop-loss limit, though. This is a set amount that he was allowed to lose before his trading would be frozen for the month. He figured out that he could manipulate his check for this value by faking the currency exchange rate that was used to calculate it. Like the other, he supplied this spreadsheet to management himself. Unlike the other, the Treasury office independently confirmed this value. Rusnak was savvy though; he convinced his management that he needed current exchange rates downloaded directly to his computer from Reuters. Because this feed cost $10,000, the bank thought they would save money by copying the foreign exchange rates from Rusnak's computer to any others (including the Treasury office responsible for auditing his calculations). This gave Rusnak the control he needed to fraudulently validate their calculations.

NOTE

Value at Risk (VaR) is a calculation used as a metric to determine the risk associated with a trading portfolio. It is used in most any industry that holds liquid assets such as banks, energy traders, commodity companies, and financial firms. The purpose is to define an acceptable loss for a particular group or individual that guarantees their single losses will not significantly impact the organization as a whole.

http://www.riskglossary.com/link/value_at_risk.htm

Around the end of 2000, Rusnak's supervisors began to notice that something was not quite right. They cut his cash by restricting his use of the balance sheet. At this point, though, his losses had more than doubled up to $300 million. He had to change his strategy to try to get ahead; he sold deep-in-the-money options for more trading cash. The premiums for these options were in the millions, yet the likelihood that they would be exercised was extremely high. One example was an agreement he made with Citibank in early 2001. Rusnak agreed to set the strike (that is, selling) price of yen at 77.37 yen to the dollar.[5] At the time, the true exchange rate was 116 yen to the dollar, and as the previous figure had illustrated, the probability of this rate occurring was highly unlikely. The value of the dollar would have essentially had to drop almost 35% within one year. The premium for this "loan" was $125 million. He did this at a number of other institutions, including Bank of America, Deutsche Bank, Bank of New York, and Merrill Lynch, and he did not hide why he needed the money from these banks. In an e-mail discovered after he was apprehended, Rusnak wrote "I have come to you with a problem; we need to outsource our balance sheet funding."[6]

In the five years Rusnak traded with losses that should have been detected, there was only one audit. The audit staff did question one of his trades, but he was able to outsmart their scrutiny. They asked to confirm a trade that he entered. Because this entry was fraudulent, there was no legitimate sponsor to send the confirmation. He instead went to a nearby Mail Boxes Etc. and purchased a fax account under the fake name "David Russell." When the auditors faxed the confirmation to "David Russell," Rusnak had the store reply with a confirmation.

In December 2001, Rusnak's supervisors began to get concerned. When Treasurer David Cronin saw that the balance sheet for January 2002 was $50 million higher than he had approved, and that the foreign exchange trading volume had been $25 billion, he temporarily froze Rusnak's authorization to trade. Rusnak was asked to prove authenticity for several of the trades, and once again he produced fraudulent confirmations. This time, however, his supervisors were suspicious. They questioned him, and he lost his temper, saying, "I'm the guy who makes money around here."[7] This was Friday, February 1, 2002. Once he regained composure following a walk, he said he would call them on Sunday with the phone number of someone that could confirm the trades.[8] However, this never happened and he never showed up for work on Monday. Instead he consulted a lawyer and turned himself in to the FBI. Rusnak pled guilty to bank fraud and was sentenced to 90 months in prison, five years of supervised release, and $691 million in restitution.

Analysis

Like other rogue traders, the prime motivation is to continually, almost compulsively, try to "dig out" of the hole. Former U.S. Comptroller of the Currency, Eugene Ludwig, was commissioned by the AIB board of directors to independently investigate what went wrong in this case. He reported that Rusnak had taken advantage of the "weak control environment" and his trades "did not receive the careful scrutiny that they deserved."[9]

Although it is clear that Rusnak did not embezzle the money, Table 6.1 illustrates that he was paid large bonuses, which were based on the "perceived" profits he was reporting.

Table 6.1 John Rusnak Salary and Bonus at Allfirst Bank

Year	Salary	Bonus
1997	$102,000	$0
1998	$104,000	$128,102
1999	$104,000	$122,441
2000	$108,000	$78,000
2001	$112,000	$220,456*

* This bonus was scheduled to be paid on February 8, 2002, but never was paid because it was four days after he was discovered.

Source: The Ludwig Report at http://ftp.ncb.ie/equities/Ludwigreport.pdf
One of the "lessons learned" from this case is that basing compensation so heavily on profits of an individual may not be a good choice as a method of reward. This can encourage risk taking beyond healthy levels. In addition, Rusnak worked alone.

There was no one else that would have the opportunity to observe first hand what was happening. Even the required "vacation" period, which would have provided insight into his behavior, was overlooked. As the Ludwig Report describes:

> It is for good reason that banks in the United States are required to have a guideline that bars traders from trading two weeks per year. Having a second employee take over for even the most trusted bank employee is a mechanism for uncovering fraud. Although Mr. Rusnak did take vacations, the efficacy of the two-week rule was vitiated because Mr. Rusnak was allowed to continue trading from his computer.

Audits need to be truly independent. Staff should do due diligence on the points of contact provided for confirmations. This lesson applies throughout all organizations. As an example, if you are provided the name and number of a reference for a potential employee, the recommendation by the reference is only as good as their authenticity.

Case Study: Barings Bank Is Bankrupted by Rogue Insider

The Barings Bank was the oldest standing British merchant bank. Despite its rich history, it was collapsed by Nick Leeson, a rogue trader that lost one billion dollars from unauthorized trades.

Topic

Rogue trader runs a historic banking company into bankruptcy and ultimately causes its collapse.

NOTE

You can read more about this story in an autobiography by Nick Leeson titled, *Rogue Trader: How I Brought down Barings Bank and Shook the Financial World*.

Source

http://www.erisk.com/Learning/CaseStudies/ref_case_barings.asp

Details

This case brought down the oldest standing British merchant bank. Despite surviving 232 years of trading, which included significant financing of the Napoleonic wars, French reparations after Waterloo, financing of the Louisiana Purchase, and Argentine railway bonds that went awry, Barings Bank could not survive Nick Leeson.

Nick Leeson started his working career as a clerk at Coutts & Co. Bank in 1985. Shortly thereafter he moved to Morgan Stanley and learned how trades were conducted. Barings offered him a job in 1989 as a clerk, but three years later he was offered an even better position in the firm's Singapore office. Almost immediately afterward he passed his exam and qualified to trade on the Singapore International Monetary Exchange (SIMEX). By the end of this year (1992), he already had secretly lost £2 million. One year later it was £13 million. By 1994, Leeson had accumulated £185 million in hidden losses.

Leeson used a trading called "straddle," which generally produces a profit when the markets are stable. However, because of an accounting error caused by the mismatched exchange rates, he lost 20,000 pounds of sterling. He created a computer record named "Account 88888" that he used to hide/write-off his initial loss. Leeson thought that he would be able to make up for this small loss with unauthorized trades. Unfortunately for him, like Rusnak he was burned by the fall of the yen in 1995. His losses quickly increased to about £742 million.

On February 26, 1996, he disappeared with his family. Leeson was caught and arrested in Frankfurt and was sentenced to six and one-half years in prison. (Note: Nick Leeson developed cancer while in prison, and was released for medical treatment.)

Explore More...

History of Barings Bank

Barings Brothers & Co. banking company was established in 1762 by Sir Francis Baring. It was this bank that helped to finance the Louisiana Purchase in 1802, at the same time that it financed Napoleon's war effort against France. Barings had problems after the Brazilian revolution and was rescued by a consortium including the governor of the Bank of England. While this near bankruptcy significantly impacted the equity and strength of the company, it pushed forward.

Continued

> A close tie with the British monarchy was formed with King George V, and unlike many banks, Barings survived the great Depression. What Barings did not survive was Nick Leeson, whose rogue trading cost the company $1.4 billion that it did not have. The bank collapsed on February 26, 1995, and was purchased by the Dutch bank ING who paid only one pound. In March 2005 this portion of ING named Baring Asset management was sold to Mass Mutual and Northern Trust.
> http://en.wikipedia.org/wiki/Barings_Bank

Analysis

This case is nearly identical to the previous one. A high-risk trader was in a position that enabled him to compromise the checks-and-balances oversight of the back office. Because of this, many analysts are quick to point out that Barings too failed, and that Leeson is not the only person at blame.

Besides a basic lack of auditing and accountability, top Barings managers demonstrated that they did not have a firm grasp (or did not care) of the type and level of risk that Leeson was taking. Analysis shows that the profits he was reporting were too high for what was possible. Instead of taking these reports as warnings, the manager rewarded Leeson. The old line that if it looks too good to be true, it probably is, holds accurate in this case. The same shows for each of these rogue traders. Unbelievably high profits were reported. At one point in time each of the traders was viewed as the "golden boy" of the organization. It should be a lesson that even when things appear to be better than possible on the surface, they should be audited and their accuracy confirmed.

Another fault in this case was that Leeson did not have one single line of reporting. He reported to a supervisor in London when it came to his proprietary trading, and then to yet another office in Tokyo for trading requested by customers. By not having one single person or entity that looked over his activities, he could hide his activities.

NOTE

According to www.trading-glossary.com, Back Office refers to:
Brokerage House clerical operations that support, but do not include, the trading of stocks and other securities. All written confirmation and settlement of trades, record keeping, and regulatory compliance happen in the back office.

Case Study: Daiwa Bank Loses $1.1 Billion to Rogue Trading

The rogue trader in this case study lost $1.1 billion for Daiwa Bank, nearly as much as Nick Leeson did for Barings. Unlike Barings, Daiwa Bank was able to remain in business despite the significant losses. In addition, unlike previous cases, senior managers were held accountable for these losses.

Topic

Rogue trader loses $1.1 billion and senior officials are forced to pay.

Source

UNITED STATES OF AMERICA
V.
Toshihide Iguchi
Case Number: 1:95-cr-00914-LAK-1

Details

Toshihide Iguchi was a Japan-born U.S. citizen who lived in New York. After college, in 1977, he joined the Daiwas New York branch. With an academic background in psychology from Southwest Missouri State University,[10] Iguchi was started in securities for the back office of the branch. Business for the branch greatly increased in the mid-1980s. Partially because of this growth, Iguchi was promoted to be a trader in 1984.

Like many of the other rogue trading cases, management made a critical mistake when promoting Iguchi. His back office position was never refilled, so he was able to trade and continue his previous responsibilities. This put him in the very dangerous position of making trades and being the person responsible for auditing them. For obvious reasons, this practice is not recommended.

Shortly after Iguchi was promoted to trader, he had lost several hundred thousand dollars from his activities. He tried to cover up his losses by selling U.S. Treasury bonds that were purchased on behalf of customers in a sub-custody account at Bankers Trust. By virtue of his back office responsibilities, Iguchi was responsible for keeping track of this account. To further conceal that the securities had been sold, he falsified Bankers Trust account statements.

This continued for 11 years with compounding losses that were continuously concealed by more than 30,000 forged trading slips. The losses grew increasingly large when customers began requesting to sell some of their securities. Iguchi had already sold them, and these customers were owed accumulated interest that had never actually been earned. To pay this interest, Iguchi sold additional securities, continuing a loss situation that was impossible to overcome. He had lost approximately $377 million in customer securities and $733 million of Daiwas' own investment securities.

On July 13, Iguchi wrote a 30-page confession letter to Daiwa. In this letter, and others that followed by Iguchi, he suggested that supervisors had assisted him with the cover-up of losses. In the early fall (September 18), Daiwa reported the problem to the Federal Reserve Board. Because of this delay, the United States government filed a multiple-count indictment and complaint against Daiwa Bank.[11] In particular, one of the issues was that on or about July 31, 1995:

> The New York Branch submitted to the Federal Reserve Board a quarterly, "Report of Assets and Liabilities of U.S. Branches and Agencies of Foreign Banks" for the period ending June 30, 1995. This report falsely stated that the assets of the New York Branch included $615,987,000 of "trading assets," a number that included approximately $600 million of short-term United States Treasury obligations that Iguchi had sold and therefore were missing from the Bankers Trust account.

Unlike Barings Bank, Daiwa Bank had over $200 billion in assets and $8 billion of reserves that enabled them to financially survive these losses. However, their reputation was significantly damaged. Their entire business strategy of moving into international markets was lost, and they refocused their future business in Japan and Southeast Asia. In addition, following legal action by shareholders, a Japanese court punished board members and executives that had failed to provide appropriate oversight, and in some cases attempted to cover-up the problem. These senior managers were collectively required to pay $775 million in damages.[12]

Iguchi was sentenced to four years in prison, five years parole, and $2.6 million restitution. While Iguchi was in prison, he was interviewed by *Time* magazine. He made an interesting comment when he was asked, "When this started, did it seem like a crime?"

> To me, it was only a violation of internal rules. I think all traders have a tendency to fall into the same trap. You always have a way of recovering the loss. As long as that possibility is there, you either admit your loss and lose face and your job, or you wait a little — a month or two months or however long it takes. No one ever goes into the market thinking he is going to lose money.[13]

Analysis

In any industry, risk is necessary. However, those that take the risks should not have the opportunity to cover them up. Again in this case we see the important lesson learned that risk-taking must be kept separate from record keeping. This goes in almost any environment and is not restricted to the financial sector. Sales numbers and the "health" of organizations must be analyzed and confirmed outside of those reporting them.

With the separation, losses can still occur, but they can be detected before they are compounded and grow to be out of control. This case is different from the others because the managers that exercised lax control were also penalized in the end. It was Iguchi that said he confessed because he was afraid that there was no end to the fraud. He was never afraid of being caught because he didn't think he was breaking any laws; Iguchi was more afraid that he wouldn't be caught.

Case Study: Insider Helped In Armed Bank Robbery

This next case is something that you expect to see in Hollywood. A young bank supervisor (still in high school) conspires with others to orchestrate a staged, armed robbery.

Topic

Weekend bank supervisor provides inside information and assistance to armed robbers during a staged hold up.

Source

UNITED STATES OF AMERICA
V.
Ean Wolf
Case Number: 1:01-CR-00260-SMO-1

Details

Ean Wolf was an 18-year-old senior at Cherry Hill West High School in Cherry Hill, NC. When he was not in school, he was a weekend bank teller at the local branch of Commerce Bank on North Kings Highway. Wolf was well respected at the bank and was given the position of weekend teller supervisor. This meant he had keys to the bank and the combination of the vault.

Minutes before it was scheduled to open on Sunday, June 11, 2000, the bank was robbed. When interviewed by investigators, Wolf admitted that he had told Quinzel Champagne insider information about security at the bank. In addition to telling Champagne the number and location of security cameras and number of employees, he told him how much money was in the bank on different days.

According to court documents, Wolf took part in the actual robbery by pretending to be a victim. He said that the day was orchestrated so that Champagne approached him in the parking lot wearing a ski mask and carrying a gun. Wolf acted as if he was "forced" into the bank through a back door by Champagne. Once inside, Champagne instructed everyone into the vault and "ordered" Wolf to assist him in gathering the money. When he left, he had taken approximately $308,815 in cash.

Wolf admitted that Champagne agreed to pay him $35,000 for his part in the orchestrated robbery.

Analysis

The point of this story is to remind you not to overlook the obvious threats. In this day and age it is easy to throw money at technological solutions for prevention, but in reality it is the person that is the weakest link. Perhaps a background check could have exposed a questionable history, or perhaps pre-employment screening could have demonstrated that he was not mature enough for the responsibility, or that he had financial obligations beyond his means. Just because you purchase security cameras and a vault does not mean you are safe.

Case Study: Insider Sold Consumer Credit Information

A new employee at TCI quickly turns into an insider, supplying conspirators with secret passwords and codes, and training so that they could access thousands of confidential credit reports.

Topic

Help desk insider participates in "what authorities believe to be the largest identity theft case in U.S. History."[14]

Source

UNITED STATES OF AMERICA

V.

Philip Cummings

Case Number: 1:03-cr-00109-GBD-1

Details

Philip Cumming was an employee of New York–based Teledata Communications Inc (TCI). As the TCI Web site (www.tcicredit.com/) explains, "Companies all around the country rely on our products for efficient and affordable access to credit bureaus, and as links to public records. TCI saves our customers countless hours by automating the process for conducting background checks, employment screenings, tenant screenings, and more." The company essentially provides computerized access for banks and other organizations to check the credit histories of individuals quickly. TCI has access to three of the biggest credit history bureaus: Equifax, Experian, and TransUnion.

Cummings was a help desk employee at TCI and had access to confidential passwords and secret codes needed to access credit reports from these bureaus. In his short time in this position (mid-1999 through March 2000), he participated in what authorities believe is the largest identity theft case in U.S. History. A co-conspirator, Linus Baptiste, dealt with at least 20 different people in New York who would then go on to request credit reports for specific individuals. Cummings downloaded their credit reports and supplied them to the co-conspirator who sold them for $60. Baptiste split this profit with Cummings.

When Cummings moved to Georgia in early 2000, he kept the scam alive by periodically traveling to New York to download the requested credit reports. Eventually, Cummings provided Baptiste with a laptop that had been set up with the proper software, passwords, and codes. With this laptop, the co-conspirator was able to directly retrieve records from Equifax, Experian, and TransUnion. As passwords and codes changed, Cummings provided updated versions so that the theft could continue.

In addition to the cost associated with fraudulent charges and identify theft of the individual victims, the entities whose passwords and codes were used also suffered losses. These organizations were billed for each credit record that was retrieved using their password. As an example, the Ford Motor Credit Corp. in Grand Rapids, Michigan, noticed their bill included approximately 15,000 records that were falsely retrieved in a 10-month period using their subscriber code. Thousands of other fraudulent charges were billed to other organizations, such as Washington Mutual

Bank, Washington Mutual Finance Company, Dollar Bank, Sarah Bush Lincoln Health Center, Personal Finance Company, Medical Bureau in Clearwater, Vintage Apartments, Community Bank of Chaska, and Central Texas Energy.

Court records site more than 30,000 victims in the case with a confirmed loss at more than $2.7 million. Many of the individual victims had the money in their bank accounts fraudulently withdrawn, had the addresses of their bank account changed without authorization, and found illegitimate charges on their credit cards. Additional participants in the theft ring such as Eniete Ukpong would purchase expensive merchandise using the stolen credit card information, and then resell them to others such as Ahmet Ulutas.

In the indictment, James Comey, the United States Attorney for the Southern District of New York, said:

> With a few keystrokes, these men essentially picked the pockets of tens of thousands of Americans and, in the process, took their identities, stole their money, and swiped their security. These charges and the potential penalties underscore the severity of the crimes. We will pursue and prosecute with equal vigor who may be involved.

On September 14, 2004, Cummings pled guilty to: (1.) Conspiracy to Defraud the United States, (2.) Fraud by Wire, and (3.) Fraud with Identification Documents. He faces a sentencing of 5 years in prison on count one, 14 years in prison on the second count, 14 years on the third count, and 3 years of supervised release. The prison terms are to be served concurrently with each other. In addition, he was sentenced to $15,386,673 in restitution.

Analysis

When interviewed about the case, Linda Foley, the executive director of Identity Theft Resource Center in San Diego, said:[15]

> How much screening did (Cummings) go through before being hired for the help desk?... This situation was a problem waiting to happen.

However, when the TCI president and co-founder realized one of his past employees was a participant in this theft ring, he replied, "We were devastated; we do background screening, checking of people, but it's very hard to stop when you've got someone who's a bad apple."[16] Instead, the company has changed the way their business is done. The help desk employees no longer have access to the subscriber passwords — the subscribers must interface directly with the credit-reporting agencies. In addition, since the incident, they have developed a specialized online software program, Employmentscreener.com, to help companies screen their employees.

Explore More...

Your Computer Might Be the Insider

Nearly every case in this book is about an insider, a person that has chosen to take actions that negatively impact their company or organization. However, the insider might actually be your computer. Deceptive spyware or malware can secretly send your most trusted secrets across the Internet. While this software is often used in connection with insiders that install it secretly, it can be *you* that mistakenly downloads a program and causes the damage. One of the more recent cases illustrating this is the attempted heist of the London branch of the Japanese Sumitomo Bank in March 2005. Although police have not determined if someone on the inside installed the malicious software, they did determine that keystroke logging software was installed and used to gather the information needed to try to steal from the bank. This particular attempt was orchestrated in a sophisticated manner. Passwords and login information was acquired and used to try to transfer money to ten bank accounts all around the world. Luckily, these fraudulent transactions were detected before they were successful and the bank did not suffer any losses.

http://www.crime-research.org/news/18.03.2005/1059/

Case Studies: Numerous Cases of Financial Insiders That Fraudulently Use Customer Account Information

Because there have been so many cases in recent years of financial insiders fraudulently using customer account information, we chose to briefly touch on several of them and to offer one combined analysis of the general problems. As you read these cases, you may quickly notice that nearly all of them are from California. This is most likely due to the fact that California has the only (current) state law that forces companies to disclose this information.

Insider Sells Customer Information Used To Generate Fake Identification Documents

UNITED STATES OF AMERICA

V.

Dorian Patrick Thomas

Case Number: 2:03-cr-00215-WBS-1

Dorian Thomas is a former financial institution employee who acquired confidential customer information including names, addresses, dates of birth, driver's license numbers, Social Security numbers, credit card information, and account balance information. He then sold this information to someone that obtained false documents under these names. Thomas pled guilty to one count of 18 USC 371 Conspiracy to Obtain Unauthorized Computer Access to Information Contained in a Financial Record, Commit Fraud and Related Activity in Connection with Computers, Unlawful Use of a Means of Identification of Another Person and Commit Bank Fraud and one count of 18 USC 1030(a)(4) Fraud and Related Activity in Connection with Computers. He was sentenced to six months imprisonment for each count, to be served concurrently and $90 thousand in restitution (also to be paid by the co-defendant).

Insider Uses Customer Information to Open Fraudulent Credit Card Accounts

UNITED STATES OF AMERICA

V.

Charmaine Northern

Case Number: 2:03-CR-00009-EJG-1 and 2:03-CR-00409-EJG-1

Charmaine Northern worked for Schools Federal Credit Union in Sacramento, California. While working at the bank, she acquired confidential customer information using the computer system in her office. This information included names, Social Security numbers, driver's license numbers, and addresses of the victims. She used this information to fraudulently open up credit card accounts and charged approximately $53,376 in illegal transactions. She pled guilty to Unauthorized Computer Access to Information Contained in a Financial Report and Misdemeanor Bank Larceny; Aiding and Abetting.

Information from an Insider
Nearly Leads To $121 Thousand In Damages

UNITED STATES OF AMERICA

V.

Kimberly Molette Smart

Case Number: 2:02-CR-00122-DFL-1

Kimberly Smart worked for a financial institution in Sacramento, California. She used her insider access to obtain confidential customer information that she provided to others. The people she provided the information to attempted to cause approximately $121,146.63 in damages. On December 5, 2002, she was sentenced to serve one year and one day in prison and three years of supervised release for Unauthorized Computer Access to Information Contained in a Financial Record.

NOTE

According to Rhode Island legislation:
    § 19-9-27 (c) A "check kite" or "check kiting" means the practice of taking advantage of the time that elapses between the deposit or negotiation of a check, draft, or other negotiable instrument in one regulated institution or other depository and its collection or presentment in another regulated institution or other depository with the intent to defraud.
    http://www.rilin.state.ri.us/Statutes/TITLE19/19-9/19-9-27.HTM

Credit Union Insider Commits Check "Kite"

UNITED STATES OF AMERICA

V.

Lynn Booker

Case Number: 2:02-CR-00362-EJG-1

Lynn Booker was an employee at a credit union in Sacramento, California. Using unauthorized access to customer account information at this credit union, she committed check "kite" fraud between December 20, 2001, and January 2002. One account belonged to her, and one was to a person that she co-signed for. She forged checks from the other person's account and deposited them into her own. She then deposited checks from her account into the other person's account, making it appear as if both had sufficient funds. Using this "kite" she used Automatic Teller Machines (ATMs) that were not affiliated with the bank, which enabled her to have additional kite time.

Credit Union Insider Assists in Defrauding Priceline.com

UNITED STATES OF AMERICA
V.
Curtis Luckey and Tifane Roberts
Case Number: 2:02-CR-00038-GEB-1 and 2:01-CR-00507-GEB-1

Tifane Roberts was an employee of a credit union in Sacramento, California. She used her access to acquire confidential customer account and credit card information. Roberts provided this information to Curtis Luckey who used the information to make fraudulent purchases on Priceline.com, which totaled approximately $116,869.30.

Former Chase Financial Corp. Employee Pleads Guilty To Computer Fraud

UNITED STATES OF AMERICA
V.
Makeebrah A. Turner
Case Number: 2:01-cr-00382-SO

UNITED STATES OF AMERICA
V.
Patrice M. Williams
Case Number: 1:01-cr-00382-SO-2

Patrice Williams and Makeebrah Turner were employees of Chase Financial Corporation in Cleveland, Ohio. According to court documents, both Williams and Turner confessed to being involved in a scheme to defraud their company between November 1999 and December 12, 2000. They admitted to accessing computers beyond authorization and stealing account information (including credit card numbers) for 68 customers. They then faxed this information to one or more individuals who lived in Georgia that used the credit card accounts to purchase items. In this scheme, $99,636.08 was fraudulently charged to these accounts.

Both parties were charged on 18 USC 1030(a)(4) computer fraud and sentenced to 12 months and one day in prison, two years supervised release, and restitution of $99,638.08.

Wachovia Corp, Bank of America, PNC Bank, and Commerce Bank Insiders

In New Jersey, eight employees or ex-employees of major banks have been arrested in connection with a theft ring that allegedly produced $2 million in fraudulent costs.[17] According to Captain Frank Lomia, head of Hackensack, New Jersey police detectives, the personal data of at least 675,000 customers was stolen. It is alleged that it was Orazio Lembo, who operated a collection agency named DRL Associates that paid the bank employees for the information. This acquired information was combined with workplace information from another participant who was a labor department employee, and together was resold to numerous law firms at collection agencies. Luckily it does not appear as if this information was used to defraud the victims financially like the other cases.

Analysis

Story after story, each of these cases is the same. An employee used his or her access to acquire identity information that they used in a fraudulent manner. The information was either used to open up accounts or to misuse funds by the employees themselves, or the information was sold to others that conducted the identity theft. This is a serious problem that increases with each database that gets populated with this information.

Technological means can be used to assist in the prevention of this problem with the institution of auditing software that reports a list of accessed accounts to a supervisor. In addition, means such as encryption and copy-protection can help ensure that information cannot be easily transmitted onto removable media and walked out of the building.

Explore More...

Accidents Happen That
May Expose You and Your Organization

In December 2004, Bank of America shipped backup tapes, which included information on 1.2 million accounts to their data center. The problem was that the
tapes never made it. They were shipped on a commercial airline, and the tapes
themselves were not encrypted. Anyone that acquired them could easily access
the sensitive names, addresses, and Social Security numbers of accounts that
belonged to U.S. Government employees. As best said by Jim Stickey, the CTO of
TraceSecurity, "The Bank of America incident was absolutely stupid."
        http://www.tracesecurity.com/news/2005-05-01_1.php

Case Study: Finnish Bank
Wireless Hacker Suspected To Be An Insider

The Helsinki branch of GE Money was "robbed" across a wireless network in a local
neighborhood. Luckily, the wire transfers raised suspicion and the funds were secured
before any money was lost. The most devastating aspect is that the prime suspect in
the robbery is the head of data security—an insider.

Topic

Helsinki GE Money head of data security is suspected of malicious insider activity
that leads to the attempted theft of €200,000 ($245,000).

Details

The former head of data security at the Helsinki branch of GE Money
(www.gemoney.fi) was arrested for allegedly stealing €200,000 ($245,000) from his
company.[18] He allegedly copied software and passwords from the bank onto a laptop
that belonged to the company. With two others, he purportedly used the unsecured
wireless access from a neighbor to access the network without any attribution, and
illegally transfer money from the bank.

   At first the police thought it was the administrator/owner of the wireless network that had committed the crime. However, a search of his apartment led to

analysis of logs for the access point. These logs had recorded the MAC address for a computer that was registered to GE Money, and then this laptop was allegedly connected to the security officer. Jukkapekka Risu, the Helsinki police officer investigating the case, said, "After a while, there were too many leads pointing against him, and after we found the laptop, that was it."[19]

This investigation is ongoing and although the security officer has not yet been charged, he has been dismissed from his position. According to the Helsingin Sanomat,[20] the data security chief confessed during interrogation and said that an accomplice with a criminal background had forced him into the crime. According to reports, the accomplice threatened his family and forced him to bring the laptop to a video store a few days before the event. The reported accomplice denies involvement. Pekka Pattiniemi, general manager for GE Money in Finland, said, "I can confirm that our local security officer was involved."[21] The transaction was immediately considered to be suspicious, and all of the stolen money was recovered.

A fourth suspect was later arrested after he attempted to withdraw €5,000 ($6,110) from the account.

Analysis

When questions about prevention were asked, Helsinki police officer Risu said, "I suppose they could make their recruitment process more airtight."[22] It is not yet known if the suspect in this case had a prior criminal record. While this case has just started, and there are not any charges yet, the person suspected of the crime reportedly used a company laptop loaded with the necessary software and passwords. Strict regulations should be instituted on how enabling technology should be used (that is, perhaps the laptop should never have been allowed to leave the building, or perhaps audit logs could have immediately flagged the MAC address when it appeared on the network trying to illegally transfer the funds).

Legal Regulations

Suddenly instances of identify theft caused by mistakes within companies have appeared on the radar. The question is: are these events something new, or is the practice of public disclosure new? You be the judge.

Federal Laws

Here are some recently passed, and recently proposed, federal laws related to identify theft and required notification.

Gramm-Leach-Bliley Act (Financial Services Modernization Act)

www.ftc.gov/privacy/glbact/glbsub1.htm

This act is primarily focused on setting guidelines for how organizations should handle sensitive confidential identify information. An example of one subsection of the act follows:

> (b) Financial institutions safeguards
>
> In furtherance of the policy in subsection (a) of this section, each agency or authority described in section 6805(a) of this title shall establish appropriate standards for the financial institutions subject to their jurisdiction relating to administrative, technical, and physical safeguards—
>
> (1) to insure the security and confidentiality of customer records and information;
>
> (2) to protect against any anticipated threats or hazards to the security or integrity of such records; and
>
> (3) to protect against unauthorized access to or use of such records or information which could result in substantial harm or inconvenience to any customer.

It is generally aimed at ensuring that financial institutions do not disclose identity information to third parties.

Health Insurance Portability and Accountability Act (HIPAA)

www.cms.hhs.gov/hipaa/

HIPAA is a broad act that amends the Internal Revenue Code of 1986. It includes provisions to provide portability and continuity of health insurance coverage to people that change employment. In addition, and more relative to this book, it includes regulations to combat fraud from identity theft.

> (2) SAFEGUARDS—Each person described in section 1172(a) who maintains or transmits health information shall maintain reasonable

and appropriate administrative, technical, and physical safe-guards—

(A) to ensure the integrity and confidentiality of the information;

(B) to protect against any reasonably anticipated—

(i) threats or hazards to the security or integrity of the information; and

(ii) unauthorized uses or disclosures of the information; and

(C) otherwise to ensure compliance with this part by the officers and employees of such person.

State Laws

In this section we briefly describe the California Notice of Security Breach Law.

California Notice of Security Breach Law

www.privacy.ca.gov/code/cc1798.291798.82.htm

A quote by Joanne McNabb, chief of California's Office of Privacy Protection, gives the best description of how the California Notice of Security Breach Law impacts citizens: "It was because of (our) notification law that anyone knew about the ChoicePoint breech. They wouldn't necessarily have been telling anybody."[23] California has led the way in the first (and only, at the time of this book) state law that requires organizations to notify citizens when their confidential identity infor-mation has been compromised. Nearly 30 other states have proposed similar legisla-tion, using California as the model.

Proposed Federal Laws

In this section we describe proposed federal laws related to identify theft and required notification.

Schumer–Nelson ID Theft Bill

http://schumer.senate.gov/SchumerWebsite/pressroom/press_releases/2005/PR41586.ID%20Theft%20Drop.041205.html

U.S. Senators Charles Schumer (New York) and Bill Nelson (Florida) have introduced a bill that they believe will help prevent identify theft, better empower the Federal Trade Commission to oversee organizations, and mandate more disclosure requirements when compromises do occur. Schumer said his motivation for the bill is, "What bank robbery was to the Depression Age, identity theft is to the Information Age. Identity theft has become so pervasive and out of hand, that we must make a real effort to prevent it before it happens. When a company like LexisNexis so badly underestimates its own ID theft breaches, it is clear that things are totally out of hand."[24]

Some of the provisions are directly related to the handling of Social Security numbers and include provisions such as one that prohibits them from being displayed on employee IDs and bans the purchase and sale of Social Security numbers by non–law enforcement entities.

Notification of Risk to Personal Data Bill

http://thomas.loc.gov/cgi-bin/query/z?c109:S.751:
On April 11, 2005, Diane Feinstein (California) introduced this bill which basically intends to provide the same protection as the California Notice of Security Breech Law nationwide. An example of requirements following a breach of database security is below:

(a) Disclosure of Security Breach—

(1) IN GENERAL—Any agency, or person engaged in interstate commerce, that owns, licenses, or collects data, whether or not held in electronic form, containing personal information shall, following the discovery of a breach of security of the system maintained by the agency or person that contains such data, or upon receipt of notice under paragraph (2), notify any individual of the United States whose personal information was, or is reasonably believed to have been, acquired by an unauthorized person.

Summary

Activities of financial sector insiders are similar to those observed in previous chapters. They conduct sabotage, steal proprietary information, embezzle money, and unlike other cases we studied, they cause damage by taking undue risks and covering them up. Repeatedly, the lessons learned call for auditing and outside accountability. This is true in all cases, but is especially necessary for employees whose jobs require high levels of risk.

This chapter also highlighted the threat of identity theft and what institutions can do to help prevent insiders from participating in fraud rings. It also points out the benefit of legislation such as the California Notice of Security Breach Law that protects citizens by forcing organizations that have incidents to expose them to the victims.

1. William Leith. "How to Lose a Billion." The Guardian (October 26, 2002). www.guardian.co.uk/business/story/0,3604,818620,00.html (accessed November 2005).
2. "Ex-IT worker charged with sabotage." Computer Crime Research Center, www.crime-research.org/news/2002/12/Mess2001.htm (accessed November 2005).
3. Conor O'Clery and Siobahn Creaton. Panic at the Bank: How John Rusnak Lost AIB $700,000,000. Dublin: Gill & Macmillan, 2002: 73.
4. "Committee Letter on Historical-Rate Rollovers." (December 26, 1991): 119. www.fed-newyork.org/fxc/annualreports/fxcar95.pdf (accessed November 2005).
5. Sharon Burke. "Currency Exchange Trading and Rogue Trader John Rusnak," 11. www.publications.villanova.edu/Concept/2004/John_Rusnak.pdf (accessed November 2005).
6. Promontory Financial Group LLC. "Ludwig Report." (March 12, 2002): 17. http://ftp.ncb.ie/equities/Ludwigreport.pdf (accessed November 2005).
7. William Leith. "How to Lose a Billion."
8. William Leith. "How to Lose a Billion."
9. Heather Harlan. "Ludwig: Rusnak was 'unusually clever and devious.'" Baltimore Business Journal (March 14, 2002). www.bizjournals.com/baltimore/stories/2002/03/11/daily29.html (accessed November 2005).
10. Rob Jameson. "Case Study: Daiwa." ERisk (August 2001). www.erisk.com/Learning/CaseStudies/ref_case_daiwa.asp (accessed November 2005).
11. "11/95 Criminal Complaint & Indictment against Daiwa Bank." http://www.lectlaw.com/files/cas60.htm (accessed November 2005).
12. "Daiwa Bank: Ex-Execs to Pay 83 Billion Yen for Illegal Dealing by Employee." http://bankrupt.com/CAR_Public/000922.MBX (accessed November 2005).
13. "I Didn't Set Out to Rob a Bank," Time 149, no. 6 (February 10, 1997). http://www.time.com/time/magazine/1997/int/970210/interview.i_didnt_set.html

14. "U.S. Announces What Is Believed The Largest Identity Theft Case In American History; Losses Are In The Millions." US Department of Justice Press Release. (November 25, 2002). www.usdoj.gov/criminal/cybercrime/cummingsIndict.htm (accessed November 2005).

15. Paul Festa. "Feds charge three with identity theft." ZDNET News (November 2002). http://news.zdnet.com/2100-9595_22-971196.html (accessed November 2005).

16. "The Great Data Heist." Fortune (May 2005). www.tracesecurity.com/news/2005-05-01_1.php (accessed November 2005).

17. Jonathan Krim. "Banks Alert Customers of Data Theft." Washington Post (May 2005): E05. http://www.washingtonpost.com/wp-dyn/content/article/2005/05/25/AR2005052501777.html (accessed November 2005).

18. René Millman. "Wireless hacker was bank insider." SC Magazine (August 2005). www.scmagazine.com/us/news/article/492078/wireless-hacker-bank-insider/ (accessed November 2005).

19. James Niccolai. "Finns urge better Wi-Fi security after bank break in." Infoworld (August 2005). www.infoworld.com/article/05/08/18/HNfinnwifisecurity_1.html (accessed November 2005).

20. "Data security chief of large credit company suspected of computer hacking and fraud." Helsingin Sanomat. www.helsinginsanomat.fi/english/article/1101980633083 (accessed November 2005).

21. James Niccolai. "Finns urge better Wi-Fi security after bank break in."

22. James Niccolai. "Finns urge better Wi-Fi security after bank break in."

23. Kathleen Hunter, "California Law on ID Theft Seen as Model." Stateline.org (April 2005). www.stateline.org/live/ViewPage.action?siteNodeId=137&languageId=1&contentId=22828 (accessed November 2005).

24. "Schumer Introduces Comprehensive ID Theft Bill Today; Identity Theft at Lexis Nexis 10x's Larger than Expected." Senator Charles E Schumer Press Release (April 12, 2005). http://schumer.senate.gov/SchumerWebsite/pressroom/press_releases/2005/PR41586.ID%20Theft%20Drop.041205.html

Chapter 7

Government Subcontractors

Topics in this chapter:

- **Compounded Threats at Government Subcontractors**

- **Trusted Air Force Master Sergeant Retires and Joins TRW**

- **Chinese National Accesses Sensitive Passwords on Critical AF Logistics System**

"If I commit esponage [sic] I will be putting my self and family at great risk. If I am caught I will be enprisioned [sic] for the rest of my life, if not executed for this deed."

— Brian Regan in a letter to Saddam Hussein where he demanded $13 million for the classified information he offered

"The insider threat is inherent in society's strive toward finding better, faster, cheaper, and simpler ways to pass information, accomplish business objectives, and survive in a fast-paced instant and impatient society."

— Valerie L. Caruso, USAF, Master's Thesis titled, "Outsourcing Information Technology and the Insider Threat"

Introduction

Statistics show that employees of government contractors are responsible for roughly 24% of espionage cases.[1] However, preventing and detecting insider threat here is perhaps more difficult than any other environment, and for this reason we suspect the number of undiscovered cases in this area is significantly large. Government contracting brings a mix of complicating characteristics that greatly compound the chance that insiders will be successful at their activity without detection. Generally it is the very characteristics that make contractors appealing to the government that leaves them vulnerable to this threat:

- **Same work, less money** Government contractors often have to accomplish the same type of activities as the government, but without the seemingly unending federal resources to do it. This means that in the end, whereas the government may accomplish a specific task to the extent necessary, with burdening levels of oversight and bureaucracy, a company must always be mindful of the bottom line financially. Levels of security and auditing are only applied to the extent that the activity remains profitable and within budget.

- **Faster, more agile, and less bureaucracy** When compared to the government, contractors make decisions and take actions faster with less bureaucracy. Almost always this is a positive statement, but on the few occasions that the person making the decisions is a malicious insider, the results can be catastrophic because there is no oversight.

- **Experienced and proven employees** Often defense contractors hire retirees that have had "proven" careers within the government. To the company, this is a great move because it makes their solutions more operational and realistic to the true needs of the government, and to the customer these employees come with their own bona fides and do not need to be "vetted" like unseasoned employees from other backgrounds. This trust can be a mistake if the insider's credentials do not match their intentions.

- **"In-office" services support** Unlike companies that sell commercial "products," many government contractors provide "people" time instead. These contracts are generally referred to as SETA (Scientific Engineering and Technical Assistance) and the contractor physically reports to the sponsoring government organization's office space. This can be most efficient for the government, because the person is available to continuously provide solutions, but it also means that the chain of command and auditing by the company becomes less clear. While there are many regulations that govern who the contractor can officially take orders from on a daily basis, more often than not that person's supervisor is a program manager that does not reside in the same space, and is not aware on a day-to-day basis of the person's activities. This leaves room for error and lack of oversight on what the person is doing, and roughly resembles the lack of clear back office auditing in the previous chapter on rogue traders.

Threats

The threats faced by government contractors are the same for any company, but with the complication that they *also* face the same threats faced by the government organizations their employees are detailed to. Employees of government contractors have the capability both to sabotage their company's systems and to sabotage the systems of the government organization that is sponsoring them. In addition, because in the end contractors are profit-driven companies, they are always searching for less expensive ways to accomplish the same task. In one of the cases we will talk about in this chapter, a large prime contractor subcontracted out to a company that brought employees from mainland China to Dayton, Ohio, for a job. Most of these employees were only paid $500 a month, a fraction of what a programmer from the United States would have cost. This trend to outsource information technology needs is not new, but it is an increasing trend that is analyzed in depth in a master's thesis titled, "Outsourcing Information Technology and the Insider Threat."[2]

Explore More...

Stay Alert at Trade Shows

In Chapter 5: Commercial, we highlighted the need to be mindful of accidental disclosure at trade shows. For government contractors, the threat is two-fold: 1) Government contractors need to guard trade secrets like any other company, and 2) Governments do not attend trade shows, but government contractors *do*. This means that people may try to get to government secrets through you.

There are countless reports of incidents involving overzealous foreign nationals approaching contractors at these shows (I just experienced one last month.) An excellent detailed account of one such incident is found in the Office of National Counterintelligence Executive Archives from September 2001. This story describes a contractor attending a booth at the American Institute of Aeronautics and Astronautics (AIAA) and Ballistic Missile Defense Organization (BMDO) Technology Conference and Exhibit July 23-26, 2001, in Virginia.[3]

All attendees of the conference were required to have a security clearance of at least Secret level. Outside of the classified conference, unclassified (but sensitive) booths were set up in the exhibit hall for attendees of the conference. In this case, the contractor was manning the booth for his company when a man walked up and began taking copies of the hand-outs available for the attendees. The attendee of the booth could see that the man did not have a badge. When he was questioned by the contractor, he explained that he was part of the press and was allowed to be there without a badge. The contractor then asked what media organization he was affiliated with, and he replied, "Beijing Daily News." The contractor asked to view his invitation to the conference, and when he could not provide one he took the documents from the man's hand and walked him to the security desk. Details of the incident were later turned over to the FBI and the 902nd Military Intelligence Group. They later determined that the man had come in through a back entrance near the kitchen and was a Chinese national "known to target U.S. technical information."[4]

Case Study: Trusted Air Force Master Sergeant Retires and Joins TRW

This is a case of an employee that is treated in an overly trusted manner because of his background and past access to classified information. Luckily, it appears as if all the detection and warning systems in place detected his behavior prior to significant damage being done. He was detained and arrested by the FBI as he was boarding a flight overseas with classified information.

Topic

A trusted Air Force E-7 (Master Sergeant) retires and continues his career involving intelligence and signals for defense contractor TRW.

Source

UNITED STATES OF AMERICA
V.
Brian Regan
Case Number: 1:01-CR-00405-GBL-1

Details

Brian Patrick Regan was a patriot. When he turned 18 he enlisted in the United States Air Force (USAF) and served in it continuously until he retired as an E-7 (Master Sergeant) twenty years later. As part of his enlistment, Regan took the following oath of office:

> I ... do solemnly swear that I will support and defend the Constitution of the United States against all enemies, foreign and domestic; that I will bear true faith and allegiance to the same; and that I will obey the orders of the President of the United States and the orders of the officers appointed over me, according to regulations and the Uniform Code of Military Justice. So help me God.

While in the USAF, he specialized in the field of signals intelligence analysis and had tours of duty that included:

- 1991–1994: As a Communications Denial Analyst and an Air Defense Analyst at USAF Intelligence Support Group at the Pentagon
- 1994–1995: As a student at Joint Military Intelligence College
- 1995–2000: Assigned to the Signals Intelligence Applications Integration Office at the Headquarters of the National Reconnaissance Office (NRO)

While in these intelligence-related positions, Regan was exposed to extremely sensitive compartmented programs and on or about November 25, 1991, he signed a Classified Information Nondisclosure Agreement that included the following text:

2. I hereby acknowledge that I have received a security indoctrination concerning the nature and protection of classified information, including the procedures to be followed in ascertaining whether other persons to whom I contemplate disclosing this information have been approved for access to it, and that I understand these procedures.

3. I have been advised that the unauthorized disclosure, unauthorized retention, or negligent handing of classified information by me could cause damage or irreparable injury to the United States or could be used to advantage by a foreign nation. I hereby agree that I will never divulge classified information to anyone unless: (a) I have officially verified that the recipient has been properly authorized by the United States Government to receive it; or (b) I have been given prior written notice of authorization from the United States Government Department or Agency … responsible for the classification of the information or last granting me a security clearance that such disclosure is permitted. I understand that if I am uncertain about the classification status of information, I am required to confirm from an authorized official that the information is unclassified before I may disclose it, except to a person as provided in (a) or (b), above. I further understand that I am obligated to comply with laws and regulations that prohibit unauthorized disclosure of classified information.

For Regan, it was the tour at NRO that changed the direction of his career. While in the USAF he learned about the NRO and had access to significant amounts of sensitive classified information. According to the charging documents, he worked in a group that was responsible for "focusing signals intelligence support for tactically deployed military units." When he retired, he became employed by defense contractor TRW and continued being assigned to NRO.

Despite his repeated oaths and signed agreements, somewhere between 1999 and 2001 Regan wrote a letter to Saddam Hussein, the President of Iraq, or the intelligence chief of Iraq, sealed it in an envelope, and prepared it for Iraqi intelligence agents. He also included a second letter that contained instructions for the Iraqi agents. Excerpts of the original letters follow (note that both letters contain uncorrected spelling errors).

The "instructions" letter from Regan to the Iraqi agents:

```
This letter is confidential and directed to your
president, ( ) or intelligence chief, ( ). Please
pass this letter via diplomatic pouch and do not
discuss the existence of this letter either in
your offices or homes or via any electronic means
(phone, telex, fax,). If you do not follow these
instructions the existence of this letter and its
contents may be detected and collected by U.S.
intelligence agencies. Do not open the internal
letter prior to it reaching the intended recipi-
ents, if you do and the contents are compromise
you will have to answer to your president as to
why you were so curious.
```

The second letter to Hussein contained the following instructions:

```
This letter (AA12194107) has been encoded to pre-
vent the comprising of the information it con-
tains. The codes to decode this letter were sent
to the following address listed below prior to
sending this letter. That letter had similar
instructions on how to handle the sealed letter it
contains. If the break out codes are not delivered
let me know by placing the ad listed below in the
Sunday Washington post (automobile classified sec-
tion). If I see that ad I will resend the codes
either to the same address or a new one. Please
secure both of these letters and limit access to
only essential personnel. Should the contents of
these letters be comprised to any foreign intelli-
```

gence agencies your country will lose a great opportunity.

The decoded letter included:

I AM A MIDDLE EAST, NORTH AFRICAN ANALYST FOR THE CENTRAL INTELLIGENCE AGENCY (CIA). I AM WILLING TO COMMIT ESPOSINAGE AGAINST THE UNITED STATES BY PROVIDING YOUR COUNTRY WITH HIGHLY CLASSIFIED INFORMATION. I HAVE A TOP SECRET CLEARANCE AND HAVE ACCESS TO DOCUMENTS FROM ALL OF THE US INTELLIGENCE AGENCIES (NATIONAL SECURITY AGENCY (NSA), DEFENSE INTELLIGENCE AGENCY (DIA), CENTRAL COMMAND (CENTCOM), AS WELL AS SMALER AGENCIES. I HAVE BEEN WITH THE CIA FOR OVER TWENTY YEARS AND WILL BE RETIRING IN TWO YEARS. I FEEL THAT I DESERVE MORE THAN THE SMALL PENSION I WILL RECIVE FOR ALL OF THE YEARS OF SERVICE AT THE CIA. I HAVE INCLUDED THE COVER PAGE TO A CLASSIFIED CIA INTERNAL NEWS BULLITEN, AS WELL AS TABLE OF CON-TENS TO THE JOINT-SERVICE TACTICIAL EXPLOTAION OF NATIONAL SYSTEMS (JTENS), AND SOME SATELIGHT PHOTOS AS PROOF OF MY POSTION AND WILLINGNESS TO PROVIDE YOUR COUNTRY WITH CLASSIFIED DOCUMENTS.

IF I COMMIT ESPONAGE I WILL BE PUTTING MY SELF AND FAMILY AT GREAT RISK. IF I AM CAUGHT I WIL BE ENPRISIONED FOR THE REST OF MY LIFE, IF NOT EXE-CUTED FOR THIS DEED. MY WIFE AND DAUGHTER WILL BE DISCRASED AND HARRASHED BY EVERYONE IN OUR COMMU-NITY. CONCIDERIN THE RISK I AM ABOUT TO TAKE I WILL REQUIRE A MINIMUN PAYMENT OF THIRTEEN MIL-LION US DOLLARS WIRE TRANSFERRED IN SWISS FRANS, THE EXACT AMOUNT (( )) BEFORE I WILL RISK MY LIFE. THERE ARE MANY PEOPLE FROM MOVIE STARS TO ATHEATHS IN THE US WHO RECIVEING TENS OF MILLIONS OF DOLLARS A YEAR FOR THEIR TRIVIAL CONTRABU-TIONS, IF I AM GOING TO RISK MY LIFE AND THE FUTURE OF MY FAMILY I AM GOING TO GET PAID A FAIR

PRICE. THE INFORMATION I AM OFFERIN WILL COMPRISE
US INTELLIGENCE SYSTGEMS WORTH HUNDREDS OF BIL-
LIONS OF DOLLARS. THIRTEEN MILLION IS A SMALL
PRICE TO PAY FOR WHAT YOU WILL RECIVE.

I WILL PROVIDE YOUR COUNTRY WITH THE JTENS
MANUAL. THIS TOP SECET DOCUMENT WILL PROVIDE YOU
WITH HIGHLY SECRETIVE INFORMAION ON US SATELITES,
AIRBOURN AND GROUND INTELLIGENCE SYSTEMS. YOU CAN
SEE FROM THE TABLE OF CONTENS AND THE SIGNATURE
SHEET WHAT AGENCIES PROVIDED INFORMATION TO BE
INCLUDED IN THIS DOCUMENT AND THE LEVEL OF DETAIL
AND IMPROTANCE. YOUR FIRST THIRTEEN MILLION WILL
BUY YOU VITAL INFORAITON ON SYSTEMS THAT COST THE
U.S. HUNDREDS OF BILLIONS TO BUILD, OPERATE AND
MAINTAIN.

I WILL ALSO PROVIDE YOU WITH A LIST OF THE ACTUAL
LOCATIONS AND ORBITS OF ALL OF THE US SPY
SATELITES, WHICH CAN BE LOADED, INTO ANY STANDARD
OBITALGY SOFTWARE PACKAGE. THIS TOP SECRET INFOR-
MATION WILL PROVIDE YOUR COUNTRY WITH THE SCHED-
ULED TIMES US SATELITES WILL BE OVERHEAD AND
COLLECTIN GAGAINST YOUR COUNTRY AND WHEN THESE
SYSTEMS ARE OUT OF RANGE OF YOUR COUNTRY.

I WILL ALSO SEND YOU A NUMBER OF INTELLIGENCE
REPORTS AND DOCUMENTS FROM A NUMBER OF INTELLI-
GENCE AGENCIES ON A VARIETY OF TOPICS RELATED TO
IRAQ. THIS WILL GIVE YOU INSITE INTO WHAT THE US
KNOWS ABOUT YOUR COUNTRY AS WELL AS EXAMPLES OF
THE QUALITY OF THE SIGNALS INTELLIGENCE (SIGINT)
AND IMAGERY INTELLIGENCE (IMGINT) SYSTEMS THAT
SPY ON YOUR DAILY. THAT INFORMATION ALONE IS
WORTH MANY TIMS WHAT I AM REQUESTING . . . .

AS A BONUS I WILL ALSO PROVIDE YOU WITH A NUMBER
OF INTELLIGECE REPORTS AND DOCUMENTS ON YOUR
ADVISARY IRAN.

THRITEEN MILLION IS A SMALL PRICE TO PAY TO HAVE
SOMEONE WITHIN THE HEART OF US INTELLIGENCE
AGENCY PROVIDING YOU WITH VITAL SECRETS. THE
KNOWEDEGE I WILL PROVIDE YOU WITH CAN SAVE YOU
BILLIONS, BY IMPROVING YOUR WEAPON SYSTEMS TAC-
TICS, WHICH WILL LIMIT THE US CAPABILITY TO
TARGET AND DESTRY YOUR EXPENSIVE AND VITAL WEAPON
SYSTEMS AND FACILITIES. I DOUGHT THIS SMALL
AMOUNT OF MONEY MEANS THAT MUCH TO YOUR GOVERN-
MENT BUT IF YOU ARE NOT WILLING TO PAY THE PRICE
DON'T BOTHER CONTACTING ME, THE PRICE IS NON-
NEGOTIOALE. I AM SURE YOU WILL RECOGNIZE THIS
OFFER A SA CHANCE OF A LIFETIME AND WELL WORTH
THE MONEY.

IF YOU ARE NESISTANT TO INVEST THE THIRTEEN MIL-
LION BECAUSE YOU DONT KNOW IF THE TRANFER PROCE-
DURE WILL WORK SUCCESSFULLY THEN I WILL ALLOW YOU
TO TEST OUT THE PROCESS TO SEE HOW SAFE AND
EFFECTIVE IT CAN BE. INSTEAD OF SENDING THE DOCU-
MENTS LISTED ABOVE AS THE FIRST SHIPPMENT I WILL
SEND YOU THE ( ) AS PROFF OF THE SOUNDNESS OF THE
PROCESS. THIS WILL COST YOU ONE MILLION DOLLARS
IN SWISS FRANS SEND THIS EXACT AMOUNT (( )) TO
TEST THE PROCESS AND ONCE YOU ARE SATISFIED YOU
CAN RECEIVE THE INFORMATION AND GET IT OUT OF THE
us WITHOUT BEING DETECTED BY THE FBI OR CIA, WE
CAN PROCEDE WITH THE THIRTEEN MILLION DOLLAR
TRANSACTION.

The letter continues on with several paragraphs of discussion and instructions
and contains one significant line that should be highlighted:

IF THE US GOVERNMENT FINDS OUT WHAT IS GOING ON
THEY WILL SHUT DOWN YOUR VITAL FLOW OF INFORMA-
TION AND ATTEMPT TO NUTRULIZE AS MUCH OF THE COM-
PRIMISED INFORMATION AS POSSIBLE. THEY WILL
ATTEMPT TO PUNISH YOUR COUNTRY AS WELL AS ME FOR
THIS ACTIVITY. **THIS RESPONSE IS WHY VERY FEW**

**WITHIN THE US INTELLIGENCE COMMUNITY WOULD EVEN
THINK OF SPYING AGAINST THE US.**

At the same time Regan produced an almost identical letter delivered to Libyan agents for delivery to Muammar Qadhafi. For Qadhafi, Regan offered to sell a document named "Libyan Capability Study, Libyan Air Defense" as well as sensitive satellite, early-warning systems, and communications information. Court records indicate that on or about Wednesday, June 13, 2001, Regan used a computer at the Crofton Public Library in Crofton, Maryland, and conducted the following searches on the Internet:

"Embassies of the Arab World"

"Embassies: Laos thru Luxembourg Embassy Resource"

"Foreign Embassies in Paris"

"Foreign Embassies in Switzerland"

"Libyian Embassies and Consulates of Libya @ Embassy World"

"People's Bureau of the Socialist People's Libyan Arab Jamahiriya"

From these searches he accessed a Web site that had the addresses and phone numbers of Embassies for Iraq, Libya, and other Arab countries located in Washington, DC. Then on or about Sunday June 24, 2001, he returned to the same library and conducted the following Internet searches:

- Iraqi embassy"
- Iraqi embassy swiss"
- "Embassies in Switzerland"
- "Foreign Embassies in france"
- "Foreign Embassies in germany"
- "Foreign Embassies in germany of iraq"
- "Foreign Embassies in germany of libya"
- "Swiss hostels"

Two days later (June 26, 2001) he boarded a Lufthansa Airlines plane at Dulles International Airport and flew to Germany. He flew back on July 3, 2001. His suitcase contained glue and packing table.

NOTE

Intelink is a large, classified network used to share information among different Intelligence organizations that is modeled after the Internet.

A demonstration of the interface for the network is at: http://www.topsecretnet.com/intelink/. More about the network's creation can be found in the book, "Top Secret Intranet: How U.S. Intelligence Built Intelink – the World's Largest, Most Secure Network," by Fredrick Thomas Martin.

On July 30, 2001, Regan began working in the NRO facility in Virginia for TRW. He was first required to take part in several months of NRO computer-based training. On August 1, 2001, at approximately 8:00 A.M., he reported to his NRO-assigned computer system to being his training of the day. Despite being outside of his official duties, forty minutes into his training session, Regan accessed the classified system named Intelink. According to court records he "opened and viewed several Intelink files containing classified information relating to a particular Libyan missile test range." Just days after this, on August 2, 2001, he applied for a temporary duty position located in Europe, but was rejected. Then nearly every day that he was in his office from August 6, 2001, to August 23, 2001, he "accessed Intelink and viewed classified information relating to military facilities in Iraq, Iran, Libya, and the People's Republic of China, as well as classified documents related to current United States intelligence-collection capabilities against those countries." This activity was not part of his official duty at TRW.

The next timeline details the days up to his arrest for attempted espionage:

- August 11, 2001. Regan purchased a plane ticket to Zurich, Switzerland (departing August 23 and returning on August 30, 2001); about the same time he told his TRW supervisor that he would be vacationing with his family in Orlando, Florida, during those dates.

- August 15, 2001. Regan accessed classified information outside the scope of his work from Intelink. This information included classified images (one was of a mobile surface-to-air missile launch facility in Iraq and another was a surface-to-surface missile facility in China).

- August 17, 2001. Handwritten geo-coordinates and other notations from the images viewed on August 15, 2001, were found discarded on a torn piece of paper in the burn bag in Regan's office.

- August 23, 2001. Regan accessed Intelink at approximately 8:03 a.m. and viewed an image dated "21 August 2001." This classified image was of the same surface-to-surface missile facility he had viewed previously, and this time he wrote handwritten notes from the image in a small notebook he carried in his pocket. Around 10:49 a.m. he left his office and checked his luggage in at the airport. Shortly after that he returned to spend several more hours at the NRO. At 3:55 p.m. he left his office for good and checked in for his flight destined for Switzerland. However, while he was riding on the shuttle to his plane, at approximately 5:05 p.m., he was approached by an FBI agent and placed under arrest. When he was searched, the notebook containing the handwritten geo-coordinates he had recorded early in the day was found in his pockets. Several pages of annotations were found, as well as paper containing a coding system he had used for the coordinates. In addition, his wallet contained a piece of paper that had the addresses and telephone numbers of:

- Embassy of the People's Republic of China in Bern, Switzerland
- Embassy of the People's Republic of China in Vienna, Austria
- Embassy of Iraq in Vienna, Austria
- Iraqi Interests Section in Paris, France

A second piece of paper concealed in his right shoe contained several other addresses of embassies.

When his residence was subsequently searched, evidence related to his queries about "offshore IBC and bank accounts/credit cards" was found. Brian Patrick Regan was sentenced to life in prison for Attempted Espionage (Iraq), Attempted Espionage (China), and Gathering National Defense Information.

Analysis

The problem with this case is that Regan's résumé does not show his true intentions. His credentials highlight a patriot that enlisted in the Air Force at the age of 18, retired, and then continued to serve the country as a government subcontractor. Despite this illusion, his true intentions come out in his letters when he wrote that people within the intelligence community do not spy because they are afraid of being caught. Perhaps we are more optimistic than we should be, but we sincerely hope that the vast majority of the people in this community do not spy because they are loyal to their country.

> **NOTE**
>
> One classic case of past dangers associated with insider threat and government subcontractors is the story of Christopher Boyce. His activities are detailed in the book *The Falcon and the Snowman* by Lindsey Robert, 1979, and in a slightly more recent (and sensationalized) movie of the same name.

Case Study: Chinese National Accesses Sensitive Passwords on Critical AF Logistics System

Unknown to the colonel in charge of the REMIS system, a subcontractor of defense giant Litton PRC has hired Chinese nationals to work on his software. One of those employees, Zhangyi "Steven" Liu, discovers lax security and he easily obtains full access to the computer system and a copy of all the passwords.

Topic

Chinese National employed as a subcontractor to Litton PRC

Source

UNITED STATES OF AMERICA
V.
Zhangyi Liu a.k.a Steven Liu
Case Number: 3:97-CR-00003-MRM-1

Details

Zhangyi "Steven" Liu was a computer programmer from mainland China who worked for a company (Shanghai Tandem Software Systems) that subcontracted to Litton PRC in Dayton, Ohio. He was a single child born to poor parents in Shanghai, China. Academically he was a good student, and he graduated in the top 10 percent of his class with a bachelor's degree in electronic engineering from Shanghai Jiao Tong University in 1994. The job at Shanghai Tandem Software Systems was his first, and he was brought to the US by the company and paid $500 a month plus about $35 per diem. Liu's rent (apartment shared among four people), utilities, insurance, and use of an older (shared) car were also provided by the company. He lived modestly and sent the money he earned back to his parents in China.

In his position at Shanghai Tandem Software Systems he was responsible for working on software improvements to the unclassified software system named REMIS at Wright-Patterson Air Force Base. REMIS stands for the Reliability & Maintainability Information System and is a "$148M logistics system used for tracking aircraft and weapons systems mission capability data, such as maintenance information, missile and communications-electronic information, and aircraft inventory data."[5] REMIS is unclassified but is considered to be highly sensitive.

While working on the software, Liu looked around at the files on the computer that he had access to. One of those files was a program named "ffup," which gave a user access to all files on the computer system. He used this program that had been left behind as a shortcut by another developer to copy all of the passwords on the system.[6]

Two weeks later, alert system administrator Jeffrey Wood discovered the intrusion. Just one day before Liu was scheduled to return to China he was arrested. Air Force's Col. William Colmer, who is responsible for managing over 170 information systems, testified that access to REMIS could provide an adversary with "a general sense of the overall reliability and available of crucial weapons systems."[7] Furthermore, Colmer testified that more than $350,000 was spent making thorough checks to search for backdoors and changes in software that could have been installed by Liu with his elevated access. One federal official interviewed by the *Dayton Daily News* said:

> The real fear was not that (Lui) had discovered something helpful to a foreign government. The fear is that he was in a position to put bugs in the program and cause the program to go down at a critical time. What happens if you can't fly planes because nobody can tell the status of the planes? [8]

In court, Liu told U.S. Magistrate Judge Michael Merz that he was sorry and that he was "like a kid who found a toy… (he was) allowed to walk in a room of secrets. They put the tools in the room without ever telling me not to use them, and just expecting that I wouldn't." However, OSI Special Agent Karen Mathews said that Liu told her he "wanted to own the system" and that he shared the passwords he found with another Chinese programmer. In addition, according to reports, Liu and five other Chinese nationals working on this project failed lie detector tests.[9]

Initially, in May 1998, Liu was sentenced to six months in jail with a fine of $5,000. But with concerns that Liu was not properly counseled when he confessed, the judge allowed him to withdraw his plea. At the same time, public defender Randolph Alden request a new trial quoting the results of the Air Force Office of Special Investigations report that "levels of access (on REMIS) had not been established; therefore, it was impossible for Liu to have exceeded his authorized access." The judge ordered that his confinement could be served concurrently on work-release in California, where he was offered a job by XYPRO Technology Corp. The job offer was prompted by Dale E.S. Blommendahl, who is an executive member of the XYPRO staff, and is the designer of a software package named "Safeguard" that would have protected the REMIS system from this event. Safeguard was installed following Liu's arrest.

On January 14, 2000, Liu was re-sentenced to four months in prison and one year of supervised release. At the sentencing, Liu told the judge, "This is probably the most terrible mistake I've ever made in my life."

Analysis

In court, Col. Colmer, who directs the REMIS system, testified that he was unaware that Liu and 10 other Chinese nationals were on a subcontract by the USAF. Beyond the significant problem of lack of security applied to the computer systems themselves, there was also a lack of personnel security and a lack of clear communications.

This is possibly also a problem caused by the financial motivations of companies attempting to provide the least expensive solution. Dayton attorney Gary W. Gottschlich, who previously represented Liu, said:

> Steven is a scapegoat for their own stupidity and laziness. It's just simply economics. There are many foreign nationals from around the world working on such projects. They're available and they're cheap.[10]

Just today my company (a small government contractor) received an unsolicited call from a business offering to outsource our computer programming needs to Russia at a rate of $16/hour. Good or bad, offshore programming is on the rise, and security procedures need to be changed to account for these scenarios.

Summary

Government contractors face the same threats as both government organizations and corporations combined. They are pressured with conducting the same type of sensitive, high-level security activities as the government, but with the additional demand of turning a profit. In addition, the lack of bureaucracy that makes companies appealing to governments can mean lack of oversight and enable lone insiders to hide their activity like rogue traders without a visible back office.

Employees operating within government contractors need to be especially aware of the danger of insider threat and have management support for the resources necessary to combat it.

Endnotes

1. Richards Heuer, Jr. and Katherine Herbig. "Espionage by the Numbers: A Statistical Overview." www.wasc.noaa.gov/wrso/security_guide/numbers.htm (accessed November 2005).
2. Valerie L. Caruso. "Outsourcing Information Technology and the Insider Threat." (Master's thesis, Air Force Institute of Technology, 2003). http://research.airuniv.edu/papers/ay2003/afit/AFIT-GIR-ENG-03-01.pdf (accessed November 2005).
3. "Alert Employee Thwarts Overt Intelligence Collection Attempts by a Chinese National." Counterintelligence News and Developments (CIND) 3 (September 2001). www.nacic.gov/archives/nacic/news/2001/sep01.html#99 (accessed November 2005).
4. Ibid.
5. Valerie L. Caruso, 109.
6. "Hackers' Victims Often All Too Willing." Inter@active Week (July 1997). http://www.image-in.co.il/HTML/NETECT2/sec-5.htm (accessed November 2005).
7. Wes Hills. "Hacker Had AF Spooked." Dayton Daily News, December 12, 1997, 1A.
8. Wes Hills. "Security Breach Penalty Stuns AF." Dayton Daily News, April 11, 1999, 1B.
9. Wes Hills. "Hacker Had AF Spooked."
10. Wes Hills. "Security Breach Penalty Stuns AF."

Part IV
Analysis

Chapter 8

Profiles of the Insider Threat

Solutions in this chapter:

- General Types of Profiling
- Base Profile
- Limitations
- High-End Profile
- Categories of Inside Attacks
- Foreign Intelligence
- Stance

Introduction

"Trust no one, suspect everyone, and make counter accusations" is a saying you hear often in the insider threat community. While it is often said as a joke, there is some inherent value to it. Oftentimes companies suffer large amounts of damage and problems because they have too much trust. "Johnny would never do anything wrong; he is our most loyal employee." Then, after there is a financial loss, you hear the reverse of "how could Johnny have done that to us after everything we have done for him?"

While a dose of healthy paranoia is a good thing, you have to strike a balance between trusting everyone and trusting no one. Too much of either will cause problems and lead to unsuccessful organizations and business relationships. If you never trust anyone, from a personal standpoint you will never fully get to enjoy what life has to offer. From a business standpoint you will often frustrate and annoy your employees because they will not be given the additional responsible they deserve because you do not trust them. From a personal sanity standpoint you will never feel empowered enough to ever delegate any work and will feel stressed and burnt out from matters that others could easily handle for you. This is often the reason that really smart, intelligent people make such poor managers: they are afraid to delegate. They do not trust than anyone can do the job as well as them or they do not want to give away the control of information. Knowledge is power but only if you share it in a selective manner. Not willing to trust anyone else with the information will actually decrease the value of the data because no one else can use it to make effective decisions. On the other hand, not properly controlling it and giving it away to everyone has its own series of problems.

This brings us to the other extreme: trusting everyone. There are certain cases where restricting information is a good thing to do. Sometimes, if people have information they do not need, they can be more tempted to do harm with it than if they didn't have it. While it is tempting to walk through life thinking no one is going to cause any harm or do anything malicious against you, this mind-set will often backfire on you. Therefore, it is good to realize that some selective measures need to be put in place to determine whether someone can be trusted or not.

The way most of us do this is through profiling. We know what to look for in a person and if someone acts a certain way we are more or less likely to trust them.

General Types of Profiling

We profile all the time and do not even realize it. When we meet a new person and we walk away thinking that person is a jerk, a mean person, etc., it is usually because there were certain things that we examined or picked up on that led us to that conclusion. It would take a much longer period of time to truly know a person's personality and how they act, but there are indicators and signs that we use to make a determination. Even though in an hour-long meeting, the person could have had a bad day or been very tired, you can still do a pretty good job of figuring them out in a short period of time. One key management technique that people use that is a form of profiling is: if someone does not impress you in the first week they are on the job, they most likely will not impress you. Now, this technique can have a lot of holes punched in it because the person might not have been given the right opportunities, they might be shy, there could be numerous reasons, but you are taking actions they perform and forming a profile of that person and judging that person based on the profile, no matter how right or wrong it is. The interesting thing is most people do a pretty good job at profiling people.

My father-in-law was a police officer when my wife and I got married and I knew that he invited several of his fellow officers to the wedding. Even though I had never met them before, I went up to most of them, introduced myself, and said, "So how long have you worked on the force with my father-in-law?" They usually gave me a weird look and said, "How did you know?" My answer was that I could just tell. People in different professions look and act a certain way and if you know to look for those behavior traits, you can easily profile someone and make a determination about their background, personality, and profession. Yes, I am one of those weird people who by looking at you can tell what you do for a living.

Profiling is the whole concept of the game Spot the Fed that is played at DefCon each year in Las Vegas. The idea is that you watch how people act, what they do, and how they look, and you try to spot the federal enforcement officials who come to the conference each year but are dressed in civilian clothes. One of my friends who is a fed goes every year and even though he dresses to fit in with t-shirts, ripped shorts, and purple hair, and looks like everyone else, he always gets caught every year. It is hard to put into words, but even thought he looks the same, he still sticks out like a sore thumb.

There are many ways of profiling, but the general methods that work with detecting the insider threat are the following:

- Actions

- Appearance

- Instinct

People that are lying tend to not look you in the eye when they are talking, start playing with their fingers, twirling their hair, and start to look uncomfortable. Now these are all extreme examples but they highlight the point that there are behavior patterns associated with different actions that someone is performing. Typically, with the insider, we are looking for actions that would indicate nervous behavior or behavior that shows someone is uncomfortable in a given situation or trying to cover something up. Anyone who is a parent can attest to this, that if you walk in the room, based on the expression on your kid's face or how he looks, you can tell he did something wrong or he is up to no good.

You can also see this with employees when you walk into someone's office and she jumps up from the keyboard quickly or starts clicking rapidly on the screen or even turns off the monitor if you start to walk around to the back of her desk. Her actions are telling you that she is trying to cover up something or is up to no good. While there can also be reasonable explanations for why people do certain things, actions speak louder than words.

A great example of profiling someone based on actions is with the Scott Peterson trial. Many people thought he was guilty and when you asked them why, they said, "Did you see the picture of him on the news during the trial?" He showed no remorse, he was not upset, his actions or lack thereof showed that he must be guilty. Now, hopefully the jury listened to all of the facts, but we as humans are going to judge people right, wrong, or indifferent based on their behaviors and corresponding actions.

The key thing with profiling an insider is if you see actions that look suspicious, the next step is to monitor the person closely. Remember to make sure you have proper policies in place, that you have taken away the expectation of privacy, and that you do it in a consistent manner. If it continues, talking to the person in a non-confrontational way could also cause the person to show other actions that could be watched to help determine their true intent.

Now, before we go further, I want to point out that profiling is a science that takes years of professional training and expertise to perfect. This chapter is meant to just touch the surface on different things to look for and to be aware of.

The next way that we profile people is based on appearance. While I do not like this method because it could cause you to jump to false conclusions, people do it. If you look at my class picture from when I was in 4th grade, your immediate response is "What a geek." Yes, I was the pudgy-faced kid with the green pants, yellow shirt, and plaid jacket on: I was a stud. If people come into work with sandals, jeans, and a t-shirt, we profile them differently than if they are wearing a pressed suit and a stylish tie. However, this one you have to be very careful with in regards to insider threat. As you will see, an insider attacker can play any role, so just because someone dresses sharp or does not dress up does not make them any more or less likely to be a potential attacker.

The last type of profiling we perform is based on instinct. You're not sure why you feel a certain way but you really like that person or you cannot explain why but you really do not trust that person. This is sometimes referred to as the gut test, the smell test, or trusting your instinct. You are not always sure why, but something just does not seem right about the person or how he acts. If you have been around for a while and have worked with enough people, you can usually become a pretty good judge of characters and people.

Base Profile

We have talked about there being no set demographic profile of people likely to commit insider threat, but there are some basic characteristics of those people that have been caught. This section will look at the similarities in the insiders that have been caught and potentially prosecuted. This section is what we are calling the lower-end attacker. The reason being is that the high-end attacker does not get caught. The base characteristics of the people who have been caught are the following:

- They had minimal technical knowledge.
- They worked at various positions.
- Their attacks focused on IP.
- They were money driven.
- They did not fully understand repercussions.
- They somehow tipped other people off about what they were doing.
- Anger played some part in their attack.
- External indications of their attack were evident.
- Their actions make an adverse impact on the company.

Minimal Technical Knowledge

Most of us have probably watched too many movies and too many re-runs of James Bond to think that the insider is highly technical using the latest and greatest gadgets to sneak into the facility and escape in the same stealth, covert manner. While there might be one or two high-tech insider attackers, they are definitely not the norm. Most people committing insider threat use low-tech methods with high effectiveness.

There are many reasons for this, but one reason is that an attacker is always going to attack the path of least resistance or look for the weakest link to try to break in. Since most companies are not set up or prepared to deal with the insider, their organizations are wide open. Remember, the security of most companies is built around a strong perimeter to protect from external attacks. They have minimal, if any, protection against an attack that occurs within the trusted walls of their organization.

Therefore, the easiest way to compromise an organization from the inside is as simple as copying, e-mailing, or deleting a file off the server. Attackers are not using any special tools or techniques. They are using the normal methods they use to do their jobs, but change their motive to do harm instead of helping the company. Most people have access to some information, data, or systems that, if it were destroyed, modified, or compromised, could cause harm to the company. Now, instead of accessing the file in the normal course of their jobs, they purposely delete it or attach it to a hotmail e-mail so that it gets sent to their personal accounts or an e-mail account of a competitor.

While the high-tech methods make great movies, things are so bad at most organizations that just utilizing the standard operating procedures will yield the end results the attacker is looking for. The problem with insiders using existing tools that they use to perform their everyday jobs is that there is nothing outwardly suspicious about what they are doing. If your company does not sanction steganography as an authorized tool (which very few companies do), the mere fact that you have it running on your system is highly suspicious and in some cases enough evidence to take further disciplinary action against the individual.

I have actually worked on investigations where the insider used steganography. When I tell people about the case, they think it is very cool; however, it was actually very simple. The company ran spyware-like scanning programs on all the desktops. One of the checks it performed was to look for stools.exe. It found it on a computer. Since there was no valid reason for this program or type of program to be on the system, it led to an immediate investigation, which determined that the person was extracting information out of the organization. Because this insider left a suspicious exe on the desktop, he was caught. It would be easier if attackers were using high-tech, non-sanctioned tools, because it would be easier to catch them. However, the fact that they are using normal tools that should be on the computer makes it very difficult to trace and detect.

Hopefully, as organizations implement stronger security measures against insider threat, insiders will be forced to install new and different tools, which will make it easier to detect them. However, now they are in essence not doing anything out of the ordinary or different from what they would normally do, which enables attackers to fly under the radar and be harder to detect.

Worked at Various Positions

One of my favorite magazine advertisements states at the top of the page, "We just caught the latest computer hacker at your company." At the bottom of the page are the words, "Betty from accounting," followed by a mug shot of an innocent-looking lady with a smirk on her face. Once again, it is probably the influence of movies, but we have this impression that someone who is going to commit insider threat has to have body piercing, cut-off jeans, and long hair in order to do harm to the company. We think there is no way a well-dressed executive would ever do anything to hurt the company. It is not the outer appearance that determines whether someone will be an inside attacker, it is their inner appearance, which is very hard to tell.

If you look across the board, there is no single position in the company that will make someone more likely to commit an insider threat than another. There is something within the insiders themselves that makes them turn on the company and to justify what they are doing as morally just. From the entry-level data-entry clerk to the senior VP, they all have been known to perform actions that will cause harm to their companies.

Based on my investigation and clients, I have found more and more that the people you would not normally suspect are the ones committing the attacks. The simple reason is: *because* they would not be suspected. In addition, if they are fairly well trusted and high up in an organization, there is also a good chance that they will be brought into the trusted inner circle when the company is investigating the attack. If the insider is also involved with the investigation and knows every step that is being taken, it is trivial for her to stay one step ahead and never get caught. Now, unsolved problems at organizations usually cause uncertainty, so an alternative strategy is for the insider to either plant evidence or start targeting someone who would be a likely target for the attack and have him be the fall person.

The funny thing is that it does not take much to start a witch hunt. If you have someone in an organization of whom everyone is a little leery and there is a major insider investigation occurring, it would probably not take much for the insider to add some uncertainty to the equation and say, "Did anyone else notice so-and-so acting strange?" Most likely, people will jump in and say, "Well, now that you bring it up, I saw that person doing this," and everyone will pretty much jump on top as if they are playing a virtual version of kill the guy.

Therefore, when investigating an insider threat case, do not ever let position or appearance impair your judgment. Judge the facts and only the facts and try to eliminate and filter out any hearsay or information that has not been validated. The difference between a good insider handler and a great insider handler is the great insider handler will look for factual information that can be validated and will base their investigation solely on that information and nothing else. Staying focused is critical to making sure you don't head down the wrong path. Falsely accusing someone of a crime is bad and should be avoided at all cost, but the more disturbing fact is that the real attacker is still at large within your company and most likely knew about the investigation. Since they knew that the company was looking for an insider, most likely they have watched their actions even more closely and the chances of catching them now are even more difficult. When investigating an insider attack, I always say that you only have one chance to catch the person. Why? Because if you do not catch them the first time, there is a good chance you will never get a second chance to catch them. They will either stop or go even more covert so that the chances of catching them the second time are almost impossible.

Attacks Focused on IP

Almost every insider attack at one level or another is focused on intellectual property or IP. This should logically make sense because if the attack was not focused on revealing, modifying, or destroying something of value to the company, then it most likely would not be classified as an insider attack. From the disgruntled employee who wants to cause harm to the company to the advanced attacker who wants to have financial gain, IP is the end state that they are going to focus on.

If I am a disgruntled employee, I want to do something to harm or damage the company. Spray painting the walls in my office, stealing my office furniture, and saying nasty things about my boss in a chat room are really not going to accomplish anything. If I want to cause harm to the company I want to cause monetary loss either directly or indirectly. In most cases if I am going to cause monetary loss, IP has to be involved at some level. If I take a sensitive piece of information like client credit card numbers and I post them to a public site or send them to a newspaper, this is going to cause embarrassment which will result in monetary loss. If I destroy a proposal that the company has been working on for five months, it is due in three days, and I destroyed all copies including backup tapes, that is going to cause monetary loss to the company. If I find a high-end drug and I am able to change the formula so it is no longer produced correctly, that will cause huge monetary loss both directly and indirectly through potential litigation and lawsuits. In any of these cases, without even realizing it, the disgruntled employee is focusing on intellectual property because he knows that is where they he will cause the most pain for the company.

High-end insiders committing corporate espionage are usually directly targeting IP, because that it what will give the companies they are really working for a competitive advantage. If they are going to steal something, they want to steal something that is worth a lot of money so they can either use it for their own personal advantage or sell it off. Why steal a server and try to sell it for $20,000 when anyone can buy a new server for a similar price? However, the formula for a soft drink, a client list, a special way to solve a complex problem, are all things that could be sold for high value because they cannot be bought anywhere else and in essence are one-of-a-kind items.

Money Driven

Donald Trump isn't the only one who cares about money. Money is the driving factor for most insider threat attacks. Either indirectly or directly, money usually plays some part in driving the insider to perform the attacks against the company. It is amazing what money or the lack of money can cause people to do. I have seen cases where people who committed insider attacks were caught and then claimed that it wasn't their fault because they had no choice. They claimed that if they hadn't committed the insider attack they would have lost everything and their families would have been living on the street. While some of these stories can be heart wrenching, money was the primary motivator that caused these people to commit their attacks.

Some argue that in the case of a disgruntled employee that there was no monetary gain for them to destroy a proposal, which is usually correct. However, money was probably a catalyst that caused them to decide to launch the attack in the first place. Many employees become disgruntled when they are not given a raise or are passed up for promotion. So the lack of money is usually a driver for launching the attack. Also, the attack itself is driven by money. It is not driven by the positive influx of money in the pocket of the attacker, but it is driven by the negative money or the loss of revenue that the attack will cause to the company. For some reason, causing the company monetary harm makes attackers think they will feel better about being passed up for a promotion.

Also, as insider attacks continue to grow, you will see the same maturity and evolution that occurred with external attacks. Originally, external attacks were focused on defacement of a Web site or a denial-of-service attack. These attacks caused the company some embarrassment and potential loss but little gain to the attacker. Then they started taking attacks to the next step and breaking in and gaining control of systems to extract data or cause more direct monetary benefit to the attacker.

The same pattern is going to continue to occur with insider threats. Most early publicized attacks were focused on the destruction of resources with a heavy emphasis on the disgruntled employee, with reduction of money to the company as a primary motivator to pay the company back for the harm that was caused to the insider. As time moves on, we will see these attacks begin to mature and become more motivated by money. Instead of the disgruntled employee only causing loss to the company, the employee will decide to make money from the attack to make up for not getting that raise. Now the style of the insider attack will start to look more like the high-end attack where they are stealing sensitive information and selling it to the highest bidder. If you do not think there is a market for this, you have to look closer at what is happening in the dark corners of the Internet.

Insider mercenaries are being sought out and pitched to extract critical assets that organizations are after. One of the prime targets for inside attacks are executives' laptops from different corporations. There are "ads" on the Internet that offer $100,000 dollars for the delivery of a laptop from a vice president of company x. This might seem extreme and risky but it really isn't. If you think about the amount of information that would be on a laptop from a VP at a Fortune 100 company, it easily is worth a million dollars if not more. In cases like this you might have internal employees that see little risk of taking a laptop and let all those zeros blur their vision. They do not even realize the harm they are causing for the company and the potential harm they are causing for themselves.

Not Fully Understanding Repercussions

To most people, the concept of: "you break the law, you go to jail" seems pretty straightforward, it is amazing how people justify their actions and do not think what they are doing is wrong. There have been many studies that show that even in cases where someone is clearly wrong, in their minds they still feel justified with their actions and think they are right. This is the reason it is usually not beneficial to argue with someone, because you are never going to win. They think they are right and you think you are right and that is the foundation for major feuding to occur.

Many people who commit insider attacks do not truly understand how much trouble they could get into if they are caught and more basically do not even realize they are breaking the law. I have seen time and time again insiders not understand why they were arrested. "I was only playing around and deleting some files to get the company back for not promoting me. What is the problem and why am I getting into trouble?"

In one case, where the individual was sentenced to more than eight years in prison, the person had no idea he could actually get arrested and have to go to jail. He thought if he got caught he would be fired but that was it. He had no idea that what he was doing was so bad. This is also an area were policies can help to make sure the line between good and bad are black and white. A policy can clearly lay out what is expected of users and what could be the repercussions if they do not follow the rules.

Gentle reminders are not a bad idea to remind employees that any criminal activity will be punished to the full extent of the law. More and more companies are putting up security policies with reminders to employees that the company takes insider threat seriously. One of my favorite posters says that if you take corporate secrets and share them with a competitor you will receive this gift absolutely free and it has a picture of handcuffs.

Another problem is the addictive nature of insider attacks. With drug addiction, the first time people try a drug they have a small amount. Then, as they become addicted, they slowly increase the dosage and frequency. Before they know it, the problem has gotten out of hand. With insider threat, the attacker might first just take a newsletter and give it to a competitor. This is a public document that is freely distributed across the organization so there is nothing wrong with that. Then the insider might take a sensitive company memo and think that since the newsletter wasn't a big deal, the company memo isn't either. This process continues and before you know it, very sensitive information is being handed over to a competitor. Then, instead of one or two documents a month, the insider is leaking information on a weekly or daily basis. Since it slowly got worse over time, in the attacker's mind it is still not that bad, yet in reality she has gotten in way over her head and the problem is out of control.

While it will not work for everyone, quarterly one- to two-hour awareness sessions reminding people of the dangers of insider threat and what could happen if they get caught could potentially nip some of these problems in the bud.

Other People Knew

In almost every case, someone besides the attacker knew either explicitly what was going on or had an idea that something suspicious was occurring. In the cases where people explicitly knew what was occurring, it is usually because the attackers told them. This is usually the case with a spouse or a trusted friend. There are many reasons the confidants never said anything, but the first is that they thought the attackers were justified in doing what they did. "My husband worked loyally for that company for 10 years. How dare they not promote him? He has a right to take action and be upset." In some cases the spouse or trusted person might have even encouraged the person to do something and provided a support channel that they were doing the right thing. Once again, after the fact, we find that most of the spouses or trusted parties failed to realize the impact the actions would have. In one case, a wife was in tears because she never realized what her husband was doing would put him in jail and ruin their lives. If she had realized that beforehand, she would have stopped him or forced him to get help.

Another reason a trusted third party does not do anything is because they are loyal to the friend or spouse and do not think it is their place to breach that loyalty. "My friend is going through a hard time and needs encouragement and support. He does not need someone to rat on him or get him in trouble." If we are talking about something minor, that logic might hold up, but with major insider attacks, people need to ask themselves how they would feel if their friends' lives are ruined, they are going to jail for five years, and they could have stopped them. Thinking about the big picture is really key in these situations. Sometimes being a true friend requires being put in an uncomfortable position even if your friend might not see it at the time.

The second way people find out about insider attacks is by observing the person do something they shouldn't do. Even in Fortune 50 companies that are very large, it is very difficult if not impossible to do something that no one else knows about or no one else sees. This comes up time and time again where the attacker wonders how in the world someone could have known what he was doing, thinking there was no way anyone could have found out about it. The world is a small place and most attackers are not as good as they think they are. Also, the longer people do something, the sloppier they get. In the beginning they might have covered up their tracks, but over time they get cocky and have a greater chance of getting caught.

If other people knew something was going on, why didn't they say anything? People are afraid to put their noses into someone else's business. They could be afraid there could be retribution against them from the individual or that it is just not their place to start trouble. These people need to step back and realize that if the company loses money, the result will directly affect them: they will not get their raises. If the company goes out of business and they are out of work, it really hits home. As an employee of the company, it is your responsibility to do what is morally right and make sure you watch out for the best interest of the company.

Anger Played Some Part

At some level anger and frustration usually contribute to the reason the insider is committing the attack against the company. It could be a major reason in the case of disgruntled employees who are so frustrated and angry that they feel like they have no other solution but to take that anger out on the company. With a corporate espionage attack, anger usually plays a much smaller role, but could also be the straw that broke the camel's back that causes the employee to turn on the company. Even with the temptation of money, it might not be enough for most people to steal from the company; however since their boss pissed them off and they're a little upset, they decide to make some extra money and give it a try.

The important point about anger is that it is a factor that can be used to detect someone who is or more likely to commit an insider attack against a company. Anger is not something that could easily be hidden and is usually fairly obvious to co-workers, bosses, and contractors. Therefore, if you see someone showing a high degree of visible anger and frustration in the workplace, you might want to keep a close eye on them and see about getting them some sort of anger management or help.

If you think a problem is beyond hope, removing the person from the situation, usually through termination of employment, is the best option. However, if you catch the problem early enough it could potentially be saved. Indications of anger in the workplace should be identified and dealt with quickly to reduce the chances of them turning into major problems and getting out of hand.

External Indication

After a devastating insider attack, many executives say that if there had been some way they could have known that something was going on, they could have acted earlier or prevented it. We know in the case of insider threat that prevention is fairly difficult, but there are some things that can be done to try to prevent it, like strictly controlling access and properly protecting critical assets. However, the more important question is, was there anything that you could have seen that would have helped to detect that there was a problem? In most cases there is usually some external indicator that tells us that someone is about to or in the process of committing insider threat.

It is not uncommon for people to carry around an umbrella even if it is not raining because there are indicators that it might rain. It does not make sense to wait for it to rain and then try to find an umbrella. Planning is much better. With planning we look for indicators of what is going to happen and then plan for those events to occur. In this case it is better if it looks like it is going to rain to bring an umbrella and not need it than to not have an umbrella and get rained on.

The important thing to remember with predications and indicators is that there is some uncertainty involved with these decisions. Sometimes rain is guaranteed, but usually there is some chance but it is not 100%. If the weather forecast say there is a 30% chance of rain, you have to decide whether to bring your umbrella or take a chance. There is the possibility that you react to an indicator like a cloudy sky and it never actually rains. This same thing can occur with insider threat and reacting to external indicators.

Now the good news is that with most insider threat cases there are some indicators that can be used to determine that there is a problem. These external indicators can be broken up into two general categories: business indicators and personal indicators.

Business indicators are things that are happening to the company that could be an indication of a problem. The following are some potential business indicators:

- Poor quarterly earnings

- Loss of key contracts or key customers

- Change over in employees in a given area or department

- Increase in number of attacks or reported incidents

These are all examples of business indicators that could show there is some problem in your organization and with some investigation could point to an insider threat. The good news with business indicators is that they are always present when insider threat is occurring. The bad news is it might not always be obvious that the problem is being caused by insider threat because with any of the aforementioned indicators there are numerous reasons why they could occur, many having nothing to do with insider threat. Therefore, while there are indicators, none of the indicators are exclusive to insider threat.

Going back to the good news, if we can even call it that, if there is an insider attack of any proportion, there will always be an indicator. If there is no impact to the company, it means that the attack did not do any harm or cause any problems for the organization. While harm is usually the end result in the case of a disgruntled employee, if there was no harm or any impact to the company, then in the case of a disgruntled employee the attack did not really work. They might have deleted a file that no one cared about or thought they deleted a file but actually didn't. The bottom line is if they actually targeted critical information and were successful, there will be a business reaction or an indicator.

In the case of a high-end attacker, harm is not usually a short-term goal. One can argue that it is a longer-term goal but if a competitor is targeting a company to give themselves an economic advantage, then ideally over the long term if the company suffers enough harm or goes out of business they have achieved the ultimate competitive advantage. However, the actual attack itself is not usually designed to cause harm. The primary objective is usually to acquire a piece of critical IP. If the insider targeted and successfully acquired a critical piece of IP, there should be some impact to the company. If there was no impact at all, than I would question whether the IP was really critical and why a company was spending money and resources to keep it confidential when there was no reason it needed to be kept secret. The whole reason information needs to be kept protected is that if the information was made public, it would cause harm to the company. Harm can come in the form of losing market share or revenue, suffering embarrassment, etc., but the bottom line is there has to be some repercussions; otherwise, it does not make sense to put energy into protecting something.

We do not want to get into the syndrome where our new hammer is insider threat and everything is a nail. I am sure we have all seen this occur where someone drinks a little too much of the "Kool-Aid" and now everything must be caused by that one problem. A system goes down; it must be insider threat. Johnny does not show up for work; he must be committing an insider attack. The list could go on and on. What we want to do is just keep insider threat as an option. For example, if the company did not make as much on a new product release, which contributed to the fact that the company did not make their numbers, a little investigation should be done. If the main reason has to do with a competitor beating them to market and no one can figure out how the competitor did this, then insider threat should be considered as an option. However, if the reason the product did not make money was because there were design problems and the company admitted that they rushed and made mistakes, then blaming it on insider threat would probably not be appropriate because there is a logical explanation. However, there could also be a fine line between the two. Let's slightly modify the last scenario. In this case, let's assume that the product did not make money because there were lots of problems and bugs with the system. After analysis, no one can figure out how this could have occurred because the design was solid and everything was properly tested and despite a lot of analysis no one can give a logical answer to how this occurred. Now insider threat could be considered as an option.

Notice the key wording I used in all these cases. Based on business indicators you could consider insider threat as a possible cause. I never said it must be insider threat. I would need to do a lot of additional analysis to make the call 100%, but the point is when you see indicators and no other explanation makes sense, insider threat should be put on your list of possible causes for the problem.

The second type of indicators is personal indicators. Unlike business indicators, personal indicators are not always there and can be hard to find, but the good news is that when they are there, they can usually be traced back to insider threat more directly than a business indicator. We talked about anger as one of the types of personal indicators, but there could be several others. Some of the key personal business indicators are:

- Frustration/anger
- Change in business patterns
- Change in personality
- Rash decisions
- Sense of urgency

Frustration and anger we talked about in the previous section. Not always, but especially in disgruntled employees, the driving factor or indicator is an increased frustration towards the company. When dealing with indicators and personal behavior we have to remember the straw that broke the camel's back paradigm. I have seen companies that say, "We knew John was angry, but we did not know he was that angry. We told him he would get up to a 10% raise and we gave him a 7% raise and he flipped out. How could we have known?" While that seems responsible, what you have to remember in almost every situation is that the person justifying it is not going to give you all the facts. In this case, if you dug deeper you would realize that over the past year the company did a series of other things to anger John. They did not give him a bonus' they passed him up for a promotion; they took away his paid overtime; and they refused his vacation. Now you can better see how his anger got to a point were he snapped. Anger usually grows over time, so if you can catch it early you can stop a problem before it occurs.

The next personal indicator is a change in business patterns and how someone operates and works in the office. While personal issues could result in a change in business patterns, this could also be an indicator of insider threat. If all of a sudden an employee is coming in early or staying late or spending more time in the data center when no one else is around and as soon as people come in, leaves, those are patterns that should be watched very closely. Anything involving business practices relating to access should be watched very closely. If someone is going to the boss or even directly to the help desk asking for access to information she never needed access to before and her job has not changed, this could be an indicator. In this situation the best thing to do is to follow up and ask why. There is nothing wrong with a boss saying, "Mary, I noticed that you have sent me forms for approval to access new directories. I was just wondering what the business reason is or why you need that access." If there is a logical explanation, then at least you can validate the request.

Now, if once you confront Mary she gives vague answers or acts uneasy, you should take note. Especially if she becomes openly frustrated or angry, that is now a combination of indicators. If you are doing your job as a boss to follow up on a request and Mary responds by getting angry and saying, "All I do is work my butt off around here and you always question me and accuse me! I can't take this anymore!" all that should be compiled together as indicators of a much bigger problem.

Some managers prefer not to deal with it just deny the request and not ask why. Even if you deny the request, you should still validate it because if this is an indicator of insider threat you could be doing several things with just denying the request. First, you could be increasing the anger of that person. Second, if this person is committing or planning an insider attack, your denying her request is not going to stop her. She tried the easy route and now she will become even more covert to get the access she needs and these actions you might not be able to see. So it is better to act on an indicator than make it go away because the next approach might be so much better that you have no chance of catching it.

Personality changes are another big indicator that there is a problem. Performing insider attacks is like a drug that lures people in. Most people that are heavily addicted to drugs are not happy and know they have a problem, but they do not know how to fix it because they are in over their heads. The same problem occurs with insider threat. Once people are actively engaged in committing the crime, they are in over their heads. They like the money they are getting for doing it but they know it is wrong and that they need to stop. But they don't know how. This causes anxiety which can result in changes in personality.

Personality changes can also be more subtle, like not socializing as much in the office or not wanting to go out to lunch with co-workers. If the whole department goes out to lunch on a weekly basis and one person stops going and they do not give a good reason, that could be an indicator that you want to examine closely. If you notice someone going outside more to talk on the cell phone, that could be an indicator, especially if they take some calls in the office. The question you have to ask is why that person took one call in the office but had to step outside so no one heard the other calls. Especially if it is a full-time employee and the company is paying for the cell phone, all calls should be work related. There are always personal calls that need to be made, but if the frequency of secret calls is increasing, these are indicators that should be watched closely.

Other personality changes involve stress-related changes like being more prone to aggravation, not thinking logically, not attending or participating in meetings. A good example on a recent case I worked on was the insider's e-mail style. Before he started causing harm to the company, this person used to write very positive, well-thought-out e-mails. As he continued in his insider activities, his e-mails became very snappy and illogical. They would jump around and not be complete thoughts. Stress can also cause this, but the bottom line is, if someone's personality is changing so much that you can see it, whether it is an indication of insider threat or not, this person is asking for help. Even if it turns out it had nothing to do with insider threat, you need to care about your employees and take care of them. If they are having problems, provide the help and guidance they need.

Two other changes to watch out for are someone making rash decisions and all decision or actions having a tight sense of urgency. If some of these are personality traits that someone has always had, that is less of a concern. What we are looking for with indicators is a change in behavior.

If someone is committing an espionage attack, the demands of the competitor will increase over time. In the beginning, the competitor is going to want to acquire anything, even if it has no value, but the more value content the insider provides, the more demanding the competitor will get. Therefore, if the company the insider is ultimately working for is getting more demanding, the insider will get more demanding in his personality. He will start acting more rashly, demanding that his boss make a decision on something or questioning why it is taking the IT department so long to get him access. This intense sense of urgency is usually a flag that there is a problem or issue.

The important thing to remember is that these are only indicators; they are not guaranteed indicators that someone is committing or planning insider attacks. Just like clouds do not always mean rain, someone showing one of the aforementioned indicators does not mean she should be fired. There could be many other reasons for these things to occur. But the point is they should be watched closely because they potentially could be an early warning sign. Especially if many of these are happening together. You have to look at the facts because there could be other logical explanations, but the point is to at least look and listen and perform some analysis to try to prevent any insider problems before they occur or limit the amount of damage if they are already occurring.

Impact to the Company

If someone is going to commit insider threat, he is usually going to do it to cause harm, for financial gain, or both. Therefore, there is going to be some impact to the company. The problem is twofold. First, the initial impact to the company could potentially be minor. Not always, but many insiders test the waters when performing their attacks. They start off slow and see what happens and slowly increase in intensity over time. Therefore, the initial results could potentially be hard to see and because they are minor there could usually be a lot of other more logical explanations for why something is occurring and insider threat is usually either at the end of the list or not on the list at all for logical explanations. We have to keep everything in balance, but just putting a small dot on the insider threat radar screen might not be a bad thing just in case that small dot starts becoming a much bigger dot.

The second problem with the impact is that there can be a delay between when the attack occurs and when the impact occurs to the company. If an insider deletes a proposal that is due tomorrow, the impact of the attack will be known immediately. When the company goes to submit the proposal and it is gone, they will know there is a problem. Since the contract was not going to be awarded for another 12 months and the company was planning on the revenue, they will not see the financial impact for another year, but at least they know they are going to lose and have a year to plan for other business. However, this is not the norm. Normally, the attack occurs and the impact is not realized for several months or several years later. It is much harder to trace back a financial problem to events that occurred a year prior.

An example is an insider falsely changing the numbers on a huge, multi-year contract. Since this contract could take six to nine months to evaluate before a winner is even announced, the company might think they are guaranteed to win the contract and nine months later find out they lost. In performing the post analysis, almost a year later, they find out all of their financials were incorrectly modified. Now the company feels the impact and knows it was an insider problem, but going back a year can be very difficult. This is where things get really scary. You know you have an insider and that they are screwing up your financials, but over the past year, how many other proposals did you submit that you are still waiting to hear back on? That can give you a real sick feeling in your stomach not only knowing you lost this contract but also knowing that you are going to lose the last five you submitted. The only potential benefit is, the more lead time you have to know you are going to lose a bid, the more time you have to spin up the sales cycle and find new work to make up for the lost work.

The previous example is still not very likely. In the last example, even thought it took a while to realize that you have a problem, you still were able to easily trace it back to the fact it was an insider, find out who worked on the contracts, and launch an investigation. Normally, not only does it take a long time to realize there is a problem, you usually have no idea what caused the problem and have no idea if insiders had anything to do with it.

Poor market projections are a perfect example. If your company has poor earnings for a given quarter or year and the stock price dropped, what caused it? Insider threat should definitely be on the list, but you have no proof or clues at all to indicate that was the case. You might know that certain projects did not live up to their expectation, so analysis can be performed on those projects. However, some of those projects could have been on-going for multiple years, so trying to not only go back that far in time but also to analyze all that data could be impossible. Another problem that is occurring today is with M&A (mergers and acquisitions). If you buy a company and project their product to perform at x level and it didn't, it is very hard to determine the cause. During an acquisition there could be so many factors at play that could impact the decision. Plus, usually there is a high turn over in employees so the people might not even be around to provide the information you need. Finally, when a company is purchased there is usually some amount of frustration and dissent towards the parent company. This could also lead to fertile ground for an insider attack to occur.

Limitations

In the previous section we covered profiles or characteristics of known insider threat. Taking this logic to the next level, how do we know that someone is an insider? The only way to know for sure (even in some cases we are not 100% sure) is if they are caught and found guilty. Therefore, the previous section looked at characteristics of insiders who were caught attacking their company from within. Some of these cases were covered in the previous chapters in this book and others were based on published reports and cases that were worked on by the author.

While this information gives us a good starting point, we have to remember that insider threat is a new and constantly evolving area. Just because we know how an insider attacked a company six months ago, because the means and methods that insiders are using are constantly evolving, there is a chance that the techniques might no longer provide good indicators today. However, it is a starting point and that cannot be overlooked. Remember that there is no secret formula that can magically be used to catch an attacker. Even if there were, as soon as the attackers found out about it, they would change and the formula no longer would work all of the time.

The key thing to highlight with the known cases is that they represent a base methodology for performing an attack. It is not perfect, but you can use that information as a starting point and at least apply the lessons learned to stop those types of attacks from occurring against your company.

The second important limitation to point out is that these people were caught. The really good ones are still out there, still being successful and not getting caught. While having a base knowledge of how these attackers were caught is good, we just have to remember that no matter how good we get, there is always someone better than us. If you want to be really good at security and incident response, that is a point that will serve you well. Never let your ego get the best out of you. No matter how much you learn and how much you know, there will always be someone who is better than you and therefore you have to out think, out maneuver, and out fly them in order to catch them and keep your company secure.

Some good people get caught and the investigators are constantly increasing in skill and technique to be able to stay one step ahead. However, even with the best skills and techniques, there is still a chance that attackers will get away. Remember, the end goal of the company is not to catch the attacker. That is a nice-to–have, but that is not their end goal. Their end goal is to stop the attack from occurring, minimize the financial loss, and make sure it does not happen again in as cost-effective manner as possible. Therefore, many of these attackers focus their methods and attention on not getting caught. Ideally, they do not want the company to even know anything is going on, but ultimately they want to make sure it is never traced back to them. Combining the company's goals and the attacker's goals, you can see that with the current generation of insider attacks, companies are finding out about them, but not catching the people who are performing them.

Since the previous section focused in on known attacks or attackers that were caught, the question comes down to how attackers are getting caught. There are many ways, but the general breakdown of why most attackers are caught is the following:

- Greed
- Boastfulness
- Sloppiness
- Stupidity

In almost everything we do, we keep pushing ourselves to be able to do more and go further than we did previously. If you exercise or run, your ultimate goal is to be able to increase the speed and distance you run or increase the weights or number of reps that you perform. While consistent increase is good, this leaves the door open for being too cocky or greedy and trying to do too much or take on too much. When you see people who have gotten injured at the gym, it is usually because they got greedy. They were steadily progressing on the weights they were lifting and they were up to 90 pounds and they wanted to get over the 100-pound limit, so they put a little extra weight on the bar, used bad form to try to lift, and they suffered an injury.

You can also see this behavior with children who would sneak a cookie before dinner and not get caught. Instead of being happy with the thrill of getting one cookie, they go back for a second and a third and on the third cookie they hear noises, they rush, and the cookies fall all over the floor and they get caught.

Greed is part of human nature and plays a role in everything we do, including insider threat, and is usually one of the reasons someone gets caught.

The attacker starts e-mailing out one document a month to an outside account and she gets away with it for a while. Then she starts doing it every week, then twice a week, and starts thinking how easy it is because no one is looking at anything she is doing and she slowly gets greedy to the point that someone notices and takes action and she gets caught.

One of the cases I worked on, the insider was taking equipment home over three-day weekends or when he was going to work from home so he could be as productive as possible. The equipment contained sensitive information and was not accessible from the Internet. So the company could either open up a big hole through the firewall or, since they trusted this individual, they figured it was less of a risk to let him take the equipment, so he could be productive. This continued for a while and then the person started getting greedy. It got to the point where he would leave with the equipment at eight in the evening and be back at work at seven in the morning without the equipment and then two days later return with the equipment. The reason the company agreed to let him take the equipment home was because the person wanted to work from home. Clearly, if he is putting in 13-hour days and leaving the equipment at home while he's at work, something else is up. They opened an investigation and found the person was giving the systems to a competitor so they could image them, then he was bringing the systems back into work. Now, as you will see, in many cases stupidity also plays a role, but the main factor here was greed. If the attacker had just kept taking the equipment at a slow rate, no one would have ever noticed.

One of the advantages to not having good protection against insider threat is that it could possibly lure the attacker into a false sense of security. If attackers feel that they have total control and can do whatever they would like with no chance of being caught, there is a good chance they will get greedy and then you can catch them. While this can work, this is not the ideal way to operate, because while the person may eventually be caught, the amount of damage caused could be enormous. The goal is to reduce the bleeding and in most organizations there is a strong cost-benefit incentive to catch the attacker much sooner in the process.

We mentioned earlier in this chapter that one of the indicators of the people that are caught is other people knowing to some extent what was going on. One of the reasons other people knew or found out is because the attacker started bragging. Depending on the grade of the attacker, some insiders are doing it to get back at the company, for personal recognition, or for pride. Therefore, if no one else knows that it is happening, they are not getting full satisfaction out of the attack. Typically, the high-end insider committing corporate espionage is more disciplined and will never tell anyone.

Since bragging is something that could occur, it is critical that the rest of the employees and trusted insiders at your organization understand the need to report this information or let managers know if they see something is going on. In one company I worked at, many of the people knew that a given employee was harming the company because he would brag and forward e-mails but no one ever said anything. After the person was fired and we found this out I asked the other employees why they did not say anything. They indicated they either thought we knew or they did not think it was their place to say anything. After I explained to them that anything that could cause monetary loss to the company could impact them directly because if the company makes less money that could impact their bonuses, etc., and that as an employee of the company they have a right and obligation to watch out for the company, most people understood. The other important follow-up is that the trusted employees have to feel that they can have a confidential conversation and that it will not be made known that they were the ones who said something. You never want to punish people who are doing the right thing and if they request that you do not tell anyone that they told you, I recommend respecting that; otherwise, no one will pass on information to you.

It is very important that there is a method for anonymous reporting to occur, especially with regards to insider threat. I know some companies get frustrated with this and demand that employees do what is in the best interest of the company and without regard to remaining confidential. While that is all well and good, you cannot forget about human nature. You have to create an environment that takes advantage of the fact that some attackers brag and make sure that when they do that you find out the information in a timely manner.

Another aspect that is tied with greed is, as people continue to perform attacks and not get caught, they eventually get sloppy. For example, in the beginning of launching an attack, the insider takes sensitive documents, uses stego to hide the information, and sends it to an account that looks like his spouse's or friend's account and even writes text in the message to make it look very legitimate. Then, as time goes on, he starts getting sloppy and decides to stop using stego and stop using cover text. Over time, the attacker essentially just starts attaching the sensitive documents directly to e-mails and sending them out. I have even been involved in one case where the attacker got so sloppy that he even started sending the documents directly to the competitor, which was easily traceable and how he was eventually caught.

I was involved in the investigation and it was amazing to see how this person progressed in his attack methodology over time. The attacker started with a very meticulous well-thought-out plan. If he had continued with that plan and stayed diligent and never deviated, he would have never gotten caught. Knowing what I know about the company in question, I know that they would never have been able to find or catch this attacker. Over time, he starting gaining so much confidence and thought that he was so good that he starting getting sloppy and taking chances that he should not have been taking. The attacker's view of the company decreased and he thought their security was so bad and incompetent that he starting making the justification that there is no way possible that they would ever catch him and he thought he was invincible, so he started to take more chances. He kept taking chances that he should not have taken and his sloppiness increased to such a point that he eventually got caught.

Once again, the fact that he got sloppy was the only reason the company was able to catch him, so it was a good thing that the attacker got sloppy. However, I also fault the company because this person's care eroded over time and the company should have caught him a lot sooner. If they had, they would have saved the company a significant amount of money.

While we alluded to it when we talked about getting greedy and bragging, one thing that also typically occurs is that the attacker becomes stupid and makes mistakes. It is usually tied into being sloppy, but no matter how good people are, they will eventually make mistakes. Even the best quarterbacks in the NFL will eventually fumble the ball. There is no such thing as perfect. Regardless the reason, people will eventually make mistakes. In some cases, the mistakes could be accidental, and in other cases, they could be intentional. If organizations are set up correctly, even with very good high-end attackers, companies can still detect and find when the attacker does something stupid and makes a mistake. It does not happen often, but when it does, it is a perfect opportunity to monopolize on the opportunity.

In another case I worked on, they had an insider that was planted at the company and worked there for more than five years. This attacker was so good the company would have never known and never suspected him. However, there was a day when the organization the insider was ultimately working for really needed a piece of information and the insider was getting very desperate and really needed to get the information out. In hindsight, the attacker admitted it was a stupid thing to do, but he e-mailed the sensitive document from his work account. His initial thought was that he would only do it once and no one would notice. However, the company had a filtering system. The e-mail was flagged by the system, investigated, and the insider was caught. The attacker's one stupid mistake ended a five-year run that could have gone on for another five years. This is good news for us and bad news for the attacker, but the bottom line is, eventually attackers will make stupid mistakes and we have to be ready to catch them and take appropriate action.

Although the goal is to stop attackers and prevent them from causing any harm, this is not practical across all attacks. There are some attacks that cannot be prevented. Companies need to put policy, procedures, and detective measures in place so that when attackers get greedy, brag, become sloppy and make mistakes, they can be caught in a timely manner. While it would be better to stop attackers, detecting them using the aforementioned measures is better than nothing.

High-End Profile

We started off this chapter by looking at the profile of known attackers. While that provides a starting point, it might not paint an ideal picture of the high-end insider threat that is going to cause the most damage to your organization. Therefore, based on experience and analysis, in this section we are going to present the profile and characteristics of the high-end attacker to give you an idea of their profile and what to look for to prevent the insider threat from harming your company. The following are critical characteristics of the high-end insider threat profile:

- Hard worker
- Quickly promoted
- Leader
- Dedicated
- Trusted
- Has special access

Disgruntled employees view their mission as an insider threat to be very short lived. They want to cause disruption and move on to their next job. High-end insiders see their position as an insider as a career and life decision. It is not short lived in any way shape or form and in most cases their sole goal is your company and to compromise and extract sensitive data for 30-plus years. The days of saying that someone has worked here for 10 years, therefore they must be trusted, is no longer valid. In large Fortune 50 companies it is worth the investment to have someone act as a sleeper for three to five years before causing any harm or damage. We also talked about the ultimate goal in some cases being to put the company out of business. With the high-end attacker, the goal is to sustain the competitor. The reason is simple, if I have a competitor and they are performing all this high-end research and I am stealing the results, if they go out of business I will eventually go out of business because I have no one to pay for my research. Therefore, I want that company to stay around so I can keep taking advantage of their work to my financial benefit and the best way to do that is to plant someone at the company.

While companies can recruit someone from inside a target company to perform insider activities, the better method that is usually focused on at most companies is to train someone, get him hired at the target company, have him get promoted, and have him under your control the whole time.

Therefore, one of the first characteristics is that the planted insider is usually a very hard worker and the reason is simple. There is a direct correlation between hard worker and trusted entity, which leads to more access. If a worker is lazy, if he doesn't get fired, he is probably not going to be put on good projects or be given much responsibility; therefore, the access he gets will be minimal. If the insider wants to know the deepest, darkest secrets of the company, he needs to get put on the best projects and be trusted with this data. While it is easier for an insider to steal information than it is for an outsider, the easier method is to have the company give you the access based on how hard you have worked for them.

If you are a hard worker, other characteristics will normally follow, the main one being greater chance of being promoted. Once again, promotions feed right into the hand of the inside attacker because the higher the position, the more control he has over what is happening. Access is important, but control is even more important because that not only gives the insider the chance to access information, but also the possibility to modify information or perform other high-grade attacks.

Foreign governments or competitors who plant high-end insiders at your company do not just randomly pick people. There is a long process including personality tests that are performed to enable the organization to pick just the right person who will perform what they want but also be effective and influential in their position. Therefore, a key characteristic is to be a natural-born leader. A leader can convince people to do things a certain way and can in essence control a situation. The more control an insider has, the better chance she has of obtaining access performing her job as an insider. In some cases, one insider at a company is not enough. Based on the size and the amount of data, a competitor might need multiple people to keep up with the workload. Someone who is a leader would have a better chance of recruiting other people within the organization to join the dark side and help him out.

Being a leader implies other natural characteristics: dedication and trust. Now, to be fair, I should say implied dedication and implied trust. The ultimate dedication and trust is to the company the insider is ultimately working for and who is paying them off. The company who they are spying on should have an implied level of dedication and trust, but since the attacker is ultimately stealing from that company, it is false when you peel back the layers. Just on the surface it seems legitimate.

The more loyal and dedicated someone seems, the better the chance she will have and an easier time of spying and covering up her tracks than if she were thought to be suspicious and did not have the company's best interest at heart.

Finally, as we have alluded to and stated several times, the key pivot point for the insider is access. That is ultimately what they are after and what enables them to be as effective as possible in accomplishing their mission. It should not come as a surprise that usually the people who are inside attackers are in positions that require special access. While it might seem coincidental, it is by design. Attackers carefully plan out their career paths so they will be in a position to access sensitive information and ideally even control the access to make it easier to cover up their tracks.

This section presented the critical attributes of the high-end insider threat. You probably noticed as you were going through this section that many of them dovetail with the list of attributes that you want in your ideal employee. This was something that was not purposely done but shows you the problem and why the problem of insider threat will continue to get worse over time. The high-end person committing these attacks looks and acts just like legitimate employees at your company. Actually, the better the attacker, the more he is going to fit the profile of your best and ideal employees.

This means that you can decide to hire only slackers and never run the risk of having an insider, or you can be very careful to watch and control access, so you can still discern the good from the bad even though they might have similar characteristics in how they act and perform.

Categories of Inside Attacks

Based on the previous analysis, there are three general categories of insider threats that could exist at your company. While every case is unique, the general categories of people that will most likely cause harm from an insider perspective are the following:

- **Level 1** Self-motivated
- **Level 2** Recruited
- **Level 3** Planted

I used levels to describe the categories to show the potential for harm and the danger that each one poses. While at the end of the day any of the three could cause significant monetary loss and potentially put the company out of business, the higher the level, the more dangerous.

At the lowest level, you have the self-motivated attacker. This is the insider that does not require any external motivation or incentive; they just decide for some reason that they want to use their access to cause harm. While I have seen cases were the self-motivated insider will start to extract secrets and try to sell them to the highest bidder, this is not typical and in the cases I have seen they are not very good at it. Most people that play in the corporate intelligence arena are very skeptical and careful who they deal with and have connections that create the lifeblood of their business. If an individual wakes up one morning and decides to sell corporate secrets, there is a good chance he is not connected correctly and won't be taken seriously. Therefore, the most common form of level 1 or self-motivated insider is a disgruntled employee that is out mainly for revenge and self satisfaction.

A level 2 attacker is someone who, on their own, does not decide to become an insider threat, but are recruited and convinced by someone else to commit the attacks. While recruited insiders would never have started to perform corporate espionage on their own, they have weaknesses that an external entity took advantage of to recruit them. We covered the motivators in a previous section, but the primary motivator in most cases is money.

With a level 2 situation, it is risky for both sides initially. If someone approaches an employee and offers to pay for company secrets, most people would be highly suspicious. Therefore, it is usually a slower process that has to occur for both sides to be comfortable. While this will work in some situations, the preferred method for many entities is to just plant their own person.

Thus, the level 3 insider, in which an organization will find someone, train him, get him hired at the company, allow him time to get situated and earn trust, and then start exploiting him for information, usually works better.

Types of Motivations

Many things may motivate an insider to turn to the dark side, but when all the analysis is performed on all the different cases, there are three motivators that appear over and over again in almost every case and they are the following:

- Financial

- Political

- Personal

Whether you like it or not or whether you are willing to admit it or not, money is a very powerful thing and will cause people to behave in ways you never thought possible. Therefore, it should not come as a big surprise that financial motivation is a key driving factor in insider threat cases.

Based on this, it should not come as a surprise that when organizations are trying to recruit people to perform insider attacks for them, the one thing they look for is people with financial trouble or who enjoy a lifestyle that their current paycheck cannot handle. By targeting people in this category, they know there is an immediate need which could create a win-win situation for both sides.

Political views are another motivator that drives people. People feel very strongly about political views and if an organization is working against those interests, employees could have a strong reason to cause harm or want to cooperate with people who are out to cause harm to the company.

In one situation there was a large research company who hired a new CEO. The CEO decided to take the company in a different direction and perform research in areas in which the net result was harmful to the environment. Everything the company was doing was legal; it just was not in the best interest of the environment.

Because of the prior research the company had done, some pro-environmentalists worked at the company and were very passionate about their beliefs. Instead of just quitting, they felt it was their moral right to stop this from occurring. They ended up launching a huge insider attack against the CEO and the new research areas. It ended up causing the CEO to be fired and almost put the company out of business. Yes, the company did pursue legal proceedings, but the point is when your company is on the edge of financial ruin, lawsuits will not do a lot to help you.

The last motivator is personal. This can come in many shapes or sizes but usually involves some form of blackmail. The attacking company finds someone with personal secrets that he does not want anyone to find out about and threatens to reveal the information if the person does not cooperate. This is a dangerous one and can cause people to get into a lot of trouble and cause a lot of problems for the company very quickly. This is one of the reasons why background checks and personal interviews are critical. If there is anything that someone has that they are ashamed about, it is better to know about it and see how bad a risk it really is. This motivator is one in which the person is usually put between a rock and a hard place. With the other two motivators, the attackers are making a decision to knowingly cause harm to the company. Either they need the additional money or they want to stand up for what they believe in, but the decision is still theirs.

In the case of blackmail, the person is being forced into a decision that he does not want to make. Either his entire life will be ruined or he will hurt the company and he does not want to do either. While the person might be very loyal to the company, most people would pick sacrificing their company over ruining their lives.

Personal motivators can occur in one of two ways. In the first way, the person that wants to recruit you will dig deep into your past and try to find out your deepest, darkest secrets and then use them against you. They know that you have a criminal background and will publicize it to all of your friends and co-workers unless you cooperate.

The other way personal motivators work is to set you up. An entity that wants to recruit you would target you and figure out that you are the person who needs to perform an insider attack. However, you are financially well off and do not need the money. Therefore, they need to find a personal reason to get you to cooperate. A typical scenario is that they follow you to a bar one evening and have a very attractive person seduce you and entice you to go to a hotel or back to their place for a one-night stance. You have had a hard week and a couple of drinks and they are able to convince you to participate. During the events that follow, someone is filming and taking detailed pictures. A week later someone else approaches you and asks you to cooperate and if you refuse they say that they will send these pictures to your spouse and at that point reveal the pictures that you had no idea were taken. This is why it is very important to be careful what you do on your personal time because if you are in a position of influence someone will try to use that against you.

Foreign Intelligence

While it has steadily been in the rise in recent years, a key area of heavy emphasis in the past year is foreign governments actively engaging in corporate intelligence against firms in other countries to give the local companies an economic advantage. This is scary because with foreign governments getting more involved it is becoming a different ball game. If a competitor is going to engage in corporate espionage, they have to be careful because if it is ever publicized, it could look extremely bad for them and actually cause more harm than good. So if a company is going to perform corporate espionage, they will probably use freelance insiders who in essence sell the critical IP of a company to the highest bidder.

However, foreign governments have completely different models and financial structures and in many cases if they get caught it does not matter. Since they have different incentives, are very well trained, and have large financial backing, the chances of them getting caught are slim, but the damage they can cause is huge. Know thy enemy is a key principle in building any defensive model. It is important to realize who your company could be up against, especially if they are a large company.

Unlike freelance insiders who want to steal critical IP and make money as soon as possible. Foreign governments are willing to plant someone at a company for five to ten years before they get any benefit from that person. This means that there will be no indication of the person's true intent for three to five years and the only thing the organization will see is a leader who works hard and is very dedicated. Then, once they earn the company's complete trust, they will use that for their own advantage.

While the threat landscape is always changing, this is an important enough change to keep a close eye on. Because this method is very hard to track and is done from a very deeply entrenched insider, once they are inside it is impossible to catch them.

Stance

For your company, your executives need to decide what stance your organization is going to take on insider threat. This is important in how you handle the cases and what level of investigation you are willing to spend to run the problem to ground. It is also important that whatever stance you take, that you clearly communicate it and implement it in a consistent manner across your company.

For example, in the U.S. legal system and as a citizen of the U.S., you are presumed innocent until proven guilty. If someone or law enforcement wants to take away your innocence, the burden of proof is on them to prove that you are guilty; you do not have to prove your innocence.

However, this stance is not necessarily taken by all companies and all countries for that matter. While as a citizen it is a very nice freedom, it can be costly to have to prove guilt. Companies who have a large number of insider attacks can see that the price tag in running every problem to the ground can be expensive. They question the benefit of spending a lot of money to prove someone is guilty only to fire them when they have enough proof. Instead, if they are suspicious of someone, they just fire him and hire someone else. This is very much an assumed guilty stance, but from a monetary standpoint it is a more cost-effective measure for companies to take. I am not saying that it is the right way to go and it can be very unfair if someone is innocent and fired; however, a company has to make business decisions that its employees do not always like.

Therefore, it is important that companies have formal procedures and follow them consistently across the company. Even if the measures are extreme, if they are followed consistently, the company is usually protected. It is in cases where the company makes the decisions on the fly and is inconsistent that they can get themselves into a lot of legal trouble very quickly.

While it is more costly to prove guilt before action is taken, there is one situation were it is beneficial and that is if prosecution is desired. If the company decides that they want to pursue prosecution, then they need to have proof to win the case and therefore they might be willing to let the person continue their actions while they gather the needed evidence. However, this can be painful because, as you are watching the person to get proof, they are causing harm to your organization.

A related scenario is if criminal actions were committed and the case is being pursued by law enforcement. In this situation, your company is no longer running the investigation and it is your company's role to cooperate and provide assistance. Your company might want to take one set of actions, but since it is a formal investigation, you are at the mercy of law enforcement to make the ultimate call.

Summary

Profiling and catching an insider is not easy, but the more you know about their profile, how they act and how they operate, the easier it is to prevent and detect them and minimize the overall loss to your company. As the saying goes, in order to catch an attacker you have to think like an attacker. The more you understand their characteristics, their motivators, and how they act, the better chance you have of tracking them down.

Most often the people that are researching, analyzing, and catching the insiders are within the security department and quite often have technical backgrounds. There is an inherent danger associated with this. Since they are technical or have technical backgrounds they tend to think the way techies think. However, many of the attackers are non-technical, so you have to think out of the box in order to find and catch them. Instead of always thinking of high-tech solutions, think how a low-tech person would solve the problem or how is could be solved without the use of technology.

For example, I was working a case where we knew the individual was working for a competitor but we could not prove it. Through many of the methods and techniques outlined in this book, we were able to pinpoint the individual but we could never catch the person red-handed. The company's stance was that, because this was a fairly senior person, the company wanted to be able to pursue legal action for all the money the company lost due to this person's actions. In order to be able to pursue legal action, we needed proof. The problem was getting bad, so we were working almost around the clock to catch this person. We were watching e-mail, Web, and every form of electronic communication possible. We even had hidden cameras to make sure the person was not taking the documents home with him and we were coming up empty every time.

One evening we were working late and it was around two in the morning and I was all out of ideas. I heard one of the phones ringing and I asked my colleague whose phone it was. When I work late, if there is an emergency, I always want my wife to me able to get in touch with me. Since no one calls at 2:00 A.M., I just wanted to check and make sure it was not an emergency or my wife trying to track me down. The person I was working with said it was probably the fax machine, that the fax machine rang all day long and drove him crazy. At that point I jumped out of my seat and said, "We got it!" I think the group I was working with thought I had lost my mind. They couldn't understand how the fax machine ringing could cause me to figure out the problem. I said, "He is using the fax machine to get the data out of the company." We were so caught up in thinking within the box and looking at technical solutions that we missed something as obvious as a fax machine. Sure enough, when we pulled the log from the fax machine, there were numerous faxes to our competitor and to the person's home. The total page count across the two exceeded 2,000 pages, and since the fax machine had memory, we were able to re-create the faxes we needed and have the proof to close out the case.

Another reason that thinking out of the box is important is that most of us would never think of causing harm to our company, so when we try to think of how this would be done or think like an attacker, our mindset creates natural limits because we could never imagine doing any of the things the person we are trying to catch is doing. Therefore, it is sometimes very hard to dig deep enough or go far enough out of the box to catch them. This is why understanding profiles of how people operate is critical. The information can be used to make us much more effec-tive at catching the insider threat.

Chapter 9

Response: Technologies That Can Be Used to Control the Insider Threat

Solutions in this chapter:

- **Understanding and Prioritizing Critical Assets**
- **Defining Acceptable Level of Loss**
- **Controlling Access**
- **Bait: Honeypots and Honeytokens**
- **Die Pad for Data**
- **Mole Detection**
- **Profiling**
- **Monitoring**
- **Anomaly Detection**
- **Signature Analysis**
- **Thin Clients**
- **Policy, Training, and Security Awareness**
- **Background Checks**

Introduction

The biggest problem at most organizations is convincing management and executives that there is a problem. Hopefully, at this point in the book we have convinced you of that point. If we hadn't convinced you of that point, you probably would have stopped reading way before this chapter, so making the argument again will do little value.

Insider attacks are happening all the time even if companies do not realize it. The problem with insider threat is that it cannot be prevented as with other attacks. If someone is running a buffer overflow attack against your system, you can patch the system and prevent the attack from occurring. If someone is connecting to your Web server and exploiting port 80, you can close down port 80 or block it at the firewall and stop the attack from occurring. Taking that logic, a simple way to stop the insider threat is to remove all insiders. We all can see that is not a practical solution, though. By removing all insiders, while it will effectively control insider threat, means your company will go out of business, because no insiders means no employees and there is no way you can run even a small company without some employees.

When we talk about prevention, we mean 100% prevention. Applying a patch will 100% stop that specific vulnerability from occurring. However, insider threat is much like resource-exhaustion denial-of-service attacks. While you can do things to prevent certain types and minimize the damage, there is no way to 100% stop a resource-exhaustion denial-of-service attack. The reason is that traffic has to be allowed to flow and cutting off that traffic will completely stop functionality. Insider threat is very similar. Although some prevention measures are in place, there is no 100% way to prevent it because employees need to be allowed to have access to resources so the company can function.

With insider threat, prevention is ideal but detection is a must. You try to do as much as you can to prevent the attacks, but in cases where you cannot prevent the attack, you have to make sure you detect it in a timely manner. Ideally, you would like to stop a fire from occurring in your house; however, if it does occur you want to make sure you can detect it in a timely manner. That is why you install smoke detectors. This raises a critical issue with detection.

Detection does minimal benefit if someone does not respond. A smoke detector will detect a problem but it will do nothing to put the fire out. If no one responds, the fire will keep burning, which highlights a distinction between prevention and detection measures. A preventive measure will prevent a problem with no intervention or human involvement. A detective measure needs some intervention and it is usually human based. Ideally we want to prevent problems but if we cannot, we need to deploy detective measures in such a way to make sure that a human will respond in a timely manner to the problem or issue at hand.

Insiders must be allowed in your organization. The question is how you can respond to the ever-growing threat of insiders attacking and stop them from destroying your organization. This chapter will look at how you respond to the problem of insider threat by looking at technologies and concepts that can be used to control and limit the damage that insiders can perform. Ideally, you would prevent an insider threat from occurring, but that is not always practical. In cases where it cannot be prevented you want to control and limit the amount of damage that can occur.

Understanding and Prioritizing Critical Assets

It is very difficult to protect something when you do not know what it is you are trying to protect. What has so much value to your organization that is worth putting time and energy into protecting? Not everything is worth protecting. At my house I have a small statue in the front yard that I paid $50 for. If something happened to it I would not be heartbroken. By having it in my front yard with no fence or other protective measures, I am saying that this asset has very low value to me. I sure would not leave a gold block worth millions in my front yard. The assets that I do not care about protecting I will leave in my front yard; the assets that I want to protect, I will keep locked up in a safe. Really valuable assets, I would lock up at a bank.

In real life, based on our actions, we prioritize assets and determine the criticality of items in our possession and we do this without even realizing it. However, in the cyber sense, we do the opposite without even realizing it. We keep critical data and critical assets available for anyone to compromise, copy, or delete and then we get frustrated when we have an insider compromise them. If you took no energy to protect your information, how can you be upset when someone steals it?

The first thing an organization has to do to control insider threat is to determine the criteria that are used to determine value. Monetary worth, future benefit to the company, and competitive advantage are sample criteria that could be used. Whatever the criteria are, they need to be determined first. How can you say that one asset is more critical than another asset if you do not have a criterion that is used to make the determination?

Once you have the criteria determined, you then need to go through your organization and score all your assets according to the criteria. It is important to note that not all criteria will be black and white. There could be some criteria that are very subjective. This is why this exercise must involve the executives at the organization. Only the person or people who are ultimately responsible for the success of the company can truly determine the worth or score a given asset should get. If you do not believe me, try this simple exercise. Go up to the VP of sales and ask him to score the assets in the company. I can guarantee you that all the sales-related assets will be scored high and all the other assets will be scored low. If you try this with multiple directors or VPs, you will see this trend continue.

After all your assets are scored, you need to prioritize them based on the criteria. After you are done with this portion, you should have a list of all the critical assets across your organization. These assets represent the crown jewels of your organization and need to be properly protected. Once the list of assets has been determined and you know the critical assets that need to be protected, ask yourself what you are protected from. This is where threat analysis comes into the picture. Threat represents possible damage and is the point of compromise for a given asset. Understanding the likely attack points and how an attacker would compromise the asset is the Know Thy Enemy portion of the equation. A valuable lesson on insider threat can be learned from *The Art of War* by Sun Tzu. A key passage from it states:

> If you know the enemy and know yourself, you need not fear the result of a hundred battles. If you know yourself but not your enemy, for every victory gained you will also suffer a defeat. If you know neither the enemy nor yourself, you will succumb in every battle.

Translating into our terms, you need to know your critical assets and know the risk to your critical assets in order to be properly protected against insider threat.

Defining Acceptable Level of Loss

Understanding and knowing what an organization's critical assets are is important, but being able to define acceptable level of loss is just as important so appropriate measures can be developed. No matter what you do, you have to be willing to accept some level of loss. Risk is all about understanding what an acceptable level of loss is and building defense mechanisms around it. While on paper this concept makes sense, it is often a difficult one for executives to understand.

If you ask an executive what level of loss they are willing to accept, most will answer none. However, even if it was possible to build security measures in such a way that there was no loss, it would be cost prohibitive to do and clearly not practical. There is always the possibility of loss and the sooner we can change our mindset to understand that, the better off we will be.

There was once a king who lived in a castle and this king was very paranoid. He started getting concerned that the people who worked for him were trying to steal from him, cause him harm, and potentially kill him. (See, even kings had problems with the trusted insider.) He decided that the potential loss was so great that he took his faithful servant who he trusted and the king went and locked himself in a cave in the middle of the woods. No one knew about the cave or knew that the king was there except his servant. The king thought this would remove all risk and take away any potential for loss. The door to the cave was locked from the outside and the only person who had the key was the servant. The servant would come four times a day to bring the king food and check on the king.

Many years later when people were exploring the woods they found a locked cave with a dead king inside. After two weeks of being locked in the cave, when his servant was coming to deliver food, the servant had a heart attack and died. Since no one else knew where the king was, the king starved to death inside the cave. While at the beginning of the story it seemed like the king was reducing all risk, he actually increased his risk by creating a single point of failure. The king would have been much happier and lived a longer life, if he had just accepted some risk and, for really high-risk items, performed proper risk mitigation.

The possibility for loss is all around us and risk management becomes a driving factor in determining what efforts should be focused on by an organization and what can be ignored. As difficult as it may seem for all critical assets, an acceptable level of risk needs to be defined. This will help an organization focus on what should or should not be done with regards to insider threat.

Cost-benefit analysis is a typical method of determining acceptable level of risk. The general premise behind cost-benefit analysis is determining what the cost is if the asset is lost in part or in whole versus what the cost is to prevent that loss from occurring. While this is hard for some people to swallow, there are actually many situations where it is more cost effective to do nothing about the risk than to try to prevent or reduce the risk from occurring.

Typically, there are two methods to deal with potential loss: prevention and detection. Preventive measures are typically more expensive than detective measures. With a preventive measure you stop the risk from occurring. With detective measures you allow the loss to occur, but detect it in a timely manner to reduce the time period in which the loss occurs. Defining an acceptable level of loss will enable an organization to determine whether they should implement preventive or detective measures.

If your acceptable level of loss is low, which means you have a very low tolerance for a loss to a given asset, a preventive measure would be more appropriate to stop the loss. You would have to be willing to spend the extra money on appropriate preventive measures.

If your acceptable level of loss is high, this means you have a higher tolerance and would most likely spend less money on a solution and implement detective measures. Now you are allowing the loss to occur but you are controlling and bounding it.

Therefore, performing calculations on acceptable level of loss plays a critical role in controlling the insider threat.

Controlling Access

After you determine what your critical assets are and your acceptable level of risk, the best method for controlling the insider threat is limiting and controlling access. In almost every situation in which an insider compromise occurs, it is usually because someone had more access than they needed to do their job. There are usually other factors at play but the number one factor is properly controlling access. Based on this, it should not be a surprise that one of the number one recommendations that I make in terms of securing an organization is Principle of Least Privilege. This principle states that you give someone the least amount of access they need to do their job. Some key parts of this principle are that you allow people to do their jobs but take away all other access. Figure 9.1 illustrates how access is often granted at most organizations.

Figure 9.1 Granting Access

Usually, the access that someone has contains at least 35% more access than what is actually needed to perform their job function. Most compromises are caused by someone using that additional 35%, which means if we took away the access that is not needed, we would also be limiting the number of compromises because we would be taking away the access that is utilized to cause harm.

Ideally, an organization should roll out a new system or network and implement least privilege from the very beginning; however, we know that is not practical. While not ideal, performing least privilege after the fact actually has some hidden benefit. Since least privilege is taking away access someone does not need, if the person is performing their job and doing what they are supposed to, they will not notice. So the first piece of good news is that least privilege can be implemented without impacting job performance or functionality at all. Second, by implementing a principle of least privilege across your organization, you can actually help catch or reduce the insider threat. If you go in and implement least privilege, taking away the extra access that someone does not need and they scream or question why that access has been removed, you now have a suspect. If you are taking away access they did not need to do their job and they noticed or complained, it meant they were using that extra access. Now the question is if someone is only performing legitimate functions, why were they using the extra access? The answer is, they were using the extra access outside the realm of their job and potentially causing harm to your organization.

Bait: Honeypots and Honeytokens

A typical way you would catch something is to set a trap. If you have a mouse in your house, you would set a mouse trap to capture the mouse. Even a mouse is not stupid enough to blindly go into a trap, so you have to put bait on the trap to lure them in. The bait must be carefully selected to be something that you know the mouse is after. A good way to figure out what the mouse is after is to ask why the mouse is in your house in the first place. In this case, the reason is usually for food. So if you bait the trap with food, especially food that mice like, you have a good chance the mouse will go after the bait, be lured into the trap, and caught.

Just like a mouse is a pest in your house, an insider threat is a pest within your organization that needs to be caught. Most insiders are after information, so if you set a trap where you bait them with information that seems important, you have a good chance of catching them. These traps are often referred to as honeypots and honeytokens. Both are traps that are set. The difference is one is set at the system level and one is set at the file level.

A honeypot is a system that is put on your network that has no legitimate function. It is set up to look attractive to attackers and lure them in. The key thing about a honeypot is that there is no legitimate use for it, so no one should be accessing it. If someone accesses the honeypot in any way, they are automatically suspicious because the only way they could have found it is if they were wandering around your network looking for something of interest. If they were only doing what they were supposed to, they would have never found the system.

For those familiar with honeypots this might seem like a slightly different concept or different use. Most people think of honeypots as being deployed externally. While that is traditionally how they have been deployed, internal honeypots also play a key role in the defense in depth arsenal. The big advantage of internal honeypots over external honeypots is reduced liability. The problem with an external honeypot on your DMZ is a honeypot is meant to lure in attackers. Since there are a ton of attackers on the Internet, in essence you are making your site more attractive to them and pulling them into your DMZ. This is not usually a good thing to do. However, with internal honeypots it has a different effect. On your internal network there ideally should be no attackers and if there are there should only be a small number of them. Therefore, putting in a system that will lure attackers when there is only supposed to be a small number is a positive thing. In will help find the needle in the haystack and focus in on the most likely targets of insider threat. A great example of this is scanning. Port scanning and vulnerability scanning is a norm on the Internet and is happening all the time. If you deploy an external honeypot you are going to see this activity and it should be treated as noise. However, scanning should only be done by authorized people on your internal network and definitely should not be treated as a norm. Therefore, if your internal honeypot sees any scanning occurring from a non-authorized host, it should immediately set off an alert. Although there are other ways to perform insider threat beyond scanning, if you seeing someone violating the policy and doing things they are not supposed to do, this is usually a good indicator that you have a problem on your hands. If someone is going to violate security policies and try to find vulnerabilities on a network, they are more likely going to be an insider threat or are more likely to be lured to the dark side.

Some people criticize honeypots for various reasons but most of those reasons no longer apply when you are talking about internal honeypots. One of the biggest issues honeypots raise is that of entrapment. Technically, it is not because entrapment can only be done by law enforcement. If I pull up to you at a light in my sports car and start revving my engine and when the light turns green we starting speeding down the highway, and since I drive that road a lot I know that there is usually a police car over the hill, so I purposely slow down and let you fly by me and as you go over the hill you get caught in a speed trap and pulled over, when you are being handed the ticket you cannot claim entrapment. Maybe stupidity, but not entrapment. On the other hand, if I pull up to you at a light and we take off racing at the light and we get to 80 mph and I slow down, pull behind you, and put on my lights because I am in an unmarked police car, now you have a chance of claiming entrapment. In the case of honeypots, especially internal honeypots, since it is being set up by your company and law enforcement is not involved, entrapment does not even come into play.

I always thought the big issue with honeypots was liability. You set up something vulnerable on purpose, and someone uses your system as a client in a DDOS attack. A honeypot is an entire system that has no legitimate value on the network but to lure in attackers. While scanning efforts will be caught, your higher-end insider threat usually will not be caught by a honeypot because there is nothing to lure them in. Real data and real business process is what is attractive and in many cases they will be able to tell that it does not contain the critical IP or anything of high worth. Therefore, a popular variant of honeypots that have evolved are honeytokens. Honeytokens take the concept of honeypots and scale it down.

A honeytoken works the same way as a honeypot, but instead of being an entire system, it is done at a directory or file level. You put an attractive file on a legitimate server and if anyone accesses it, you just caught them with their hand in the cookie jar. This usually has a higher pay off. Insiders are really good at figuring out a certain system or even a certain directory that contains critical IP for the company. If you add an additional file to the system or directory, there is a high chance someone might stumble across it. Once again, since this is not a legitimate file, no one should be accessing it. There is no speculation involved if someone accesses the honeytoken file. They are clearly up to no good since there is no reason anyone should be accessing it. Therefore, setting them up correctly, honeytokens can enable you to set up a virtual minefield on your critical systems. If you are a legitimate user and know the files you are supposed to access, you can easily navigate the minefield and not set off any mines. However, if you are an insider trying to cause harm, there is a good chance you will be tempted by a honeytoken, misstep, and set off a mine.

The important thing to remember with any of these techniques is that they are not 100% foolproof. But if each method increases your security, by putting them together you have a robust solution.

Die Pad for Data

In many situations, when you are looking for solutions to a given problem, you do not have to reinvent the wheel. Most likely part of the problem has already been solved in another domain and if you look carefully enough you can apply a solution from a different domain to the current problem you are trying to solve. When dealing with insider threat, you are trying to limit, control, stop, or detect information from leaving your organization.

A domain that has a related problem is the banking industry. Talking at a very abstract level, one of the problems that banks have is to prevent someone from stealing their money and if they cannot prevent the bank robbery, being able to find out who stole the money is the next best thing. One solution that banks (use to) utilize to try to detect potential banker robbers is called a die pad. It is a very basic but effective technique. While it is an effective technique, based on the new techniques of robbery, die pads are no longer common practice. However, they teach us a valuable lesson that can be applied to insider threat.

At banks, there is a stack of money that is properly wrapped and looks like all the other money at the bank. The idea is that if someone comes in to rob the bank they would steal this stack of money along with the rest. Or if the robber was holding a teller at gun point he/she would put this stack of money in the bag.

On the surface, there would be nothing about this stack of money that looked unusual. However, when the robber went back to his hideout and unwrapped the money, there would be a pressurized canister of ink that would explode and cover the person in permanent ink. Now in a small town if a certain person was covered in ink, it would be pretty obvious that he was the one who stole the money. As I stated early, while this might no longer be scalable for banks, the general concept applies to insider threat.

The idea is to add something that is not correct but insignificant to a document or a piece of data and if it gets revealed you can trace back who the insider was. The trick with a digital die pad is to add something to a document that is not correct so there is no chance that it could have accidentally appeared, but on the other hand it should not change the accuracy of the document or cause any potential harm to the organization. Therefore, there is a fine art of creating an insignificant inaccuracy that could be traced back to either a group of people or a single individual.

An example of how this could be used is with a book publishing company that publishes electronic books. A big problem today is one person buying the electronic book and then violating the copyright and posting it to the Web for anyone to download. In this particular case, you would know it was someone who bought the book that was doing this, but if you sold 5,000 copies, how do you pinpoint who it? The trick is with each version of the book that is sold, you introduce a unique inaccuracy. After the book gets pirated and available publicly, the publisher would look through a series of errors and when it found one that matched, they would know which person's version of the book violated the copyright and therefore which individual to go after. Examples of errors that could be used include a double period after a sentence on a given page or any extra space between sentences. These are examples of minor changes that would not take away from the reader's experience, but provide tracking capability.

The big advantage of the digital die pad is that people would not know that they are being tracked. With the traditional ink example, if you look in the mirror and your face is blue you know there is a problem. In this case, even if the person knew that the organization was using a digital die pad, finding it could be almost impossible.

The problem with a digital die pad is in an ideal sense, it has to be unique for each person; otherwise, the accountability is not present.

Mole Detection

Mole detection, while similar to the die pad idea, is slightly different. With a die pad, in essence you are hiding something within a piece of data so you can trace it back to the person who compromised the information. With mole detection, you are giving a piece of data to a person and only that person and if that information makes it out into the public domain, you know you have a mole.

If you suspect that someone is a mole you could "coincidentally" talk about something within ear shot of him and if you hear it repeated somewhere else, you know he was the mole. Mole detection is not technically sophisticated but can be useful in trying to figure out who is leaking information to the public or to another entity.

To show the effectiveness of this method, this was used on a recent insider threat case that I worked on. An attempted coup was made at a medium-sized company that failed and the people attempting the coup were fired. However, information was still leaked out to them and the people that were fired put up a Web site in which they posted information about the company. After internal-only meetings, information from those meetings would appear on the Web site, so we knew we had a sleeper or a mole inside the organization. As part of the process to put everyone at ease, the company held meetings with each department. What I started doing was to have the executive tell different stories and anecdotes in each of the meetings and then watched the Web site of the ex-employees. After doing this we quickly knew that someone from department x was the mole. Without their knowledge we then slowly targeted smaller groups from that department. If we saw four of them go to the lunch room, we would happen to have a conversation that they could overhear and we would wait to see what happened. After doing this several times, we were able to narrow down the three moles and terminate their employment. Not high tech but it got the job done.

Profiling

An ideal way to control and detect the insider is by understanding behavioral patterns. At the end of the day the behavior patterns of someone who is performing their job legitimately versus someone who is committing insider threat is going to be different. While they might seem very similar on the surface they have to deviate at some point since one is causing harm and the other one is not causing harm. It is at these deviation points that an inside attacker can be tracked and caught. The trick is being able to understand and figure out what those patterns are.

A common way of understanding behavior and looking for deviations is profiling. Profiling is not a new area of research and has been around for a long time. Law enforcement typically enrolls the help of criminal profilers who understand how certain types of criminals act and behave to be able to determine who is a potential suspect or who the ultimate criminal was in a particular case. While profiling has value, it is not perfect and there are always potential ways around it.

With insider threat profiling you are creating cyber profiles. You are creating time and motion parameters to be put in place to understand what legitimate behavior is and what goes outside of the norm. To do basic, generic profiling, profiles need to be created for a user or group of users. A simple example would be for the call center for a major credit card company. For a credit card call center you have people answering the phones who can access credit card numbers. Clearly this leaves the door wide open for insider threat. What stops someone from going into the database, extracting all the credit card numbers, and either using them for personal gain or selling them to the highest bidder. One solution is profiling. Call statistics can be gathered to determine that the average call desk employee can take 20 calls per hour and for an average call they have to access two credit card numbers. This means over the course of an hour a single operator would access between 30 and 40 credit card numbers. A profile has been created that, spread out over the course of an hour, 30 to 40 credit card accounts will be accessed.

If a given person accesses 30 credit cards within a three-minute period, it would set off a flag. If someone accessed 300 credit cards in a given hour, that would also set off a flag. By looking at this simple example, you can see that this is not foolproof. Profiling provides some level of protection but it is not perfect. For example, attackers could perform a low and slow attack where they access one to two credit cards every three to five minutes and continue this attack for eight hours a day for 40 days, thus gathering a significant number of credit card numbers. This type of attack would fit within the profile and not be flagged. Additional profiling could be created to help thwart this, but you can quickly see how we would get into a cat-and-mouse game if we are not careful.

Defeating profiling is one concern, but catching legitimate hardworking employees is another potential problem. What happens if an organization has a very hard worker who spends a lot of time in the office and they figure out a way to handle a call every minute? This worker is accessing 60 credit cards per hour and this would set off a flag. If a company is not careful, the message this is sending to the employee is, if you work too hard you will be flagged. This, however, creates a more serious problem, which is you are tipping your hand to what you are looking for. If an employee has a very successful day and answers 60 calls and their boss questions it, this immediately tells the employee that profiling is being performed. If they pass the word on to other people, every employee with know that if you go above 40 accesses in an hour it will be flagged. Anyone who is going to commit insider threat will quickly know how to defeat being caught and lay low.

It becomes very tricky to create profiles that can still work even if people know about them. One answer is to keep the profiles secret, but the longer you use them and people get caught by them the greater the chance that people will find them out. Once people know that profiling is being performed, it will act as an immediate deterrent. However, as they quickly learn ways around it, the usefulness of the measures will be defeated. A good example to illustrate this is Web surfing and monitoring. Many organizations have a problem with people surfing to inappropriate sites. If organizations are monitoring this behavior, if the company announces that they are now going to monitor everyone's Web access, you will see the number of people going to inappropriate sites drop significantly. After a little time you will see it starting to creep up, where people test out the bounds of the monitoring. In the worse case, if people continue to their normal level of inappropriate surfing and nothing happens, over a three-to-six-month period you will now see the level of inappropriate surfing back to the original level because everyone realized it was a false claim. However, if people start surfing and get caught, how they got caught will spread, and as people figure out ways around it, this knowledge will also spread across the organization.

Therefore, with any measure, but especially profiling, it is critical that you understand the effectiveness of the methods you are deploying. Another method that helps solve the above problem is to have many types of profiling that is performed and rotate them on a random basis. Yesterday if someone did x they did not get caught, but today when they did they got caught. This unpredictable type of profiling will usually keep the attacker and people who are trying to bypass the system on their toes.

There are two general types of profiling that can be performed: individual and group. Individual profiling is tied to a specific person and how they operate. Every person is unique, so individual profiling will learn the pattern of normality for a given individual and if it falls outside of that norm that person is flagged. The advantage of this method is that it more closes matches to an individual and is more customized to how a single individual acts. The problem is that it changes with the person so if the attacker knows that individual profiling is being performed and makes slow, minor adjustments to their behavior they could slip through the system.

For example, if I logged into the network between 7:00 A.M. and 8:00 A.M. every day and logged out at 8:00 P.M. every evening, this would create a profile that would be tracked. If a given day I logged in at 2:00 P.M., it would set off a flag. This is a very simple example so it might not seem practical, but it is meant to illustrate the point. However, if I knew profiling was being performed, for a week I would log in at 8:05 A.M., then a week later I would log in at 8:10 A.M., etc. If I slowly changed my behavioral patterns, I would be able to bypass the profiling, because as I made minor adjustments over a long period of time my profile would adapt and change to that new behavior.

Group profiling is tied to averages of how a group of people in a similar job perform.

Instead of profiling a single person, you would take a group of people who perform similar functions and create a profile based on how the group performs as a whole. The advantage of this method is that a single person cannot skew the results and it is easy to calculate. Even if a single person tries to slowly change their behavior, if the group maintains the norm, then that person's behavior will have little bearing on the overall profile. The disadvantage is that it assumes everyone has similar if not identical patterns within the group and anyone within the group who is an outlier would be flagged.

Monitoring

While profiling has benefit, there is also a lot of required effort that needs to be put against the problem in order to solve it. Instead of jumping directly towards profiling, many organizations decide to start off with a more passive method: monitoring. Monitoring is easy to do and provides a starting point for profiling. With monitoring you are just watching behavior. In watching the behavior you could inspect the information either manually or automatically but you are looking for a specific signature in the information you are monitoring. In order to profile a given person and flag exceptional behavior, you have to perform monitoring as the base. Therefore, in many cases, it is better to start with monitoring to see how bad the problem is and then move toward profiling if that is deemed necessary at a later point in time.

Before an organization performs monitoring, it is critical that they do it in a legal and ethical manner. From a legality standpoint, it is critical that an organization determines whether information has an implied expectation of privacy. If something such as e-mail or Web is determined to have an implied expectation of privacy, that expectation must be taken away prior to monitoring. While taking away an expectation of privacy might seem like a big hurdle, it can easily be achieved with a well-executed security policy. A security policy can take away the expectation of privacy so that everyone knows that their activity can be monitored and acted upon. In addition to taking away the expectation of privacy, it is important that an organization performs monitoring in a consistent, fair manner across the organization. Ideally, all methods and processes for performing monitoring across the organization should be written down in procedures that everyone follows in a consistent manner. If it is written down, there is less chance for misunderstanding than if it is verbal. If you do not believe me that the written word has less chance of being misunderstood or changed, then I suggest you play the telephone game with your co-workers. I can guarantee you that if you say something about how monitoring should be performed to one co-worker and they tell someone, who tells someone, who tells someone, after five to six people, what the last person says and what you said will always be different.

Different types of monitoring can be performed:

- Application-specific
- Problem-specific
- Full monitoring
- Trend analysis
- Probationary

Application-specific monitoring focuses on looking at a specific application for potential signs of abuse. The two applications that typically top the list are e-mail and Web. Many people send inappropriate e-mail or attach content that should not be sent out of the company. Monitoring all e-mail traffic can give a good indicator of potential problems. E-mail monitoring, just because of the wide range of information and material, is usually done with some manual methods. Web monitoring is focused more on people wasting time or going to inappropriate sites. Typically, these sites can just be flagged or blocked so in most cases Web-based monitoring is done with more automated methods.

Organizations will have problems or issues that pop up from time to time. Monitoring might be performed to reduce or get a handle on the problem. One of my clients was having a problem with employees running hacker tools on their network. It started off as one or two people just playing around and quickly turned into competitions and was impacting network performance and job performance. To get a handle on this problem, they started monitoring for people using and running these tools and took disciplinary action against people who were not following the policy.

Full monitoring is where all information or traffic is monitored. This is the most comprehensive method of monitoring but is also the most time consuming. Typically, when full monitoring is performed, it is usually passively gathered and only analyzed if there is a problem down the road. The general philosophy behind full monitoring is it is better to have the information and not need it, than to need the information and not have it. Usually if an organization is performing full monitoring, it is in conjunction with another method. A great combination is problem monitoring with full monitoring. The full monitoring will gather all the data and then where there is a problem, the full dump can be monitored to see where the problem is and take appropriate action. This is an example where it is easier to take too much data and whittle it down, than to take too little data and magically create the information you need.

Trend analysis is an analytical capability that is usually tied into full monitoring. With full monitoring, you would capture every packet on the network. With trend analysis you would just show the high-level trends leaving out all the details. Then, once you find a problem, you can dig into the details. To show you the power of trend analysis, look at the following example.

```
0000   00 00 5a 98 d3 3c 00 d0 59 ca 86 b7 08 00 45 00    ..Z..<..Y.....E.
0010   00 2e c4 3f 40 00 80 06 9f d3 0a 01 32 86 40 0c    ...?@.......2.@.
0020   1a 24 06 8f 14 46 b7 e8 10 e2 cc de 5e 37 50 18    .$...F......^7P.
0030   43 06 3d f4 00 00 2a 05 5f 5a 00 00                C.=...*._Z..


0000   00 d0 59 ca 86 b7 00 00 5a 98 d3 3c 08 00 45 00    ..Y.....Z..<..E.
0010   00 28 18 a8 40 00 2e 06 9d 71 40 0c 1a 24 0a 01    .(..@...q@..$..
0020   32 86 14 46 06 8f cc de 5e 37 b7 e8 10 e8 50 10    2..F....^7....P.
0030   40 00 ca 61 00 00 40 00 00 00 00 00                @..a..@.....


0000   00 00 5a 98 d3 3c 00 d0 59 ca 86 b7 08 00 45 00    ..Z..<..Y.....E.
0010   00 30 c4 44 40 00 80 06 36 3b 0a 01 32 86 c0 a8    .0.D@...6;..2...
0020   03 19 09 09 00 19 3c 30 1f 67 00 00 00 00 70 02    ......<0.g....p.
0030   40 00 de 1d 00 00 02 04 05 b4 01 01 04 02          @............
```

```
0000   00 d0 59 ca 86 b7 00 00 5a 98 d3 3c 08 00 45 00    ..Y.....Z..<..E.
0010   00 30 00 00 40 00 3e 06 3c 80 c0 a8 03 19 0a 01    .0..@.>.<.......
0020   32 86 00 19 09 09 ef f8 e4 e8 3c 30 1f 68 70 12    2.........<0.hp.
0030   16 d0 32 5b 00 00 02 04 05 b4 01 01 04 02          ..2[.........
```

```
0000   00 00 5a 98 d3 3c 00 d0 59 ca 86 b7 08 00 45 00    ..Z..<..Y.....E.
0010   00 28 c4 45 40 00 80 06 36 42 0a 01 32 86 c0 a8    .(.E@...6B..2...
0020   03 19 09 09 00 19 3c 30 1f 68 ef f8 e4 e9 50 10    ......<0.h....P.
0030   44 70 31 7f 00 00                                  Dp1...
```

```
0000   00 d0 59 ca 86 b7 00 00 5a 98 d3 3c 08 00 45 00    ..Y.....Z..<..E.
0010   00 81 d7 02 40 00 3e 06 65 2c c0 a8 03 19 0a 01    ....@.>.e,......
0020   32 86 00 19 09 09 ef f8 e4 e9 3c 30 1f 68 50 18    2.........<0.hP.
0030   16 d0 02 3b 00 00 32 32 30 20 6d 61 69 6c 2e 69    ...;..220 mail.i
0040   77 63 2e 73 79 74 65 78 69 6e 63 2e 63 6f 6d 20    wc.sytexinc.com
0050   45 53 4d 54 50 20 53 65 6e 64 6d 61 69 6c 20 38    ESMTP Sendmail 8
0060   2e 31 31 2e 36 2f 38 2e 31 31 2e 36 3b 20 4d 6f    .11.6/8.11.6; Mo
0070   6e 2c 20 31 37 20 4d 61 72 20 32 30 30 33 20 31    n, 17 Mar 2003 1
0080   36 3a 34 32 3a 30 39 20 2d 30 35 30 30 0d 0a       6:42:09 -0500..
```

```
0000   00 00 5a 98 d3 3c 00 d0 59 ca 86 b7 08 00 45 00    ..Z..<..Y.....E.
0010   00 28 c4 46 40 00 80 06 36 41 0a 01 32 86 c0 a8    .(.F@...6A..2...
0020   03 19 09 09 00 19 3c 30 1f 68 ef f8 e5 42 50 10    ......<0.h...BP.
0030   44 17 31 7f 00 00                                  D.1...
```

By looking at the preceding binary dump, can you tell me where the problem is or what packet you should look at to find additional information? You probably can't. Now look at Figure 9.2.

Figure 9.2 Trend Analysis

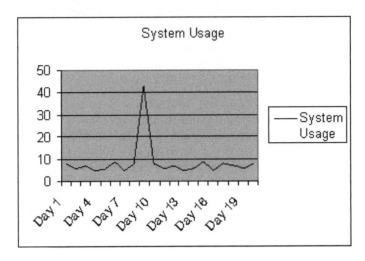

Looking at Figure 9.2, can you tell where the problem is? Clearly, doing trend analysis makes it very easy to be able to spot the high-level trends and look for problems and figure out where to go for further analysis.

The last type of monitoring is probationary monitoring. Probationary monitoring usually has to be tied with a strong security policy or monitoring procedures to be effective. If someone does not follow the policy and is put on probation, you want to watch their actions more carefully. In these cases, anyone who has violated a policy or performed an action that is suspicious will be watched and monitored.

Anomaly Detection

Anything that is not normal or is out of the ordinary could potentially be a problem. Just because something is not normal does mean it is a problem, but it usually means that further analysis should be performed. Hopefully in your organization insider threat is not a norm. Therefore, in order to commit an insider attack, someone will have to do something that is not normal. Hopefully, if the detection piece is done correctly, the person is flagged, follow-up work is performed, and the insider is caught before significant damage is caused.

While anomaly detection does work, it is not as easy as it sounds. First, in order to be able to say something is an anomaly, you have to be able to define what normality is. This can be very difficult to determine, depending on the organization and the specific area you are talking about. Normality is constantly changing at most organizations and what is normal today might not be normal tomorrow. The trick to doing this correctly is to be able to distinguish between static and dynamic behavior and patterns. A static behavior is something that stays the same for a long period of time and a dynamic behavior is constantly changing. For example, when people go to meetings is a very dynamic process. Just because I have a meeting today at 1:00 P.M. does not mean I will have a meeting tomorrow at 1:00 P.M. If you try to do anomaly detection on dynamic behavior you will constantly get false results.

Static behavior is more constant and usually is tied to more critical assets. For example, the people who can issue payroll are probably pretty constant. There might be some turnover in the department, but it does not happen that often. So if only three people in the company should be accessing payroll data, that is static behavior and is perfect for anomaly detection. If anyone outside of those three people try to access payroll, it should set off a flag and the chances that this is a malicious insider are probably fairly high.

When talking about anomalies, it is important to compare and contrast anomalies and malicious behavior. Some people use these words interchangeably, but that is a very dangerous practice. Just because something is not normal does not mean it is malicious. Things are constantly changing, and just because something is different than it was yesterday does not necessarily mean the activity is malicious or will cause harm. On the other hand, just because something is malicious does not mean it is anomalous. File access is normal and happening all the time, but if I go in and access a file and give it to a competitor, that is malicious, but probably won't be flagged as anomalous.

While both are important terms, be careful to use them appropriately in the realm of insider threat.

Signature Analysis

Signature analysis is a basic but effective measure for controlling insider threat or any malicious activity. Signature analysis is also called pattern analysis because you are looking for a pattern that is indicative of a problem or issue. Someone walking around your neighborhood with a ski mask on carrying a gun is a signature of malicious activity and if you saw this signature you most likely would call the police immediately. If you pick the signatures correctly, you have a high chance of catching malicious behavior. The drawback, however, is there could be other variants or forms of that malicious behavior that would not fit that pattern. Someone wearing a ski mask and carrying a gun is an extreme pattern of someone who is going to rob a house. There are many other people who are going to rob a house that would not fit that pattern. Therefore, only looking for that pattern yields a high chance that attacks would be missed.

The problem with signatures is that you must know about an attack in order to create a signature for it. The first time an attack occurs it will be successful because you will not have a signature. After it is successful and you perform incident response and damage assessment you can figure out how the attack occurred and build an appropriate signature the next time. However, if the next time the attacker changed the attack slightly, the signature might miss the attack again.

This brings up two important points with regards to signatures. First, they will only catch known attacks; they will not catch zero day attacks. A zero day attack is a brand new attack that has not been publicized and is not well known. Second, signatures are very rigid. If you have a signature for an attack and it occurs the exact same way each time, you will be able to detect it and flag it. However, if it is morphed or changed there is a good chance the signature will no longer be effective.

The last problems with signatures is that they take a default allow stance on security. A default allow stance says we will list what is malicious and anything else that falls through will be flagged as good. By itself, signature detection says if you see a signature that is bad behavior but there is not a signature match, then the behavior must be good. This is illustrated in Figure 9.3.

Figure 9.3 A Default Allow Security Stance

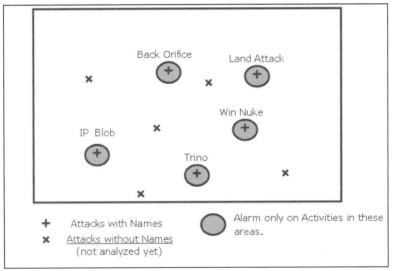

Clearly this has limitations and highlights the point that if there is not an exact signature for the given behavior, the attack will be missed. A better way to implement security is by using a default deny stance. Default deny states that anything that is not explicitly allowed is denied. Anomaly detection is more robust in that it takes a default deny stance with regards to security. It says that it will determine everything that is normal and anything that does not match a normal pattern is classified as an attack. This is illustrated in Figure 9.4.

Figure 9.4 A Default Deny Security Stance

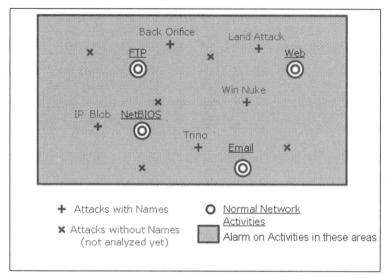

In this case you can see that with anomaly-based protection you achieve a more robust approach to the problem.

While signatures and anomaly detection are not perfect, they do have their value and can be useful when combined with other methods for controlling the insider threat.

Thin Clients

There are many factors that lead to the ease with which an attacker could commit an insider attack across the organization, but one key factor is local storage and portability of information. A laptop, while a very powerful tool for employees and mobile workers, is also a very powerful tool for someone who is trying to commit an insider attack. Why would an attacker try to send data across the network or use advanced techniques like stego when he can just walk out the front door with his laptop and then do whatever he likes with the information? A potential for reducing the liability is to remove the problem.

A technology that was used in the early days of computing has proven valuable again. In the early days, when they were connected to mainframes, they were called dumb terminals. Now, when they are connected to servers to better control systems and reduce the chance of insider threat, they are called thin clients. A thin client is a system without a hard drive and in some cases without a USB drives or other writable drive. Thin clients connect to the network and everything, including the desktop image and all software, is automatically downloaded to their system. Since there is no hard drive, nothing is stored locally. When you shut down the thin client nothing is kept locally and anything that has not been saved to the server is lost. It does not matter what happens to the client since it does not contain anything sensitive. It also makes it much harder for someone to extract data from the organization.

Policy, Training, and Security Awareness

I could just see Dorothy skipping through the cyber yellow brick road singing policy, training, awareness, oh my. While that might be a far stretch, these three items work very closely together.

The easiest way to think about the problem is: policy tells you what to do, training teaches you the skills for doing it, and awareness changes your behavior so that you are willing to do what you are suppose to be doing. While each one is critical and important by itself, when you put all three together they play a key role in controlling, reducing, and stopping insider threat.

Every organization says they have a policy but very few implement them correctly. When I think of security policies the analogy I like to use is security policies are a lot like sex when I went to high school. When I went to school, everyone was talking about sex, everyone was claiming they were having sex, in reality very few were having sex and those that were having it were not doing it correctly. You get the picture with security policies. Most companies like to claim they have policies, but they are cumbersome and hard to read. For a policy to really help combat insider threat, it has to be readable and understandable to the average employee; otherwise, it will not do any good.

Training complements the security policy by teaching users the skills they need to do their jobs in the most efficient manner. Even with proper training, some people will still not do the right thing. Awareness is meant to change someone's behavior and explain to them the importance of a given policy statement and do it in such a way that they will change their behavior and follow the policy moving forward.

Background Checks

People who have done bad things in the past will most likely do bad things in the future, and people who have never done bad things in the past most likely will never do bad things in the future. There are always exceptions to the rules, but this general premise holds true. While there is no set indicator of someone who will commit insider threat, one of the best indicators is if they have something in their past or even potentially a criminal record.

There is nothing that is foolproof, but doing a quick background check of employees and applicants to make sure nothing stands out is probably not a bad idea.

Summary

With any security problem, there is never a single solution to solving it. The only way to solve difficult security problems is with defense in depth – multiple layers of protection. This chapter showed that there are many methods that can be used to control insider threat. No single method is perfect, but by combining multiple methods an organization can maintain a secure environment and properly control insider threat.

Chapter 10

Survivability

Solutions in this chapter:

- Risk

- Limiting Failure Points

- Increasing Redundancy

- Controlling and Limiting Access

- Psychosocial Factors

- Educating Employees

- Reacting to Insider Threat

Introduction

At the end of the day, survival is the name of the game. While you hope and pray that no damage ever occurs to your organization and that it operates and sustains a high level of profit, when attacks hit, you want to be able to make sure your organization survives and that there is still a piece left standing that can continue to operate after all the dust settles. While operating at 30% revenue is not as ideal as operating at 100%, it is better than operating at 0% or going out of business.

In this last chapter of the book, we summarize everything that we have talked about and revisit some issues. We also examine how does a company goes about surviving insider threat and increasing their defenses over time to minimize the amount of damage it will cause.

Risk

When talking about survivability, a key point to start with is risk. Risk is the possibility for suffering harm or loss and survivability is making sure that an organization never has complete loss. Therefore, balancing the two together with insider threat, the key is to figure out the areas where an organization is suffering harm or loss and making sure that controls are in place so the organization cannot be completely destroyed. As we talked about in the previous chapter, critical intellectual property is what gives an organization net worth. If that IP can be destroyed, then the company could also be destroyed. While we understand the importance of having a prioritized list of IP, what is the next step that needs to be performed? The next step is looking at what potentially could happen to the IP and what are weaknesses that we have that would allow that to happen. In doing this analysis, what we have just defined is the general formula for risk. While many different formulas for risk are available, the one that I like to use in insider threat, because it is very comprehensive, is the following formula:

Risk = (threat x vulnerabilities x probability x impact)/countermeasures

Understanding and calculating risk enables you to better understand your exposure points. If you are going to survive, it is critical that you are able to protect and limit the damage an exposure point can have. If you want a good lesson in survivability and risk management, play chess, or even better, play Risk. In either of these games you have to make risk decisions and allow your pieces to be taken. However, the real skill is survival, it does not matter in chess whether you have one piece left or 10 pieces, if your opponent has no pieces left, then you have won. There are not different degrees of winning, you either win or lose. And when the stakes are high, which they are in insider threat, losing must be avoided at all cost.

Threats

Threats represent possible danger and come in many shapes and sizes. When you are putting together the risk formula, threat is what drives the train. Threat is the starting point that is used to calculate all the other variables that are needed to come up with a formula for risk.

We could make an almost infinite list of different areas of possible danger, but the key is to focus in on realistic threats. For example, a general threat that represents possible danger would be a hurricane. If you live in Florida or Mississippi, this is a real threat that should be analyzed closely and risk should be calculated for it. However, if you live in Montana or Colorado, a hurricane is not a real threat. Based on location and weather conditions it is not something that is going to happen and therefore spending any energy on analyzing that threat is wasted effort because it is not realistic. However, planning for heavy snow and blizzard conditions is a must. Just like different states in the U.S. have different threats, different companies have different threats. There is no way we could create a generic list of threats, since it has to be tied very closely to your organization. The vertical market you perform business in, and what your critical intellectual property is are all used to focus your attention on the correct area.

While the identification of threat enables us to focus our effort, in many cases there is nothing we can do about a particular threat. The threat tells us what to worry about in the risk formula, but to lower the overall risk, you cannot reduce the threat; rather, one of the other variables has to be lowered. If you think in terms of hurricanes, this will make sense. A hurricane represents possible danger and is a key threat for certain areas in the U.S. While the possible danger that a hurricane could cause is devastating, can you stop, prevent, or do anything about a hurricane? The short answer is no. Trust me, if there were a way that we could control a hurricane, we would have done so this past year. Unfortunately, there is nothing we can do to stop the threat.

Threats from insider attacks come in many shapes and sizes. The general areas of threat for insider threat are the following:

- Revealing sensitive data
- False information
- Loss of an asset

I want you to look at the list very closely, since another way to write the list is:

- Disclosure of information
- Alteration of information
- Destruction of information

What we are really talking about with the aforementioned lists are:

- Confidentiality
- Integrity
- Availability

Without even realizing it, we quickly were able to map our key threats in insider threat back to our three core areas of network security: confidentiality, integrity, and availability.

Confidentiality

Confidentiality deals with preventing, detecting, and deterring the unauthorized disclosure of sensitive information. Every company has information that gives them a competitive advantage and needs to be kept secret to the company. This information is usually called intellectual property at a high level and the more specific form is called a trade secret. Whether a company formally calls it a trade secret or not is secondary, but every company has them. A trade secret is information that provides a company a unique market share or unique competitive advantage that if publicly revealed could have dire impact to the organization. One of the best examples is the formula for Coca-Cola. This is a trade secret and lots of time and energy have been put into protecting it. With insider threat, breach of confidentiality is a big concern. This is probably the main means of attack for a high-end insider committing espionage against the company. If you look at all the insider threat examples with the government and any ones involving a commercial entity, all revolve around some trusted insider giving away sensitive information to another government or a competitor.

Integrity

Integrity deals with preventing, detecting, and deterring the unauthorized modification of information. Anything dealing with data consistency or alteration of information falls under integrity. If a company is writing a proposal and the cheapest company wins, integrity becomes a key issue. If someone could either accidentally or deliberately modify the numbers, it could impact the ability of the company to win the contract. Database consistency in a distributed environment also falls under integrity.

While integrity is usually not the main focus of high-end insider threat attacks, it could be a secondary goal. If a competitor of mine has a key piece of information that I want to compromise, what I could do is either increase the value to me or decrease the value to them. To increase the value to me, I must compromise the confidentiality of the information. By stealing it, I can see it and use it and increase my competitive advantage. However, there are some cases where I might not be able to breach the confidentiality. In that case, if I cannot increase the value to me, I would want to decrease the value to my competitor. The main way of decreasing the value is by compromising the integrity of the information. If I cannot find out the formula for Coca Cola, but I could go in and change the formula, I am still giving myself a competitive advantage. By changing the formula, customers are going to stop buying it. If they are not buying my competitor's soda, they have a better chance of buying mine. In this case I have just decreased the value of a company's intellectual property through an integrity attack.

Availability

Availability deals with preventing, detecting, and deterring unauthorized destruction of information. Denial and theft of information is the primary availability threats. The problem with attacks that destroy information is that they are very easy to do. Destroying a server could be as simple as pouring water on top of it. Purposely deleting backup tapes or not backing up any data and just storing blank tapes in their places would also be a simple yet effective attack.

Availability attacks are usually done by low-end attackers with the main group being disgruntled employees. This is considered a low-end attack because there is no direct benefit for the attacker except the satisfaction of seeing a company destroyed or lose money.

In some cases, availability attacks can be used by the high-end attacker, but they offer low re-use value for the attacker, so they aren't that attractive. For example, if we are competing against each other, one way to give myself an advantage is to destroy your facility with a bomb or fire. However, you will eventually rebuild the facility and there will be other competitors, so this is not a huge value or return on investment. Planting someone on the inside to slowly extract data over a long period of time is usually a much better payoff.

From a threat perspective, all three could represent danger to a company. Breaking it down by attacker you have the following threats from highest to lowest:

High-End Attacker (Most Damage)

- Confidentiality
- Integrity
- Availability

Low-End Attacker (Least Damage)

- Availability
- Integrity
- Confidentiality

This presents an interesting dilemma in terms of threats. If you are worried about a high-end attack, the most likely threat is confidentiality; however, if you are worried about the low-end attacker, the most likely threat is availability. Since both can cause damage, you have to worry about both high-end and low-end threats, which means a company must pay attention to threats across all three areas: confidentiality, integrity, and availability.

Vulnerabilities

Vulnerabilities are weaknesses that enable a threat to manifest itself against an organization. Threats are all around us and, as we pointed out, there is little we can do to minimize or prevent a threat. However, since vulnerabilities become the portal that enables a threat to cause damage, reducing the vulnerability will reduce the overall risk to a given threat. Therefore, vulnerabilities are the items that we fix across an organization to reduce risk.

What is important to remember is that threat drives the train. So once we determine a list of high threats for an organization, the next step is to identify the corresponding vulnerabilities that could be exploited or compromised. If the answer is that there is no vulnerability for a given threat, then we are not concerned. What we are looking for are items where there is a threat and vulnerability. A threat without vulnerability is not a concern because there are millions of threats around and tons of items that represent possible danger, but if we do not have a weakness then who cares?

The same holds true with vulnerabilities. If there is a weakness but not a threat, then we also are not concerned, but we should never get to that point, because we are starting off with threats and only looking for vulnerabilities that correspond to a given threat. Therefore, if there is not a threat, then we are not even going to bother looking at vulnerabilities.

The most common vulnerability or weakness at an organization is access. Giving someone more access than what they need to do their job is the most common portal that attackers use to compromise an organization via the use of an insider. Access can come in many shapes and sizes, but the more common weaknesses are:

- Access to critical files or IP
- Access to physical computers or systems
- Access to physical buildings
- Access to storage medium
- Access to sensitive file in printed form
- Access to sensitive conversation or transmission

If organizations can learn to properly control access, they will reduce their vulnerabilities and reduce the ways that threats can manifest themselves.

Probability

While knowing that there is a possible danger (threat) with a corresponding weakness (vulnerability) is important, the next important thing to ask is what is the probability or likelihood of this occurring. You could have a devastating threat and vulnerability, but if it is never going to happen, why worry? In determining likelihood, the situational environment that a company operates in becomes critical. If I tell you that I have a house that cannot support the weight of snow and if more than two inches of snow falls on the roof it will collapse, is this a problem? It depends. Clearly we have a threat and clearly we have a resulting vulnerability, but the question is where is this house located? The environment or location will help us determine the probability of whether it will snow, which will determine whether this is a concern or not. If this house is located in Boston, where it snows several feet each year, this is a major risk. If the house is located in the tropics, where it never gets below 50 degrees Fahrenheit, then it is a low risk. Therefore, probability must be added to the equation to get an accurate risk rating.

When some people talk about risk, they use only the following formula:

Risk = threat x vulnerabilities

They plot each risk on a risk matrix where they include likelihood (probability) and impact. Although this method is also okay, I prefer to put it together in one formula to make to not lose site of the critical components.

Impact

The next piece of the puzzle we are going to look at is impact: how bad will it be if it happens? In essence, when we add impact, we are looking at what is the monetary loss that is going to occur with a given threat. What you are really doing in this step is tying the threat and vulnerability to a given asset or system.

Saying that there is a new buffer overflow threat and our systems are not patched is a problem, but the real question is what system we are talking about. If we are talking about a test system in the lab that is only used to run experiments once in a while, then the impact to the organization if that system is taken down is minimal. However, if we are talking about the critical file server that contains all the key IP that is accessed thousands of times a day and is used to operate the company, then the impact for that system being down is very high.

At this point we have a clear picture of how bad the problem is really going to be. We know what the possible danger is, we know whether we have a weakness, we know the likelihood of this occurring, and we know against which system or piece of data this is going to happen to. Now that we have a clear picture of the risk or loss, we need to know what we can do to reduce it.

Countermeasures

Countermeasures focus in on the solution piece. Now that we have a clear picture of the problem, what can we do to fix the problem? When dealing with risk, there are three general solutions:

- Accept the risk
- Reduce the risk
- Transfer the risk

Accepting the risk is different from avoiding the risk. Risk avoidance is where you do not care about the risk and just want it to go away and in essence will say anything to make that happen. That is not an acceptable solution and is not considered part of the risk countermeasures because it is something that you never want to do.

Risk acceptance is where you fully understand the risk and make a cost-benefit analysis in which you compare the cost of the risk with the cost of fixing or reducing the risk. If the cost to fix or reduce the risk is more than the cost of the risk, it makes sense to accept the current risk. Even if the risk occurs, it will still be cheaper than if you had prevented it. When performing these calculations, the biggest mistake that is made is to not calculate the full cost of both the risk and the countermeasure. In calculating the cost of the risk, it is critical to calculate the annualized loss. In many cases if you have a potential worm as a risk, an organization will only calculate the single occurrence of the worm as the cost of the risk. However, if this worm could occur six times a year, then the number that was calculated must be multiplied by six to get the real value. In terms of calculating the cost of a counter-measure, it is important to calculate the TCO or total cost of ownership. In many cases, organizations will say that they can reduce or fix a risk by purchasing a new appliance that cost $50,000 and use that to calculate the cost of the countermeasure. The cost of $50,000 is the cost to just get the appliance delivered to your doorstep. As soon as someone in your organization starts to unpack it, the cost is more than $50,000. As someone configures it, troubleshoots it, and maintains it, the cost is probably easily three to five times that of the single appliance. Therefore, it is critical to always use accurate and complete numbers; otherwise, the cost-benefit analysis will be flawed.

The next option for dealing with risk is more common: reducing the risk. Typically, risk acceptance is done after the risk has been reduced to an acceptable level. Some people, when they look at the ways to deal with risk, say there is one that is missing: eliminate the risk. Actually, risk elimination is a subset of risk reduc-tion. If you reduce the risk to zero, you have successfully eliminated the risk. In most situations it is better to reduce many risks than to eliminate one risk. In some cases, if the risk is very high, it might make sense to eliminate the one risk, but in most cases if you are going to spend effort and energy, it is better to reduce many risks than to eliminate one. Figure 10.1 illustrates this point.

Figure 10.1 Risk Reduction

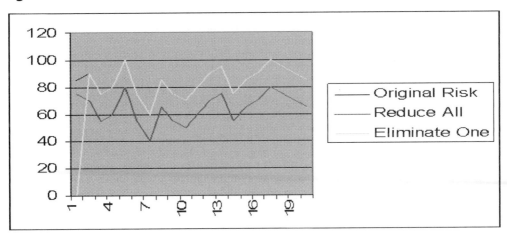

From an organizational risk perspective, would you rather have the top or bottom line? I know that I would rather have the bottom line where all my risks are reduced than the top line where one risk is zero, and I have done nothing about the other 19 risks. With limited resources, we have to look at the big picture. Instead of focusing on just one risk, look holistically and fix or reduce them all in a coordinated fashion.

The final countermeasure is to transfer the risk. This is often called the insurance model because instead of assuming the risk you are transferring it over to a third party who will assume the risk for you.

When you buy insurance for something, the way they determine the premium is by using risk formulas. If you have never had an accident and never had a speeding ticket, your premiums will be lower than someone who has had accidents and multiple speeding tickets. Why? Because the insurance company feels that the first driver is less of a risk than the second driver. The greater the chance that an insurance company is going to have to pay out, the higher the premiums. Insurance companies are still in business because they manage to make money.

Risk Analysis

Now that we have covered the key components of risk, we can move onto to how we perform general risk analysis. Risk analysis deals with analyzing the risk and figuring out which items require more attention than others. There are two general types of risk analysis that can be performed:

- Qualitative
- Quantitative

Qualitative

Qualitative risk analysis is where you categorize risk but you do not assign exact values. Qualitative risk analysis is easier to perform and much quicker because you are just performing a general rating. The easiest method of performing qualitative analysis is using the scheme of high, medium, and low. Although this works okay, I personally feel that three categories do not give enough room for discretion. I prefer to use the scheme shown in Table 10.1.

Table 10.1 Quantitative Risk Categories

Category	Description
1	Configuration issue that does not impact security
2	Non-critical security risk but should be fixed
3	Low security risk
4	Medium security risk
5	Major security risk

I feel that using a five-degree rating scheme gives a little more flexible. With qualitative you perform the analysis very quickly, rating items into one of the five categories.

Some argue that you are going to miscategorize items, which is correct, but the important thing to remember is that this is a self-correcting model. Since qualitative analysis is such a quick process, you would actually perform it on a regular basis. If I accidentally put a risk in category 4 when it should be a 5, it does not matter, because the next time I do the analysis it will bubble up to 5. The other neat thing about this model is you are really only concerned with level 5 items because the way this works is you will fix the level 5 items and re-perform the analysis, fix the level 5 and re-analyze. With this trick in mind, it becomes even easier. For each item, you are just determining whether it is 5 or below and if it is below it does not matter where you put it because you are never going to focus on anything below 5. This provides a nice trick for performing a quick analysis that is self-correcting, just in case you make a mistake.

Quantitative

Quantitative is the more time-consuming method in which you assign an exact number to each item. While this takes a lot longer to perform, the results are usually more useful for overall strategic and business planning. While getting exact numbers for each risk can be beneficial in certain circumstances, in most organizations the extra benefit is not worth the extra effort.

The criticism is if I am going to spend eight months figuring out exact values for each risk item and four months fixing the problems, I am not focusing my energy in the right areas. I should be focusing as little energy as possible on figuring out what the problem is and the most energy on fixing the problem. In this example I spent two-thirds of my time figuring out what the problem is and only one-third of my time fixing it.

The other criticism of quantitative analysis is that organizations are very dynamic and always changing. Most organizations are a lot different today than they were three to four months ago. Since quantitative analysis takes so long to perform, by the time you calculate exact numbers for each risk, the risks have changed and the values are no longer accurate.

Calculating Risk

Risk analysis is very helpful, and in most cases provides the information that you need. However, in some cases it is beneficial to be able to perform actual calculations on risk. In performing actual calculations, two formulas are used:

- SLE
- ALE

SLE stands for single loss expectancy and calculates the cost of a single occurrence of the risk. SLE is calculated by taking the exposure factor multiplied by the asset value.

While SLE provides a starting point, is does not tell you the true loss. It tells you the loss if it occurs only once. Many risks, as with viruses and worms, occur many times in a given year. Therefore, what you really want to know is what the cost is over an entire year. To find this, you calculate the ALE, or annualized loss expectancy, which is the SLE times the ARO, or annualized rate of occurrence.

Let's look at an example to show how these formulas can be used to make a cost justification for security. A key aspect and focus for insider threat is access. At your organization, a proposal that will bring into your company $10 million in revenue is currently being worked on. Of the last six proposals that you submitted, you lost three because the competition outbid you. When getting the results, it almost seemed that they had inside information and knew details of your proposal. That brought up concern and the potential for insider threat. In this example, if we calculated the SLE it would be the asset value, which is $10 million, times the exposure factor. In this case, based on historical data, three of the last six proposals were suspect to insider threat, so we will use an exposure factor of 50%. Therefore, the SLE in this case is $5 million. In performing a cost-benefit analysis, we need to know the true loss and not just the single occurrence.

One of the problems with cost-benefit analysis is if you use too low a number or an incorrect number for the loss you will not be able to make correct calculations. If you are going to work on six additional proposals this year, all around the same potential revenue, then the ARO is six. So the true cost of this loss is really the

SLE times the ARO, which is $5 million times six, or $30 million, for the ALE. For calculations, the true loss over a year is represented by the ALE not the SLE.

Here is a good example that illustrates how performing the wrong calculation can give significantly incorrect numbers and results. In this case, if the cost to fix the problem or reduce the risk was $4 million, if you used the SLE it would be a low return on investment, but if you used the correct value of the ALE, it make a stronger case. Spending $4 million to fix a $5 million problem is not nearly as compelling as spending $4 million to fix a $30 million problem. Therefore, understanding the difference between SLE and ALE is critical to making sure the proper values are being used.

The second half of the cost-benefit analysis is the TCO or total cost of ownership of the solution. Just like people would mistakenly use the SLE instead of the ALE, organizations also mistakenly use the cost of the product instead of the total cost of ownership of the solution.

In this situation, let's assume that the current problem (and the reason we think proposals have been compromised by an insider) is that proper authentication is not being performed and everyone uses weak passwords and access permissions are not properly set up. We cost out a solution to use token-based authentication and the cost for the server and the hardware tokens for all users is $800,000. We also cost out authentication software that can better control and track IP across the organization at $200,000. Therefore, we predict that we can fix this problem by spending $1 million. However, we all can see that we did not price out the complete cost of the solution, but only the direct hardware and software costs. The $1 million is the cost for the delivery person to drop the boxes at the front door. As soon as employees start unpacking boxes and configuring the software, the cost is going to dramatically increase. In both of these cases, not only are the systems time consuming to set up, but there is a lot of maintenance and a lot of integration costs involved. This $1 million software/hardware outlay will probably cost the company six to ten times that over a year when you calculate in the total cost of ownership and maintenance.

It is important to remember that when you calculate risk and countermeasures that you pay careful attention to what is being calculated. I know some people purposely play games with the numbers, but there are also a lot of people who accidentally miscalculate the numbers and lead the company to make bad or incorrect decisions.

Nonetheless, quantifying certain risks and presenting them to executives go a long way toward making a case for why the insider threat needs to be addressed and fixed as soon as possible. I have found that by performing monetary calculations that can be validated, it is easier to sell security solutions to upper management.

Many security people complain that their management and executives won't spend the money that is needed to make the organization secure, and they walk around frustrated and in some cases bitter. When I ask them what they are asking for and what management says, they usually tell me that they ask for x but management won't give it to them. I then ask what the benefit is to the organization and the cost savings that will be realized by purchasing this item. They usually give me a dirty look and ask, "Whose side are you on?" My answer is, I am on the side of the company, but I can usually clearly see that the reason most security departments are under-staffed and under-resourced is because many people do not know how to sell and do not know how to talk the language of business.

Security is always changing and there are always new threats and corresponding vulnerabilities at an organization. There is no way that executives can keep up with this changing landscape and insider threat is a perfect example. If security departments do not make the case and sell management on the importance of paying attention and dealing with the insider threat, how are they going to know it is important? In many cases we assume that the executives already understand and know the importance of a problem, but if the experts do not tell them, how do we expect them to know? As I stated earlier, part of our job is to be evangelists for the cause. We have to be careful and make sure that we do not turn into Chicken Little screaming that the sky is falling. But by staying up on the news, gathering facts and data points, we will be able to make a compelling case to executives of why a problem needs to be addressed before it gets out of hand. In terms of insider threat, we are quickly approaching that time period. While few companies are publicizing it, by talking with partners with whom you have executed NDAs (non-disclosure agreements) and looking at public sources, you can make a strong case that this is happening. The Secret Service and CERT are publishing a series of insider threat reports, many of them covering commercial sectors. Why? Because they recognize this is a big problem and they need to raise people's awareness.

Awareness based on factual data is the key. If you start running around screaming about each problem with no data and no follow-up, you are going to quickly lose credibility. However, if you find out the facts, perform analysis across your organization, and present a clear business case on the dangers of insider threat, the impact it has had to other locations, and the impact it could have at your organization, people will start to listen. Putting together clear business cases is a good start, but you have to make sure that you have a solution you can present. One of the biggest problems I see is that security will present a strong case, but when an executive asks how to fix it or how much it will cost, security does not have an answer. Whenever you are going to present a problem and raise awareness on a situation, you always want to make sure you have a solution in your back pocket. You might not always present it, but just in case someone asks for it, you want to make sure it is available.

The second mistake that is often made is running the problem to ground or validating the solution. Often when a problem comes up, we like to look at a small segment of it and sell a solution instead of a problem. I have seen cases where people say they need an intrusion prevention system (IPS) and when asked why, explain that it is a new security component, the company needs defense in depth, and everyone else has one. Although the defense in depth argument has validity, you still have to run it ground and ask what the problem is. Figure out the problem and then see what the appropriate solution is. Insider threat is a perfect example: analyze your company and see what your true threat and corresponding vulnerabilities are to insider threat and then figure out different possible solutions. Perform cost-benefit analysis across the different solutions and pick the best solution and present that to management. Also be prepared to present the reason for choosing that solution and potentially an alternative solution.

The last issue is the need to speak the same language. If I am speaking English and you are speaking Spanish, although audible sounds are coming out of our mouths and we are hearing those audible sounds, they have no meaning since we speak different languages. We are not communicating because we are speaking different languages. That is often what happens when security people and executives talk. Security is speaking security and the executives are speaking business. There is no wonder that when these meetings occur everyone leaves frustrated and nothing gets accomplished.

If you want to be able to communicate and sell, you need to be able to speak the language of business and the common ground is money. If you can show a validated business case talking dollars and cents, you have found a common language and you will be more effective in your communication.

Limiting Failure Points

If the ultimate goal is survivability, a key way to accomplish this is by limiting failure points. Once again, almost everything we do with security and insider threat revolves around risk and therefore every decision that you make you have to ask yourself what do I have to gain and what to I have to lose by making a given decision. Since insider threat is focused on controlling or limiting access it is critical to make sure that the access control measures do not fail. If other measures that are not as important fail, they are less of a concern. In essence, we are identifying what the critical business processes are and making sure those security controls do not fail.

When talking about failure points, it is often useful to perform an analysis between automobiles and airplanes. If a component fails in a car, while it could cause an accident, usually you can pull over to the side over the road. If a component fails in an airplane at 30,000 feet, you have a much different problem. That is one of the reasons that components between the two are designed much differently. In addition, with airplanes the primary maintenance that is performed is called preventive maintenance. Instead of waiting for a component to fail, the component will be fixed prior to a problem. Although this tends to be more expensive, it is well worth the extra cost. Compare this to automobiles. While some people do some basic preventive maintenance like changing the oil, in most cases people wait for a problem before they bring it into the shop. Since there is less at risk with a car, there is less need to do preventive maintenance. Since there is more at risk with an airplane, it is more important to perform preventive maintenance.

Even with an airplane, the preventive maintenance schedule focuses on the critical failure points. There are many systems, but two that come immediately to mind are the engine and landing gear. If either of those failed, there would be major issues and potential loss of life. In an airplane scenario, the driving factor is to prevent loss of life and to focus on critical failure areas to prevent them from failing.

With insider threat, the driving factor is loss of significant revenue or profit or, to be more direct, prevent drastic loss so the company will not go out of business. In any situation, although it is ideal to minimize loss, the key component is to make sure the organization continues to function and stay competitive both short term and long term. This balance between the two is critical. I have seen organizations be so focused on short term that they never realize the long-term impact something could have. If you cannot get past the short term, you might never make it to the long term vision.

Taking this focus of keeping a company in business, you can quickly see that the focus of keeping a company in business would tie back to what gives a company a competitive advantage. In most cases, the answer would be the intellectual property of the organization is what makes a company unique or a differentiator in the market that enables the company to continue to be successful and thrive. Therefore, that is going to be what is targeted. In previous chapters we have covered identifying critical IP; now we have to look at the failure points across that IP.

Where are the areas that your IP can fail or be compromised? The three general areas are in the disclosure, alteration, and destruction of it. Hopefully, you are starting to see some similarities in what we are presenting, which is meant to show you the importance of this key information. When it comes to reducing the failure points of disclosure and alteration, access control or the lack of access control is usually a key culprit. On the surface it seems easy to understand that if you stop someone from getting to a piece of data they cannot disclose it or alter it; however, you still have to strike that fine balance between functionality and security and enable your organization to function. Too much functionality increases your failure points and too little functionality causes other problems. Neither is good since both could result in loss of revenue and loss of competitiveness for the organization.

The other area to focus in on is limiting the failure points for destruction or denial of access to information. The best way that is handled is through redundancy.

Increasing Redundancy

We started off the previous section by talking about airplanes and limiting failure points. While preventive maintenance is a critical aspect of that, one of the best ways to limit failure points is by implementing redundancy across a system. Preventive maintenance is based on the mean time between failures. If a certain component on average fails every two years, if you replace it every year the chances of it failing are very low. However, this is playing with averages. If I play baseball, I could have a very high batting average but there are times I strike out and go way below the average and there are times I hit home runs and go above the average, so on a given day there could be a huge fluctuation even though at the end of the season my average is high.

The same thing holds true for mean time between failures. While there are some components that fail in four months and other components will last for four years, the average when you put all of these together is two years. There is no guarantee that even with preventive maintenance that a component will not fail before the maintenance is performed; it is just not very likely. However, defense in depth teaches us that you never want to rely on a single measure to be secure, so an alternative solution is redundancy. This is prevalent in airplanes but is very prevalent in the space shuttle. All mission-critical systems in the space shuttle have redundancy built in so if they fail it will still function properly. Even landing sites have built-in redundancy. Since the shuttle has strict requirements in terms of weather and other conditions for landing, they want to make sure the shuttle is never stranded or has to land in unsafe conditions. Landing site redundancy means that if it cannot land at one site, there is an alternative site where it can land.

IP is the life blood of your organization and if it is destroyed your company could potentially be destroyed in direct response to the compromise. Therefore redundancy plays a key component with destruction or denial of access to information. A low-grade insider such as a disgruntled employee does not want to get any direct benefit by their attack other than to cause harm to the company. These attacks could include encrypting a hard drive on a key server and not giving the company the key unless they pay a large amount of money, typically referred to as extortion.

They could also steal a hard drive or physically destroy a system or facility. With all of these problems, redundancy plays a key role in the solution.

Even with a competitor or government who is planting or compromising an insider, they could also resort to availability attacks if all else fails. If we are competing against each other for a new product, ideally I would like to get your IP and use it to build a better product. However, there could be situations in which I am unable to do that. There could also be cases where even though I have the IP, you still have too much of an advantage for me to compete. In those situations, an alternative would be to destroy the information. An insider would have better access to destroy information and do it in a way that either the company does not know who did it or that it looks like an accident. In this situation, redundancy will help protect your data so that if a single copy is lost your company can still survive.

As with any solution, there is always a positive and a negative. While redundancy will help prevent data loss if a single copy is lost, redundancy also increases your exposure points. Instead of your data residing in one location, it is now in multiple locations, and there is a good chance those other locations do not have the same security or access control as the primary location. One of my clients had a primary computing facility that had very tight security and access control. To plan for an attack against the facility under their disaster recovery plans, they assumed that with a large-scale attack, their primary facility could be destroyed. Therefore, at one of the remote satellite offices they put a redundant server in which all the information was backed up, including critical IP for the company. The satellite office was never designed for tight security since the original idea was that it would house some sales and marketing people who all had laptops and took them home every evening, so even if someone broke in, there would be nothing of value to take. With the backup server located there, they never changed or upgraded the security at that facility. Whenever they had risk assessments and penetration tests done, they always focused on the primary site and thought everything was fine. They suffered a major insider attack and the insider compromised the remote facility because he knew it would be much easier than the primary facility.

This is a situation where you have to make sure you always look at the plus and minus with every solution. While redundancy can help increase your security, if it is not done correctly and the backup site is overlooked, it could actually do more harm than good.

Full redundancy at the server or data center is ideal, but it can be very expensive and if not carefully thought through could actually increase your exposure points which would decrease your security.

Other alternatives are file backups. While this is not real time, it would still enable recovery in a shorter time period than having to re-create it from scratch.

Tape backups run into similar issues as backup servers. If you only store them locally, you have the physical security protection of the main facility, but they are vulnerable to the same disaster you are trying to protect against. Fireproof safes with limited access is an alternative to this, in which the tapes are still on site and locally protected but have control to limit the number of insiders who could get access to them and even if the facility were destroyed, the tapes and safe might be okay. Offsite storage is another option in which the tapes are stored offsite. Now they are remote and harder for an insider to access and in the event of a major disaster they would still be protected. The problem is if the person who controls the tape inventory at the offsite facility is an insider threat, they could still request the tapes.

A potential solution to the problem of a single ill-intentioned insider causing harm is to utilize a security triad that I refer to as the following:

- Least privilege
- Separation of duties
- Rotation of duties

Least privilege starts off the process by stating that you give someone the least amount of access they need to do their job. You need to create a matrix identifying the minimal subset of people that need access to the tapes while allowing your organization to still function. On the one hand, you never want the number to be one because that creates a single point of value. On the other hand giving 200 people access is probably too many. Essentially, you are looking for a number greater than one so there is some redundancy but as low as possible to be able to maintain control. Whenever you have more than one person who can do something, you must also keep accountability in mind.

Accountability enables you to determine the specific person who performed a task and track it in a way that they are held responsible for their actions. If you have 10 people who have access to the tapes and the tapes are stored in a locked cabinet that opens with a standard metal key, every one of the 10 people would have the same key. If you went in one day and a tape was missing or a tape was intentionally destroyed or corrupted, you would know one of the 10 people did it but you would not know which one. While you could keep an eye on all ten, you want to make sure you can isolate the one person and hold each individual responsible for the actions they are performing. As you will see, separation of duties also helps with the accountability piece.

Gong back to least privilege, you would give employees the least amount of access they needed to perform their jobs. However, in some cases that access is still too great or poses too big a security threat, especially in the arena of accountability.

The next step in the security process is to take a function and break it up across multiple people or perform separation of duties. In this situation, to access a tape, two people need to be involved. Now this adds checks and balances into the equation. The chance of one person being an insider threat is low, but the chances of two people both being insiders are exponentially lower, so you are increasing your odds and providing better checks and balances.

Here's a story to drive home this point: A statistician would always pack a bomb in his suitcase whenever he traveled. One of his friends noticed that he did this and asked him why. The statistician explained that the chance of there being a bomb on an airplane is .01 percent. The chance of there being two bombs on an airplane is .0000000000000001 percent. So by carrying a bomb, he great reduced the odds that there would be a second bomb.

Now with that story to tell at cocktail parties, how could anyone ever say that geeks are not fun and math is not cool?

With backup tapes, a common way to perform separation of duties locally is by utilizing two safes. Most organizations already have one large safe, so purchasing a second smaller safe will not be a great increase in cost. Put the tape in the small safe and give the combination to one group of people. Then take the smaller safe and put it in a larger safe and give that combination to a second group of people. As long as the same people are not in group one and group two, you have achieved separation of duties. In order to access the tape, at least two people need to be involved; no single person can gain access to the system. The reason you put multiple people in each group as opposed to a single person is redundancy. As we stated before, you never want to have a single point of failure and if there is only one person who knows the combination and they are not around or on vacation, then you have just caused a denial of service attack to occur because you cannot get access to your safe and recover your data.

Another way to perform separation of duties is across multiple sites. If you are performing incremental or differential backups you would need more than one tape in order to recover the data. If your company has multiple locations, you can store each of the tapes at different locations, each being locked and controlled by a different person. If there is a problem and the data needs to be recovered, two people need to be involved.

While separation of duties works well, it has the potential to deteriorate over time. Instead of one person performing a job, two people work together to perform the job. In the beginning, the two people do not know each other very well. As they begin to work together, they get to know each other and they become friendlier. The longer they work together, the stronger the potential friendship grows, and the greater the chances that they might work together to launch an attack against the company. So while separation of duties is powerful, the benefit decreases the longer two people work together. Therefore, you want to rotate people's positions so the chance of them becoming comfortable is reduced, which brings us to the next principle.

Rotation of duties is the last part in our chain. You start off by giving someone the least amount of access they need to do their job and if that access is still too great you then break the job up over multiple people and perform separation of duties. The longer people work together, the greater the chance of them becoming friends, which reduces the value of the separation of duties. Rotating positions on a regular basis reduces the chances of this occurring. Rotation of duties is a fairly common practice with the goal to reduce collusion among people in the workplace. While this could require some re-training, usually there is a large base of people trained in a given task so rotation is more feasible than it might seem on the surface.

So far in this section we have been focusing on redundancy across data. We looked at redundant servers, databases, and tape backups for the data. While it was not covered we could have also covered RAID, redundant array of inexpensive disk which is meant to set up local redundancy on a system, that if a single drive stops working the system will suffer no data loss. Although it is important to focus on the data, we have to remember that if you cannot get to the data, then it does not matter how protected it is.

Therefore, we will finish up this section by looking at redundancy across your entire network and infrastructure. No matter how protected your data is, any single point of failure in your organization could be used as a point of compromise by an insider. Typically, the logic that many companies used was that while there are single points of failure within their network, an external attacker does not know what they are, cannot find out about them, and cannot get access to them. While I was never a big fan of security through obscurity, which says if you hide the inner workings of your system you will be secure, the argument holds some water. However, with an insider, that entire logic falls apart because the insider knows your network, knows how to compromise it, and has access to perform the attack. Worse case is, even if you have a fully redundant network, since the insider has full access there is no reason that he cannot take down multiple points of redundancy or create a situation where he creates his own single point of failure.

If I wanted to stop a city from functioning, I could target the people, which would be equivalent to the data. I could go in and destroy every single car in the city so no one could drive, which would stop the city from functioning. The problem is that there are so many people and cars that this would not be possible. The second option is I could take out the bridges and key highways in and out of the city. This would be equivalent to the routers and firewalls. People's cars would still function, but I took down the infrastructure so people could not go anywhere or do anything, which in effect stops the city from functioning.

While targeting the data is one method of causing harm to an organization, a potentially simpler way for an attacker is to make the data inaccessible to those who need it by taking down the routers and firewalls. If an attacker can disrupt the infrastructure, he can still cause harm, and the insider has the means to do this fairly easily. On an e-commerce site, which of the following would be more damaging?

1. Giving the customer list to a competitor
2. Publicizing all the customer credit card numbers
3. Making the site inaccessible for multiple days

They are all bad and trying to prioritize such a list is like choosing whether you want to be shot in the arm or the leg. At the end of the day, though, item 3 is probably the worst because no customers, means no business, means no company. While 1 and 2 could lead to the company going out of business, item 3 will guarantee it.

Controlling and Limiting Access

One of the best ways to prevent, detect, and survive an insider attack is by properly controlling access. On the surface this seems like an easy thing to do, but it is extremely complicated and difficult. Essentially every piece of data in most companies, which is easily in the millions, has to be controlled. Proper system design in which directories are well thought out and built in a hierarchical manner, and groups that are properly created make it easier to control and manage access. Most organizations fail to realize that things that work well for functionality also work well for security. Therefore, spending the time up front to properly design a server and putting together a well-though-out plan for breaking up the file structure, setting permissions, and creating groups can go a long way in protecting against the insider threat.

Before looking at other areas that require access control, let's revisit least privilege. When assigning access, we talked about giving employees the least amount of access to do their jobs. While this works well, we can make this even better. While least privilege is a good starting point, the next level is need-to-know. Least privilege says to give someone the access to do their job and need-to-know takes it to the next level, saying give them the access only when they need it and as soon as they are done, take it away. Need-to-know adds an extra level that also helps to control insider threat.

Let's look a brief example. An HR director needs access to the HR files across an organization. Therefore, least privilege states that the HR director should be given access to all HR files to perform his job function. While this is good, adding in need-to-know is even better. While least privilege says he needs access to all HR files, need-to-know says to give him access to the HR files only when he needs it to perform a certain job function. The HR director cannot just walk in and access any HR file; he must have a need. If there is a termination or a review, then the director gets access because there is now an implied need tied to the least privilege, which makes it even more difficult for an insider to cause harm.

Once again, in the previous paragraph and this chapter we have been focusing mainly on access to data, but we should not overlook access to physical areas of your building. Even access to the network needs to be carefully controlled. All the principles we talked about with securing data can apply to any part of your organization.

Physical security is another part that can go a long way to protecting against insider threat. Many organizations have fairly strong physical security around the perimeter of the building. To put it another way, if a company has any physical security it is always going to be around the perimeter. The doors and entry points to the building is where the badge systems and guards sit. There might even be fences to get onto the grounds of the facility. However, once you get inside, physical security is usually limited. On your network you want to institute a principle of least privilege where you give people access only to the files and network resources they need to do their job. The same thing needs to be done for you building. People should be given physical access only to the parts of the building they need to access to do their jobs and nowhere else.

There are often disconnects in organizations between the real risks and the perceived risks. For example, I know many people, executives included, who leave sensitive papers on their desks and their offices unlocked when they leave for the evening. The perception is that no one would go into their office, but the real risk is huge. If someone is working late and no one else is around, what stops an insider from looking at sensitive papers on other people's desks? Most people might not do that, but it only takes one person to create a problem. In an organization of any reasonable size, the chances of there being one or two people who would do that are high.

In one company I worked at, one of my employees came up to me and said, "Did you know that x and y are occurring at the company?" I said no and asked him how he found out. He said, "I came in late last night to work with my wife and as I was working she just wandered around the offices and she found these papers in the boss' desk drawer." As he was saying this my jaw must have hit the desk because he asked me why I looked upset. I said, "Did you hear what you just told me?" His response was astonishing. He said the offices were unlocked and the drawers unlocked so there was nothing wrong with looking around. He continued to say, "It's not as if we broke into the offices or did something we were not supposed to." And the scary thing is this person was a very honest and upfront person, which can be seen by the fact that he told me with no remorse. Different people just have a different view of what is right and wrong and we have to make sure that we properly protect our information. I did not want to get anyone in trouble, but I went to my boss and asked him why he left sensitive information in his drawer and left his office unlocked. He said, "Because no one will come into my office." I said, "Is your assumption that because the door is unlocked and the desk is unlocked that someone can go through that information?" He looked at me shocked for even asking and said, "Of course not." It is at this disconnect, where one person has one view of the world and someone has a different view that we get ourselves into trouble.

To drive home the threat of insider attack and physical security, cleaning services are another example. At many offices, people lock their doors when they leave with their trash can inside their office. Later that evening, the cleaning service comes by, opens the offices, cleans the offices, empties the trash, and locks the doors. While there is a slight risk with that, most people think the overall risk is minimal. However, I have seen firsthand how this works and it is worse than you think. To minimize the risk, the cleaning company does not give the master key to the actual cleaners; they give it to a manager. A manager shows up usually around 9:00 P.M. and walks around the floor unlocking every office and then leaves. In the next couple of hours, the actual cleaners show up and start cleaning the offices. When they are done cleaning an office, they pull the door shut and lock it. However, this creates a time period in which all the offices are open, including managers' and executives'. An insider just has to work late and after the cleaning manager opens the offices, she has free reign to do whatever she likes with no one else around. What drives me crazy is that there is an easy solution to this that no one likes to follow. When you leave your office at the end of the day, put the trash can in the hallway. Trust me, if you forget the first time, the smell will remind you to leave it out the next day. If you want your office vacuumed, you would leave the office unlocked. Now, because you are leaving it unlocked, it is your responsibility to make sure any sensitive information is properly secured for that day. Some people still won't follow the rules, but the trick is to come up with a solution that will scale and people can follow if they want to.

Going back to least privilege applied to every aspect of your organization including physical security, a great example is the data center. In most data centers you walk in and all the racks and systems are sitting there in one big room. Yet if you ask who is responsible for each server, there is a different person or group responsible for each set. One set is for marketing and administered by Pat; one set is for research and administered by Sally. If that is the case, then least privilege says that

Sally does not need access to the marketing systems, yet since they are all in one big room, she can still get physical access to them. Ideally, to get defense in depth and least privilege, there should be a door to the data center and then once inside, there should be separate rooms for each group of servers. Now both Pat and Sally can get into the data center but Pat can only get into the room with the marketing servers and Sally can only get into the room with the research servers.

One last area of access to focus on is network access. If an outsider can connect to your network, either through a port in the conference room or via a wireless access point, that outsider has just become an insider with minimal effort. Therefore, connectivity to a network must be carefully controlled. Before a system is allowed to connect to a network it must be properly authenticated to make sure it is a valid system and needs that access to do its job. While the primary function of controlling network access is to thwart insider threat, it also helps to control virus and worm outbreaks. If people are traveling and their systems becomes infected with a virus, instead of them coming back, connecting, and infecting the network, when they plug into the network not only will they be authenticated, but checks can also be performed to make sure the system is secure before it is allowed to connect.

While there is no perfect security, through proper design and analysis most organizations can do a lot more to prevent the insider threat than they are currently doing today and a key way is to control and limit access at all points across their network.

Psychosocial Factors

No magic formula exists for finding an insider threat at your company. If the problem were easy, then very few companies would care about it and entire books would not have to be written about it. However, there are some basic factors to consider when identifying potential problems within your organization. People are wired a certain way and act a certain way based on their personality and psychological factors. For example, my grandfather would never speed. It did not matter if no one was around and there was no chance of getting caught; he just would never break the law no matter what because that is who he was. There are other people who, even knowing that there are police officers around, will always speed, thus the reason there are tickets.

The bottom line is people who have done things wrong in the past are more likely do to things wrong in the future. People who have done things right in the past will most likely do things right in the future. People who have been disruptive in the past will most likely be disruptive in the future. While not always a perfect indicator, looking at past problems and behavior can usually be a good indicator of people who are likely to cause problems moving forward.

Therefore, as a starting point it is usually not a bad idea to perform screening or background checks on key employees. Just because someone made a mistake in the past does not mean they are going to cause harm to your organization and just because someone has a clean past does not mean they are not going to snap and cause problems in the future, but knowledge is power. The more information you have the more informed a decision you can make.

Many times when people are disruptive in the workplace people are reluctant to say anything because it is sometimes easier to ignore a problem than to have to deal with it. However, these could be big indicators so it is critical that they are properly reported to HR and followed up on because they can be some of the best indicators to find potential attackers within the walls of your organization.

When it comes to insider attack, employees are your biggest allies and your biggest enemies. Since one or more of your employees or contractors are harming your organization, a healthy dose of paranoia needs to be used but not so much that no one is trusted and everyone hates working at your organization. Causing disgruntled employees and dissent will only increase your chances of being attacked and cause more problems. However, there is always a balance that needs to be achieved. The best bet is to carefully control access, enabling people to do their jobs but taking away any additional access. If people need additional access, carefully validate and control the access but give the access that is needed for people to be effective at what they were hired to do.

While there is always the chance of someone on the inside being an attacker, less than 5% of your employees will be, which means that 95% have the company's best interests at heart. While you want to keep an eye out for the 5%, do not let the 5% ruin it for the other 95%. At the end of the day, assuming someone is innocent until proven guilty is not a bad rule of thumb.

Educating Employees

While a small percentage of your employees or trusted insiders might have ill intentions, most of them would like to see the company succeed and do well. Therefore, knowledge is power. Employees cannot help you and in some cases they can actually hurt you if they do not know what they are supposed to do. A well-educated and trained employee is a strategic weapon that can be enormously helpful for tracking and finding inside attackers. On the other hand, a well-intentioned, poorly guided, and poorly trained employee can inadvertently cause more harm than good and result in damage to your organization.

Therefore, keeping your employees as allies is critical and is done in three critical ways:

- Policies
- Procedures
- Awareness

Policies and especially security policies are the organization's high-level stance on what needs to be done and what is expected of users to make the organization successful. You always hear people complain that no one follows policies and users always complain about them, but I would urge you to carefully analyze the data. When you really go through and add up the numbers, I bet you that the people that are complaining and causing problems are less than 10% percent of your organization. It is always easy to focus on the small number of trouble makers, but it is critical that you do not lose site of the greater good.

Training is a critical adjunct to policies in that training teaches people the skills they need to have in order to follow the policy. If your policy states that people have to do a certain thing and your employees do not have the skills to do it, how can you expect them to ever follow it? Therefore, it is critical that you empower your employees by giving them the tools they need to properly follow and obey the policies.

What makes the world such a neat place to live is that everyone has a different view of the world and different opinions. If we were all the same the world would be pretty boring. Things that make sense to me might not make sense to you. When things do not make sense you form bias and even though you might know that something is the right thing to do, you still might not follow it because you honestly do not believe it is in your best interest to do so. This is where awareness comes in. Awareness is meant to change behavior by giving you a different perspective. If an awareness session is effective, you will hear people say they never thought about the problem the way you laid it out and now it makes sense why they need to do that. Prior to that session they never understood why they had to do a certain thing. Some people are just downright malicious, but most people do not follow the policies because they think they are a waste of time and they do not understand what the value is.

While each of these three areas has value, to have a highly effective organization requires all three to work in harmony. Policies tell the employees what to do, training gives them the skills to do it, and awareness changes their behavior so they understand the value of it and follow it.

This is all well and good, but why is it important to have well-informed, policy-obedient employees? In terms of insider threat, the answer is simple: employees who are in the trenches and working side by side with the insider threat provide your best chance of detecting and finding the problem. Employees who sit in the cube next to someone, who see how they act in meetings, who hear what they talk about outside of the office, provide your best chance of finding and weeding out people with ill intentions. You do not want to turn everyone into moles, but the more people that care about the organization and understand that others can cause damage, the greater the chance they would do and act in the best interest of the company.

Reacting to Insider Threat

As with any type of adverse event that occurs at your organization, the best way to handle it is to have a plan, which is why most organizations have an incident response plan and a disaster recovery plan that are tested and people are trained on. This enables them to act with vigor and planning to see unforeseen problems. While it is never easy when there is an adverse event at your company, proper planning can minimize the bleeding.

In some sense, an insider attack fits under the general category of incident response. Therefore, some organizations will just use their incident response plan in the case of any incident, whether it is internal or external, and hope for the best. While this might work in some cases, it usually does not provide the best response because an incident response plan at most organizations was built to handle external incidents not internal. If you remember from Chapter 1, there are big differences between an internal attack and an external attack.

Because they are so different, I usually prefer to either have two separate plans or, to minimize confusion across an organization, break the incident-handling procedures into two parts depending on whether it is an internal or external event. There are many differences between the two, but in terms of incident response the following are some key differences:

- Knowing it is an insider attack
- Could involve key people
- More strict control of information
- Notification procedures could be altered
- Less chance of being publicized

- Greater chance for loss

- Less chance of knowing or catching the attacker

- Harder to fix problem or prevent future attacks

- Might not involve an actual breach

The first big difference is knowing that it is an internal attack. With most external attacks you are able to quickly identify the source of the problem being external and you can quickly tell that you are under fire. Having lived through many incidents, I can tell you that it is never a fun feeling being under fire; however, in some sense I would rather be under heavy fire and know exactly what the problem is and where it is coming from, than have a sniper that is silently picking people off. If your Web site is being defaced, if a denial of service attack is occurring, or if someone exploited a buffer overflow attack and installed a rootkit, you know what you are dealing with and you can address it.

However, with an insider attack, you usually have no idea what is going on; your intellectual property seems to always wind up in the hands of a competitor but you do not know why (is it coincidence or a real problem); you keep losing contracts by a small margin and are not sure if it can be attributed to poor market analysis. The list could go on and on. With insider threat you are not sure if you are in a war or not, sometimes even at the end when the company is closing shop you still are not sure if you are just paranoid or if there was a real problem. It is much harder to fix a problem when you do not know what the problem is or where it is coming from. This is usually the hardest problem when dealing with an insider attack.

Let's assume you know there is a problem or you have enough data points to decide to take action. Who do you enlist to help you? Since you know the problem is coming from within, you are not sure who to trust or who not to trust because the attack involves potentially key people at your organization. With an external attack, the boundary lines are clear: us versus them, and everyone at your company can be enlisted to fight off the external enemy. With internal threat, nothing is worse that involving someone who is actually involved in the attack and playing both sides. While you think they are helping you, they could be destroying evidence, covering up information, or framing someone else at your organization. Nothing is worse than to put your heart and soul into a football game and lose the game not because the other team played better, but because your quarterback was paid off to throw the game.

Typically, with an external attack, you would want to utilize internal resources because they are better trained, know your organization, and have your best interests at heart. In addition, it is usually cheaper and more effective to use internal resources. With an internal attack, it is usually recommended to use external resources to handle the incident. While it is more costly and not as effective, in essence they are unbiased and can be trusted. During an incident, having an honest broker is the most important piece of the puzzle. It is also easier to keep a low profile if external resources are being used because employees can still go about their regular business and not do anything that looks suspicious. If you use internal resources to investigate, the fact that key internal people are running around working on an incident and not performing their normal jobs is usually fairly obvious and can tip off your hand to an attacker.

Information involving the case must be tightly controlled. While in any type of incident, you always want to be careful who you give information to and always enforce a need to know, it becomes even more critical with an insider attack. Unlike what we might think, anyone at any level in your organization could be involved in an insider attack, from the lowest level to the highest level, which makes it extremely challenging to keep strict control. To be completely paranoid, how does your company or executives know for sure that you, the person leading the investigation, is not involved or behind it? How perfect would it be for the person investigating the crime to be the person who committed the crime? Now that is paranoia.

Based on not knowing who was involved, during a high-alert insider attack, normal notification procedures might be altered. For that matter, many of the standard operating procedures that you would use during an external incident might have to be suspended or altered because the attack is causing so much damage. This is the reason it is usually easier to create a separate section or plan for insider attacks as opposed to creating a long list of exceptions to your normal operating procedures. Without a separate internal attack plan, your regular external incident response plan is quickly turned into Swiss cheese based on all the changes and modifications that have to be made to it.

One of the potential benefits of an insider attack is there is usually less visible evidence of attack, which, although it makes it harder to investigate and identify the problem areas, also makes it easier to keep the details private with less chance of public exposure and embarrassment. With an external attack in which your Web site has been defaced or is not available because of a denial of service attack, it is pretty hard to deny you have had an attack because there is visible evidence. With an internal attack there is often no visible evidence and can usually be kept more contained.

The harder it is to control and identify, tied with the fact that the person committing the attack has access and is more covert, means that the bleeding is occurring at an even quicker rate and there is a great chance for loss. With an external attack, one of the key steps of incident response is containment, which is typically accomplished by isolating the infected system or infected network segment. However, with an insider attack it is usually a high-level attack against your intellectual property. How do you isolate your IP when it exists in both tangible and intangible forms across your organization? If you cannot contain something, how do you control potential loss?

Ideally, you want to be able to catch or stop the person who is attacking you. With an external attack, even though sophisticated attackers will use relays and other decoy measures, you still have an IP address of the next hop. Yes, IP addresses can also be spoofed, especially in DDOS attacks, but at least you have an IP address or something to use as a starting point. With an insider attack, you usually have few if any facts and in most cases no information to even use as a starting point. Unless you invest money and have trained experts, the chance of catching the insider with only internal resources is minimal.

One of the other key steps in the incident response phase is eradication, which means you have to fix the problem before you put the system back on line. With external attacks, you can usually trace the breach back to a missing patch or misconfigured system and worse case you can put additional defense measures in place to stop or minimize the attacker from coming back the next time and being successful. With an internal attack, besides firing all your employees, the problem lies in the inherent nature of people having more access than they should. While controlling and limiting access can be fixed, it is not something that can be done in a reactive fashion and it surely is not something that can be done in a short period of time.

Finally, with an internal attack there might not actually be a security breach. If someone has legitimate access to a resource and uses it to perform his job and one day he decides to give that information to a competitor, where is the breach? Besides not hiring that person, what else could the company have done to prevent that from occurring? Very little, if anything.

While insider threat is completely different from external attacks, you still need to have a plan to enable the least amount of monetary loss. Based on the differences between the two, it is highly recommended to either create a separate section in your incident response plan to cover insider attacks or to create a separate insider plan. Especially since different resources will be used and there is a high reliance on external resources for an internal attack, different training and test procedures are required. The first time a plan is written it will never be correct. The only way to maximize the efficiency of a plan is by truly understanding the problem and performing detailed testing.

Summary

Insider threat is a big problem and will only increase in intensity as more and more hostile entities start to understand and realize its value as it applies to digital assets. Governments have long known the value of insider threats and the fundamental principle behind spying and espionage. Now commercial entities are starting to realize the value. More and more cyber-mercenaries and cyber-hit-men will pop up, which for the right price will get you whatever information you need all through the power of computers and technologies.

The first part in dealing with any problem is acceptance. Hopefully you have accepted that insider threat is occurring, it will continue to get worse, and measures must be put in place immediately at your organization to solve it. Hopefully, if you are an executive and reading this, you know you have to push this knowledge down throughout your organization, raise awareness, and implement changes. If you are not an executive and reading this, you have an even more important job to become an evangelist for the problem and make people aware so that changes can be implemented. Selling upper management and executives on new problems and issues that they do not understand or see is not an easy job, but do not give up. The rewards will be well worth the journey.

Once you accept that there is a problem and you have raised awareness so key components and division across your organization understand the criticality of the problem, the next step is to figure out your exposure point. Identifying and prioritizing assets is critical. If you do not know what is important, then how can you go about protecting it? If you are having trouble figuring out the critical assets, another trick is to ask, "If I were an attacker, what would I go after?" Asking yourself questions like what would have the most value to the competition or what information if it appeared on the front page of the *Washington Post* would cause the most monetary loss or embarrassment to the organization, helps to scope the problem. Wording the problem in different ways is a helpful clue to be able to figure out the real answers.

After you identify the critical assets, you then calculate the risk exposure starting with threat, working through vulnerabilities, and tying in likelihood and impact. Once the full calculation has been performed, you figure out what the appropriate countermeasures are, and you implement the solution. Remember that the ultimate goal is survival.

Remember, this is a new area so there is no right way to solve the problem, just many ways that do not work or are not effective. The trick is through trial and error you will find the solution. Work hard, be diligent, document your results, and I look forward to reading the book that you are going to write once you figure out all the answers.

Index

Syngress: *The Definition of a Serious Security Library*

Syn·gress (sin–gres): *noun, sing.* Freedom from risk or danger; safety. See *security*.